PARADISE
in RUINS

EAST ASIA W

CHINA

BURMA

LAOS

HAINAN

SIAM

INDOCHINA

CAMBODIA

*ANDAMAN
SEA*

*GULF OF
THAILAND*

Acheh (Atjeh)

MALAYA

Malacca

Sarawak

o Singapore

Du

SUMATRA

Pladjoe o

DUTCH EAST INDIE

Soenda   Soebang
Batavia (Djakarta) *o o*
8 Tjiater Pass
Bandoeng   JAVA
Tjilatjap

KOREA *JAPAN*

MAP AREA

*o Lourenço
Marques*

LDER NAMES

FORMOSA

PHILIPPINES

esselton
North Borneo

*CELEBES
SEA*

eo

o *Celebes*

Hollandia o

DUTCH NEW GUINEA

ja

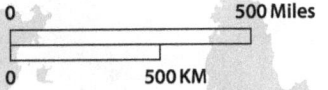

0   500 Miles

0   500 KM

PARADISE
in RUINS

A NOVEL (VIEW) OF THE PACIFIC WAR

ANTWYN PRICE

ARPress

ILLUMINATING IDEAS,
EMPOWERING VOICES

ARPress
45 Dan Road Suite 36
Canton MA 02021

Hotline: 1(800) 220-7660
Fax: 1(855) 752-6001

Ordering Information:
Quantity sales. Special discounts are available on quantity purchases by corporations, associations, and others. For details, contact the publisher at the address above.

Printed in the United States of America.

ISBN-13:   Paperback   979-8-89330-289-9
                    eBook   979-8-89330-288-2
                    Hardcover   979-8-89330-290-5

Library of Congress Control Number: 2024901484

Dedication

This edition of *Paradise in Ruins* is dedicated to Admiral Joseph J. "Jocko" Clark USN (ret), whose leadership as a Carrier Group commander in WWII greatly contributed to US air superiority during the Battle of the Philippine Sea, a.k.a. *The Marianas Turkey Shoot*. Admiral Clark's exemplary naval service is commemorated by a plaque at the National Museum of the Pacific War in Fredericksburg, Texas, and by the portrait shown below, painted for the Oklahoma State Capitol by Mike Wimmer. He was inducted into the Oklahoma Hall of Fame in 1952, and the Claremore Oklahoma Hall of Fame in 2019. The Guided Missile Frigate *USS Clark* (FFG-11) was named in his honor.

Admiral Joseph J. "Jocko" Clark USN

* Born 12 Nov 1893 Cherokee Nation, Indian Territory (now Oklahoma)
* First Native American graduate of the US Naval Academy, Class of 1917
* Became a naval aviator after his World War I service
* Air Officer of USS *Lexington* (CV-2) "*Lady Lex*"
* XO of USS *Yorktown* (CV-5)
* CO of escort carrier USS *Suwanee* (CVE-27), Battle of Casablanca
* CO of USS *Yorktown* (CV-10) "*Fighting Lady*"
* Rear Admiral of Task Force 58.1 under Vice Admiral Marc Mitscher
* Chief of Naval Aviation training (Intermediate) after WWII
* Vice Admiral in charge of the US Seventh Fleet in the Korean War
* Retired in 1954 as a full admiral
* Died 13 July 1971 New York City
* Buried at Arlington National Cemetery
* First admiral in the US Navy of Native American origin

Epigraph

They will live a long time, these men of the South Pacific. They had an American quality. They, like their victories, will be remembered as long as our generation lives. After that, like the men of the Confederacy, they will become strangers. Longer and longer shadows will obscure them, until their Guadalcanal sounds distant on the ear like Shiloh and Valley Forge.

James A. Michener, *Tales of the South Pacific*

CONTENTS

INTRODUCTION

★ ★ ★

Flags of the original United Nations (US
Office of War Information, 1942)

This historical novel, *Paradise in Ruins*, strives to recreate a world that began fading away over seventy years ago, after the most disruptive and wasteful cataclysm in human history, the Second World War.

Although that war officially began in Europe on August 30, 1939, when Nazi Germany invaded Poland without warning, the United States was not directly involved until Japan devastated the US naval base at Pearl Harbor in Hawaii on December 7, 1941—likewise without warning—with the aim of destroying the US Pacific Fleet.

Japan, with an emboldened military establishment, had been at war for many years with China by then, but despite Japanese atrocities in China—and even anti-US provocations by Japan, such as sinking the gunboat USS *Panay* on the Yangtze River—the United States population at home was by and large still bent on neutrality, until Pearl Harbor happened.

Although an aggressive move of some sort by Japan was expected eventually, having become almost inevitable after the Netherlands and USA cut off oil supplies upon which Japan was heavily dependent, Japan shocked the US and its allies by attacking not only Pearl Harbor but a host of other US and Allied bases in the Pacific region on the very same day.

The oil embargo had been in retaliation for Japan taking control of the French colony Indochina, after France capitulated to Germany. So it went, one thing after the other, until Pearl Harbor shattered the US isolationist mood altogether.

The great land, sea, and air battles of the Pacific war have been—and continue to be—depicted in several excellent books, many of which are listed in our bibliography. *Paradise in Ruins* provides the reader with an insightful backdrop to those battles and their aftermath, as the Japanese onslaught was finally contained, and the Pacific war progressed toward its ghastly climax in August 1945.

With eye-opening surprises for all readers—and perhaps a touch of nostalgia for those who grew up closer to the era—*Paradise in Ruins* stitches together the many complex events in the Pacific war zones, helping the reader to visualize the geography, the peoples, the logistics, and the strategies.

Ghosts of many historical personages flit through these pages, helping to guide the fictional actors that portray ordinary people of various nationalities, both civilian and uniformed, who were nudged or propelled out of their comfort zones by unforeseen events and adventures, leaving them better or worse off for their experiences.

Since it may not be obvious to the reader which people are historical and which are fictional, please refer to the End Notes for a list of the fictional ones. Should any of those happen to resemble actual persons, living or dead, it is accidental and unintentional.

Verisimilitude–All other named characters are historical, to whom various words or actions may have been attributed by the author with the utmost respect, to enliven their known public personae. Geographical settings for the novel are depicted as they likely existed in the early 1940s.

Orthography–US spelling is used in this novel. Please see technical notes in the Postscript regarding such details.

Further Reading–This historical novel *Paradise in Ruins* covers the American campaigns of the Pacific conflict, including those of Admiral Chester Nimitz and General Douglas MacArthur. In a companion book of the series, *Colonies in Ruins,* the author explores the history of French, British, Dutch, and American colonies in the Pacific region, their occupation by Japan in WWII, and their eventual transformation into independent nations.

PROLOGUE

Boeing 314 of Pan American Airways in San Francisco Bay
(courtesy Pan Am Historical Foundation–PAHF)

*** *THE PAN AM CLIPPERS* ***

Early on December 5, 1941, a huge silvery Pan American Airways (PAA) seaplane eased slowly away from its boarding dock inside the atoll lagoon of Canton Island, big US emblems boldly emblazoned on either side of its nose, and its registration number NC18602 prominently displayed on the tail fins. It was not long past dawn, and already a sea breeze fluttered the official British and American flags that had just been hoisted up their respective poles on the coral encrusted strip of land that fringed the lagoon.

Inside the cautiously throttled behemoth, a Boeing B-314 'Clipper Ship', were a Pan Am crew of seven and two dozen or so US military and civilian passengers bound for New Zealand via Fiji and New Caledonia.

Joining the US-origin passengers on this flight was British High Commissioner for the Western Pacific Sir Harry Luke, who had decided there at Canton to catch a quick ride back to his station on Fiji, rather than return aboard the government ship that was moored offshore.

Two days before, everyone but Sir Harry had departed from Pan Am's seaplane base on Treasure Island in San Francisco Bay, commencing a lengthy flight to Pearl City, Oahu, in the Hawaiian Islands. There they spent the night ashore in a well-appointed Pan Am-owned hotel. After another weary all-day flight from Oahu to Canton Island, the surprised passengers were awarded certificates on crossing the equator, in accord with a long-standing maritime tradition that their flying Clipper Ship had borrowed for the occasion. When the giant aircraft had finally splashed down onto Canton's calm lagoon, which was roughly halfway between San Francisco and Auckland, New Zealand, the final destination, passengers were billeted at Pan Am's newest little hotel for a delicious meal, an evening stroll, and a very welcome night's sleep.

Captain Bob Ford and his flight crew also slept, while Pan Am ground staff refueled and inspected their seaplane, as had happened in Hawaii and would happen twice more in Fiji and New Caledonia, before they were finally safe and sound in Auckland.

In view of the early morning departure for Fiji, Sir Harry Luke also slept at the Pan Am Hotel rather than aboard the Royal Colonial Ship *Viti*, which was still rocking at anchor outside the reef. RCS *Viti* had brought him to Canton Island after a month-long official tour of the Phoenix group, of which Canton was one of eight small islands.

After sunset and dinner the previous evening, Sir Harry and the Pan Am transient visitors had learned that it was customary to take a brief stroll along the ocean side of the atoll. Like other twice-weekly passengers before them, they were invariably fascinated to find themselves on a remote island 'in the middle of nowhere,' with its small cluster of buildings and storage tanks spread out tidily around the southwest corner of the dark lagoon, close to a small lighthouse.

Refreshed by an evening breeze, the strollers were particularly alert to the powerful crash of ocean surf against the protective reef that enclosed their now-dormant seaplane, scarcely visible in the rippled reflection of a lonely floodlight as Pan Am mechanics checked its vital statistics and fueled it for the morning's early departure.

Outside the reef, the surf beat slowly and steadily like the heart of a giant beast, alerting the strollers to their personal vulnerability. Underlying the rhythmic crash was a peculiar odor of bird droppings.

"It is called guano," Sir Harry explained to his strolling companions, "a hallmark of all the Phoenix Islands with their huge seabird populations. You may be surprised to know that it is quite valuable as a source of phosphates for fertilizer."

Before each such bi-weekly group began its evening stroll, Pan Am hotel staff would inform them that Canton Island was not named after Canton, China, but by American whaling captains of the nineteenth century to honor one of their fraternity whose SS *Canton* of far-away New Bedford, Massachusetts, had run hard aground on the mischarted atoll in 1854, close to where the visitors were at that moment standing.

The whaler's plucky captain, they were further informed, had led his shipwrecked crew to safety in the *Canton's* whaleboats, eventually reporting the misadventure at the Spanish colony of Guam far to the northwest, after forty-two days and nearly three thousand miles adrift on the endless ocean, with scant food and water to sustain them.

Such gritty folklore seldom failed to intrigue the Pan Am guests, who would instinctively scrutinize the reef for shards and driftwood. Some of the present group, in the hotel bar for a nightcap afterwards, were further intrigued upon learning from Sir Harry that Amelia Earhart's mysterious

1937 flight had disappeared near these Phoenix Islands, just weeks before British and American solar eclipse expeditions brought about the first modern-day settlements on Canton Island.

"After each country's astronomers reported on what a fine seaplane base the Canton atoll could become," Sir Harry explained, "there was an Anglo-American rush to develop it because travel by air was just then coming into vogue.

"The problem," he advised his rapt audience, "was that both countries claimed to own the island, but happily a peaceful joint-ownership solution was eventually found through negotiation. Canton Island was granted an unusual Anglo-American condominium status, to be administered jointly by on-site representatives of both nations. You will doubtless meet the current ones tomorrow before we depart for Fiji!"

Quite early the next morning, December 5th, a tasty breakfast was served by Chamorro waiters who had been brought from the former Spanish, now US colony of Guam where Pan Am maintained a hotel training school. After breakfast, whoever so desired could watch through the glass louvers or step outside to witness the respective flag-raisings. That December of 1941 it was the Union Jack first, followed by the Stars and Stripes, and in the reverse order of flag etiquette during alternate months.

Those who stood outside the hotel could see clearly in the daylight that Canton was not the lush green Pacific island of travel brochures but was instead a barren white coral-fringed atoll just a few feet above sea level, with scarcely a tree standing. A sketch on the hotel wall showed the island to be around nine miles long and four in width, with an irregular-shaped circumference of some thirty miles. The sketch revealed much more water surface than land, and a notation stated that most Phoenix Islands had a similar topography.

After flag ceremonies were completed, US-origin passengers were asked to kindly board the docked seaplane for its next leg to the Fiji Islands. The official US Government Resident on Canton Island—in his other, much busier and more lucrative persona as Pan Am's station manager—was there to shake hands and occasionally pose for photographs with the departing guests.

His somewhat recluse British counterpart was usually absent from the Pan Am departure routines. In fact, noting the discomfort that the

British Resident and his wife displayed with the frenetic activities of their American partners, playwright and fellow countryman Noël Coward had earlier in the year spent a fortnight on Canton, writing away in the Pan Am Hotel while attempting to cheer up the British couple in the evenings.

On this particular morning, however, the resident Britisher and his wife were standing outside the hotel with Sir Harry Luke, who was himself feeling a bit neglected by the busy Pan Am staff, all anxious to get their regular paying customers off and away without further ado. Until those passengers were aboard and in their previous seats, only then was Sir Harry invited to join them. *The Condominium administration of Canton Island has its limitations*, Sir Harry would later note in his diary, although he had enjoyed meeting some of the American passengers the previous evening.

On most mornings during the year, a handful of other people enjoyed the hotel breakfasts as well, for which a modest charge was debited against their monthly stipends. They were a collection of splendidly fit young and middle-aged men of varied nationalities, deeply tanned, who worked at various jobs on Canton to keep the island (meaning mostly Pan Am) running smoothly.

On that December 5th morning, a group of such men stood outdoors to watch the big seaplane crab its way carefully to the west end of the atoll, not far from a natural channel through the reef that allowed daily tides to flush the lagoon and reenergize its thousands of marine life-forms. It was close to the reef channel that the little lighthouse stood.

The tide was rising inward at that moment, which helped Captain Ford position his large machine for takeoff. Soon with a deafening roar of four massive engines at full throttle, amid the screeches of terrified sea birds, the massive plane gradually gained speed along the lagoon, its prop wash drenching the boarding dock and a moored flotilla of small boats, even managing to stir the handful of scraggly palm trees that poked up beseechingly from coral-encrusted ground near the hotel entrance.

A sturdy old Tahiti ketch named *Zanzibar,* moored off the British compound west of the Pan Am buildings, bobbed perceptibly at its mooring buoy inside the lagoon.

The Pan Am Clipper eventually broke free of the lagoon surface, circling back around to climb slowly onto a westerly heading that would take it by afternoon to Fiji's main island with its colonial capital, Suva. An occasional hand could be seen waving from a porthole, being answered by the group of Canton residents below.

As engine noise was gradually replaced by surf cadence and the shrieks of agitated boobies, frigate birds, and terns, another workday had begun on Canton Island, and the equatorial sun was already hot.

No one on Canton or Hawaii knew it yet, of course, but driving hard, day and night, in a direction opposite that of the departed Pan Am Clipper, was a large Japanese war fleet under the command of Vice Admiral Chuichi Nagumo. The fleet was bound for Hawaii, where his six aircraft carriers would launch their planes against the anchored US Pacific Fleet.

CHAPTER ONE

★ ★ ★

Canton Island

Old Map of Canton Island (Edwin H. Bryan, Jr)

At Pearl Harbor the naval and military facilities were in a shambles, with dozens of planes destroyed on the ground. Over two thousand people were dead, including some civilians.

*** THE CALM BEFORE THE STORM ***

"Peter, would you have a moment this evening?" the official British Resident asked a fellow countryman, who was still standing with the mostly American group by the lagoon shore, that had watched the Pan Am seaplane disappear.

"Of course, Graham, I could pop around about half six if you like. We'll be working this side of the lagoon all week."

Graham Overwood smiled and nodded his thanks. "Lois and I look forward to your visit, Peter. Thank you."

"Many thanks to you for the invitation. Is it about the new runway project, by chance?"

The most recent American intrusion into British sensibilities on Canton Island was a team of Army Engineers that had arrived in October, aiming to build a 6,000-foot runway for land planes at the northwest corner of the Canton atoll, far across the lagoon from Pan Am, thereby swelling the American population to nearly fifty. *At least that project is also far across the lagoon from the British compound*, Peter could imagine the Resident pair smiling intimately to each other.

"Oh no, nothing like that. We'd just like to see how you're getting on, and perhaps suggest an outing on *Zanzibar*."

"Absolutely brilliant," replied Peter. "See you tonight, then."

Peter Perry was an English civil engineer in his late thirties, dark-haired, well-tanned, reasonably handsome and athletic-looking, with evidence of a broken nose from rugby football. He was nearly twenty years younger than Graham Overwood, the reclusive British representative, who was slightly balding and often wore a wide-brimmed hat in the tropical sun.

Trained in England, Peter had spent a decade with the Municipality of Singapore, overseeing complex water and sewage construction projects, only to be coerced by His Majesty's Government into a temporary job on the British-American condominium of Canton Island (wherever that was; no one had been quite certain).

Peter, who was by nature adventurous, rose to the occasion with his wife Wendy's reluctant blessing, leaving her and their six-year-old son behind on the island of Singapore, a century-old British colony heavily involved in trading such commodities as tea and rubber, and in 'showing the flag' to the nearby Dutch colonies of Java and Sumatra. The British government liked to refer to the island as 'Fortress Singapore', which imparted a certain sense of invincibility.

Upon arrival at Canton Island, halfway eastward across the Pacific Ocean from Singapore, Peter learned that his assignment was to work with US Army engineers on some new land-based aviation facilities, for an expected influx of US soldiers in the near future. The Americans having finally asked for British assistance, Peter was the result of a hurried search through British colonies in the Pacific region for the right sort of expertise, which was water engineering.

'Hurried' was apparently a time-honored keyword for Canton Island projects, which had grown steadily busier right from the time of the 1937 solar eclipse expeditions. That was the time when all the competitive flag raising had started. A handful of British settlers with wireless equipment arrived soon after the scientists had left.

Not to be outdone, a noticeably larger handful of American settlers with their radio sets came along the following spring, building a little brick lighthouse tower next to the reef channel. They officially dedicated the little tower to Captain Edwin Musick of Pan American Airways, the airline's chief pilot who had died with his crew in a tragic air accident off Samoa.

In more modern times, when they occasionally met for drinks after work, British Resident Graham Overwood—who had actually attended the long-ago lighthouse dedication—often groused to Peter Perry about the bustle of activity that followed it.

"Not long after the Musick event, a Pan Am construction team suddenly appeared in January '39. They came to develop the Canton lagoon into this refueling base for their new seaplane route from Hawaii to New Zealand. I think they brought twenty or more people, which at the time seemed a lot but of course that was nothing compared to nowadays. The ruddy Yanks even have a baseball league now!"

Graham would usually carry on: "Try if you can to imagine this charming atoll as a Roman coliseum with us Brits as the Christians, being only four hardy souls—including our two Gilbertese helpers—then imagine the Yanks who have surrounded us since the beginning as a Pride of Lions, with their twenty-nine or thirty Pan Am members," he would often say, buying Peter another pint at the cozy little hotel pub.

"After the seaplane base became operational in the summer of 1940, it was still 'Christians four' but the ruddy Lions had grown to forty or more! They didn't seem to know or care anything about our war in Europe with the sodding Krauts and Eye-Ties, but there was no end to their fancy new projects for the seaplane base!"

Peter would usually shake his head and cluck in sympathy, though both men knew that Pan Am had done something similar back in 1935, turning Wake Island, Midway, and Guam into northern hemisphere refueling stops on the seaplane route between Hawaii and Manila in the Philippines, and that Pan Am engineers were probably the world's foremost experts in lagoon development and fit-out.

Eventually, the original northern Pacific seaplane route even extended from Manila to far-away Hong Kong and Singapore, and Peter recalled going to Singapore's Padang sports field earlier in 1941, to watch the first B-314 Pan Am Clipper splash down offshore within clear view of St Andrew's Cathedral and the Raffles Hotel, not far from Kallang Aerodrome where the flight would dock.

"It was spectacular," he told Graham on more than one occasion; "the whole British community turned out, yours truly and lady wife included. In fact, that's how I managed to get here so fast; I started on one of those big fat island-hopping Clippers from Singapore to Honolulu via Manila, Guam, Wake, and Midway, then back this way on Pan Am's new southern route for New Zealand. When I saw the first Clipper splash down at Singapore, I never dreamed I would actually be a passenger in one of those luxurious machines soon afterwards."

"Quite so," Graham had agreed, during their most recent pub session on December 1st, "And we were mightily pleased to have you bump up the Christians from four to five. Quality, not quantity, that's what we Brits are all about, eh? Cheers! And by the way, thank you ever so much once again for being the stand-in British representative here, while Lois and I took our delightful four-week leave on *Zanzibar* to Tarawa Atoll in the Gilberts. It was marvelous to get away from the Yanks for a while, and we love handling our wonderful old ketch out on the deep blue sea."

"Think nothing of it, Graham," Peter had replied; "I don't often get the chance to run a flag up and down or play with a wireless set. How *was* your cruise, for that matter? Did you have a chance to see your people at the Colonial Office?"

"Oh yes, we were just fifteen days under sail to Tarawa and back, which gave us another fifteen ashore for business and chin-wagging with old friends, and of course re-provisioning *Zanzibar*. I'll tell you more about it in a few days, actually, once the next Pan Am Clipper arrives from Hawaii on the fourth."

"Fine", Peter had replied, slightly puzzled, "I'd like to learn more about Tarawa in any event. They say it's marvelously primitive and relaxing. Perhaps I can take some leave there on the way back to Singapore, if the supply ship calls in here at a convenient date and offers me a lift. I may be able to wrap up here sooner than expected, as a matter of fact, now that those Army chaps have brought over some bulldozers and whatnot."

Graham had nodded, suddenly lost in thought, as Peter waved good-night and left the hotel pub that December 1st evening.

Pan Am even built a nice little four-star hotel on this barren atoll, Graham mused, draining the last of his beer, *complete with Chamorro staff from Guam, and a personable young American couple to manage it.*

It invariably gave Graham a headache to compare the comfortable hotel to his own humble quarters, that until recently had vaguely resembled an oversized packing crate. He had tried to improve the residence after Lois joined him, and although it was at long last being enlarged by Sir Harry's work crew from Fiji, he knew that it still wouldn't win an architectural prize. The cozy little Pan Am Hotel by comparison was something like a desert mirage.

Graham's thoughts returned to the 1940 start-up days of Pan Am once more. Amazingly, the first B-314 seaplane had glided onto the Canton lagoon in July of that year, he recalled. On board was a visibly proud Juan Trippe, founder of Pan Am, keen to accompany his VIP passengers to

Auckland, and to inspect his new seaplane facilities firsthand at Canton and Nouméa (Fiji was not then operational). *They say he had placed orders with Boeing for twelve of the big 314s by then*, Graham remembered.

Although Pan Am's frantic activities often bewildered him, Graham—who had arrived on Canton Island from Fiji back in 1938 to replace one of the original British wireless operators—nonetheless managed to stay on friendly terms with the bustling Americans and had even shaken hands with Juan Trippe during the inaugural flight (thinking to himself: *have a nice trippe*).

Graham, having become the sole British wireless operator by then, desperately hoped to see the British Colonial Office augment its tiny presence on Canton as well. This was despite a promotion in early 1941 by Sir Harry Luke, making Graham the legal British Administrator-in-Residence for the entire Phoenix Island Group—*a hollow advancement but a few more pounds in the bank*, Graham often thought.

Now Sir Harry was about to reach Canton from a tour of the six other Phoenix Islands, without having invited Official Representative Graham Overwood to accompany him.

Most of those British-only islands were struggling with an ambitious colonial resettlement program in danger of failing from a lack of fresh water and would probably soon be vacated.

And to think there are still people who expect to find Amelia Earhart and Fred Noonan somehow surviving on one of those islands after five years as castaways!—Graham's thoughts tended to wander sometimes; four years on Canton Island could do that to a person's mind, but after waving good-night to Chamorro Joe the bartender, he knew the pathway by heart back to the British compound in the dark night.

*** *A SECRET PHOTOGRAPH* ***

Unbeknownst to Graham but occurring around the time of his 1941 Phoenix Islands 'promotion', a slightly-built junior lieutenant in the Imperial Japanese Navy (IJN) was ordered to lock away some official photographs taken inside the Kure Naval Arsenal near Hiroshima, Japan, a large shipyard that was strictly off limits to visitors—especially foreign ones. The photos, developed and printed by a senior colleague of the young lieutenant, had been reviewed and approved by the shipyard commandant. They recorded that day's progress on a highly secret naval construction project, which happened to be the mightiest such undertaking in the entire world at the time.

But instead of proceeding directly to the secret archive room as ordered, the junior IJN officer slipped down one more floor to an equally secret Fuji Film Company laboratory, to which he had a pass key. He selected one of the photoprints and quickly duplicated it at very high resolution. If not apprehended in the meanwhile, the nervous young man would return to convert the unauthorized copy into a micro-film image, which was the latest development in the scientific field of photography. Japan excelled in photography to quite a high degree.

He glanced at the calendar on the laboratory wall: it was the twentieth day of the ninth month in the sixteenth year of the Showa period, Showa being the reign of Japan's present Emperor Hirohito. Showa-16 was known in the West as the year 1941.

The secret copy hidden safely away, the junior-in-years but senior-in-cunning IJN lieutenant then scurried back upstairs to the archive room, to duly file and log that day's photography collection. He was pleased that his hands were steady, in spite of a pulse that he could feel racing as if from intensive exercise.

*** ALLIED PREPARATIONS ***

More than three thousand miles to the east of Japan, and three months after the clandestine microfilm had been made, a group of hyper-confident Americans were continuing their frenetic development of the Canton Island atoll. Noël Coward had come and gone by then; Juan Trippe was pleased to see the twice-weekly Pan Am flights to and from New Zealand showing a profit; and Peter Perry had recently arrived from Singapore to start working on Pan Am's latest development phase for the island. *Even the American Army, Navy and Coast Guard seem to be working for Pan Am,* Peter had noticed, *or is it vice versa?*

But there was still no sign of new projects on Canton Island by the British, apart from occasional modifications to the Overwood dwelling.

Eventually some of the Americans, with whom Graham Overwood had been on fairly friendly terms, began to look pityingly at him.

"Well Graham, I guess you Brits will be closing up shop soon, eh?"

It was mortification, and Graham pleaded for guidance from his immediate colonial superiors in the Gilbert & Ellice Islands.

"Terribly sorry, Overwood", they said. "It's the war in Europe, y'know."

Which it was. France had capitulated to the Germans. Troops from Great Britain, and Commonwealth allies Australia and New Zealand, had their backs against the wall at that time. Fighting against the Germans in North Africa was intense; hence the Pacific Ocean was far from the minds of most Whitehall planners. Nonetheless, against the wishes of the Admiralty—which preferred to keep its fleet intact to fight against Hitler—the British Prime Minister, Sir Winston Churchill, had on impulse dispatched a pair of capital ships to Fortress Singapore, for boosting the defenses and reassuring the residents.

Japan had been in open warfare with China for a decade, so one couldn't blame people in the Pacific colonies for being nervous about Japan's long-term intentions. Singapore, after all, had a very large Chinese population, in addition to its many British expatriates.

Sir Winston did not in any way concern himself with the lack of an expansionist British presence on Canton Island, however, as he probably had not heard of it either.

So it was left to Graham and Lois to badger Noël Coward, when he had visited Canton Island, about the dismal lack of cooperative British planning. Graham often wished that Peter Perry had also met the author even briefly, so they could discuss the amusing poems he left behind for 'the British Resident.'

The fact remained, though, that the only real concession Graham had ever managed to coerce from the Colonial Office during his lengthy tenure was an approval to bring Lois—and their thirty-foot ketch *Zanzibar*—to Canton from Fiji in 1940, where Lois had been living aboard the yacht and visiting her colonial relatives.

Thus, Lois Overwood was among the first few women to live on Canton Island—the others being the Pan Am station manager's wife and the hotel manager's wife—although Lois was on the verge of fleeing back to Fiji by the time Peter Perry arrived, and the Americans started openly pitying her and Graham for their seeming abandonment and inertia.

But it was no longer this problem, which had been somewhat mollified by his house being at long last enlarged, that Graham needed to speak to Peter about as soon as he could. Instead it was a burning discovery that he had made during the recent sailing trip to Tarawa. Even as November 1941 drew to a close, he could still reveal nothing, as the two men downed chilled pints of watery American beer during their latest get-together at the pub.

Then a few days later, when Sir Harry Luke returned from his month-long Phoenix Islands tour, and Pan Am Captain Ford's Boeing Clipper had arrived from Hawaii, Graham could finally invite Peter to supper and a chat at the remodeled residence.

I shall ask him over tomorrow, after the plane leaves; that will be best, Graham had decided.

*** *THE BENJO SYSTEM* ***

The evening after the Pan Am seaplane's departure for Fiji, Peter was prompt at 6:30, calling a soft 'halloo' as he approached the Overwood bungalow within the British compound. It was not very far from Pan Am's facilities—though some wags said the properties were 'poles apart', referring to the flag-raising formalities.

There would still be daylight for another thirty minutes, hence the myriad seabirds were chattering away and adding their contributions to the smelly guano deposits. Being scarcely south of the equator, evening would fall quite suddenly on the island, so Peter carried a small battery-powered lantern to find his way back to the guest quarters where he slept.

Not only was the equator quite near, but Canton Island was also close to another important reference point, the International Date Line. The island was slightly to the east of the arbitrary north-south reference line, the same side as more distant Hawaii. Peter reminded himself that the Pan Am Clipper, which had departed westward from Canton that very morning, would have recorded most of this day's log entries as December 6th, although it was doubtful many of the passengers would notice anything

9

until they deplaned at Fiji for the night. *Perhaps Pan Am presents certificates for the dateline crossing too*, he chuckled.

"Good evening, Peter", called a woman's voice. "Let us perhaps sit on the veranda for a Gimlet, and watch the sun vanish from the lagoon."

"Yes indeed, Peter," echoed Graham's voice, "how was your day, old sport?"

"Quite interesting, actually," Peter replied as he reached the veranda steps and shook hands, admiring the enlarged house that had only just been finished by the Fiji Public Works crew. A faint smell of varnish still hung in the air. *Well, that's a whiff of progress*, Peter thought.

In addition to bringing a crew to rebuild the residency, Sir Harry Luke's kind munificence had also restocked the Overwood pantry with long-absent provisions, including ample gin and whiskey, and of course English cigarettes—Craven-A and Players.

"Hullo Lois, what is that marvelous aroma?" Peter asked.

"Filet de Wahoo au beurre, mon brave," Lois offered, handing Peter a drink and inviting him inside to inspect the kitchen. "Fresh from the tidal channel this very day."

Lucky sod. Peter eyed Graham, envious of the nuptial comforts. "But, must I really bore you both with today's development of the Great Pacific Thunder Box Drama? I thought Graham had something quite important to tell me."

"Yes you must," Lois replied, lifting her Gimlet: "Cheers, all. Do sit here with Graham, Peter. I'll keep an eye out for the sunset and an ear open to your report. Graham's announcement can wait until you have finished telling us about your projects."

Lois Overwood was attired in one of her precious but faded sun dresses for the occasion—the formerly blue one. She was nearly as weathered looking as Graham, and close to the same height and age. They were both born in England, but had met in France after the Great War, where Graham had briefly been a flier. *Their strong mutual support is clearly what keeps them going*, Peter quietly observed as he took a seat.

"Cheers. All right then," Peter began, speaking loudly enough for Lois to hear from the veranda, "as you seasoned colonials well know, your humble servant was brought here to Paradise Atoll because of a certain unmentionable expertise, gradually acquired in the faraway Straits

Settlement of Singapore. Drat; why can't we talk about something more interesting?"

"Do go on, Peter. Lois knows about thunder boxes, y'know."

"Right, then. Well, my civil engineering speciality is water supply and treatment, including, um, sewerage control. It's quite simple, really; on the supply side one seeks to transfer clean water from points A to B, without it leaking or becoming contaminated; then on the treatment side one strives to dispose of the, er, 'night soil' as the Chinese call it, usually with the help of some clean water."

Peter paused for effect, sipping his Gimlet in appreciation, then startled Graham and Lois by observing casually but dramatically: "Finally, if one had additional resources, one could even convert the output slurry back into clean water again."

From the veranda came a shriek. "What!! You mean ... make the sewerage drinkable? Good gracious! Is that what you've been up to with the Yanks?"

"Quick thinking, Lois. That's exactly it, except the Yanks call it sewage!" exclaimed Peter, glancing at Graham's contorted expression. "But not to worry; we shan't be drinking treated effluent on Canton Island. The process isn't economical for a few hundred or even many thousands of people. It hasn't even been tried in Singapore, though perhaps one day it could be since the economics there are more attractive.

"Here on Canton it is still more economical—though not inexpensive— to generate electricity or steam to distill fresh water locally from seawater, and of course the more we can collect from occasional rains helps the economics even further."

"That's something to be grateful for, at any rate," Graham ventured. "One never knows what the Yanks might get up to. I'm pleased it doesn't include recycling their thunder boxes."

"Ha! Well, with our growing island population, we must get everyone to stop emptying bed pans into the lagoon, as a first step. If we can't afford to treat the waste properly—which even Pan Am cannot afford—then we must at least get it dumped into the much larger ocean, and not spoil the pretty lagoon where we like to swim—and eat the little fishies. Agreed?"

Agitated, Graham slurped his Gimlet. "Of course we agree, Peter, but how to manage that? One can't very well expect people to rinse their potties in the surf and risk being swept out to sea, or dangle their bottoms out over a coral ledge in the teeth of a howling gale, or in plain view of Pan Am passengers, now can one? I suppose our effluent, as you call it, could be collected by a cart somehow, and taken in batches to the ocean from time to time, but it sounds rather complicated, not to mention primitive. Perhaps we could just sell the night soil to the 'other Canton', in China! And what a lovely job for some poor sod to collect the stuff here on the island! The ruddy Yanks would probably assign it to us."

"Too true," Peter smiled, "but today we worked out a system with the Army blokes that will enable us to 'pump the poop in batches,' so to speak, using salt water from the lagoon as a vehicle for the slurry, and several big stainless steel grinder-pumps to move it into the ocean, through a series of trench designs that we've been experimenting with over the past few weeks."

Peter carried on, beginning to sound somewhat pedantic: "Using sturdy coral trenches will save us from having to bring in shiploads of ceramic sewer pipe from afar. Tapered trenches are used all over Singapore as storm drains for rainwater, by the way, where they are called *benjos*, a Japanese name, apparently. Here we'll install wooden *benjo* covers to contain the smell, but the brilliant Gimlet-refilling point this evening," he emphasized, waving his empty glass, "is that we have figured out how to carve and smooth out the trenches using some of the amazing American machines. Those special pumps will move the, er, flotsam to the sea in batches, and even rinse the trenches afterwards."

"'Flotsam', that's the name! It sounds too good to be true, Peter," said Lois, coming inside to mix a second round of Gimlets, "but where do the people, um, deposit their contributions?"

"At a series of out-houses here and there, or in major buildings like the hotel and airplane terminals. Separate systems will be used both north and south of the lagoon, discharging right through the reef into deep water," Peter advised. "First priority will be Northside, however, because it's likely that lots of American troops will be sent here in the event of war with Japan, which I'm sure Graham will agree is not too far-fetched a possibility. In such eventuality, this Pan Am Paradise on Canton Island would immediately become a crucial military refueling point, for both land and sea planes."

Thanking Lois, Peter took the offered Gimlet carefully with both hands as she hurried back to watch for the sunset. "There may be a thousand more Lions on Canton before long, Graham," Peter quipped.

"Bravo, Peter, how wonderful it's been to have you here at this critical time. It is uplifting to see such a valuable British contribution to the spiritual and social development of Canton Island. I feel truly exhilarated. But could we perhaps change the subject to something less—shall we say—technical?"

"Thank you, Graham, I'm sure," Peter laughed. "Actually, it was an interesting challenge, and really quite a pleasure to work with the Pan Am team and the Army engineers. I hadn't had much to do with Americans before, but find that we get on well together. The new runway is nearly completed, by the way, and people in Hawaii have sent over plans for a terminal building. But a really big engineering job still lies ahead. Sorry to bring up another technical subject, but you really must hear about this one. I'll be quick about it."

"Peter, I'm taking rough notes of all you've told us. May I report onward to Tarawa and Suva—in code, of course? And what is the really big project ahead? The Yanks have already built a small community hospital and a little fire station, not to mention the hotel pub; now what more have they dreamed up?"

"I can't answer the reporting question. The problem with wireless, as we all know, is unwanted eavesdropping, and I wouldn't have a clue how secure the current British codes are. What about conferring with your American counterpart, and deciding how to handle that aspect? He must surely be wondering what to report as well and could perhaps use your help."

"Thank you, Peter, good suggestion. I'll get onto that in the morning. Now what about the ...."

"Hurry you two, here comes a cloudless sunset for a change," Lois shouted from the veranda, as brilliant red streaks in the sky lit up the lagoon surface for the briefest of moments. The men rushed to join her outdoors and caught the final display of a blood-red lagoon.

"Fantastic!" Peter exclaimed. "For some odd reason you can't see this from everywhere on Canton, not even standing right next to the lagoon. At least, I've never seen it from the Pan Am Hotel or thereabouts. Wonder why that is?"

"According to hearsay in colonial circles," said Graham, "the incredible sunset reflection was one reason our predecessors chose this particular spot for the British compound, back in 1937, before any American settlers had arrived. I suppose the eclipse astronomers had something to do with it. Just a friendly little secret, eh?" They all chuckled. Lois stood, and led them inside from the imminent darkness.

*** *A FUTURE HARBOR* ***

During the delicious meal that followed, discussion turned to the other major project to which Peter had alluded.

"There will be an artificial ship channel cut into the lagoon, right through the reef, not very far from the existing natural channel that flushes the lagoon at every tidal change, once or twice a day," Peter explained. "The new channel will allow small tankers to enter the lagoon, reverse direction in a marked turning basin, and then tie up at a new dock to discharge bulk quantities of aviation fuel, diesel oil, and petrol for the north side of the atoll. Other supply vessels can use the new dock for delivering food, building materials, heavy equipment, and even water if necessary."

Graham began one of his "bloody Yanks again" tirades, but Lois silenced him with a hiss.

Peter continued: "There'll be no more manhandling of heavy fuel drums and materials onto shallow-draft lighters offshore, then towing the overloaded lighters carefully back into the lagoon for still more manhandling at the seaplane docks. The result, in eighteen months or so, will be what the Americans call a 'tank farm', connected by road to the new airport at the northwest corner of the island. It will be aimed at supporting future landplane operations, but the Southside seaplane base will also benefit to some degree. Pan Am will acquire a little tanker-barge to bring aviation fuel over to their docks across the lagoon from the tank farm," Peter concluded.

"Why eighteen months?" Lois asked. "That seems a long time for your Army supermen to wait."

Peter explained that the existing tidal channel couldn't be modified, because it would be too damaging to the lagoon's marine life over several months while it and the turning basin were being dredged and stabilized at the same time. The new channel would be cut a hundred yards or so north of the natural one and would be much deeper.

"The project will take quite a lot of money and personnel, but actual construction would probably be just six months after all is ready to go. Unfortunately, it will probably be a bit too late for the influx of Army planes they are expecting at some point in the near future. On the other hand, if war does break out with Japan, the new channel will doubtless be started and finished sooner."

"Mind-boggling," Graham mumbled, predictably. "Leave it to the ruddy Yanks to turn Paradise Atoll into the Manhattan docks! Cor!"

Peter and Lois laughed. "Graham, you'd opt for living in a cave if the Colonial Office would approve it," Lois opined. "Why this project will be superb for Canton, and should help the lagoon flush out even better, right Peter?"

"Absolutely; and imagine having fuel facilities here for not only sea and land planes, but for small ships as well, such as Sir Harry's HMS *Viti*."

"And first-rate sewerage—oops, sewage—too, don't forget," Lois added.

"Bollocks," Graham retorted. "Anyhow, Peter, now that it is brandy and cigar time, might I bring up yet another subject for discussion?"

*** *A STRANGE SECRET UNFOLDS* ***

Graham and Lois glanced at each other, then Graham pulled his chair closer to Peter's, lowering his voice slightly:

"This is highly confidential, Peter, ... although I almost feel like laughing for having to say that. I think we're all going a bit daft from having so many military types around us, but I had to wait for Sir Harry's final approval yesterday, in order to tell you about this."

"I understand," Peter agreed, "please do carry on."

"I shall; but may perhaps wander a bit. This odd story begins in Tarawa, when we took annual leave on *Zanzibar* in October and you kindly 'watched the store' for us, as the Yanks like to say."

Peter smiled, and Lois said, "Please get on with it, Graham, it's nearly bed-time."

15

"Yes, my love," Graham fluttered submissively over his spectacles. "Actually, the story really began in Japan, but we became involved in Tarawa. Once we reached there, and had cleaned up *Zanzibar* and ourselves for a couple of days, I left Lois relaxing aboard and wandered over to the Colonial Office to report in. Not much was pending, as suspected, but then as I strolled back to the wharf a young Japanese-American chap approached me and asked for a match to light his cigarette."

"How did you know he was Japanese-American?" Peter asked. "That would be quite odd in the Gilbert Islands, I should think."

"Well, he looked Japanese and sounded American, how else? And the funny thing was—he knew my name! I didn't quite know what to say, so I fumbled for a match, and then he introduced himself as Lieutenant Naburo of the Imperial Japanese Navy!"

"Good heavens, that *is* strange. Did he bow?" Seeing Graham's annoyance, Peter hesitated. "Sorry Graham, just joking. It sounded rather like *The Mikado*, or a Charlie Chan detective film, that's all."

Lois jumped in: "Please be serious, Peter. It *is* bizarre, I agree. Graham, tell Peter about that man coming aboard *Zanzibar*. I was quite frightened at first."

"Yes, yes, coming to that. After the surprise introduction, Naburo sort of nudged me along the pathway toward the wharf, all the while asking if I'd had a nice crossing from Canton Island, and such small talk with personal details. I was really quite flummoxed that he knew both who I was, and where I had come from." Peter glanced at his watch. Graham scowled, and continued a bit faster:

"When we reached the pier, Naburo insisted—well, almost pleaded—that we let him come aboard for a discussion: '*I promise to answer all your questions, Mr. Overwood. Please, may I join you in the cabin? I would rather not be seen here on the waterfront, even out of uniform*'. Well, it was a gamble, but Lois and I rather felt we could trust him. We were both quite eager to hear what he had to say, actually."

"I shouldn't wonder. I'm quite eager as well. What *did* he have to say, then?"

"Peter, Lt Naburo grew up on one of the Hawaiian Islands, which was quite a distortion to our picture of a typical Japanese naval officer. He is around twenty-two years old. Three years ago—May '38, the same month by coincidence that I arrived here on Canton—this fellow signed on with a Japanese freighter in Honolulu, to work his passage to Yokohama. There he would stay with his father's distant cousin for a year or so, to study Japanese classics and polish up his language skills, perhaps acquire a doting wife, all that sort of thing. Naburo's father is what the Yanks call a 'Nisei', meaning second generation Hawaiian resident, which makes Naburo Junior a 'Sansei'—*ichi, ni, san* and so forth."

"Yes, Graham. We had a Japanese photographer in Singapore who taught us the basics. Goodness, perhaps he too was a wandering Hawaiian musician like Naburo."

Graham continued, unperturbed: "You may not know, Peter, that the US Coast Guard settled some Hawaiian boys on several mid-Pacific islands around here on rotating six-month tours of duty, including Howland, Baker, and Jarvis in '37, then Canton and Enderbury in '38. Except for Canton, that 'pseudo settler' program is still going on today. Bizarre, right?"

Peter shrugged, as Graham continued: "Those so-called settlers were supposed to lend credibility to American sovereignty claims so that, for example, the Yanks could instruct Amelia Earhart to land at Howland Island—which was disastrous advice in retrospect."

Peter nodded in agreement as Graham went on: "Howland, Baker, and Jarvis are not internationally recognized as part of the Phoenix group, even though they should be included geographically. Instead, the Yanks claimed those three under their silly Guano Act, and then plonked these poor lads on them to make it seem like a colonization. Every six months the lads are replaced with a fresh batch, and so on—four of them at a time, per island."

Peter yawned: "Do go on, Graham. I suppose there's a point to all this?"

"Well of course, there is!" Graham bristled. "The US settler program did in the end force Britain into a condominium agreement for Canton and Enderbury—though not the other six Phoenix Islands—so that Pan Am could build its desired Clipper base on the most suitable atoll in the region. Perseverance, what?"

"Dear, you are digressing again." *Lois and the gin.*

"Yes, my pet, but Peter will need to know that Naburo went to school in Hawaii with some of those rotating groups of schoolboy settlers. He got

17

itchy feet from knowing his Hawaiian friends were going off to see the world, or so he imagined. In spite of being a third-generation Hawaiian resident he was still not eligible because of his Japanese background. People of Japanese background were always under suspicion in Hawaii, or so I've heard."

Peter yawned again, once more looking impolitely at his watch. "So he tells his father that he wants to see the world too, and papa-san sends him off to live with an uncle in Japan, is that it?"

"Exactly, Peter. After he arrives in Yokohama, he begins his studies but also finds a technical job with a new company called Fuji Film."

"Do we know anything about this company?" Peter asked. "Everyone's aware that the Japs are dead keen on photography, and I even had our wedding photos taken by an honorable Japanese gentleman in Singapore, as mentioned. People think they are all spies for the emperor, though, but what can they possibly learn from portrait photographs of colonial Brits and their families?"

"Peter, please try to remember what I'm telling you, for future reference. Naburo said Fuji Film are quite technically advanced and were willing to train him if he would join the firm. Apparently Naburo has a clever knack for science, and the training he received from Fuji Film was in a new field called micro-filming, where high-quality photos can be shrunk to tiny sizes, then viewed at full size later on."

"Hmm, that *is* quite interesting I suppose, but what is it all about? Why do you care about Lt. Naburo, and what has this to do with Peter Perry, your friendly but temporary Canton Island colleague and tennis partner?"

"Well, Peter, I'll do my best to enlighten you now, with my dear wife's help, just as Lt. Naburo enlightened us some weeks ago on Tarawa. By the way, he easily learned who I was and where from, by simply peeking at the Harbor Master's logbook. I should have realized that. Another Gimlet?"

*** *THE PLAN OF ACTION* ***

The next morning being a Saturday, Peter slept a bit late, nursing a Gimlet-induced headache, which Graham told him in the hotel dining room was what the ruddy Yanks call a 'hangover'. Had Peter imagined last night's conversation? He asked Graham a few quiet questions to clear his memory.

"So, I'm to carry this, er, souvenir, to Hawaii, is that it?" Peter asked. Graham nodded.

"Right, then, when would that be?"

"Next available transport, as I said last night—the eastbound Clipper on Tuesday, on its way back from New Zealand, remember?" Graham looked annoyed.

"Please don't shout," Peter implored. "I am a wounded man. All right, what do I tell the US Army people here, as to why I'm leaving suddenly on the next Pan Am Clipper to Honolulu?"

"Just say you've been recalled to Singapore for some important confidential reason. After all, you would have to go first to Hawaii then westbound to Singapore, retracing the way you came here."

"That's true," Peter agreed. "Right, so much for a visit to Tarawa on the way home. I was looking forward to that. How is Lois, by the way?"

"Still asleep, I suspect. She does make a decent Gimlet, I must say. Now Peter, please remember you are to go straight to the admiral's office at Pearl Harbor in Hawaii and tell his aide that you bring a very special gift and message from the British High Commissioner of the Western Pacific, for the admiral's eyes only. These papers will supply your bonafides." Graham handed a brown envelope to Peter, with Sir Harry's colonial seal quite prominent.

"The Clipper should arrive there Tuesday night the ninth," Graham continued, "so try to get an appointment with Admiral Husband Kimmel for Thursday or Friday. Sir Harry says the admiral plays golf on Saturdays and is fairly well known to be out of the picture on weekends."

"Right, then," Peter concurred. "Let's have some more coffee, Joe," beckoning to the Chamorro attendant. "Some more 'joe' please, Joe. Ha-ha," Peter tried to smile; Graham winced.

"You look bad, boss," said Joe, bringing two more cups.

"Doesn't he, though," Graham agreed with the Guamanian. "He is from Singapore, where they usually just drink tea all day."

Chamorro Joe was sometimes assigned as evening bartender at the busy hotel bar, and knew his two English customers well, especially Graham. When Joe had withdrawn to the hotel kitchen, Graham continued:

"The so-called 'gift' that Lt Naburo left us, is apparently a high-quality Japanese geisha doll attired in a kimono, the sort of thing a discerning tourist might collect. It is elegantly gift-wrapped in a box, which you can easily pack in your luggage. Inside the doll is the microfilm that the lieutenant risked his life to smuggle from Japan, knowing he was due to be transferred to their fleet headquarters on Truk atoll, not too far from the Gilberts.

"I haven't actually seen the film," Graham added, "but Naburo said it is one of the official photos that Fuji Film was instructed to take for the IJN, of a secret new battleship—the first of four huge sister ships that Japan began building in violation of naval treaties. No other country in the world has anything like these monstrous warships, according to Naburo, so it's important for us to let the Americans know straight away. They will need to be on guard if and when war breaks out over here.

"Naburo had access to the original photo briefly, as he was still working for Fuji Film after the surprise of being conscripted into the Japanese naval reserves. He was quick-witted enough to duplicate it as a micro-film. The photo is dated 'Showa-16-9-20', which simply means 20th September 1941. It shows the battleship being outfitted at the Kure naval shipyard after launch, but before sea trials, which according to Naburo have since taken place this past October—not all that long ago. There are apparently three more such monsters under construction at various other shipyards in Japan, each hull like the first one hidden under gigantic cloth tarpaulins from prying Western eyes until they are launched."

"A fascinating story," Peter agreed, gratefully inhaling the coffee aroma. "But why didn't Sir Harry just have you pass the information to the senior American officer here on Canton? And why am I the courier to deliver it to the Yanks in Hawaii, eh?"

"The senior Yank officer here on Canton is just a ruddy engineer—oops, sorry Peter—who has absolutely no clout whatsoever up the line. He would probably just bin the package or send it home to his sweetheart. And if Sir Harry had taken it back to Fiji, well that's the wrong direction. It needs to get to Honolulu and then probably to Washington, as fast as possible. I suppose, ideally, he would like it to reach London before Washington, but Britain is in a turmoil at the moment with the war in Europe, and so forth.

"As for you being the courier, well I couldn't just go to Hawaii myself and leave you here with Lois and the gin, now could I? Sorry, Peter, a bad joke. The real reason is that you get on admirably with the ruddy Yanks, and I don't. Besides, I am the official factotum here and cannot go dashing off to Hawaii just like that."

"But what if the package is confiscated, or my luggage is lost by Pan Am? What happens then?"

"It seems our friend Naburo thought about that possibility. He made a duplicate microfilm and embedded it in this handsome necklace that I am presently wearing and have been ever since Lois and I returned from Tarawa."

"Well, Graham, I did notice that strange necklace but thought you had gone native on us. From my brief exposure to Hawaii, I would say it looks like a monkey pod seed."

"Exactly what it is, old man. Naburo brought it from Hawaii as a gift for his uncle but asked for it back when the uncle wasn't particularly interested. His thinking was that no one in Hawaii would ever imagine a monkey pod necklace being a military drop box. It does make a very hardy capsule, though."

"Am I supposed to wear that as well, then?" Peter exclaimed. "Will you lend me a Hawaiian shirt?"

"Nay, dear boy. This duplicate is to be buried somewhere around here for safekeeping, just in case your kimono doll gets lost. The only problem is, I hadn't been able to think where, until now. What with the Americans digging up Canton, it might accidentally end up in your benjo drains if we're not careful."

Peter grimaced. "Yes, that's true. What, then?"

Graham smiled broadly: "Well, after Sir Harry arrived and mentioned that *Viti* had stopped at Enderbury Island, so he could have a look around and meet the four Hawaiian boys, we both suddenly realized that isolated Enderbury would be the perfect place to bury a treasure of any sort. Enderbury Island is part of the Anglo-American Condominium too, if you recall, but it hasn't seen much activity apart from those so-called Hawaiian 'colonists'. Our monkey pod could lie there undisturbed for centuries, probably."

Peter's eyes were beginning to glaze over as Graham droned on: "I was hoping you and I could sail over there with Lois on *Zanzibar*, y'see, as it's only sixty miles from Canton, but that would be cutting it close for your flight on Tuesday. Instead, Lois and I will go over later with one of the Gilbertese, John or Gordon. As for you being a courier, young Naburo risked his all to get the microfilm from Truk to British Tarawa, on the chance he could find someone trustworthy to take it the rest of the way to America. We can't let him down now, can we?"

"Well, all right," Peter agreed, yawning, "I'll do as you wish, and deliver the doll to Admiral Kimmel. I assume I'm free to go back to Singapore thereafter?"

"Very likely, unless a Washington visit is needed. Let us go next door to reserve your seat on the Honolulu Clipper, and see if anyone else is keen for a swim in the lagoon this afternoon, which will help clear the cobwebs. On Monday we'll gather up some Yanks for a little beach party as your send-off. I checked with Madam Hostess at the Pan Am hotel, and she will be happy to lay on a special something or other with Chamorro Joe on the guitar, and so on. People will genuinely miss you, Peter m'lad, and the Army blokes especially—well, Lois and I as well."

"I can scarcely wait," said Peter. "By the way, what is the name of this monster battleship, does anyone know?"

"Naburo wasn't certain, but he heard discussions that it would probably be *Yamato*, named after an important Japanese province. The christening—or whatever they call it—should be fairly soon. "And by the way, Peter, this will interest you." Graham added, "We just learned that Churchill's two British warships reached Singapore today. They are HMS *Prince of Wales*, a new battleship, and HMS *Repulse*, an older battlecruiser. There was supposed to be an aircraft carrier too, but it apparently ran aground in the Caribbean and is delayed for repairs." At the mention of Singapore, Peter paid more attention.

"Perhaps this lot will tangle with *Yamato* one day, which should be interesting," Graham continued. "Unbelievably, Naburo said *Yamato* has 18-inch guns. I doubt our Royal Navy ships could cope with that, nor could US battleships either. You must stress this point with the admiral."

"Do you think Admiral Husband ... sorry, Admiral Kimmel will believe the Japs can build monster battleships with 18-inch guns?" Peter asked.

"Well, Sir Harry thinks that may just be why you'll need to go on to Washington from Honolulu, to speak personally with their Chief of Naval Operations. It's a strange British secret that you're carrying, Peter old chap—what the Yanks call a 'hot potato'—and you are inadvertently its advocate, like it or not. We can't get our hands on Naburo to send him along with you as evidence, much as he would like us to. The poor fellow is no doubt back on Truk, wishing he had never left the Territory of Hawaii."

After the refreshing swim on Saturday afternoon among the fascinating marine-world creatures of Canton lagoon, Peter turned in early at the tiny British guest house, glad to finally be on his own to get a good night's sleep. There would be a generic chapel service Sunday morning, which he usually liked to attend as a lay reader. The Americans seemed to like his English accent.

Peter dozed off, wondering what his wife Wendy in Singapore would think of this new assignment. Their letters to each other were delivered fairly quickly, thanks to the excellent Pan Am seaplane networks, but he still needed to tell her he was leaving Canton early next week for Hawaii and possibly Washington. Wendy's latest letters had already berated him for being away so long; she wouldn't be pleased at all about the Hawaiian extension. He fell asleep wondering just how many tropical islands there were in the British Empire.

*** THE ATTACK ON PEARL HARBOR ***

The first Japanese carrier planes struck Pearl Harbor early the next morning. Canton Island was two hours behind Hawaii-time, and there was no one on duty at either the British or American radio shacks before local dawn on Sunday, December 7. By the time Graham Overwood and a Pan Am operator had tuned into their various morning news sources, it was already mid-morning in Hawaii, and the amateur radio networks were alive with agitated blow-by-blow descriptions of the first and second waves of Japanese planes, and the terrible damage they left behind.

They had strafed and bombed Hickam Field, Schofield Barracks, Ewa Marine Air Station, and Ford Island with the neat rows of US battleships moored inside the presumed safety of Pearl Harbor's anti-submarine net. The battleships had been devastated, although a battered USS *Nevada* got up steam but then had to go aground to keep from blocking the only exit channel from Pearl. Several cruisers were lost as well, but the main Japanese thrust was clearly at the battleships, onto which dive bombers had even dropped 16-inch naval shells to penetrate the deck armor.

This, Graham thought to himself, *is what the Yanks call 'shit hitting the fan'*. The alarm was quickly raised on Canton, and people tumbled from sleep to gather at the radio shacks for news. It was clear that many had been asleep at Pearl Harbor too; the crafty Japanese choice of a Sunday morning hangover to delay American responses, was cool and deliberate.

The news grew worse and worse, though there was perhaps some exaggeration. It was clear that most of the US battleship fleet at Pearl Harbor was sunk or crippled. The naval and military facilities were in a shambles, with dozens of planes destroyed on the ground. Over two thousand people were dead, including some civilians.

Peter began to wonder how he could get back home to Singapore if Hawaii was as devastated as the news reports indicated. Was the Hawaiian Pan Am base still intact? He went for a long walk along the lagoon, scarcely noticing the tropical fish or the screeching birds.

The Pearl Harbor reports were a complete and total shock to all the occupants of remote and defenseless Canton Island, where people shuddered to think that the enemy fleet must have passed somewhere nearby, unobserved, on its way to Hawaii, and could perhaps be lurking out there on its return voyage, ready to destroy Canton Island too.

Even the Britishers—the five Christians who had been living with their own European war anxieties for two years—were taken aback. As further news and rumors came over the airwaves, many a beer was consumed on the Canton atoll the evening of December 7, 1941.

*** *TRANSITION TO WAR* ***

The next morning things were somewhat more settled, and dedicated coded messages began arriving for Canton from official British and US sources. Everyone learned that the United States had declared a state of war with Japan. President Franklin D. Roosevelt's powerful speech to the US Congress was broadcast around the world:

"Yesterday, December 7th, 1941—a date which will live in infamy—the United States of America was suddenly and deliberately attacked by naval and air forces of the Empire of Japan...." The US Congress acted immediately to make its necessary declarations in return.

With their focus on hearing more radio news, no one on Canton noticed a Japanese submarine passing the outer reef that morning at periscope depth, on its way to bombard Howland Island. Canton was easily photographed for future reference, while among the messages that the island received was a terse one from Pan Am, announcing that the recent westbound Clipper to New Zealand would not be returning to Hawaii. The decoded text was relayed to the British radio shack by Pan Am's station manager.

"But I already have a ticket! What can this mean?" Peter asked Graham.

"No idea," Graham shrugged. "Let us go speak to the Army people at the airfield and see if they have any better news." Then Graham noticed all the small boats were already in use and going across the lagoon in that direction.

"Not a problem," Peter reassured. "I have that Army jeep. We can drive around the lagoon, as I often do. Should we bring Lois?"

"I think not," Graham replied, "but I'd better ask her to listen to our wireless in case there are any instructions from the Colonial Office. Be right back."

Graham ran quickly into the house for a few moments, then struggled to put on a shirt as he jumped back into the jeep. At Peter's snide smile, Graham muttered: "I'd better look official; we might run into President Roosevelt."

"Or the Japanese Emperor, more likely!" Peter said.

It took about twenty minutes to circle just half the lagoon along the nearly thirty-mile bumpy coral track that was poorly maintained. Squawking birds were everywhere, some colliding with the windshield, and the crunch of tires on hermit crab shells was quite unsettling. There were no trees or buildings that far east of the settlements, so the view of Canton's surf and the vast empty ocean was spectacular, but thought-provoking in view of the latest news.

Not long after they had rounded the easternmost tip of the atoll and started back along the north shore, they suddenly saw a US Navy Catalina seaplane settling down into the lagoon. Apparently it was in radio contact with Pan Am, as it knew exactly where on Southside to dock.

"Whoops, we could have given someone a lift, but I see a launch going over from Northside to collect them. Just carry on, Peter; we may learn something after all."

"I thought those amazing PBYs were amphibious," Peter said. "In theory they could have landed on the new runway instead of the lagoon, correct?"

"I suppose so, but didn't your Army chum say the runway wasn't going to be officially tested until January? See there; we're just passing the east end of the runway, as a matter of fact. Not a bad job, I must say, but a fairly rough coral surface still. What is the length again?"

"About 6200 feet, I think. Could handle bombers, and now probably will."

By the time the jeep reached the tents and incomplete terminal building at the start of the runway, the Catalina VIPs were still aboard the launch. Two more jeeps waited to drive them another 10 minutes from the lagoon to the terminal.

Graham waved to the Pan Am airport manager, who was also the US civil authority for Canton. He had apparently decided to check in with the military too and must have come over by launch.

"Halloo Uncle Sam, do you know Peter Perry, our engineer who's working with your Army chaps?"

"Yes, yes, of course; the 'Straight Flush' they call him. Welcome, Peter. I'm glad you're both here so we can all find out what news the Navy has brought. Things are really in chaos at Pearl; I would hate to be Admiral what's-his-name after that mess yesterday."

"Admiral Husband Kimmel," Peter blurted out, much to everyone's surprise. Graham coughed. "I read it somewhere," Peter added feebly.

"Oh? Strange first name. You're more up to date on US Navy things than we are, Peter," the Pan Am man observed drily.

The other jeeps pulled up, bringing three Navy officers who shook hands all around. The most senior was a Captain Weaver. The Pan Am manager asked: "Shall we go into the temporary tent and get out of the hot sun, gentlemen? Lemonade and miraculous flush-toilets await. After we finish, you'll be able to catch a meal back across the lagoon at Southside before you take off again, courtesy of the Pan Am Hotel. Meanwhile it'll take at least half an hour to refuel and check out the bird."

"Fine," Captain Weaver replied, "and many thanks to Pan Am for the hospitality. You have Army people here as well, I see. Engineers? Everyone seems to get on well together."

"Yes indeed, as we're not sure which is the senior service out here— Navy, Army or Pan Am!"

"That's a good one," the captain chuckled. "Well, I'm afraid it'll soon be Army for the foreseeable future, with all due respect, although we sailors will take over Pan Am's base to set up a seaplane shuttle service under our new NATS umbrella. NATS means Naval Air Transport Service, which will be operational this month under Lt. Commander Starkey, here", indicating another officer. "The Army's equivalent is ATC, which will be operating the land plane shuttles—and also the island's defenses.

"We're here today from American Samoa," he went on, "which already has a light garrison. But a complete Marine regiment—the Seventh Marines—will be on its way to us quite soon, under their famous Colonel 'Chesty' Puller, I might add. We should sleep well at night."

"No Marines for Canton then, sir?" an Army major asked.

"No sir," answered Captain Weaver. "Your troops will be Army, about 1,200 of them, but they can't get here until mid-February '42 due to other shipping priorities and their incomplete training. But you'll be fairly safe from the Japs, with the British Gilbert Islands as a buffer zone not too far away, except perhaps for possible submarines. I understand you'll be baptizing the new runway with a small squadron of B-17s next month, for anti-submarine patrol."

"I might add something too at this point," interjected the Pan Am manager. "We were just told that Pan Am won't be operating any more civilian flights through Canton for the foreseeable future, but our boss Juan Trippe has agreed with FDR that we will assist for a week or so to keep seaplane operations running smoothly for the initial Navy flights coming through. Pan Am has pretty good fuel and food reserves, and more is on order. There's a fairly robust water distillation system too."

"What happens to Pan Am after the week is over?" asked Graham Overwood.

"Gentlemen, this is Mr. Overwood, British representative to the Canton Island Condominium. Graham, I've been told that all US civilians will be evacuated around that one-week timeframe, but we don't have an exact date yet. Meanwhile please let us know what the British departure schedule is, when you can."

Graham nodded. Peter whispered: "Cripes, there goes my ride to Honolulu. Shouldn't we just tell the Navy Captain now about the Jap battleship?"

"Shh!" Graham almost hissed. "Heavens no, we want Britain to get credit for this intelligence coup, in view of all the splendid help that FDR—as they like to call the President—has given to Mr. Churchill for the past two years."

*** AFTERSHOCKS ***

The next day, December 9th, brought more encoded sad news to Canton Island. A Japanese air raid on Clark Field in the Philippines had destroyed most of General MacArthur's air force on the ground, in spite of ample warnings and alerts from Hawaii. Later, the Cavite Naval Base in Manila Bay was heavily bombed, and all but destroyed.

It was difficult to comprehend, and the Americans on Canton seemed to lose some of their characteristic bluster, especially when they learned that Wake Island—an already-garrisoned Pan Am seaplane base—had been attacked and was barely holding.

Then too, Guam, a larger US possession in the Marianas that included yet another Pan Am base, was also under attack and would likely capitulate. The Japs were kicking everyone in sight!

Next it was the British turn to be humbled. Japanese naval forces invaded Betio in the Tarawa atoll that very day, in the 'nearby buffer of the Gilberts,' from which most British expatriates had departed in haste to the southern islands of the Ellice group, and even to Fiji. Canton seemed suddenly naked!

"Damn," said Graham. "That means we'll be within bomber range from Tarawa before long."

News came of another great disaster that befell the British, after a Japanese invasion fleet was spotted leaving Viet Nam in the direction of

Malaya and Thailand. Viet Nam, with its excellent harbors and airfields—part of the French colony of Indochina that had unfortunately sided with the German-controlled Vichy French faction—was regarded by Japan as a pro-German ally that they could bully their way into occupying, under terms of the Tripartite Pact.

The two British capital ships that had just days before reached Singapore without a companion aircraft carrier, set forth bravely with a small screen of destroyers as Force Z to attack the Japanese invasion fleet. Alarmingly, the British flotilla had no land-based air cover either, and ultimately the capital ships were unable to locate the Japanese transports due to misleading information from the Singapore garrison.

But Japanese aircraft—also from Viet Nam—managed to spot the British warships, and after a number of vigorous attacks sank them both with bombs and torpedoes off the east coast of Malaya!

Thus, at one stroke went battleship HMS *Prince of Wales* and battlecruiser HMS *Repulse* to the bottom of the sea with their admiral and more than 800 other souls, as Japan demonstrated that under the right conditions air power could dispense with anything afloat. It would be a sobering lesson for the gunboat schools of naval strategy the world over, and one that would probably be retaught several times before the war ended.

The only vague glimmer of good news from the string of recent disasters was that US aircraft carriers *Saratoga*, *Lexington,* and *Enterprise* had been away at sea on assignments when Japanese planes struck Pearl Harbor. The about-to-be-obsolete battleships at Pearl took the brunt of Admiral Yamamoto's ingenious plan of attack, therefore, and were incapable of preventing his fleet's clever escape back to Japan.

On December 10th, more alarming news rolled in. Makin Atoll in the British Gilberts fell to Japanese invaders a day after Tarawa, as did Guam in the Marianas. The Japanese were expanding their bases in all directions! Canton Island's recent nearby protective buffer of the Gilberts was now a Japanese buffer for its fleet anchorages in the Marshall Islands further west, an abrupt change of role!

Wake Island's Marines and civilians were still holding their own against great odds, evoking many cheers from the Canton listeners, but their days were doubtless numbered. Admiral Kimmel, before being relieved as CINCPAC at his own request, had dispatched a small carrier task force to help defend Wake. Vice Admiral Pye, his senior assistant—who was placed temporarily in charge of the Pacific fleet—canceled the Wake Island rescue rather than risk the loss of a precious carrier, so Wake was left to fight on ... and surrender.

After hearing the terrible news from Singapore in particular, Peter was of course worried about Wendy, and with Pan Am going out of business in the Pacific he didn't quite know how to reach her. *Will there continue to be any postal service? Can Pan Am help me send a cable to Wendy before they close down the Canton facility? Should she and young John try to get away from Singapore now, and if so—to where?*

Wendy and Peter's parents and relatives were mostly in England, which was virtually under siege by Hitler's air forces. It seemed the last place anyone ought to think of going in 1942, even if there were a way to do so. It would certainly bear some serious thought.

Next morning, Pan Am called Graham Overwood to ask what the British plan was for evacuation of Canton Island. Graham said there was still no plan, therefore the small British contingent would be staying to keep an eye on things. Graham couldn't resist a touch of smugness in his voice, but instantly regretted it. This was no time for friction with the Americans.

Some Navy people trickled in to take over the lagoon operations that Pan Am would be leaving behind, but there was not much liaison between the naval and civilian teams.

On December eleventh, Germany declared war on the United States, in response to Japan's declaration. The US Congress declared war on Germany hours later. It was a world war once again.

Then on December 12th, the complete Pan Am staff was suddenly evacuated to American Samoa by ship, leaving behind essentially everything they had worked so hard and so long to accomplish—the hotel, the housing, the storage tanks, electrical and desalination equipment; the docks, launches, and vehicles. Some staff members were quite frustrated at being ordered out, but most were relieved to be getting away from what might easily become a war zone in a matter of days. News of the civilians on Wake Island lingered, who were still under siege along with their Marine garrison.

Army engineers on Canton were rushing to complete the airport runway and terminal building, and on the nineteenth a dozen or so military ATC staff arrived to organize the site for land plane operations. The new airport was officially named *Topham Field Canton Island*, after an Army Air Corps pilot who had died in a mid-air collision.

Peter Perry carried on working with the Army on water and sewage refinements, both to keep himself busy and to see that his billable time was being duly recorded and vouchered. He had cabled Wendy in Singapore, asking her to take their son to Australia as soon as possible, and then perhaps to Canada where he hoped there might be a safe haven and he could eventually join them. Unfortunately, most people in Singapore still thought themselves safe from the war, mainly because of misleading British propaganda, so Peter had to push hard to get Wendy to agree to the 'silly evacuation', as she called it:

"After all, our friends are not planning to leave," she wrote, "and the beastly Japanese are far away in the north of Malaya where British and Australian troops will no doubt box them in."

*** *PAN AM REMEMBERED* ***

The original tiny British community of four on Canton Island represented an anomaly to the newly-arrived American military at first—apart from Peter who was well known to the Army people—but gradually they were appreciated for their detailed knowledge of Canton's past events, the hot but changeable weather, and the spartan lifestyle routine.

Although not familiar with the workings of Pan Am's comfortable hotel, Lois and Graham did know where some things were kept. With the loyal assistance of John and Gordon, they did their best as a surrogate hotel management team to train a group of Filipinos to support the incoming NATS officers who would billet there. The Chamorro employees had all left with Pan Am, although they couldn't of course be repatriated to Guam.

Graham's wireless reports were devoured by everyone, even the sad one of December 23rd when word came that the gallant survivors on Wake Island had finally surrendered, and now faced captivity. Next day—Christmas Eve—the British garrison on Hong Kong also surrendered after a final bitter fight, which threw Graham into the depths of despair.

31

Hospital nurses there were raped in a drunken orgy by Jap soldiers. Peter remembered a brief holiday that he and Wendy had taken at Hong Kong's charming Repulse Bay Hotel when John was a baby. The news was too sad for words.

The singing on Christmas Eve was quite emotional, but the holiday itself was just another workday on Canton Island.

Christmas was a workday for Admiral Chester Nimitz too, as he arrived in Hawaii as CINCPAC to immediately take command of the Pacific fleet and facilities from the temporary commander Admiral Pye, Admiral Kimmel having already returned to the US under a cloud. The Army commander, General Walter Short, was likewise soon relieved of command. Both Kimmel and Short were reduced in rank to two stars although it was generally felt that the Pearl Harbor disaster was not entirely their fault.

Fears of a Japanese attack dogged everyone's spirits on Canton Island as January 1942 arrived, but there was fortunately no such aggression. Japan had apparently failed to appreciate the atoll's future importance to the US military linkage with Australia and New Zealand. It was almost as if their brass were also saying, like the British and Americans: "Canton Island? Where on earth is that?"

Moreover, Japan was still hotly engaged in subjugating Malaya and the Philippines, in a relentless southward drive to neutralize British Singapore and capture the Dutch East Indies with its vital oil and refineries. That final prize was why Japan had launched the Pacific war in the first place, to counter the US embargo that had been announced by FDR after Japan took control of northern Viet-Nam, in their endless war against China.

Then all of a sudden, life became refocused on Pan American Airways for a short while, as an amazing report came in about the last westbound clipper flight that had left Canton Island on December 5th. Captain Ford had in due course delivered his passengers to Suva, Nouméa, and Auckland, only to learn about the Pearl Harbor raid. He was promptly instructed by Juan Trippe not to return eastward, for fear of having the plane captured or destroyed somehow by the Japanese.

"Normal return route canceled. Proceed as follows: Strip all company marking, registration numbers and identifiable insignia from exterior surfaces.

Proceed westbound soonest your discretion to avoid hostilities and deliver NC18602 to marine terminal La Guardia Field New York. Good luck."

Captain Ford promptly returned from Auckland to Nouméa, to collect Pan Am's twenty-two ground staff members from a large rented motor yacht that served as the company's surrogate hotel and staff quarters. After dropping them off in Australia, he and the flight crew flew on westward in a series of adventures worthy of the best talent in Hollywood, refueling at far-flung places with exotic names like Surabaya, Trincomalee, Karachi, Bahrain, Khartoum, Leopoldville, Natal, and Port-of-Spain, eventually reaching the marine air terminal at La Guardia in New York on January 6, 1942—just a month after leaving Canton Island!

By dint of this feat, Pan Am and its resourceful Captain Bob Ford established a record for the world's first round-the-world commercial airline flight—USA to USA!

*** A LOOK AT ENDERBURY ***

Also, in January '42, the new Canton runway, Topham Field, was finally put to use as three B-17 scout bombers began anti-submarine patrols, with some eventual successes. Having this added security in the region, Graham Overwood decided it was time to take Peter Perry on a tour of Enderbury Island, sixty miles away, to search out a secure 'vault' for the backup microfilm of the secret Japanese battleship *Yamato*.

Without of course explaining the real reason, Graham duly advised the US Army and Navy commanders of his plan to inspect Enderbury on behalf of the condominium, which resulted in good-natured smiles and comments.

"OK, Graham, we'll patrol the skies while you Brits patrol the seas. Have a care for Jap subs, although a thirty-foot wooden boat under sail should be fairly hard for them to detect."

"We'll be fine," Graham chuckled, "just tell your B-17s not to strafe us, please!"

Before leaving Canton, they had learned from NATS that a Coast Guard cutter, USCGC *Taney*, would arrive in the area by February, to evacuate the quartet of Hawaiian boys from each remaining US 'settlement island,' namely Enderbury, Jarvis, and Palmyra. *Taney* would also be escorting a supply ship for Canton Island which, after a few days unloading offshore into lighters, would carry all the Hawaiian boys back to Honolulu under *Taney's* protective five-inch guns, thereby ending the peculiar three-year US settlement program—the Department of the Interior's brainchild—once and for all.

Wanting to inspect Enderbury before *Taney* arrived in the area, Graham left John, one of the Gilbertese staff, behind on Canton to continue flag drill and wireless monitoring, while Graham, Lois, Peter, and Gordon—the other Gilbertese—set sail on *Zanzibar* very early in the day for Enderbury Island. They reached it close to sundown.

Peter, a member of the Royal Singapore Yacht Club but not really a 'blue water' (deep sea) sailor, was mightily impressed with the lapstrake-planked, double-ended Tahiti-type ketch, and even more so with the polished seamanship of both Graham and Lois, as they tacked *Zanzibar* southeast into the trade winds with exquisite finesse and timing. Because Enderbury was a low land mass like Canton, with even fewer trees, *Zanzibar* was completely out of sight of land for most of the day, but the Overwoods' dead-reckoning and occasional sun shot proved impeccable as they fetched up in the southwest lee of Enderbury Island, to be hailed by one of the Hawaiians on shore. It was clear that either of the Overwoods could sail the boat single-handed, if necessary.

Unfortunately, Enderbury was not an atoll like Canton, with a calm inner lagoon in which to safely anchor. It was just a flattish three-by-one-mile blob on the ocean, with a north-south orientation and a slight depression in the middle that on rare occasions could get swampy after an extended rainfall. Its only offshore anchorage, at the southwest corner, was subject to dragging, so everyone stood a turn at anchor watch that night.

At first light, the dinghy was launched and loaded; Lois stayed behind on *Zanzibar* with Gordon, as Graham and Peter rowed cautiously through the surf to a little sandy beach near some strange-looking wooden buildings.

The resident Enderbury boys helped Graham and Peter pull *Zanzibar's* dinghy well up onto the sand, then gave shouts of delight upon seeing the gifts and supplies that the little rowboat contained for them. Two of the boys stayed at the beach in case *Zanzibar* might require assistance, while the other two took Graham and Peter for a tour of the rather ugly little island, that had been a guano strip-mine for both American and British companies in the late 1800s. There were still some little rusting rail tracks here and there, but otherwise not very much of interest from the previous century. A few trees struggled for survival, and the island surface was for the most part a patchy blight of carelessly abandoned diggings. Peter wondered how the boys could stand to live there.

At the southwest corner near the landing beach stood a collection of odd-shaped wooden buildings, where the boys resided. The idea was apparently to give the appearance of a larger settlement, but another of those stage sets—which seemed borrowed from a low-budget cowboy film—had unfortunately attracted recent deadly Japanese air and submarine raids on Howland Island that killed two of the young settlers there. The Japs apparently thought the disused airfield built for Amelia Earhart was also for military use, which was both silly and tragic.

Peter and Graham decided not to hide the Monkey Pod micro-film on Enderbury at that time, because it would be too likely that the resident boys would retrace the visitors' footsteps and discover it. Instead, Peter would return from Canton aboard *Taney* and deal with the 'Tarawa Treasure'—as Lois had named the Monkey Pod necklace—once the boys and their possessions were aboard the escorted freighter. Peter and an officer from *Taney* would then install a plaque attesting to the abandonment of Enderbury Island. Coast Guard gunners would gleefully destroy the wooden buildings with five-inch fragmentation rounds—carefully avoiding the location of the official plaque. All this was a future plan, likely to be followed within one or two weeks.

Meanwhile back aboard *Zanzibar* around nine in the morning, Graham and Peter hauled the dinghy aboard, waved to the Hawaiian boys on shore, and immediately set sail for Canton Island. This time the passage was a fast, downwind run at 10 knots, and they were safe inside the Canton lagoon by toddy time. Far across the lagoon they could make out the American machines, still hard at work on the new airfield.

"'A fair wind and a following sea'; it feels good to be home, eh Peter?" Lois smiled and passed around some chilled beers that John had brought down on a tray from their kerosene refrigerator.

"I'll say," Peter nodded his thanks to John, then Graham beckoned Lois and Peter to the veranda as the two Gilbertese went to tidy up the yacht.

"Cheers, you lot. Look, I've been thinking about the buried treasure. How does this sound to you? If we just select a piece of solid coral, say about twice the diameter of a cricket ball, then hollow it out so the Monkey Pod can fit inside, we would have a long-lasting time capsule worthy of Jules Verne. After plugging up the hole, why no one could tell it apart from any other godforsaken lump of coral, correct? Your thoughts?"

"We'd better stain it a peculiar color, Graham, or people won't be able to recognize it, if it ever needs to be recovered," Lois observed.

"Good point," said Peter, "and we did find just the perfect spot on Enderbury to stash something like that. Almost directly on the opposite side of the island from the little settlement buildings that *Taney* will destroy—lord knows why they bother—is the base of a small broken monument that one of the guano companies left behind ages ago. It's not far from the windward shore on the southeastern side. We can dig down behind the monument shards and hide the coral there."

"Perfect, that way we can show an exact reference point on the 'treasure map', me hearties." Graham, enjoying his third beer, began singing *Hurrah for the Pirate King* from the Gilbert & Sullivan operetta.

"Graham, please shut up; you're embarrassing Peter," Lois pleaded.

"Pour oh pour the pirate sherry," Graham continued singing, passing his empty beer bottle to Lois. "You mean I'm embarrassing you, little Buttercup, isn't that it?"

At that moment a Navy jeep pulled up to the residence, halting Graham in mid-stanza on a high note that sounded like *'ing'*. A well-attired young ensign in khaki shirt and shorts, trying hard not to look askance at the salty and disheveled trio, coughed and announced to Graham:

"Beg pardon, sir; skipper's compliments. Some female officers from Pago Pago have arrived on the Martin flying boat for an overnight stay, and Lt. Commander Starkey wishes to invite your, er, excellency and guests to dine at 1930 hours." The ensign coughed again.

"Nicely stated, young man, nicely stated." Graham straightened up and assumed the dignified but slightly wobbly persona of a British Resident in full flight. "You can no doubt appreciate that we have only just returned from an ocean voyage on the residential yacht, but as one hour remains before the appointed time, please return our compliments to Lieutenant

36

Commander Starkey (stressing the 'left' in lieutenant) and confirm that we shall be most delighted to accept his kind invitation this evening."

Graham then wheeled about smartly: "And I trust that goes for Lady Overwood and Group Captain Perry as well," he added. They both nodded in wonderment. The ensign saluted and started toward his jeep. Graham called after him: "Summer-service dress, I presume?"

"Oh, sorry sir; aye, aye sir. Khaki shorts and long socks."

"Well, now, that was most impressive," Peter chuckled, wide-eyed, as the jeep drove away, "but 'Group Captain Perry' is stretching things a bit. You well know that I am merely a member of the Singapore Engineer reserves, just a civilian in disguise," he pointed out.

"Tut-tut," Graham countered. "The RAF have such lovely titles, particularly impressive to Americans. I almost said: 'Wing Commander Perry', but that might have been challenged at dinner due to your lack of the customary mustache. Furthermore, should anyone choose to address us Perrys as Sir Graham and Lady Lois, then we shall simply smile demurely, shan't we dear?"

"Oh quite," answered Lois, "but now we must rush and get civilized, as it's a ten-minute walk. Off with you to the guest house, Peter. We shall meet in the hotel at half past seven, sharp!"

"And Peter," Graham hastened to say, "now that those surly Pan Am louts have vanished, they who heckled us mercilessly for years, let's have a spot of merriment with the newly arrived anglophiles, what? Until it's time for your departure, that is, when *Taney* arrives next month. But no balderdash, mind you; we must maintain our dignity. I shall teach Gordon and John to raise and lower the flag with more aplomb. And Lois, we must have *God Save the King* on the gramophone."

She smiled: "Yes dear, I think we still have a new packet of needles."

*** *A LAST HURRAH* ***

Thus passed the last three weeks of January 1942, with the Overwoods no longer the butt of Pan Am jokes but suddenly the most sought-after advisors on the island, deferentially consulted on all manner of topics like a pair of beloved scout leaders. Graham's daily coded wireless communications, which still took a fair amount of his time, were directed to the High

Commissioner's office in Fiji now that the Gilberts were occupied by the Japanese. The busy new routine was physically hard on Graham, who was nearly into his sixties, but at first he hardly noticed the strain, so joyful were he and Lois at being welcomed back into the human race.

While everyone on Canton lived from day to day in apprehension of a Japanese invasion that inexplicably never materialized, such apprehension was further fueled by news that Rabaul, near New Guinea, had been captured by the Japanese from its small garrison of Australian militia. That provoked discussion about a possible Japanese conquest of New Guinea itself, just a hundred miles north of Australia.

Meanwhile, on Canton Island, there was always an underlying buzz of frenetic activity as newly arrived Army personnel erected a tent camp on Northside, and the Navy transformed previous Pan Am habitations on Southside to suit their new mission. Vanishing four-star-quality furnishings from the Pan Am hotel gradually lent a thin touch of elegance to various new command posts and social clubs, with some items even finding their way to bunkers that had been bulldozed underground into the coral.

Pillage was so complete that any postwar Pan Am hotel would likely be a rattan version more in tune with the informal Pacific environment. In the meanwhile, replacement hotel furnishings were metal bunks for its new role as a BOQ.

Peter continued assisting the Army on engineering matters, and thoroughly enjoyed himself. Best of all, Wendy wrote that she had purchased tickets for John and herself to Darwin, Australia. She told Peter she was beginning to realize his insistence on their leaving Singapore was the right decision, as the Japanese were still not defeated on the Malay Peninsula.

*** BORA-BORA ***

News reached Canton that the Army had chartered the liner SS *President Taylor* from American President Lines (APL), to deliver a regiment of troops between Bora-Bora, Fanning, Christmas, and Canton Islands, in that order. The escorted convoy was called *Task Force Holly*.

Bora-Bora would become the South Pacific Theater's major US fuel depot and supply point, from where oil tankers large and small would distribute the essential fluids far and wide, to combat zones, warships, and the less-deserving.

In Bora-Bora a strange phenomenon was scarcely noticed at first. Its military personnel would re-enlist, rebel, go AWOL into hiding, and even become suicidal, in order to avoid being transferred away from that lovely South Seas atoll with its hundreds of unattached Polynesian girls. Cohabitation became entrenched throughout the chain of command, and the astonishing secret was completely suppressed from the outside world.

Bora-Bora was one of the Society Islands administered by Tahiti, that fortuitously had sided with the Free French rather than the Vichy French as Indochina had done. Most of *TF Holly* would be disembarked there, poor souls. The remainder would be left at Canton and those other two pleasant rest stops.

*** CLOSURE OF THE CANTON ISLAND RESIDENCY ***

One late-January afternoon, when Graham, Lois, and Peter were sharing a drink on the veranda after hours, Graham suddenly announced: "I've had it, friends. I have resigned this very day!"

"What?" said Peter. "Oh good," said Lois.

"At long last," said Graham, "as I have been wasting away on this God-forsaken island for nearly four years and am now completely worn out."

"Won't you miss the birds, Graham?" Peter shouted over the raucous sundown chorus.

Graham snorted: "Truthfully these past few weeks have been the very best of my entire life. I love my dear Lois more than ever, I even love the ruddy Yanks, although I would never admit it publicly, and I probably love you too, you sodding Singaporean. But I've completely run out of steam, really I have." Lois moved close to Graham's chair, protectively.

"There's another reason as well," Graham went on, taking Lois' proffered hand in his. "Sir Harry is retiring from the Colonial Service this year, y'know. I suspect he is quite weary of looking after the Allied brass that float through Fiji like a tidal stream. I have no empathy at all with the new chap, Philip Euen Mitchell, whom they will be sending out from London, though he may well be a splendid fellow too. At any rate, I've managed to negotiate six months of medical leave with Sir Harry, so Lois and I can regain our health and take our sweet time finding something war-related but calmer to occupy us."

Lois kissed Graham tenderly. "Yes dear, it is a logical time to leave, I agree. Your American cowboys claimed Canton Island from the very beginning, although I must say this recent lot has been wonderful to know."

"Right, then, here's the plan."

*** FAREWELL TO CANTON ***

The send-off for the little British community, still piously referred to by Graham as "the Five Christians," was a 'real blast,' even by time-honored US Army and Navy standards. Thursday, February 5th, was of course a 1942 workday, but Coast Guard vessel *Taney* and an escorted freighter had anchored offshore early that morning, with supplies for the Canton garrison. The workday for most people began and ended earlier than usual, therefore, except for ongoing stevedoring, guard duties, and the B-17 submarine patrols that continued until dark.

Taney's arrival meant it was time for *Zanzibar's* departure. Accordingly, *Taney's* new skipper, Cdr. Louis Olson, came ashore to seek out Peter Perry and discuss the pre-arranged lift to Honolulu. They conferred at the residency with Graham and Lois present, as Graham had a long acquaintance with that fine ship going back to 1938, when supplies for the American community were delivered by *Taney's* launches to the little British dock in the lagoon, the only suitable place at the time.

"Yes," Graham reminisced, "I well remember meeting Commander Coffin's executive officer Mr. Kelliher, who led the shore party into the lagoon in *Taney's* small fleet of boats. Each of those launches was stenciled 'R. B. T.', I suppose because '*Roger B. Taney*,' the ship's official name at that time, would have looked outsized on them."

"Exactly right," the new skipper said, "but now that we're part of the Navy for a while, we are officially just 'USS *Taney* (CG),' less of a mouthful. Same ship and crew, however. Our home port has been Honolulu ever since '36, soon after the good old *Roger B* was launched in Philadelphia. The lads really look forward to these cruises out to the Phoenix and other islands, even in wartime. They call them Line Cruises; I suppose because we first reach Line Islands such as Christmas and Palmyra."

As far as everyone on Canton was concerned, Peter would be sailing off to Fiji that evening with Graham, Lois, John and Gordon, the latter two becoming official Gilbertese refugees because of the recent Japanese invasion of their homeland. But in reality, Peter would be dropped off by *Zanzibar* at Enderbury Island, to supervise the four Hawaiian settlers' preparation for leaving on the freighter a day later. Then Peter would be taken aboard *Taney* after she escorted the freighter to Enderbury, once he had quickly buried the micro-film monkey pod.

With lengthy planned stops at Jarvis and Palmyra Islands, they would probably not reach Honolulu until the end of February, some weeks after SS *President Taylor* would have delivered anxiously awaited troops and anti-aircraft guns to Canton Island. Peter would always remember the bittersweet Canton sendoff party that afternoon, courtesy of the US Army and Navy. Everyone not on duty seemed to be at the lagoon beach by the British compound, where few had ever visited before, cavorting in the water and paying only slight attention to the speeches, toasts and well-wishing.

There was, of course, a toast to Pan Am, which brought forth just the slightest of smirks from Graham, as he knew Lois was watching him closely.

Peter received a nice accolade, a certificate of appreciation and a medal of some sort from the Army engineers. The 'Straight Flush' was not mentioned, but there seemed to be a bit of laughter now and then.

Swimming and diving contests were in full flourish, while beer, gin and whiskies flowed in abundance. The din of laughter, bird shrieks, and pounding surf almost drowned out a little brass band that diligently performed *God Save the King*, as Graham lowered the Union Jack for the last time.

The flag was carefully folded and presented to Navy Captain Weaver, who had come over again by PBY from Pago Pago for the occasion. He in turn presented a folded American flag to Graham, who, with glistening eyes, said he would treasure it always. Peter clapped Graham on the back, and Lois gave them both a big hug. Graham then turned over the keys to the British compound and buildings to Captain Weaver, together with a contents list that was duly received and signed.

"Good, you'll be taking the transmitter, I see," said the captain. Graham nodded.

After the official ceremonies, when the temperature began to drop and exuberance abated, Lois began playing her collection of popular European wartime songs on the gramophone—*Some Sunny Day; Bless 'em All; I'll See You Again; Lilli Marlene; The White Cliffs of Dover*. Not all were known to the Americans yet, but they asked for repeats and soon learned the nostalgic words.

Then news of Singapore came over the wireless, and it was very bad. The Japanese Army under General Yamashita had reached the southernmost Malayan city of Johore Bahru, just across a narrow body of water from Singapore Island, having out-thought and out-fought the British and Australian defenders down through two hundred miles of jungle. A vehicular causeway connecting Johore and Singapore had been blown up by the British, after a pair of Scottish pipers in full highland regalia had marched across behind the last British stragglers.

If the Japanese managed to cross the waterway, the ultimate battle for Singapore would begin and it would be hard fought. Even then, however, fresh Australian troops and crated aircraft were arriving on the island, and there was still hope.

Peter was 'thankful to the lord above', that he had insisted on Wendy leaving for Australia six weeks beforehand. Many of their friends, who had stubbornly stayed on, might soon be behind barbed wire, or worse.

Just before sundown, the Five Christians boarded *Zanzibar* and cast off into the lagoon. Peter had already entrusted his Hawaii-destined kimono-doll luggage to *Taney's* skipper, and now in a haversack he carried the purple 'bowling ball' and an Army entrenching tool, to bring ashore on Enderbury. One micro-film would be buried on Enderbury, and the other would travel with him to Honolulu. It was indeed a strange secret, as Graham often said.

Zanzibar passed close to the Musick Light, and those aboard sang out to Captain Weaver: "For he's a jolly good fellow, and so say all of us!"

Then the sturdy old ketch, under jib and mizzen alone, eased through the reef channel at slack tide while the little brass band on shore broke forth with *The Star-Spangled Banner*. Those paying attention, stood at attention.

CHAPTER TWO

Hawaii to Fiji

大和

Yamato, an ancient Japanese province

"One measurement is worth a thousand words"
Variation on a theme

*** *THE US COAST GUARD* ***

Sir Harry Luke's office had arranged through channels for Peter Perry's passage from Enderbury Island to Hawaii with the little *Taney* convoy. Important things would no doubt be brewing in the Pacific Theater before long, and Peter was eager to hand over the kimono-clad microfilm to the US Navy, and afterwards get the three Perrys out of the crossfire. Wendy had cabled before Peter left Canton, that she and little John were booked on a passenger-freighter from Singapore to Darwin in a few days' time, which Peter was very glad to hear. They would reach Darwin before Peter got to Hawaii.

Former Coast Guard Cutter *Roger B. Taney,* now USS *Taney* (CG) under Navy oversight, Cdr. Louis B. Olson commanding, eventually returned to its base at Oahu, Territory of Hawaii, the morning of Thursday March 5, 1942. She had delivered supplies to Canton Island, and afterwards collected a dozen Hawaiian 'settlers' from Enderbury, Jarvis, and Palmyra Islands. These young men, last of a fanciful 1937 island settlement program conceived by the prestigious Bernice P. Bishop Museum of Honolulu and ordained by the US Department of the Interior, were finally home to Hawaii aboard the freighter SS *Barbara Olson* (no relation to *Taney's* skipper), that the cutter had been escorting at a slowly zigzagged twelve knots. Luckily there had been no sightings of Japanese submarines. The returning settlers would be delivered to Coast Guard Station Oahu in Honolulu Harbor. Most of the boys seemed eager to join one of the services and go off to war.

Peter Perry would likewise be delivered to the Coast Guard Station, which was situated near Honolulu's handsome Aloha Tower. Being a US ally in the British Army's engineering reserves for Singapore, Peter had been able to travel aboard *Taney* herself—rather than the freighter—and was much intrigued by the disciplined handling of the fairly new (1936) search-and-rescue cutter, one of seven sister ships known as 'Secretary

Class Three-Two-Sevens'. They were 327 feet in length, and each had been named for a former US Secretary of the Treasury.

The Treasury Department, during the rough old days of Prohibition smuggling, had acquired oversight of the United States Coast Guard, but not long before war broke out with Japan in 1941 that responsibility was transferred to the Department of the Navy—firstly just the 'seven sisters', then a month later the entire nationwide Coast Guard organization.

Taney was still fondly referred to as '*The Roger B*' by her original shipmates—the 'plank owners'—most of whom had already visited Canton Island a time or two, as Peter learned en route.

The Fourteenth Coast Guard District home port was in Honolulu's commercial harbor, rather than the nearby naval fleet anchorage at Pearl. *Taney* had been at her pier on December 7th but escaped damage while pluckily firing her five-inchers and machine guns at Japanese aircraft coming and going over Pearl Harbor and occasionally threatening Honolulu itself. One Jap sortie made as if to attack the Honolulu power plant, but energetic bursts of AA fire from *Taney* caused the planes to skitter away.

Peter became quite intrigued by the US Coast Guard after spending nearly a month aboard *Taney*. At their academy in New London, Connecticut, cadets followed a traditional maritime curriculum like midshipmen of the Naval Academy at Annapolis, Maryland, but with added specialty courses to do with Smuggling, Search & Rescue, and Immigration.

On this morning's approach to the south coast of Oahu, Peter had been invited to join the skipper and officer-of-the-watch on the bridge and was carefully keeping himself out of everyone's way. He could sense the underlying excitement there in the wheelhouse as the beautiful green island of Oahu gradually hove into view, with its tall prominent peak and shaded valleys.

British explorer Captain James Cook must have marveled at a similar view when he first saw these islands in 1778 aboard HMS *Endeavor*. He named them the Sandwich Islands, after his English patron the Earl of Sandwich, and they were known to the world by that name until entrenched American business interests in the islands forced the Hawaiian monarchy to abdicate in 1898. Soon thereafter they became the US Territory of Hawaii, or TH for short.

As *Taney's* northeastward course drew closer to the shoreline, several features were identified for Peter by Commander Olson: "That high peak off the starboard bow is called Diamond Head. The strip of sand to our right, or west of it, is Waikiki Beach. After Waikiki comes Honolulu harbor, now dead ahead where we'll be docking. You can just see the lighthouse—Aloha Tower.

"To the west of Honolulu is Pearl Harbor, where most of the Jap raids took place in December. You'll no doubt see the effect of the raids when you visit Pearl tomorrow; they really clobbered us."

The bridge signalman blinkered a message to a Navy destroyer on picket patrol, and the radio operator handed the captain a message from the harbormaster. Two Navy fighter planes flew overhead. "We're clear to come on in now," the skipper told Peter.

Then the duty officer announced to the crew: "Duty section stand by to dock, starboard side to," and rang the engine room "slow all to one third", as *Taney* slid past Sand Island into the commercial basin, followed by the freighter.

Then came "all ahead slow", as *Taney's* outside berth at Pier Six grew closer. The OD rang for "all astern" and then "neutral" as Taney continued coasting slowly toward the pier bulkhead, where guardsmen on shore were attaching extra fenders. Soon, lightweight heaving lines were expertly cast to Taney's deck crew fore and aft, who used them to pull the heavy dock lines aboard.

"Make fast forr'd." A dock line was dropped over a ship's bollard and the line was cleated on shore. At another command, the helmsman spun the wheel to port and the OD ordered the port engine momentarily ahead. The ship's stern eased to starboard toward the bulkhead and was made fast. Spring lines were then set, and a gangway was taken aboard.

The OD saluted the captain: "All secure, sir. Permission to stop engines?" *Taney* was home again and a blessed quiet descended over the ship. An entry was made in the logbook.

The freighter astern was directed to Pier Five, where arrangements had been made for the pseudo-settlers to be delivered to their former school and relieved parents. The unusual program paid those lads the rather princely

46

sum of one hundred sixty dollars per month, which parents and siblings were no doubt eyeing possessively.

After the dockside midday meal aboard *Taney*, Peter was offered lodging for the night at the Coast Guard duty offices, which contained two small en-suite rooms for such occasions. He accepted gratefully and invited *Taney's* captain and XO to dine ashore that evening.

"Very kind of you, Mr. Perry," the skipper replied, "but we will have a Navy inspection tomorrow morning, part of the general panic that still pervades Honolulu. *Itasca* is already back in port, and her crew will help us work this afternoon and most of tonight, to get *Taney* squared away. I'm sure you understand. But by the way, do you know how to reach CINCPAC headquarters tomorrow in Pearl City?" Peter shook his head.

"Well, let's see; I can let you have our staff car and driver in the morning while we're tied up with Navy brass, but he'll need to leave you there in the unlikely event that Admiral Nimitz or his aide will receive you without an appointment. Most probably they won't, so we'll ask our yeoman to tarry just half an hour, on the assumption you could catch a ride back to Honolulu from the Navy if they do invite you to stay. Otherwise he can bring you back here or drop you anywhere you like. Be sure to take your British military ID or something else official, so the driver can get you through security, OK?"

"I'll take everything I have just in case, bags and all, and thank you Commander Olson for the transportation. You have been a wonderful host," Peter said. "The trip from Enderbury to those other two islands, and here to Honolulu, was really quite special. I wish you and your fine crew the very best of adventures in future."

"And we hope you get yourself to Australia, or bring your family to the States," was the reply, "and of course we also hope our friends the Overwoods made it safely to Fiji. Do let us know if there is any news."

Peter had been thinking about the Overwoods too, and the hasty goodbye at Enderbury Island where they had left him to await *Taney's* arrival. He very much hoped they would meet again somehow, preferably aboard *Zanzibar*.

"By the way, Mr. Perry, we heard some old—and odd—news of Canton Island this morning. Apparently the chartered liner *President Taylor* did bring those twelve hundred Army troops to Canton as scheduled—shortly after we left Enderbury, as a matter of fact—but somehow she managed to drift onto the reef near the tidal channel. We don't yet know how it happened, but so far they haven't been able to float her free; meanwhile she's being slowly unloaded outside the reef. It sounds to us like she's been holed by some coral heads, in which case she may be there forever. I don't imagine APL, the owners, are very pleased."

"Cripes, quite a disaster," said Peter, "but at least it'll be easier for fliers to spot the island now—small consolation, though."

"And easier for Jap subs too!" replied the skipper. "Oh, and I forgot to mention something else. You said you were eager for some Chinese food; well there are several little places around the docks here, not too fancy of course, but acceptable. Just be sure to get back off the street by seven this evening, as these islands are now under martial law and a curfew. There should be some notices in your quarters."

"Really? A curfew in Hawaii? I had no idea," said Peter, "and what about money changers? I mostly have Malayan dollars from Singapore. Are there any places near the docks, or will I need to find a bank?"

"The restaurant owners can probably assist. This is a fairly international waterfront, as a matter of fact, although nothing like your busy Singapore. OK then, goodbye once again. Our car will collect you at 0730." The two officers shook hands with Peter and hurried off to prepare for the Navy delegation in the morning.

Peter hefted his luggage down the wharf to the little Coast Guard BOQ. He was desperate for news from Singapore, which he last heard was facing the Japanese army at Johore, Malaya, practically next door. Perhaps a Chinese restaurant would know something more, as Peter's news was already three weeks old.

He showered and dressed and pressed some clothes for the morning visit to CINCPAC, then hurried past the docks toward a cluster of buildings near the Aloha Tower. It was only two in the afternoon, but he was eager to find his way around the port city.

He also needed postage stamps to write Wendy, though he had enough American money from his card games for that. Peter had recently suggested she look for a way from Darwin down to Sydney, where she would be safe from air raids and perhaps there might be a better chance of getting passage to Canada. Their son John was now almost seven, and probably somewhat behind in his schooling.

*** *THE HONOLULU WATERFRONT* ***

The tall and elegant Aloha Tower, built in 1926, was attached to some warehouse buildings at Pier Nine. It was both a lighthouse and clock tower and held the harbormaster's offices. *Taney* at Pier Six had been ordered to defend the tower during the Japanese attack in December, which they did very well.

As Peter came closer, he could see several shops and offices as well as a vaguely oriental restaurant whose name, City Noodle Shop, did not really give a clue as to its ownership and menu. It could be Chinese or perhaps Japanese but turned out to be both. He peered through a bead curtain in the doorway and saw a dimly lit room with about a dozen empty tables and booths, and wobbly rotating ceiling fans. Nondescript pictures hanging here and there provided the only décor, except for a small red altar near the kitchen door. A delicious and familiar aroma made Peter's stomach rumble and eyes water. He called a 'halloo'.

"Welcome, sir, please. We still open for late lunch." A smiling woman in her thirties, perhaps an owner, came from the kitchen and invited Peter to a table near the window. "What to drink?" she murmured, dropping a menu onto the table.

"Hot tea, please, and can you change me some money?" Peter showed her the Malayan dollars.

"One moment," she replied, and went in search of someone else. Meanwhile a pigtailed young girl of ten or eleven brought a pot of tea and poured a cup. Peter tapped lightly on the tabletop to thank her; the girl nodded and left.

Savoring the scented tea he scanned the menu, seeing a nice variety of Cantonese dishes plus, of all things, Singapore noodles. He also saw Japanese food listed, and Hawaiian too.

The hostess returned with an older Chinese man. "This Mistah Fong," she explained. "Can help change money. You order food now, please?"

Peter stood to shake hands with Mr. Fong, who bowed slightly. "Do join me, Mr. Fong. Yes, Singapore Noodles, please," he said to the hostess.

Mr. Fong sat and offered Peter a cigarette, holding the pack with both hands, oriental fashion. Peter declined, smiling his thanks.

"Sir, you have Malay dollah from Singapore?" inquired Fong. Peter showed him the money, about $500 worth. "Sir, I so very sorry; cannot change this money no more. You know, Japanese now occupy that place."

Stunned, Peter answered that he did not know. "Mr. Fong, what happened to Singapore? I have been at sea without any news. Please tell me." Peter was almost in a panic.

"Japanese Army now control all Malaya, Brunei, and Straits Colony— Penang, Malacca, Singapore. Malaya money no good now, but maybe after war OK. No can take chance hold you money so long time, sorry. You no have American money?"

"Well, I do have a few American dollars, probably enough for my noodles," Peter said, piqued.

"No, no, noodles my treat," Fong said. "I mean, how you pay hotel, airplane or ship to somewhere?"

Finally, Peter's shocked brain began to function again. Of course! He had all those US Army vouchers from Canton Island in his luggage at the BOQ. It wasn't really cash, but perhaps he could convert it at Pearl City tomorrow.

For a brief moment Peter sensed how horrible the plight of real refugees must be, without any money of the host country. He shuddered.

"Mr. Fong, I worked for Pan American Airways and the US Army on a Pacific island for several months, and they gave me some Army vouchers as payment. Can I convert those vouchers into cash somehow, while I'm here in Hawaii?"

"Yes, yes, must be possible at some military place," Fong said, "But you know, government only allow any person carry two hundred dollah cash, and US dollah in Hawaii have special stamp mark now."

"Really? Why only two hundred dollars, and what kind of stamp mark?" Peter was really nervous about his first trip to an American territory. His noodle plate arrived, and he chose chopsticks to dig into it. Fong waved him on and ordered more tea for both of them. The young girl was sweeping the floor among the tables.

"Military want control everybody. Very bad for people. Military 'fraid of Japanese people in Hawaii. Almost half Hawaii people now Japanese, you know this? Me and wife has Japanese friend, business partner, family long time Hawaii, he Nisei, means born Hawaii. My partner and all Japanese people now has big trouble in Hawaii, but they still no like Japan country. They very ashamed for Pearl Harbor attack."

Fong continued in a sing-song voice: "Now all people in Hawaii has curfew and suffer too much control. Must get ID card, no can carry much cash, young people no can change job, only get small pay. Some Hawaii Japanese must stay military camp, something like jail. Military police everywhere."

"Cripes, I had no idea," Peter said between noodles. "Probably the same thing is happening in Singapore under the Japanese too."

Fong grew agitated at that statement. "Oh no, oh no, we hear many bad thing happen for Singapore Chinese. Those Japan *kempeitai*—secret police—kill many, many thousand Chinese. Many ten thousand even! Also put British people in jail, some also die. Maybe Hawaii bad too, but no bad like Hong Kong and Singapore. Hawaii Japanese want stay here but feel very sad for bad treatment by military.

"Military people maybe think all Oriental is Japanese, so my family also having problem. This unworthy person," he pointed to the pig-tailed floor sweeper-tea server, "the daughter of my son. School send her home, maybe think she Japanese." The girl looked up and smiled prettily at Fong and Peter. Peter smiled back.

He finished the delicious plate of seafood noodles and gestured his compliments to Fong. "Mr. Fong, I am very lucky because my wife and boy left Singapore last month, and they are in Australia now. I was hoping to bring them to Canada, but don't know how to do that yet. We are British, you see, and we don't know America at all."

"Hawaii people liking British people," Fong replied. "Your Captain Cook was here, so British flag is part of Hawaii flag, you know this?" Fong pointed to a small Hawaiian flag over the door, in which the upper left quadrant was clearly the British Union Jack.

"No, I didn't," Peter said. "That's certainly a surprise! And the Americans don't object?" Peter made a mental note to write Graham Overwood about this peculiar discovery, which was certain to amuse him. It was especially odd, since the Hawaiians killed Captain Cook eventually.

Just then a man entered the restaurant and looked about. Seeing Fong at the table, the man came over to them. Peter thought he looked Japanese but wasn't certain. He seemed somewhat younger than Fong. "Ah, my partner Naburo-san," Fong exclaimed.

Peter's eyes glazed over, and a sense of what the French call *déjà vu* enveloped him.

*** *THE US NAVAL BASE* ***

Next morning Peter left the Coast Guard station precisely at 0730, feeling most grateful to Fong for advancing him some HAWAII—overprinted US 'dollah', and for showing him the clean and comfortable little Golden Harbor Hotel near Chinatown. *That one shouldn't cost anywhere near as much as the Moana on Waikiki Beach, that Commander Olson had recommended,* Peter guessed.

He signed out of the BOQ and brought along all his luggage in the staff car to Pearl City, just in case the Navy asked him to stay out there. The gift-wrapped Japanese doll and his introduction letters lay handily on the car seat.

Not long after driving through heavy traffic from Honolulu, they passed an enormous building complex on a low hill, painted a bold pink color. "What on earth is that?" Peter asked the Coastguard driver.

"That's the Tripler Army hospital, sir. We're passing Fort Shafter now, about halfway to CINCPAC. Some say it would take too much Army paint to camouflage it, and others say they left it pink for a kind of Red Cross identity."

Peter chuckled. Then he remembered Naburo-San at the restaurant yesterday. Mr. Fong's partner was very obviously the father of Lt. Naburo IJN, a chance-in-a-million encounter. Peter had not said much after the introduction but understood the partners' agitated conversation somewhat in its funny mixture of Hawaiian, English, Cantonese and Japanese patois.

It seemed Naburo was being investigated because someone told the Army that his son went to Japan two years ago. That was enough to place the Naburo family under suspicion, and probably consign them to an internment camp on an outer island. There seemed to be a reigning paranoia on the island that Hawaii's Japanese residents were likely to become spies or militia, to support a forthcoming Japanese invasion, but the military was unwilling to meet with their community leaders and discuss the problem.

Fong and Naburo seemed to understand the Army's concerns—after all, imagine if there were a large American colony in Tokyo when war broke out—but they felt the Army was over-reacting. So did Peter, hoping to lend a moderating voice at CINCPAC if he was somehow able to see Admiral Nimitz.

Peter subconsciously noted that the road they were following had skirted inland toward the north side of Pearl Harbor, which could occasionally be seen in fleeting glimpses through the trees as they moved slowly along with the morning traffic. As they then turned west and inched along it towards Pearl City, the damage from the raid was more visible. Abruptly, they left the highway and approached a security gate, with smartly uniformed Marine guards checking the queue of cars ahead of them. Other armed Marines in combat gear with dogs were standing to the side of the road near some readily movable barriers.

"Welcome to CINCPAC sir," Peter's driver offered. Up a hill some distance away, stood the two-story Navy headquarters building with a small detachment of Sailors and Marines outside, saluting the flag. It was exactly 0800 hours.

Finally, it was their turn at the security gate. The Coastguard driver presented his identification and advised the gate guard that he had a British representative aboard to see the admiral's aide. Peter displayed the official British letters and his ID, then the car was motioned over to a parking area close by. The Sergeant-of-the-Guard arrived, who saluted Peter and asked him to kindly step out of the vehicle.

"Sorry, sir, could you please speak to the OD?" Handed a telephone, Peter explained his mission to the OD, and after a few minutes on hold, was invited to return to the car and proceed up the hill to the headquarters building.

One of the admiral's aides was waiting for them outside the main door. Peter left the car again, self-conscious in his casual English shirt and slacks, and Monmouth School rugby tie. He smiled bravely and took the extended hand.

"Captain Silvers, Mr. Perry. We had something on file about your visit, but no idea of your arrival date. I apologize but Admiral Nimitz is fully booked these days. We would like to have you meet a representative from Naval Intelligence, what we call the ONI, based on our understanding of your mission. Would you mind waiting inside a while for his arrival?"

"Captain Silvers, my driver needs to return to the Coast Guard pier shortly. I should perhaps leave with him, but if I do stay here now would I be able to get a lift back to the city later on, even by shuttle bus? I also badly need to convert some Army payment vouchers into dollars today, as I am otherwise 'flat broke', which I think is the expression. My cash just became worthless because of Singapore's demise."

"Hmm, I see," pondered the captain. "Wait one, please." Leaving Peter and the driver outdoors near the flagpole—which gave Peter a momentary flashback to Canton Island—Captain Silvers ducked back into the building and picked up a telephone. He emerged ten minutes later, while Peter was having a good look at Pearl Harbor's quite visible evidence of the Japanese raid.

"Hell of a mess still, I'm sorry to say," the Captain growled, pointing. "There's what's left of the *Arizona* and *Oklahoma,* and you can easily see the disaster on Ford Island." Peter shook his head; "I had no idea how bad it was. We were on Canton Island when the news came."

"Well, the little bastards will pay one day, that's certain. At any rate, here's a suggestion for you, Mr. Perry. They tell me the Army vouchers are negotiable at any civilian bank if you present your ID, so why don't you catch a ride back to town with your driver and have him drop you at a bank near your hotel. The bank can only give you two hundred in cash, I suppose you know, but they'll wire the rest to your home bank wherever it is in the free world, or else open an account for you here in Hawaii. You should be able to get all that settled today.

"Meanwhile, our ONI man will come meet you at the Moana Hotel for dinner tonight, which is where those sneaky fellows like to hang out. He is Lt. Commander Perkins, a jock from Dartmouth College. They call him 'Bongo' for some reason or other. Does that sound OK to you?"

"Yes sir, it does," Peter replied, much relieved, "and thank you for all the useful information. It would have taken me weeks to figure it out by myself. What time should I meet the mysterious Bongo then? I'm not staying at the Moana but will enjoy seeing it this evening."

"Darn, he didn't say, but I would guess around 1700—five o'clock—time enough to get through dinner before the curfew. Anyway, after you two chat and he reports back to me, we'll see about getting you a meeting with Admiral Nimitz, OK? It may take several days, so please tell Perkins your complete story on the Admiral's behalf."

Peter smiled and nodded as Captain Silvers continued: "We understand you also bring a special gift for Admiral Nimitz; please hold onto it as I'm certain he will want to thank you personally."

"Brilliant," Peter said, "Absolutely perfect. Thank you so very much, Captain Silvers."

"Just one more question, Mr. Perry, if I may. In the earlier message we received from the British office in, er, was it Fiji?—yes, Fiji—there was an odd instruction that we don't quite understand. It says: 'look carefully under her kimono.' Any idea what that means? Is it a code?"

"All will be revealed," said Peter, trying very hard not to grin.

*** WAIKIKI BEACH ***

Back in Honolulu, Peter was most amazed that he, as a foreign visitor, could open a bank account and convert three months' worth of Army vouchers into US dollars. He would be able to transfer most of that to Wendy, as soon as she arranged for a Sterling account in Sydney, so Peter stopped at the main post office to send a priority air letter, saying he fervently hoped she had closed their Singapore bank account, and converted its balance into British Pounds Sterling. She so far hadn't mentioned any money problems, but he still worried about that aspect.

Peter soon had a wallet full of dollars—tens and twenties, boldly over-printed **HAWAII,** which enabled him to lunch at the City Noodle Shop and repay Mr. Fong, who was quite pleased to see him. Together they strolled over to the Golden Harbor Hotel to drop off Peter's suitcases.

A comfortable room on the top floor with a view of the Aloha Tower and Sand Island was just $2.50 per night including breakfast, whereas the Moana was almost up to $20 per night according to Fong, because of all the military visitors and suppliers. Peter was not surprised to learn that Fong was part owner of the small hotel where he was staying. *Good for him.*

He took a taxi to the Moana around 3pm, as he wanted a look at Waikiki Beach before it was time to meet Bongo Perkins for dinner. The elegant Moana itself was well worth a look too, having been built in 1901 by an impatient American investor, trying to gentrify the somewhat haphazard Waikiki Beach neighborhood of bungalows and cottages, so that wealthy clients would come and pay for a view of Diamond Head and the idyllic Waikiki surf.

But not long afterwards, Lady Moana was sold to Matson Steamship Lines, which took a longer view of tourist development. Matson then built the larger Royal Hawaiian Hotel nearby, the hotel's color scheme having evidently inspired the pink hospital that Peter had passed that morning. Matson's SS *Lurline* passenger ship had recently been requisitioned by the Navy, so tourism would have to wait a while, but there was plenty of Navy traffic to fill all the hotels; indeed, the Honolulu streets seemed choked with people in uniform.

Waikiki Beach looked and sounded wonderfully inviting, with its long parallel rows of surf. Peter strolled along the palm-shaded sea wall and admired the postcard panorama of white sand and blue ocean, with iconic Diamond Head in the background. The breeze felt slightly cooler but more humid than Canton's dry equatorial heat and would doubtless cool down further after sunset—meaning after curfew, he would need to remember.

There were lots of adults and children splashing about close to shore and a small gathering of surfboard riders farther out. Peter admired the way the surfers positioned their boards to catch a wave, and then quickly stood up to ride it toward the beach. *What a brilliant idea! Hawaii is really some place special!*

He returned to the Moana lobby around 4:30 and left his name at the front desk so they could page him when the Navy man arrived. Outdoors, behind the lobby, facing toward the beach, he noticed a big handsome tree surrounded by tables, that might be a delightful place for dining. Then a light tap on his shoulder made him spin around. He almost collided with a smiling face, that he realized instantly could belong to no one else but a man named Bongo.

"Peter Perry? Yes? I'm Bongo Perkins," the face announced over an outstretched hand. The owner of the face and hand was wearing a flowery shirt and seemed the antithesis of formality. About the same height as

Peter—slightly under six feet but perhaps a few years younger—Bongo looked fit and athletic, with a short brown crew-cut hair style that Peter had noticed on some of the other Navy officers at CINCPAC.

"What an intriguing name," Peter couldn't help but exclaim. "How did you come by it? Not from your mum, I assume."

"Heavens no; she's no musician. We had a little combo at Dartmouth that kept us energized on weekends. We specialized in calypso music from the Caribbean, and I was the rhythm section until deciding to join the Navy reserve a year ago. When the career types from the academy found out I was a mathematician, they pushed me into the ONI—as a full lieutenant no less—and when the ONI checked out my background they came across a couple of the old band members, who told them I could play bongo drums given the right incentive. Occasionally I do a club gig with local bands around Honolulu; it's a good cover. What are your hobbies, Peter? Any music or sports, for example?"

"No music, sorry to say, but I'm quite keen on rowing and rugby football. I don't suppose you have either of them out here in paradise."

"As a matter of fact we have both, but only on occasion. I dabbled in rugby at Dartmouth, but more about that another day.

Shall we dine in the courtyard? I saw you admiring the famous banyan tree."

Peter smiled, and Bongo led the way. "There's my favorite spot, nice and quiet." The head waiter approached and nodded to Bongo, leading them to a lonely little table up against a side wall, far from the main traffic pattern.

A piano tinkled an unfamiliar tune near the opposite wall, and a low wooden platform on the beach side implied something more energetic to come for hotel guests who could linger past the seven o'clock curfew. A little sign mentioned hula dancing. The air smelled of frangipani and roast beef.

"This curfew business," Peter began, "Is it going to last long?"

"Afraid so," Bongo replied. "The Army and Navy brass are convinced the Japs will invade these islands eventually, and even if the brass would learn to relax there's still the FBI. Apparently Hoover planned all the martial law details way back in '39 because of anti-Japanese sentiment at the time, so the regulations went into effect the very same day as the Jap raid, December 7th—bingo! Imagine this if you will; the civilian governor resigns on the spot, and an Army general takes over by nightfall! A cool drink, Peter, or are you in training?"

"In training? I've been frying in the Canton Island sun for the past three months, a virtual slave to Pan Am and the Army Corps of Engineers. That ordeal kept us all in shape, I suppose. Well, we did have a British Resident there as well, who had a good supply of gin."

"A Gimlet then?" suggested Bongo, "or perhaps a Martini on the rocks?"

"Gimlet, by all means. The mere thought of Canton Island brings back that lovely flavor and aroma. Have you been there?"

"Not in this lifetime, but I suppose there are many war months ahead." Bongo signaled a waiter and ordered the drinks.

Peter mentioned that Pan Am was operating a seaplane base on Canton Island, while he was working with them and the Army on various civil engineering projects. He also told Bongo about landing in Hawaii on a Pan Am Clipper from Singapore and other refueling stops, then taking off again in Hawaii on another Clipper bound for Canton Island. "There were a lot of Navy ships hereabouts, I remember, so I guess the local Pan Am base must have been at Pearl Harbor."

"Indeed it was." Bongo explained that Pan Am's prewar seaplane base—in need of year-round calm waters that Honolulu Harbor could not guarantee—was located right off the Pearl City peninsula that nosed into Pearl Harbor, not far from CINCPAC where Peter had been that morning.

"For reasons of military security," Bongo said, "the Pearl City location prevented Pan Am from offering route-reciprocity to Great Britain, which badly wanted Hawaii as a refueling stop for their own conceptual seaplane service from Canada to the South Pacific. The Hawaii restriction in turn prevented Pan Am from gaining a seaplane base in England, so they had to settle for Portugal as their European gateway. Not a very steep price to pay for a virtual seaplane monopoly in the Pacific region, though, from the mid-1930s onward!

"Getting back to Hawaii's martial law," Bongo went on, munching on a bread stick, "last but not least, there's the business community. The five largest Hawaiian producers—the Big Five as they are called—lobbied hard to have wage and job freezes included in Hoover's FBI plan. Even now they keep on stoking the paranoia fires whenever they party with the generals and admirals, and so it continues. The Big Five *adore* martial law, you might say. Apparently FDR himself was in favor of it as well, although I doubt there is any legal basis for martial law in a US territory. There certainly wouldn't be in a US state, but Hawaii isn't one of the forty-eight so it's a gray area, and of course there's the war, and so on."

Peter was paying close attention, wondering if something like that had happened during Singapore's final days of British freedom, and he imagined the outrage of his friends at any suggestion of a curfew.

"Have a look at the menu, Peter; perhaps there's something you haven't tried before, although I understand Singaporeans will eat anything that moves. I imagine you had plenty of fish on Canton too, so you might like to consider some mainland delectables that the Moana sneaks in from the commissary through grace and favor—lamb chops for example, or a juicy T-bone?"

"Lamb chops would be perfect, especially with a local mango if they do that," Peter proposed. "By the way, old sport, in Singapore we know without any doubt that Adam and Eve were not Chinese; want to know how?" Bongo raised an eyebrow skeptically. "They'd have eaten the snake!"

Bongo rolled his eyes, and spotted the waiter coming with the Gimlets. He was still chuckling when they ordered the lamb and a consommé, then he lifted his glass and toasted the Anglo-American alliance.

"Peter, let's get down to business. What exactly have you brought for the Old Man to see? And please explain why something so important has taken months to reach us."

*** NAVAL INTELLIGENCE ***

Bongo telephoned the Golden Harbor Hotel next morning early. "Peter, old boy, can we meet for coffee somewhere?"

Peter suggested his hotel, so his new 'Ivy League friend' (as Perkins described himself) would see how the rest of the city lived. "Why not come over here and I'll buy breakfast. The food tastes quite good—to a Singaporean at least."

"OK, my man, I'm on the way. Feel like a run at the football field later? Saturdays can sometimes be a little crowded, but we should be able to work out somewhere."

It was by then March 7, 1942, a day that did *not* live in infamy like December 7, 1941 but was rather gorgeous and deceptively peaceful three months after the Japanese attack.

"Certainly, I look forward to a run. What about those Samoans that you mentioned last night? Can we get in a little practice with them?" Peter learned that Bongo had played for a rugby club at Dartmouth, although American football was a much more popular sport overall. Peter had yet to watch an American football match, but Bongo assured him there were vague similarities.

"Those Samoan boys are practicing in secret somewhere; even the ONI doesn't know where. And by the way, they are excellent rugger players—as are the Fijians, Aussies, and Kiwis. Anyway, see you in a little while."

After breakfast and a workout on the pitch at Fort Shafter—what Americans call a football field, Peter learned—Bongo suggested a stroll through the Foster Botanic Gardens so they could rehash the discussion from last night.

"That sounds pleasant," said Peter, "but let's stop at Fong's place first for a bite of lunch. I'd like you to meet him, and perhaps his Japanese partner will be around. Besides, I still haven't caught up on my quota of Chinese food after the Canton Island exile."

Bongo begrudgingly consented: "Are you sure I won't have to eat any sea slugs?" he grumbled.

"No sea slugs, but a plate of fish eyes and chicken lips will surely perk you up," Peter grinned. Bongo was not amused.

Fong was not in evidence at the restaurant, but the hostess—who Peter had learned was Fong's daughter-in-law—said he would be back in the evening. Peter ordered some simple shrimp-fried rice for Bongo, and Japanese tempura shrimp for himself, plus a couple of bottles of the local beer, Primo. They shared a Hawaiian fruit plate for dessert.

"That was very nice," admitted Bongo. "Pretty bold of you to order Japanese food. Let's go tour the gardens now; they are right here in the city, or rather the city has grown to surround them."

The Foster Botanic Gardens were charming, and reminiscent of those in Singapore, both dating from the mid-1800s and featuring large hardwoods and extensive orchid displays. Bongo got right to the point, once they had strolled out of earshot of other visitors.

"Peter, you said the huge Japanese battleship is one of four, correct? Are the others launched yet, do you know?"

"Not certain. I didn't meet with young Naburo personally, remember, so whatever I tell you is just hearsay from the Overwoods, who met Naburo on Tarawa. But my recollection is that *Yamato* should already be in service by now, and the second monster not far behind. Information about the final two was rather vague, but Naburo was positive that four had been ordered. The cost must be enormous. And one wonders why they keep on building battleships after what their planes did to the *Prince of Wales* and *Repulse* off Malaya."

"Excellent point. Tell me again about armaments: are you sure you heard 18-inch guns mentioned? That's quite revolutionary." Peter nodded emphatically.

"And what about tonnage and speed?"

"Not certain," said Peter. "Can you perhaps calculate from the photo? I suppose that depends on the photo, of course. I've not seen what it looks like myself, so the sooner we get Naburo's gift to Admiral Nimitz, the sooner we'll learn some more."

"That's exactly what the admiral told my boss," Bongo said, "but Admiral Nimitz is totally buried with meetings and war planning for the foreseeable future, unfortunately, and the poor man hardly gets any rest as it is. However—and this is a big 'however'—he is supposed to attend a high-level but boring civic dinner this evening with the local powers-that-be, meaning Major General Greene the military governor, the Big Five of course, and FDR's war secretary Stimson, who's just arrived at Pearl."

Bongo and Peter strolled on through the gardens, pointing occasionally at some plant or other. Bongo looked carefully around them before continuing.

"Well, buddy boy, the admiral is going to be a no-show at the big dinner and will instead dine in his private quarters with his patient wife, Catherine, and us lowly peons! My boss, Captain Silvers, will be with us, and another of the admiral's aides with a photography expert in tow, who can enlarge and print that microfilm while we wait. How's that for dedicated leadership?"

"My word," Peter exclaimed, impressed by Bongo's message. "I am overwhelmed. I've never met an admiral before. What does one wear to an admiral's dinner party?"

"Ah well, my boss told him about your sartorial splendor, assuming that what you showed up in at CINCPAC, and for our dinner at the Moana, was your best shot. Therefore, you've done us all a big favor; uniform of the evening has been officially announced as slacks and Hawaiian shirts, what we call 'Aloha Class-C'. We'd better pick up some things for you on the way to your hotel, eh?"

Peter was embarrassed about the attention his casual clothes had attracted, but before he could apologize Bongo changed the subject again.

"Oh, by the way, do you know what sort of container is protecting the micro-film? Are we going to need a safe-cracker or demolition expert at dinner?"

"I don't think so," Peter chuckled. "I haven't opened the package, but Lt. Naburo told the Overwoods that the film is inside a fancy Japanese doll dressed in a kimono. Mrs. Nimitz should like it if she collects such things, provided the photography chap doesn't mess it up when he extracts the micro-film."

"Ah so, that explains the strange message from Fiji! My boss will crack up!" Bongo grinned broadly. Peter laughed as well, remembering Captain Silvers' innocent question at CINCPAC, which he had been too embarrassed to answer.

"Bongo, I still don't understand why the admiral wants to get involved personally with such a small matter. Couldn't the ONI handle this and report the findings to him?"

"Well of course; he could have instructed you to give the film to us, but he is an old-school well-mannered gentleman who really did want to meet the nice Englishman who spent so much effort bringing a strange British secret to the US Navy. Would there were more like him in the world."

*** THE CAROLINE ISLANDS ***

By March 1942, while Bongo and Peter met in Hawaii, masses of ships and naval personnel were arriving at Truk atoll, Japan's prominent naval base in the Carolines that lay west of the Marshall Islands. Purchased in 1899 from Spain by Germany, in the aftermath of the Spanish-American War, Japan had in turn acquired the Carolines as a League of Nations mandate, after Germany's defeat in the First World War.

Truk was the main Pacific base for Japan's Combined Fleet, and it was from there that Admiral Yamamoto had dispatched Vice Admiral Nagumo to Hawaii with the attack force that nearly destroyed Pearl Harbor.

Young IJN Lt. Naburo had already been stationed at the Truk naval base for half a year before the Hawaii attack, after being called to active duty from the naval reserves that he had been coerced to join. Having risked his life to deliver the secret film to the Allies during a clandestine survey of Tarawa Atoll, Naburo still sought a way to extricate himself from the Japanese Navy and return to his parents in Hawaii.

It would not be easy, he realized. It was highly likely that he might have to become an Allied prisoner first, which carried with it the risk of being killed by the Allies while surrendering, or by other Japanese prisoners if they learned of his duplicity.

*** BACK TO CANTON ***

Strapped into one of the most iconic seaplanes of the wartime era, a Navy combat PBY Catalina, with Bongo snoring in the next 'seat'— actually a pile of duffel bags—Peter Perry was hugely relieved to be heading back westward across the Pacific Ocean in the direction of his family in Australia. It was the week after Admiral Nimitz had personally thanked him for delivering the secret Naburo photograph of battleship *Yamato*.

With a full combat crew of ten, including the two side blister gunners, Peter and Bongo were the only passengers in the replacement PBY flight from Hawaii to Pago Pago via Canton Island, and were only accepted because there was no heavy bomb load aboard.

This plane and crew would replace one that had recently been lost while taking photographs over Tarawa in the ex-British Gilbert Islands.

It had been jumped by two Japanese H6Ns, the so-called '*Zero*' that was starting to make its presence known throughout the Pacific. The doomed PBY had managed to damage one of the *Zeros* and get off a short radio alert describing a roughed-out air strip on Betio, before the terrifying silence told Pago Pago of their sacrifice.

The helpful staff at ONI Honolulu had managed to negotiate a ride for Peter and Bongo just as far as Canton Island, where the PBY would collect its weighty munitions, and where the pair of evicted passengers could theoretically catch a NATS flight to Fiji or beyond in just a few more days.

Their ultimate destination was Sydney, Australia, where Bongo would help start an ONI office and Peter would at last be reunited with his family. Peter was glad of Bongo's company on this journey into the strange world of Americana, and Bongo was glad of Peter's company, to decipher the quirky minds of the Colonial British Empire that they would meet in Fiji and elsewhere.

In Peter's experience, the ubiquitous wartime expression "just a few more days" was a highly variable one, occasionally meaning two or three days but more often a week or a month. Nevertheless, he was eternally gratefully for the admiral's kindness in authorizing him to start down a path that would hopefully get him back to his family, and not onward to Washington DC as had first been imagined.

A big surprise had been Bongo joining the PBY flight too. "Ah well, high time the ONI learned something from an expert about Pan Am's former territory. But they're going to make me sweat in Australia to pay for this little vacation cruise with you, ugly Brit."

"My heart bleeds, Perkins. Now tell me why the blazes everyone calls you Bongo? What name did your mum give you?"

"Elmer."

"Ah, I see; thanks Bongo." The Catalina droned onward.

"Bongo," Peter said again after a few minutes. "Sorry, I didn't mean to make fun of your name, old sport. Please forgive my impertinence. But what I'd really like to say now is thank you for calling off the Army blokes from their persecution of Fong's partner Naburo-san. That poor fellow certainly did nothing wrong by sending his boy off to Japan for a cultural experience. Now he's probably lost his son for good, and we can't even say that the boy is trying to help our side win the war. Doesn't seem fair."

"The kid deserves a medal," Bongo agreed. "I hope he survives the war so the admiral can pin one on him. Now listen up, clever Brit, it seems the ONI had already heard something vague about the monster battleship project, from foreign diplomats in Japan before they were kicked out, but that photo you delivered really did put things in perspective—and woke up some of the admirals.

"Whether those are really 18-inch guns is difficult to say, but our experts think they are. We've been picking up Jap radio traffic too, that seems to imply there's a new flagship in the Truk area. Could be *Yamato*, though the traffic refers to needing supplies of special 400mm hardware. That's around 16 inches, but maybe the word 'special' is a ruse, just to lead everyone astray. 18 inches would be around 460mm. Wish we could get someone to actually measure those big popguns, eh? 'One measurement is worth a thousand words', as they say. Anyway, let's hope your wife enjoys Japanese doll collecting. Mrs. Nimitz clearly thought it would be unpatriotic for her to keep it, but I don't think the admiral would have minded."

"No, and your boss was almost drooling. He kept telling everyone about the inscrutable Fiji message, and you could see he really wanted the doll as a trophy for his office. By the way, old Sherlock, remember there's a duplicate microfilm hidden out here in Phoenix-land, on Enderbury Island, in case you should ever need it. But not another kimono; the film on Enderbury is buried inside a monkey pod seed."

"Good grief, that Naburo boy is quite creative. I noticed you gave our people the Enderbury treasure map. Thanks for that."

Both of them grabbed for their harnesses as the plane suddenly banked left and dropped towards the sea, with a curt announcement: "All hands belt up. Close doors and brace for splashdown. Repeat, close doors and brace for splashdown." The PBYs were literally airships, with internal watertight doors to help them stay afloat in case of a crash at sea.

It was still dark outside, and Peter wondered how the pilot could possibly see where to go. Suddenly the Canton lagoon lights shone straight up, so as to not attract submarines, and as the plane continued to bank around toward the southeast, Peter could see the old familiar lagoon outline, shimmering inside the reef. Then the PBY leveled out to glide lower, and he crossed his fingers. With a spectacular splash they were on the water and the periphery lights went out again.

"How's that, eh?" Peter asked no one in particular. The plane rumbled over to a waving light at Pan Am's old Southside dock, and the waist door was dogged open. A smell of salt air and guano immediately filled the cabin.

"Crap", said Bongo, "this place smells like a Singapore outhouse."

"Could be," chuckled Peter.

*** HURRY UP AND WAIT ***

After daylight's eventual and sudden equatorial appearance, Peter and Bongo walked from the dock area to stand outside the NATS Quonset hut as instructed by the landing crew chief. From what he could see, Peter reckoned Southside itself had changed but little. There were a few more vehicle tracks and small buildings on the coral, certainly, but a huge visual change was sitting offshore.

The grounded steamship *President Taylor* loomed like a huge black dirigible over the low atoll. Already some lighters were being towed from the lagoon into the tidal channel in the morning light, and soon the first one was navigating the surf outside, bobbing and swinging behind a little tugboat.

"Cripes, what a disaster," Peter said to Bongo, pointing at the wreck. "That happened soon after I left here over a month ago. Look, they still haven't finished unloading all the heavy stuff."

There was no sign yet of a new channel into the lagoon, and the wrecked ship was more or less blocking the best anchorage outside the reef.

"Someone's ass is in a sling over this," Bongo observed. "Anyway, what an amazing little outpost this is. You could go crazy here in no time at all. Did you say Pan Am built it?"

"Mostly. That was their hotel, with the flagpole outside. Perhaps it still serves meals to the NATS people. And over here is the British compound, between Pan Am and the reef channel. We used to quaff Gimlets on the verandah of that larger house and watch the world's fastest sunset. They had a flagpole too; I wonder what happened to it."

"Well, here come our travel agents," said Bongo, as an ensign and two sailors sauntered over from somewhere nearby. They were all wearing shorts. Peter and Bongo wore identical navy-blue jump suits, but Peter's bore no insignia.

"Morning gentlemen," chirped the ensign, as a sailor unlocked the Quonset hut door and dogged open the windows. "Please step inside. Now let's see, the manifest shows, um, Lt. Commander Perkins and Mr. Perry, civilian, is that correct? May I please see some identification?" With that, the ensign gave Bongo a snappy salute, turning then to Peter.

"Ah, you are English, Mr. Perry. An honor to meet you, sir. I'm afraid your representatives have gone away from Canton Island, but we are supposed to allow British visitors to use their former residency as transient quarters. Commander Perkins could also stay there in your company." Peter smiled at that upstaging remark.

The ensign continued: "There is only one problem sir, for which I apologize. You see, the head … er, the indoor toilet does not work because it was never connected to what we call, for some odd reason, the Benjo System. You would have to use the hotel facilities or a bed pan for that purpose, but otherwise the British quarters are quite comfortable. Captain Weaver sometimes uses them for VIP events."

"With the afore-mentioned caveat, one supposes!" Peter had laughed aloud at the mention of 'benjos', causing his fellow traveler to regard him with curiosity.

"Private joke, tell you later," Peter said to Bongo. "Ensign, did you say a Captain Weaver is here? Was he previously in American Samoa?"

"Yes sir, he was. Captain Weaver is now the naval commander for NATS operations on Canton Island."

"Lucky man," said Bongo. "Where can we find him to pay our compliments?"

"Why, he'll probably be at the hotel having breakfast before morning colors. I'm sure he would welcome your company for the event."

Bongo tapped his watch and looked about for a clock. "Oh yessir, the local time here is 0717 at the moment."

"Good. Well, Mister Ensign, I don't suppose you'll be bringing a plane in today to get us to Sydney?" Bongo asked hopefully, nonetheless.

"No sir, but in just a few more days we should have some seats available for Fiji." Peter and Bongo smiled.

Just a few more days; someone should write a dance tune, Peter mused.

Bongo yawned: "Well done, Ensign, er…?"

"Culver, sir. Winthrop Culver, at your service." A typewriter clacked away in the back of the hut, as did a distinctly swab-type bucket.

"Carry on, Culver. You'll go far in this man's Navy. Get yourself a brass doorknob for the office."

"Beg pardon, sir?"

"Never mind, just give a shout when our bird comes in, and thank you. Oh, and could your yeoman drop our bags at the British residency, please?" Peter had prudently exchanged his battered old suitcase for a duffel bag too, but worried occasionally about the kimono doll getting broken.

"Aye, aye sir, right away sir," the ensign responded, executing a studied Hollywood-type salute. The two NATS sailors smirked at one another. Bongo returned the salute *en passant*.

Captain Weaver was quite surprised—and pleased—to see Peter again, and welcomed both visitors to his table. A Filipino messman appeared with a menu and coffee.

"What's good?" Bongo asked him.

"Spam and powdered eggs, sir, always a treat."

The captain chuckled; "By golly, you're never wrong, eh Manuel?"

"No sir. How would you gentlemen like your eggs?" "Scrambled for me, please. Peter?"

"Same, thank you."

Manuel bustled away.

"Well, Mr. Perry, what brings you back to Canton Island? Are you checking on your legacy plumbing system? Is it still in warranty?" the captain joked.

"What's all this?" Bongo picked up on the topic.

"Well, Commander, obviously Mr. Perry is too modest to tell you, but he is the inventor of Canton Island's legendary batch-process sewage system, for which the Army Corps of Engineers created a manufacturing process and operating procedure. It is called the Benjo System, which I understand is based on a bizarre Singapore experiment to outsmart the Japs. We installed it on Canton Island so the Japs would get totally baffled—in a manner of speaking—if they invaded us, and would therefore immediately return home again, thinking they must have attacked one of their own islands by mistake. But as you can see, word must have reached them about our benjo system through their excellent network of spies, as we are probably the only tropical island in the entire Pacific Ocean that has not yet been over-run."

"Peter! Or should I now call you Benjo? You should have said something in Honolulu. I can see Admiral Nimitz awarding you a special medal. What a man of many talents you are!" The breakfast plates were delivered by Manuel, with more coffee.

"Actually the Army did give him a medal," Captain Weaver continued. "I remember a palm tree superimposed on a wooden box. I think his citation read 'The Canton Island Thunder Box Symphony Award—a Tropical Movement', something like that, eh Mr. Perry?" Peter busied himself with the eggs and spam. "I believe he was known to the poker playing set as the 'Straight Flush'."

Bongo guffawed. "Wait'll we tell the *Navy News* editor about this little jewel of a story!" Peter looked askance.

"Well, gentlemen, we digress. It is time for morning colors. I usually go outdoors, but you may continue with your meal if you wish." The others stood up with Captain Weaver and followed behind.

"I wouldn't miss this for the world," said Peter, recovering his composure. "It's part of a long-standing Canton tradition that Pan Am and the British residency started years ago. I'm sorry the other part is missing today," he said, glancing toward the British compound, "but the Navy has continued the tradition, thankfully."

A Navy bugler sounded the lengthy and lively morning riff as Old Glory with its forty-eight stars and thirteen stripes slowly rose up the pole and fluttered out in the sea breeze. Everyone took their cue for the salute from two Marine guards at the lanyard.

Peter supposed there weren't many such ceremonies within the Canton Island time zone. He missed not seeing the Union Jack go up next but was glad to be back on the atoll for this special moment. Suddenly from far down the lagoon came the loud boom of a big gun, and the shrieking of a thousand sea birds.

"My God, Benjo, it's the invasion! I thought your invention was supposed to repel the enemy."

"That's the Army's anti-aircraft gun practice," said Captain Weaver. They have 90mm AA sites around the entire atoll, probably half a dozen of them, and one gets tested every—what's today?—every Monday. At least they try to wait until the flag is up; I think that's their signal, come to think of it." He pointed with pride toward the far end of the island.

"You two really must meet Colonel O'Reilly; p'raps we'll send a boat for him tonight. The Army HQ is on Northside—you may have noticed the tent camps. Small groups of their boys even take turns sleeping at the guns, in full combat gear no less. Makes a man proud of his country."

"Are there any Army engineers left here, sir?" Peter asked.

"Not the original crew that you knew, I'm afraid, only some maintenance people now," replied the NATS captain. "Never mind, it's always good to invite the Army over to Southside when interesting visitors come through. Good for inter-service morale, eh? We'll call Horace O'Reilly and see if he's free tonight. Do either of you play bridge?"

Moments later the twin-engine refueled and fully armed Navy PBY buzzed down the lagoon, and Canton Island was returned to its somnambulant state once more. Somewhere there was a war on.

*** THEY ALSO SERVE WHO STAND AND WAIT ***

This time, 'just a few more days' turned out miraculously to be only four of them before Peter and Bongo were booked to get away together on a flight from Canton to Fiji's capital, Suva. A big Martin flying boat was due to drop off a couple of Navy doctors for Canton Island (Bongo visualized Captain Weaver asking whether or not the doctors played bridge). The Martin would then go on to Fiji and Nouméa.

Either Peter or Bongo alone, even with their low 'space available' priority level, could have left on the PBY the evening after the AA gun test, because there was still a single seat available on that flight after loading the ammo, but they decided to wait it out until they could travel onward together.

In theory, they should have been assigned some administrative responsibility on the island while waiting in transit, but more or less all

70

daily tasks suitable to their rank—or to any rank at all, for that matter—
were highly coveted by the 1,500-or-so bored naval and military men
who called Canton Island home in March 1942. So Peter and Bongo
amused themselves for those few days by swimming off the docks in
the lagoon, or by walking around the water's edge and watching small
packs of abandoned feral dogs skillfully fish for young sharks and other
tempting marine life, each dog having a specific role in the capture that
was devoured by all.

The lagoon was a thriving aquatic nursery with a thousand species
of marine creatures both vertebrate and otherwise, many constantly on
the move. Usually there was little to fear while swimming, but on rare
occasions a more mature shark or ray might wash in with the tide, and
cruise the lagoon curiously before returning to the open sea. And after a
seaplane flight landed or departed, it was best to refrain from swimming
for an hour or so because of the agitated state of the fish, particularly
barracuda.

Unfortunately, but sensibly, a fairly level Pan Am tennis court was
closed down by Captain Weaver for the duration, over concerns about
Canton's wartime image. Baseball was really the only team sport that the
occupants of Canton had available, since the island's coral surface was far
too rough for football and turf was a distant memory. In the evenings,
there were endless poker games and an occasional singsong, and always
fairly current movies twice a week that the Army and Navy traded back
and forth.

Mail was delivered regularly, and war news from the radio was
uncensored, nevertheless as time went on there were often fights among
the men over seemingly trivial things. An Army stockade was constructed
on Northside to house the unruly, and not long afterwards—across the
lagoon—a Navy brig with Marine guards, including presumably the
Marines who raised and lowered the flag.

Once on a full-moon evening there had been a Japanese air raid by
a lone 'Betty' bomber, flying presumably from Tarawa. All the bombs
missed, with most falling outside the reef and two inside the lagoon, but it
added some excitement to the daily routine. The raid was such a surprise,
that not a single gun of any sort was fired before the Betty flew away again.
Next time the gunners would be ready, they vowed to each other.

71

The waiting days passed much more slowly than when Peter had worked on the Benjo project with the Army. Strangely enough, the venue now made him recall his schoolboy rowing days on the Wye River in Wales. Peter imagined what a fantastic course could be laid out on the Canton lagoon; it was really a crime not to have any doubles, quads or eights available for racing in such a perfect place.

"Would help keep the lads fit both physically and mentally," Peter explained to Bongo, who nodded absent-mindedly as if his thoughts were far away also.

Being so close to the equator, it was almost always hot and sunny on Canton although an occasional cloudy day might promise welcome rain in season. The distillation plants seemed to run full time, rain or not, as there was insufficient cistern storage in those days, especially on Northside, for rain to make much difference. The sense of creative frugality that had dictated Canton's earlier development was somehow lost in the rush to outspend the Japanese.

Unloading the wrecked *President Taylor* also proceeded slowly, Peter and Bongo noticed in their strolls. Some equipment seemed too heavy for the lighters to handle, and half the ship's cranes had been rendered useless by the angle of the wreck on the reef. Through intense skill and effort, all the 90mm anti-aircraft guns had already been lightered ashore, and also a dozen or more jeeps, but several bulkier trucks and generators had been flooded down near the bilges and became too ruined to salvage.

Although some people still preferred the small PANAIR and Navy launches for lagoon fishing, where a gaff could be brought to bear upon a heavy catch, the *President Taylor's* deck also became a fishing spot of choice for serious Canton anglers, being right in the tidal stream where the aquatic food chain invariably brought tasty wahoo or grouper to the hook. It was undoubtedly true that seafood had kept the garrison a lot healthier than it would have been on simple GI cuisine.

Fuel for the island and its visiting aircraft was still lightered ashore in fifty-five-gallon drums from supply ships, a dangerous and backbreaking routine. There were persistent rumors of the new ship channel being started in 'just a few more days', which was becoming quite urgent in view of the growing number of flights into Northside and Southside in need of refueling.

At the old British residence one evening, Peter tried out one of Lois Overwood's 78 rpm record collection on the wind-up gramophone, with its big acoustic horn on top, that she must have left behind for other people's pleasure.

Unfortunately, the small collection of used phonograph needles was well worn, which made the song too scratchy to understand and enjoy. Theoretically the needles should have been replaced after every two or three plays, but once the supply ran out the last of them became hopelessly dulled. The US Navy didn't seem to know about British gramophones, and no one thought to resharpen the needles in the machine shop.

Peter thought of all the pleasant evenings spent at the residency with the now-absent Overwoods, and related many amusing tales to Bongo of Graham Overwood's one-man battle with the Pan Am 'Lions', and gentler memories of Lois' kind encouragement to Graham and himself when they occasionally suffered from 'Robinson Crusoe Syndrome', a feeling of creeping madness like the despair that overcomes prisoners in solitary confinement.

Finally, on the Friday of that week's return to Canton Island, the eagerly awaited Martin seaplane splashed down to deposit the Navy doctors and carry Peter and Bongo onward the next morning to the British colony of the Fiji Islands. Their goodbyes were brief, but Captain Weaver seemed genuinely sorry to see them go. Ensign Culver delivered one of his snappy salutes again.

*** CANTON ISLAND GAINS IMPORTANCE ***

Although the war in Europe commanded by far the most US attention in 1942, where Great Britain and Russia were desperate for help of any sort to stem the German onslaught, and vast convoys of escorted cargo ships were doing their best to dodge U-Boats in the north Atlantic, the somewhat neglected Pacific theater was nonetheless preparing for its eventual turn to come. In expectation of that future day, Canton Island grew more and more important as a mid-Pacific refueling stop, and in March 1942 there were new pressures.

Gen. MacArthur and his family had been ordered out of the Philippines to Australia where, while still en route to Melbourne, he assumed command of a fledgling Southwest Pacific Area (SWPA) organization on March 17, the day after Bongo and Peter reached Canton from Honolulu on the Navy PBY.

MacArthur's arrival in Melbourne on March twenty-first, after harrowing travel by PT boat and B-17 bomber, underscored the decrepit condition of Allied equipment at that point in time. His wife, Jean, and young son, Arthur MacArthur IV (named for the general's father), were practically done in by the long hazardous trip, as were the general's handful of staff members who accompanied them.

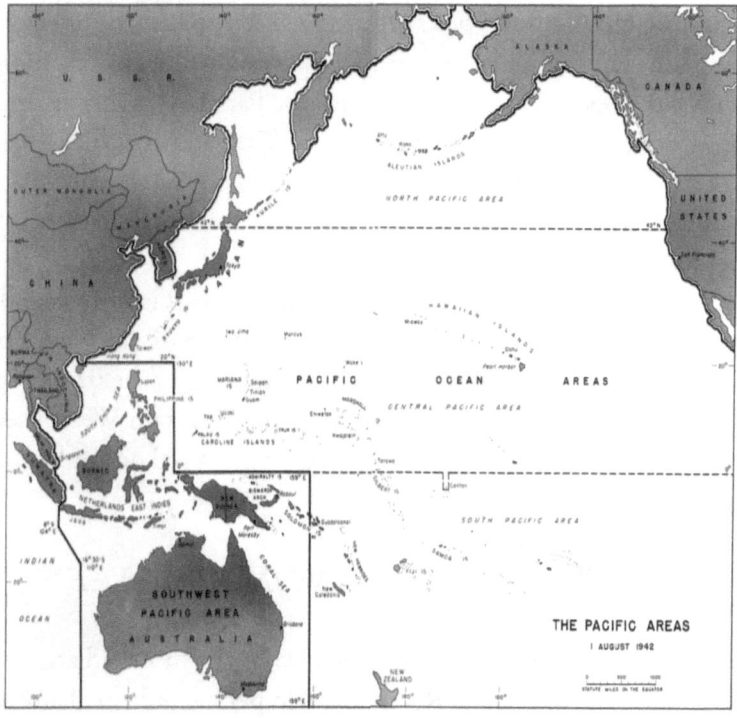

Divided Pacific Command
(https://history.amedd.army.mil/tools/privacy.html)

The ONI knew that a split command for the Pacific theater between Nimitz and MacArthur was forthcoming, and therefore sent Bongo Perkins to Australia as a liaison with MacArthur's organization, as well as to keep an eye on the Navy's historic rival service. Army Intelligence was secretly doing the same with the Navy in Hawaii.

Meanwhile Japan was preparing for an attack on Midway Island, last of the original Pan Am northern bases still in Allied hands. Ominously, the battleship *Yamato* was positively identified by ONI codebreakers as the attack flagship for the Midway strike. Were those guns 18-inch, or just 16-inch? Thanks to Lt Naburo's risky gamble, Admiral Nimitz and his staff were fairly certain they were 18-inchers, though not all experts agreed. To support the weight and recoil of nine 18-inch guns, *Yamato* would have to be nearly twice as large as any other battleship afloat, a sobering thought.

*** *THE FIJI ISLANDS* ***

It was just a six-hour flight from Canton Island to Fiji for the Martin seaplane. After a long nap, peering from a small window, Bongo eventually spotted the capital city of Suva jutting out into the ocean with water on three sides, not unlike the way Pearl City pushed into Pearl Harbor.

"Look at that, Mr. Flush." He beckoned Peter to the porthole. "Suva has a bay on each side. The smaller one to the west is a darker blue and must be the commercial harbor. The large shallow one is probably where we'll be landing in a few minutes. See the other plane parked on the water?"

"The city of Suva looks intriguing from here," said Peter, more attracted by the red tile roofs. "The little fact sheet I picked up in Hawaii says this island is called Viti Levu, the largest one in the colony, and Suva is located at its southeast corner. In fact, 'Fiji' and 'Viti' mean the same thing, so Viti Levu means Great Fiji. According to this, there are over three hundred islands all told, with just a third of them inhabited. The total land area is similar to the Hawaiian Islands. Should be interesting to take a tour, depending on how long we'll have to wait for the next flight."

"I wonder what defenses the Brits or Kiwis have put in place?" Bongo asked. "What about Singapore, for example? Could it have withstood a frontal invasion from the sea? How far are these Fiji Islands from the nearest Japs?"

The seaplane descended gracefully onto the wide shallow bay to the east of Suva, as Bongo had predicted. They rumbled over to an empty pier at the western edge of the bay, and deplaned. Another large seaplane, an unfamiliar type, was moored off an adjacent pier, guarded by two military men with a machine gun, under an umbrella. The plane bore British emblems and was labeled RNZAF.

"Some shady Kiwis," Peter pointed out, at which Bongo groaned.

Lauthala Bay, for so it was identified by a Welcome sign at the wharf, did not look like a former Pan Am base at all, but more like a hastily cobbled-together government facsimile. Peter reckoned Juan Trippe had never visited here, as the Fiji stopover was only added to the Pan Am route one month before the war started. But the rudimentary base still seemed to serve the right purpose for non-pampered passengers—non-PanAmpered, better yet—a stretch of calm water with a dock and a place to sleep.

Canton Island had a few leftover small boats from the Pan Am days, Peter remembered, identified with PANAIR signage. There didn't seem to be any of those here at the Suva base.

In addition to Bongo and Peter, there were about thirty-five other passengers and six Navy crew on board the Martin. A shore-based Navy lieutenant waited at an outdoor desk under a little roof, just beyond the dock's Welcome sign, while three seamen and a chief petty officer motored out in an unmarked launch to retrieve the bags.

Among the passengers were a woman and three young children accompanying a Free French officer to Nouméa. Everyone insisted the French family should be first in the arrival queue, for which they smiled gratefully. Passengers were already listed on a manifest, so the procedures did not take long for the entire party. People were then directed to a handsomely faded three-story hotel across a narrow-paved road, to which they gladly wandered by twos and threes. The old hotel was quite charming, with a colorful tropical garden, and a smiling Fijian team inside, directing people to their rooms.

Peter could visualize Sir Harry Luke arriving at this seaplane wharf last December, just before the Hawaii attack, being met by one or two aides attired in white uniforms, with an open-top staff car from which Sir Harry would doubtless wave paternally to the natives, donkeys, and occasional expats, as the car moved in stately grandeur to the splendid British High Commission for the Western Pacific, probably situated on a slight rise overlooking Suva. Those were the last two days of a comfortable colonial era, for now the uniforms were rumpled khakis or blue jump suits, and the future looked decidedly uncomfortable.

It turned out that Bongo was the senior-ranking officer on the Canton-Fiji flight, so they pinned a little badge to his jump suit:

Lt. Commander E. Perkins USNR

"Suits you well," observed Peter. "What do we do next?"

"Read this stuff they gave us, then look for a bar in town. I hope we can find one because this first notice says everything in the town is closed on Sundays, one of which is tomorrow."

"But today is Sunday," Peter pointed out. "Remember we crossed the dateline?"

Bongo groaned. "OK smart fellow, so we did. That means we'd better visit the hotel bartender right now because the town is buttoned up like a whalebone corset."

A cozy dining room and adjacent bar began filling up with the newly arrived NATS passengers. The French family opted for a table right away, and some other passengers did as well. Most, however, entered the smoky bar in expectation of a whiskey or sherry.

"Sorry sirs," the Indian bartender solemnly announced. "Only have Lion beer from India, or Australia replica, Fosters."

"Good grief, never heard of them," Bongo grimaced. "What now, O great colonial mind?"

"Tea, of course. It cures any longings. Let's just eat supper and forget the booze for a change."

As they started toward the dining room, they were spotted by the Navy lieutenant who had checked off their names at the wharf.

"Commander Perkins, Mr. Perry, do you have a moment?"

"We do indeed. About to partake of some tea. Care to join us?" Bongo offered.

"Why yes, that would be a pleasure, sir, but let me invite you gentlemen instead; expense account." The young man grinned, introducing himself as Lt. Michael Osborn. "Please call me Mike."

"How long have you been posted out here then, Mike", Peter asked as they were seated at a table out on an adjoining veranda where a gentle breeze blew away some of the cigarette smoke.

"Only three weeks, but it has been great duty so far. The natives and Kiwis both treat us well—I guess because we seem to have money to burn."

"So how many New Zealand troops are here?" Bongo asked, "And what are they up to?"

"Quite a few, sir, actually, including a couple of artillery companies, I think. But what they're mostly up to seems to be beer and darts, which they all love. Won't go into a pub that doesn't have a dart board or two. Suva is their headquarters, but there's another large contingent at Nadi airfield on the west coast. RNZAF actually purchased several hectares of land over there themselves, then started building the airstrip and terminal last year."

"The Kiwi Army and Air Force have been in Fiji for quite a while then?" Bongo asked.

"Yes sir, since war started in Europe. Their main job seems to be aerial reconnaissance of these islands, and defense of their own installations and the cities. I think there are around ten thousand of them all together. Originally, they were keeping a lookout for German raiders, which were sinking ships all around the Pacific, but now of course their role has expanded because of Japan. These days they hunt for submarines. Besides a couple of Short Sunderland seaplanes, like the one you saw in the bay, they are expecting some of our PBY Catalinas, which they call *Black Cats*."

"I was curious about this seaplane base," Peter said. "Was Pan Am involved in it at all, or was it set up by the Kiwis on their own? Do you have any knowledge of its history?"

"I do, as a matter of fact," the NATS lieutenant replied. "At first, the Kiwis operated a couple of seaplanes from Suva harbor, but their survey team said the harbor wouldn't be suitable year-round, particularly for larger planes, and suggested they look for another site that was calmer. Although Lauthala Bay should have been obvious from the beginning, I guess there were concerns about the bay's shallowness at neap tide, and the lack of a solid seawall on the shore. Then Pan Am came along, looking for a base, which led to a kind of joint-venture idea. I believe Pan Am kicked in funds to get things started, but at any rate there was some dredging and the new sea wall was built in a hurry; it was all beachfront here before that."

"Then what about this fine old hotel?" Peter asked. "Looks like it's been here for decades. Why was there a charming hotel here before the seaplane base came along?"

"Apparently this bay was a colonial getaway place. In the old days, it took hours to get from Suva Harbor to Lauthala Bay, which was isolated and much less developed. There is also a little camping resort out there on Lauthala Island, at the far side of the bay." Lt. Osborn pointed to the faint line of trees on the horizon.

"Expat Brits would leave their sailboats permanently here at the hotel moorings, then sail over to the island for holidays," he added. "They could also sail a bit further afield to Nukulau Island, ten miles southeast, after it stopped being the quarantine place for indentured Tamils from India, coming here to work in the cane fields."

"Tamils such as our bartender, right?" Bongo queried.

"Exactly," nodded the lieutenant. "Anyway, sometimes the expat family members preferred to stay behind at the hotel to swim, or to explore Viti Levu while the husbands went sailing, so this hotel was built to capture the holiday business. It did a fine job of it, so the bartender tells us. He said his father ran the bar before him, and even had some shares in the hotel. A Scottish family started it in the '20s."

"And NATS is a hotel tenant now, I gather," said Bongo.

"Yes we are, sir, and we also have a fair-sized warehouse down the road, where we keep the fuel and equipment, and the radio, and most of the offices. This little hotel office is mainly for receiving passengers, but the hotel also provides our Navy quarters. We are two officers, a chief and eleven sailors, and we all live here in the hotel." He smiled again.

"Thank you, Mister Mike Osborn, for all this background. Where were you stationed before Fiji?"

"Hawaii, sir; I love the Pacific islands. I'll definitely come back after the war."

"Weren't you going to tell us something, when we met in the bar?" Peter reminded him.

"Oh yes, sorry. I was going to ask whether your plan for going to Sydney was firm or not."

"What does that mean?" asked Bongo.

"Well, sir, all the other passengers who arrived with you this afternoon are heading for Nouméa in New Caledonia and will be departing tomorrow morning. Your two seats are still available, so I wondered if you might not prefer to wait in Nouméa for a Sydney flight, rather than here in Fiji. Our next scheduled flight for Australia is in five days, but I can't guarantee there will be any available seats on it. NATS doesn't do a lot of Australia business through Fiji yet, though we will in a couple of months after SWPA get fleshed out.

"The Army's ATC land plane network from Canton stops at Nadi on the drier west side of Viti Levu, and then straight to Sydney. We could of course get you over to Nadi by car if they had any seats available, but ATC have been flying full lately because of General MacArthur's priority to get his army built up."

"What's New Caledonia like then, Mister Michael, if you please?" Bongo asked. "And what are the chances of us getting stuck there too?"

"It's a French colony sir, supposedly quite nice. I don't think you would be stuck there for long, if at all. At the moment, there's more Navy traffic to Sydney from Nouméa than there is from Fiji, and they are just half a day apart by air. Admiral Ghormley will have his flagship at Nouméa soon, as you probably know, being ONI."

Bongo didn't know that and wondered why not. But then, he had been out of circulation for a whole week already. Embarrassing.

Peter shrugged. "I'd just as soon get a bit closer to Australia while we can, but it's a shame not to see something of Suva as well. Unfortunately, nothing is open in the town this evening, correct?"

"Right sir, just the hotels; but having said that, the Kiwi Colonel Percy McKee asked me earlier to bring you to their wing of the hotel this evening. They have their own hotel bar, you might say."

"What, just the two of us, or the other 35 passengers as well?" "Just yourselves, sir. The colonel wanted to meet you."

"All right then, let's go get acquainted, shall we?" Bongo instructed Lt. Michael to lead the way. Thoughts of supper were superseded by images of good whiskey and gin.

A lively event appeared to be in full swing at the third-floor wing as Lt. Osborn led them into an elaborate vestibule. A young New Zealand naval officer answered Michael's knock on the inner door. Upon seeing the American uniforms, he shouted into the smoky room beyond:

"Attintion on dick!" The noise slowly abated as a red-faced colonel approached the visitors through a mass of Kiwi Army and Navy drinkers, who were standing or leaning about in the elegant formal parlor designed for long-ago wedding receptions. He sported a bushy mustache with pointed ends and looked the part of a ferocious warrior or pirate.

"Blimey, it's the bloody Yanks! Come in Liftinant Osborn and introduce your companions."

"Thank you, Colonel McKee. May I present Lewtenant Commander Bongo Perkins, US Naval Reserve and lately of Honolulu"—the two shook hands—"and Mister Peter Perry, a reserve captain in the Royal Singapore Engineers."

"A ruddy Pom then, disguised as a Yank. What's all this about, eh?" Without waiting for Peter's reply, the colonel shouted for drinks.

"Three good whiskeys for our Allies, and quick about it!" An Army corporal with a little tray appeared as if by magic.

*** ZANZIBAR'S *TRAGIC VOYAGE* ***

Next morning Peter and Bongo joined Lt. Osborn and some NATS sailors to watch the Martin flying boat take off for Nouméa.

They themselves were not aboard because in the din and shouting of last night's Kiwi party at the hotel, Colonel McKee had offered them a direct ride to Rose Bay in Sydney Harbor, aboard the New Zealand Air Force seaplane that would be departing on Wednesday morning, two days hence.

This offer seemed like a wonderful compromise between waiting in Fiji for the next NATS plane in five or so days, possibly finding it already full, or else departing on the Nouméa bird that had just taken off, leaving them possibly stuck in New Caledonia without an ongoing ride to Sydney.

They jumped at the Colonel's offer, perhaps primed by two more glasses of fine Scots whiskey. The garrulous Colonel McKee, his splendid mustaches dancing energetically, quizzed them over and over about their backgrounds, and what they thought of the war.

He had fought in the Dardanelles as a young subaltern, y'see, and was not as a result particularly fond of the English, but he made a good effort of accepting Peter as a sort of honorary Kiwi as the evening wore on. Bongo and Michael, being ruddy Yanks, were beyond redemption, but the colonel was entranced by their tales of the Hawaiian Islands, which he longed to visit one day.

Lt. Mike promised the necessary paperwork for transferring two passengers from NATS to RNZAF custodianship, and the deed was done. Someone had thoughtfully ordered a buffet of Indian curries, with condiments and poppadums, which arrived at the reception room just in the nick of time as the whiskey ran out, and a stirring riff from a bagpiper rent the air. At 2100 hours, the visitors took their leave amid much good-natured and unintelligible banter.

At breakfast after the NATS plane departed, Peter was very pleased about the two days they now had available to explore Suva, and to possibly track down Graham and Lois Overwood so that Bongo could meet his old Canton Island friends. Peter had no idea where in Fiji they might be living but assumed the Colonial Office should be able to help. They stopped by during their walking tour of the old city.

It was a good guess. A female CO clerk informed them the Overwoods were still on medical leave and presumed to be living aboard their yacht *Zanzibar* over at Nukulau Island, the former quarantine station. As there was no telephone connection to the yacht, and the daily ferry had already left, she suggested hiring a motor launch and paying a visit to Nukulau themselves, a one-hour ride, more or less, depending on sea conditions.

This they did, and around noon they were deposited by their hired launch and native Fiji driver at a sturdy wharf near a little Nukulau village, hidden among bougainvillea, frangipani and palm trees. As they walked along a dirt road toward the beach moorings, Peter spotted *Zanzibar* right away among a cluster of masts and buoys, its dinghy tied alongside.

Attempts to gain someone's attention on the yacht were unsuccessful. Peter was on the verge of returning to their boat for a lift when an ancient motorcar stopped beside them. Its driver, a grey-haired Fijian of some evident importance, offered to assist.

"But how will you reach the boat?" Peter asked.

The old Fijian laughed: "Watch, sir, and you will see." The car had an old squeeze horn with a rubber bulb, like similar ones Peter remembered from his youth in Wales. The man squeezed the bulb hard, and it produced a duck-like call of fairly loud intensity. He repeated this steadily every couple of seconds, and after a dozen or so quacks, heads would pop up from the boats that had people aboard.

Peter kept pointing toward *Zanzibar,* but it seemed ages before Lois finally appeared from below and saw him. With a wave she disappeared again, then was up on deck followed by Graham. They climbed into their dinghy and began pulling slowly at the oars.

Thanking the Fijian driver effusively, and searching for a coin, Peter was surprised when the fellow turned away any thought of compensation.

"No indeed, sir. It was a pleasure to be of service. I am the Postmaster on Nukulau, so please stop in at the office if I may be of further service." With that he quacked off down the road.

"What a splendid bloke," Peter observed, "But look, here come the ancient residents of Canton at last. Do try to be on your best behavior, Bongo, old thing."

Graham and Lois, clad in rather skimpy and faded boat attire, looked tired and thin to Peter. After a hug and a handshake, he was certain they were not well. Bongo caught Peter's concern and was gentle with his greetings.

"Come back to the boat in our dinghy," Graham suggested faintly. "Then we can have a drink and talk."

Bongo countered: "Look good people, we have a motorboat and driver chartered for the day. Let us go back to the pier and have him bring us over to *Zanzibar.* Could he then tie up to your mooring and wait there until it's time for us to return to Suva? Would that be acceptable?"

It was Peter's turn. "Bongo, be a sport and bring the launch over without me. Then I can take the oars and get the dinghy back to *Zanzibar.*" Bongo agreed at once, apologizing for not having made the suggestion himself.

After the dinghy was tied up at the old Tahiti ketch—which looked somewhat the worse for wear—and they had climbed aboard, Peter voiced his concern quickly, before Bongo and the launch arrived.

"Dear friends, you both look unwell. Is there a problem?"

"Oh Peter," Lois replied, "we had a dreadful cruise back to Fiji from Canton. Didn't want to bother anyone afterwards and didn't know how to reach you. We were stopped by a Japanese submarine, the last thing we expected. It surfaced and fired a machine gun near us, so we dropped sails and stopped. Then they sent over a rubber boat, and of course searched *Zanzibar*.

"They found Graham's wireless transmitter and tried to force him to show them the codes, which he had already chucked overboard. So they beat him up, quite badly. The two boys from Tarawa—John and Gordon—stood up for Graham and threw one of the Japs over the side after knifing him. Then they were both shot dead by another Jap; and one of the shots hit me in the arm."

"Wait Lois, here is my friend Bongo. He needs to hear all this so he can report it to the US Navy."

The launch pulled alongside, and Bongo climbed aboard, asking the driver to move to the mooring and wait for them.

Peter gave Bongo a synopsis. "Where did the attack happen, Mr. Overwood?" Bongo asked.

"About 400 miles east of Funafuti in the Ellice group, as I remember; it's in the logbook," Lois replied on Graham's behalf. "About halfway to Fiji from Canton. It was almost three weeks ago."

"Did you see the sub's number on its tower?" Bongo asked.

This time Graham responded, feebly: "Damned certain; it was I-23. They eventually hauled away my transmitter, and left Lois and me to die. Wouldn't even waste a shell on us to sink the boat. I remember that boarding-party officer grinning as they cast off. Well, in spite of her bandaged arm, Lois sailed us onward, bless her, and here we are, bloody well battered but thrilled to see you again, Peter, and your ruddy Yank friend too." Whenever Graham spoke, he seemed to double up.

"What is it, Graham. Are you in pain?" Peter asked.

Lois again replied for him: "Peter, they broke three of Graham's ribs, which aren't healing properly—but at least he's stopped smoking!" Graham glowered on the bunk.

"We told the Colonial Office about it all after we managed to get to Fiji, but they wanted so much paperwork filled out that we decided to just come over here and lick our wounds. I don't know how to find out whether John and Gordon have any family here. Being Gilbertese, it's not very likely. They were such wonderful friends too, and gave their lives for Graham—well, not really for Graham himself, but for the British Resident of Canton Island."

"But Lois, Graham needs medical attention, and what about you? Is your arm healed? You seem ill as well. What happened?"

"I don't know, Peter, and please don't worry. It's just some female problem, that's all. Can we get Graham to a hospital somehow, without the Colonial Office being involved? But if we do, who will look after *Zanzibar* while we're away?" She was shaking with fatigue and anxiety.

"Graham and Lois, listen: Bongo and I have to fly out to Sydney on Wednesday morning, but we can try to get things settled for you this afternoon and tomorrow. I can suggest two names to look after you when we leave. The first is a wonderful gent we just met when trying to get your attention from shore. He is the Nukulau postmaster; do you know him? He could keep an eye on Zanzibar while you two are in Suva getting treatment. We can talk to him today."

"Yes, we know Cyril," Lois said, "But not very well. He does seem like an honorable man, I agree."

"Good, the other one is a 'ruddy Yank', if that's alright with Graham. He is Lieutenant Michael Osborn who is in charge of the US Navy seaplane transportation office—what they call NATS—over there on Lauthala Bay. I think Commander Perkins here, who outranks him and can get his attention, would probably agree that you would be in good hands with Mister Osborn looking out for your interests, as a valued ally of the United States."

Bongo stepped in: "Graham is still a colonial officer on medical leave, right? So let's make the most of it. They have no choice but to get you both healed and back to work. Are you ready to give it a try? We can take you to Suva in the launch this afternoon and speak to the Colonial Office on your behalf tomorrow."

Lois was almost in tears. "Yes, of course. It's just that we've both been feeling drained and useless. We were even thinking about a Viking funeral in *Zanzibar*. But let us by all means follow your plan, bless you both."

Peter nodded his firm agreement, and Graham turned his head to the bulkhead, eyes glistening.

CHAPTER THREE

★ ★ ★

Australia Fair

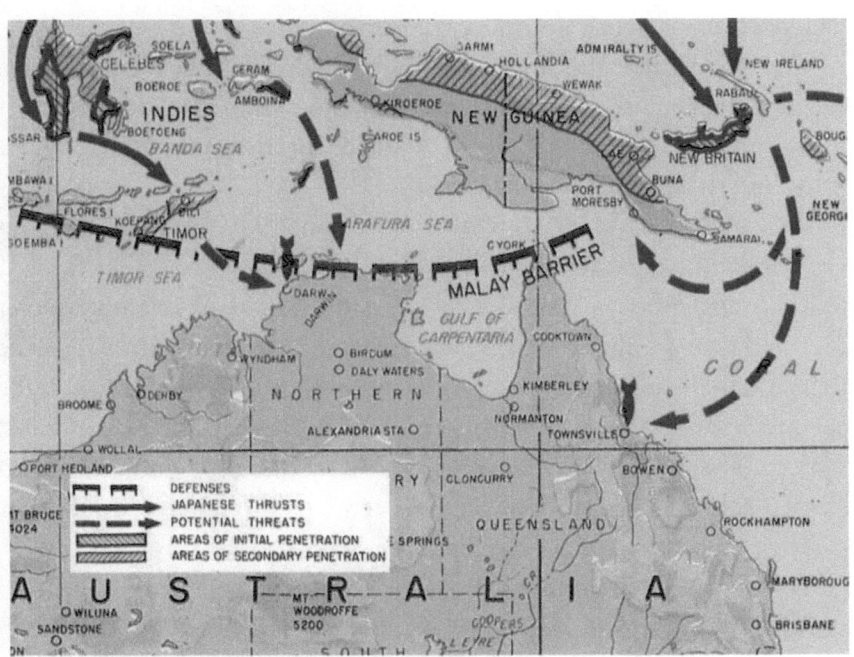

Malay Barrier
(https://history.amedd.army.mil/tools/privacy.html)

"Where's that jolly jumbuck you've got in your tucker bag?"
From *Waltzing Matilda*, Australian folk song

*** THE LAND OF OZ ***

Australia, whose name is derived from the Latin *Terra Australis*, meaning Southern Land, is the world's sixth-largest country by total area. Located within the Southern Hemisphere, most of Australia is an island so large that it is usually classified as a continent. Its landmass is nearly as great as that of the continental United States. Six of Australia's seven states comprise the island-continent itself, while the seventh is a separate and much smaller island-state to the southeast, called Tasmania.

Dutch explorers discovered this interesting part of the Pacific Ocean ahead of the English, calling it New Holland. They named the smaller island Van Diemen's Land, but it was later changed to Tasmania in honor of an English explorer, Abel Tasman.

The Dutch made some coastal river explorations here and there on New Holland, before the English chased them away.

Claiming at first just the eastern part of the land—the English explorer Captain James Cook having mapped the eastern coastline in 1770—the English established a penal colony in New South Wales to replace the one in Georgia that had recently been lost with the rest of their American colonies. The Australian colonies grew steadily thereafter and accelerated during a gold rush in the 1850s. The last convict ship arrived in 1848, after which penal servitude was abolished by Britain.

Some modern Australians, by 1942, fondly referred to their beloved land as 'Oz', a phonetic derivation of the collective noun 'Aussie' which is itself a diminutive of 'Australian'. This nickname was also, of course, a tribute to the Wonderful Wizard thereof, for which the Aussies developed quite a liking after the 1939 American film that took the English-speaking world by storm.

Anthropologists (at least Australian anthropologists) say that Australia was once attached to a mega-continent called Gondwana, from which the Land of Oz broke away ages ago, thereby marooning its life forms on a drifting continental plate. If that is true, the breakaway rupture event must have been an absolutely hellish experience for all life forms that survived it, but the reward was a sort of dusty Garden of Eden afterwards—until the Europeans arrived.

Before those explorers came, Australia was occupied for some fifty thousand years by Stone Age hunter-gatherers, whose descendants became known in modern times as Aborigines. Those skittish folks were not well respected by the newer Caucasian population, many of whom still call them 'Abos' in a sort of affectionately disdainful manner. Their old way of life, like that of North American 'Indians', was severely disrupted by European immigrants.

Australia is also populated by a host of strange (to the rest of us) animals and birds. World-renowned among the former are several species of marsupial (pouch-bearing) mammals, such as the kangaroo, wallaby, koala, wombat, possum, opossum, and Tasmanian Devil. Some other local mammals are not marsupial, for example the placental dingo, which is a wild dog. The oddest mammal of all is the egg-laying, duck-billed, beaver-tailed, other-footed platypus, an extremely shy creature that inhabits riverbanks.

Then there are the non-mammalian crocodiles, speaking of rivers. Monstrous crocs are found in northern tropical rivers and are not to be trifled with unless your surname is Dundee.

Australian birds, of which there are hundreds of species, include the emu, a huge flightless thing rather like an ostrich, and the kookaburra (in the gum tree), whose laugh is both infectious and unforgettable.

There are also vast communities of marine creatures, ranging from the great white shark down to tiny mollusks, many of which take shelter along the Great Barrier Reef, a sixteen hundred mile-long offshore phenomenon of nature that parallels a great part of Australia's eastern seaboard.

Insects abound as well, like mosquitos—or 'mozzies' in Oz-speak. They can, and do, transmit malaria in the tropical north.

Most US military personnel sent to Australia for General MacArthur's SWPA buildup, had difficulty visualizing its unique geography—let alone that of the mighty oceans which surround it. A diligent reader or writer nowadays can easily find an atlas for reference, but good ones were quite scarce in the war years.

A modern atlas, if you have one handy, will show that most of Australia's human population is still distributed up and down the east coast, in the cities of Melbourne, Sydney, Brisbane, and Canberra. The first three are state capitals of Victoria, New South Wales, and Queensland respectively, while Canberra, a purpose-built thematic city located within New South Wales, is the national capital.

These somewhat humid cities lie to the east of high mountain ranges—some southern peaks of which are snow-capped—that block most moisture from reaching their semi-arid western slopes, the extensive grazing lands of sheep and cattle.

In Australia the people who tend cattle are called stockmen, rather than cowboys; they carry enormous bull whips instead of pistols, and they brew tea in billy cans—yes, tea.

Far west of the cattle country, the vast central intrastate region of Oz is mainly desert, where hardy towns like Alice Springs provide the occasional 'fair dinkum' (reliable) oasis.

Perth and Adelaide are the capitals of Western Australia and South Australia. The capital of the small island of Tasmania is Hobart.

Darwin, finally, is the principal city of the Northern Territory, where Peter Perry's wife and son arrived from Singapore and remained for nearly a month. Darwin was heavily bombed on several occasions by Japanese aircraft flying from East Timor (check your atlas), right after they captured the Dutch East Indies.

Wendy and John found bus transportation from Darwin to Sydney shortly before the bombings, when she learned that Peter and an American friend called Bongo Perkins were due to arrive there from Fiji. Wendy knew the men would come by plane, so she was glad to find a rental cottage near Rose Bay in Sydney Harbor, where both seaplane and landplane bases were then located.

Sydney looked quite attractive to her. Its temperate climate was a welcome change from tropical Singapore, which lay almost upon the equator, and was an even grander change from her memories of frigid English winters. And one could probably get used to the funny Aussie accent and vocabulary, she supposed.

Southern Hemisphere seasons took more getting used to, Wendy realized. In Australia at the end of March 1942, which it then was, the middle of autumn was approaching; Christmas Day would appear in the middle of summer!

*** FAREWELL TO FIJI ***

The Royal New Zealand Air Force (RNZAF) seaplane at Lauthala Bay departed as scheduled on Wednesday, March 25, 1942, with Peter and Bongo aboard as authorized Allied supernumeraries, meaning passengers who could be put to work if necessary.

The combat-ready plane's eventual destination was Sydney, Australia, but its mission en route was to briefly join a search for Japanese submarines off western Fiji, then to overfly the New Hebrides and New Caledonia islands afterwards. Those island chains lay on a straight-line path to Australia from Viti Levu and made for convenient fueling or emergency landing stops accordingly.

In the prior two weeks, there had been vague but mounting evidence of an enemy submarine at work near Nadi (pronounced Nandi), site of the new airfield on the southwest side of Viti Levu. The seaplane's flight was coordinated that morning with two RNZAF land-based bombers and a fast frigate armed with depth charges.

Around 11am, when the sun was high enough to illuminate the ocean depths, the four hunters converged onto a planned grid to search the immediate area. If nothing was found right away, the seaplane would simply carry on to Sydney, leaving its companions to continue for a few more hours on a more northerly sector.

Unlike rival branches of the services in other Allied nations including the United States, New Zealand's armed forces used compatible wireless equipment whereby ships, planes, and ground units could readily communicate with one another. This was both a planned strategy and a practical necessity for a country with a limited military budget and a vast international responsibility.

On this particular morning the strategy would perhaps pay off, as the frigate was reporting sporadic asdic (sonar) contact with a possible enemy target. The ship vectored the three planes into a focused search pattern. Peter and Bongo were given earphones, enabling them to hear the ship-to-plane conversations, though they could only converse with their plane's crew, not the whole network.

"Tally Ho, mates!" It was the ship, reporting a solid contact less than five thousand yards away. The sub must have been stationary and silent on the bottom, hoping to avoid detection, but now realized it was a definite quarry. It was making tracks out to sea for deeper water, but the speedy frigate closed rapidly, leaving the audio circuit open so the planes could faintly hear the 'thump, thump' of depth charges exploding underwater.

Fifteen minutes later, another pass, more thumps, then still another. "I think we've got the blighter; can you planes see anything?"

The sub became gradually visible as it was forced to the surface. "Blimey, there she is!"

Next, the bombers made a run one after the other, to drop near misses that shattered the enemy hull. The sub broke to the surface and began to list.

The frigate slowed near the battered I-boat and launched a prize crew of armed sailors to try boarding before it could be scuttled.

Japanese poured from the conning tower and a deck hatch, racing to clear the deck gun for action. Machine guns were fired from the tower at the frigate's boarding party.

Multiple machine guns on the frigate fired back, raking the deck and the conning tower. Several Jap sailors fell, but others were still fighting.

The conning tower was clearly visible to the seaplane now, and Bongo could see a rubber boat being launched on the far side, that probably wasn't visible to the frigate. "See that little boat, skipper?" Bongo asked excitedly.

"Aye, that I do," the pilot replied. "Let's git 'im!"

The seaplane dove and circled the sub and frigate. Bongo shouted to Peter: "Look, it's the *I-23*, the bastards that shot up the Overwoods in their sailboat." The number was clearly visible to all.

Bongo shouted again: "Can we catch those two in the rubber boat, skipper? We have a score to settle with that sub."

The pilot said he would put the plane down near the little boat and send two men over in the plane's own fast boat.

"Let me go along on this gig," Bongo insisted, cocking a round into his .45 pistol.

"Right, then; these two lads will take you along. They have Sten guns."

The Sunderland was throttled back, to splash down on a collision course with the two Japanese and their rubber boat, which swerved to avoid a crash. At the last minute the seaplane also turned, and its side door quickly opened.

The two Kiwi sailors launched their craft and jumped in, starting the outboard motor as Bongo tumbled in close behind them. They raced after the Japs, who were going flat out toward the distant shore. The seaplane cruised around to get inshore of the quarry, and the little Kiwi boat closed the distance from seaward. Trapped, the Jap boat slowed and stopped, and the two men aboard raised their hands.

Bongo and the Kiwis slowed as they drew close to the enemy, when suddenly both Japs ducked down to grab weapons and open fire. They were no match for the British-made Sten gun, a lightweight submachine gun which killed them instantly, but Bongo had been hit by a Jap bullet and was slumped down in the boat. One of the Kiwi airmen took the Jap boat in tow, while the other started them toward the nearby seaplane. He noticed Bongo's bloody shirt, but saw he was conscious.

"Hold on sir, we'll have you back aboard the plane in half a mo." He fished a compress from the aid kit on his web belt and passed it to Bongo.

"Hold this on the wound sir, please." Bongo nodded but drooped his head.

The seaplane pilot could see the situation, and had willing hands waiting at the open door to lift Bongo aboard, where Peter helped lay him onto a stretcher. It was a messy shoulder wound but apparently spared the lung.

Meanwhile others were searching the pockets of the dead Japs and sliding their bodies into the water. A short blast from a Sten gun shredded the captured rubber boat, then the seaplane door was closed and the plane began to move.

The pilot shouted to Peter over the din of the engines: "We've drifted a fair bit from the frigate, which now has the sub almost under control, and we could use some more fuel for the run to Sydney. I'm taking us to the island of Efaté in the New Hebrides, which is not much farther ahead than going back to Suva." Peter nodded.

The pilot continued: "A new US Navy hospital is soon to open on Efaté. They have enough medical staff there already to take care of your

Yank friend and send him along to Sydney when he gets well enough to chase the nurses. Sorry about him getting hit, but he's stable now and sleeping."

"Thanks very much," Peter replied, moving up so he could be heard.

"You know, skipper, Commander Perkins and I are very pleased that you chaps have put that damned sub out of commission. *I-23* stopped a friend's yacht a few weeks ago near Funafuti and left him and his wife for dead. He was the British administrator on Canton Island. They are in a Suva hospital now. I hope your chums will capture the sub's logbook."

"That's very bad form for the Japs; I'm glad your friends are still alive," the pilot answered. "Tell me, Mr. Perry, where exactly is Canton Island?"

*** *SYDNEY AT LAST* ***

The Australian coast of New South Wales gradually emerged out of a pencil-line smudge on the horizon. Peter, who had been standing behind the two pilots chatting, returned to the rear of the aircraft.

He thought in amusement of the now-absent Bongo, whom they had left on Efaté under protest until he was spoken to by a Navy nurse from some southern US state, whose sugary drawl and fluttering eyelids subdued him more than any sedative possibly could.

"I'll be along soon, ugly Brit, don't worry," the anesthetized patient grinned. "Leave a message at Sydney Base where to find you."

Port Vila, the New Hebrides capital, had been spread around a gorgeous little bay on the island of Efaté, Peter remembered later, with government residences discreetly tucked away on a tiny offshore islet within the bay. *The high and mighty could only come and go by launch, but that inconvenience let them sleep more securely. It was rather like having a castle moat*, Peter imagined.

That peculiar thought made Peter recall Bongo chiding him during one of their chats, when they had whiled away the hours on Canton Island waiting for a ride to Fiji:

"You Brits have a 'thing' about small offshore islands to control your colonies, right?" Bongo had teased. "Consider Hong Kong off China, Singapore and Penang off Malaya, and Tulagi off the Solomons; I reckon the idea must come from your natural insularity within the British Isles. Not a bad idea though, but what drives it—prejudice, or paranoia?"

The New Hebrides Islands were another British condominium creation, Peter had learned during the overnight stopover to offload Bongo, but unlike Canton Island, which was a British and American union, this much older condominium in the New Hebrides was, astonishingly, British and French. Some residents called it a 'pandemonium,' Peter recalled with amusement.

Luckily the French, in this case, did not seem to harbor pro-German Vichy sentiments, because both condominium partners had worked hard to suppress any such public sentiment among the colonial expatriates.

At Havannah hospital on Efaté, where Bongo had been deposited, a doctor told Peter that individual outlying islands of the New Hebrides tended to foster either Gallic or Britannic customs and loyalties, but seldom both. Port Vila, the capital, where Peter and the seaplane crew were taken to dinner by boat, was seemingly an exception—a uniquely bicultural place with genuine cordiality between the two condominium representatives, the doctor opined. "Yet there are so many committees….."

Getting an American seaplane base and hospital constructed at Havannah Harbor on the far side of Efaté must have taken a wizard in diplomacy, so everyone said at dinner. Peter overheard further snatches of conversation at adjacent tables:

"… and soon there will be land-based planes, and an American admiral, *mon Dieu….*"

"… but at least they won't be here at Port Vila," someone else had smiled slyly, being that Havannah Harbor wasn't accessible to Vila by road, thus the Americans could be kept away from their wives and daughters.

Port Vila was so charming that Peter halfway wondered whether Bongo would ever reach Australia. He felt somewhat guilty for deserting him but knew his friend would be quite relieved to get up to date with the ONI at long last, at an American facility with secure communication.

Then there was the nurse, many more of whom would be arriving once the hospital was completed. What was her name again?—Forwood?—Norbush?—Something like that.

*** BEAUTIFUL SYDNEY HARBOR ***

The Short Sunderland approached Sydney from the northeast, cutting across Manly Beach and the north headland of the harbor mouth. Having permission to enter the air space, the plane made a gentle gliding turn toward Rose Bay at the southeast side of the magnificent harbor. Peter could glimpse the iconic Sydney Harbor Bridge briefly, as they descended to calm water. Soon they reached the seaplane dock.

Wendy and young John were there to meet him. She wore the old light blue windbreaker that she often liked for sailing regattas in Singapore. It went well with her customary wind-blown hairdo and serious expression, which for the moment revealed a slightly quivering chin and somewhat reddened eyes. Young John, who at age seven was attired in his school uniform, was waving enthusiastically to Peter.

It was an emotional reunion, as so much had happened to all of them since Peter left Singapore for Canton Island about six months before. Above all, the Perrys had lost their comfortable home and lifestyle, not to mention Peter's important engineering job that he had held for a decade. They had also been torn away from their international friends in Singapore, and the wonderful Chinese staff who were almost like family. The Pacific War—a misnomer if ever there was one—had done all of that.

"You look wonderful, darling," Peter told Wendy as they embraced. "And John-O, you must have grown a foot, young man. Almost time for a birthday, right?"

"Hullo Pops, I'm four foot one now," the boy announced proudly. He was dressed in gray shorts and cap, a white shirt and navy-blue tie.

"What about school; then, do you like it?" Peter asked his son, his arm still around Wendy's shoulders.

"It's alright, but I don't know many boys yet," was the reply. "One of them called me a pom-pom yesterday. Is that something bad?"

"Nothing to worry about," Wendy chimed in. We're all Poms in our family now. It just means English, not Australian. Come on, let's show Daddy our new home near Rose Bay." She dabbed her eyes. "And what of your friend Bongo?"

Peter explained briefly what had happened, as they collected his luggage and strolled to the exit door. Outside the terminal building was a black 1939

Ford with a charcoal-burner attached to the back. A pretty, freckle-faced woman, in a sun dress like Wendy's, got out to shake hands with Peter.

"G'day Peter, how d'you do? I'm Doris your neighbor."

"Peter, Doris is a lifesaver to bring us here and fetch you home. She and Fred live across the road from our cottage, and up the hill a bit. Their lovely place has a view of the bay," Wendy went on.

Doris smiled and opened the doors. "Right, in you go, Master John, back seat with the luggage. Hop in everyone, three up front. Sorry we can't easily stow anything in the boot now, what with the nasty charcoal thing on the back. Petrol rationing has started y'see. There'll be other things before long, I'll wager."

"This is awfully kind of you, Doris," Peter said, "Where is your husband then, still at work?" It was around 5pm.

"Oh yes, Fred is a banker. He works in the City and can't reach home before half six, usually. Often it's later these days, especially on a Friday like this. Well, here we are. Let's unload at your place, Perrys." Doris parked across their drive, then pulled into hers after the goodbyes.

"What a nice neighbor. This seems quite a pleasant place, Wendy dear. You chose well." Peter looked over the garden then took a little tour inside with John. Wendy put the kettle on.

"Peter, there are half a dozen other Singapore families here in Sydney, and a few still in Darwin. We heard that some women and children got away to England or Sumatra and Ceylon at the last minute, and others died trying, but apparently there were masses of English and Australians still on the island when the Japs crossed over from Malaya—mostly men, but many families as well. We can't find out what's happened to them." Peter listened carefully, as Wendy continued.

"There is a refugee center in Sydney that I went to because, well, that's what we officially are now—refugees! I doubt we'll ever see a penny for our things left behind—the furniture and clothes, the car, your book collection. And poor Amah, Cook and Syce, and the houseboys; who knows where they are now. The wonderful Andersons took them on when John and I left—and thank heaven you insisted we get away. It's still like a very bad dream. Everyone thought we were mad to leave Singapore. I did as well."

"I know, I know. The whole thing is ghastly," Peter answered. "Most of our friends must be interned by now, if not dead. And think of all the British and Australian prisoners of war, including General Percival, who had to sign the surrender. They won't have an easy time of it. 'Fortress Singapore' was certainly a misnomer if ever there was one. But, tell me, how is John bearing up?"

Wendy thought about her answer: "Luckily, he doesn't understand the depth of the problem, but he misses his friends and the servants. Of course, I haven't told him what I think may have happened to them all."

"Of course," Peter said. "Wendy, another disaster is the Singapore Chinese. A chap in Honolulu told me they were being executed by the thousands if they had any British connections, which many did. The Japs appear to be fiendish, all of them. Let's try not to dwell on it, for John's sake as well as our own sanity. Now tell me how you found this well-appointed cottage, and then how we are going to pay for it."

Wendy poured them some tea and waved a finger at John to remove his muddy sandals.

"Well, I did salvage our funds at least, and had started on that even before you wrote about it. I collected all your back pay from the Municipality, and a pro-rata home leave allowance and severance pay when I told them we would be leaving Singapore for good, because you had been commandeered by the Americans. I had it all wired to Barclays Bank in Australia, to hold for us.

"Then I received your funds from Hawaii, after the Barclays account was opened here. We'll be all right for quite some time if we're careful. Of course, it would be nice to have a car, but heaven knows how we could manage that. Doris says you have to know somebody just for the chance to even bid on one, they are so scarce with all the Canadians and Americans coming over. And of course, there are no new ones any longer."

"That's true. Well done on the money side of things, though, my love. But the cottage—whose is it? This certainly is an attractive neighborhood. Oh, and what was it like in Darwin, when the raids started? You haven't mentioned that yet."

"Peter, the cottage and Darwin go together, sadly," Wendy spoke softly. "I met a Sydney couple at the Darwin hotel a few weeks after John and I arrived. The husband was a government inspector of some sort, and she always traveled with him on his assignments. They were past middle age, with their children both grown.

"When I told her about our circumstances, she said 'Oh, you must stay at our house on Rose Bay for as long as you like. We shan't be needing it for at least a year and will be happy to have someone living there.' That sounded divine, and she asked only a modest rent. We signed a simple agreement, and she posted a copy to their son in Sydney."

"How wonderful!" Peter exclaimed. "That's wonderful too, young John," he added, admiring his son's drawing of a kangaroo.

"John and I left the very next morning for Sydney by bus," Wendy went on, shooing John out of the room, "And made our way to the cottage eventually, perhaps a week after meeting the nice couple. We contacted their son for the keys, and when he brought them he told us the hotel in Darwin had been bombed soon after we left, and both his parents were killed on the spot! Can you imagine?"

"Oh my God, Wen, this awful war," Peter groaned. "And so the son let you stay on, is that it?"

"Exactly, he was so nice about it and I felt terrible for him and the sister, whom I met later. Some are blessed, and some are cursed and there's no way to know what happens next." Wendy wept at the sad memory, and the contrast to their own relatively good fortune. "*Yin* and *Yang*, as the Chinese used to say in Singapore," she sobbed.

"Well, chin up dear. I can't bear to think about Singapore either; it's like a vanished dream. I simply cannot imagine it populated by the Japanese, can you?" Wendy shook her head quietly, wiping her eyes.

Peter tried to cheer her up. "Look, love, tomorrow's Saturday, so let me get unpacked now and help get supper going. Can we take John for an outing in the morning? Should do us all good. As I begin to remember things, I'll tell you all about your dear husband's adventures on Canton Island and beyond. It all seems surreal, looking back. Oh, but before I forget; I brought you a present."

Peter rummaged through the duffel bag and found the re-wrapped gift box, handing it over. "Sorry it's a bit rumpled looking. Our luggage was tossed about a lot."

"What on earth is it?" Wendy asked, unwrapping the box, and lifting out the ceramic doll in its elegant kimono. "Peter, where did you get this?

I can't possibly display such a thing in our home, after what those people did to Singapore! What's come over you? Is it a memento of someone you met, a Japanese girl in Hawaii perhaps? Really, it is all too much to bear!" She sobbed and left the room.

*** *THE DOOLITTLE RAID* ***

Three more weeks into 1942, on April 18th, a surprising announcement came over the wireless. People in Sydney would generally gather around to hear the news after supper, and this particular Saturday evening report was electrifying.

US planes had bombed Tokyo, Kobe, and Yokohama, and flown on towards China! This first Allied strike on the Japanese homeland cheered Australian civilians immensely and startled Japanese civilians by an equal measure. Later it turned out that sixteen B-25 bombers had been launched from aircraft carrier *Hornet*, led by USAAF Colonel Jimmy Doolittle. Land-based bombers had never been launched from a carrier before; it was a harebrained idea that worked!

Peter was still scouting around for employment a fortnight later, seeking some meaningful war work, when Bongo telephoned to say he was at Rose Bay and "where the hell are you staying?"

Peter gave him the address and invited him to dine with Wendy and John, if he could find transportation.

"No sweat, pal. I'll be there in twenty minutes." And he was; a US Navy staff car delivered a smiling Bongo, strikingly attired in Navy dress whites, sporting his Purple Heart and campaign ribbons, and the three shiny new shoulder board stripes of a full Navy commander.

"Pay attention, ugly Brit. This is how you get ahead in the war theater; don't you know?"

After hurried introductions, Bongo pecked Wendy on the cheek—at which she drew back—and solemnly shook hands with Master John, who was eyeing the white uniform with evident awe. "Well boy," Bongo removed his hat and bent down nose to nose, "Does this establishment serve Gimlets?" John looked flustered and glanced at Wendy for guidance.

"Certainly it does," she confirmed. "An excellent suggestion.

Can your driver wait while we dine?"

"Oh, I'll let him go for a few hours, as long as you don't need him to fetch some gin first." Bongo spoke to the yeoman, who drove off.

"So Wendy, did Peter show you his medal from Canton Island? Actually I haven't seen it myself, Peter old thing. Where is it displayed?" Peter fetched the silly thunder box award from a drawer.

"A work of art," Bongo whistled. "Just what a Mexican bandit would die for. Cheers to you, Mr. Benjo, and also to you, lucky Wendy. This clever man is a fine friend to the downtrodden masses. I have seen him in action."

"I shouldn't wonder," Wendy smiled icily, at which point Bongo deflated a little, and sipped thoughtfully from his Gimlet.

"Well," he coughed at last, "What are you doing with yourself Peter? I assume you've found gainful employment, no?"

Peter confessed that he had not, which brought forth a frown from Bongo.

"What's the matter with the Aussie government? Don't they need any and all kinds of specialists to run this peculiar nation, now that their boys are in German or Japanese prison camps? Especially super plumbers like your good self, Peter."

"I can't seem to find the right people to ask," Peter said, morosely. "There's a militant labor government here, as in New Zealand, which is very protective of jobs for the lads until they return home. Meanwhile Australia is falling farther and farther behind on military projects. You Yanks are intent on opening six or seven new bases for MacArthur, but so far nothing has been started."

"That figures," said Bongo. "The US military will end up doing it themselves, you watch. I'd be surprised if they don't take over the Aussie nation and put it under martial law like Hawaii. However, I do know of somewhere not too far away that is desperate for civil engineering talent, and has a budget underwritten by Uncle Sam—who as you may know is the King of America."

"Where is this, then?" Peter asked. Wendy was listening attentively.

"Well, I'm not sure Wendy would be too happy about you leaving again, but the pay is good and you could make a real contribution to beating the damned Japs. It's New Caledonia, where neither of us managed to get to after the Fiji tour, but I went to Nouméa from Efaté after you left me to waste away in that horrible hospital."

"With those horrible nurses," Peter couldn't help saying.

Wendy sniffed and left the room to check on dinner.

"Anyway, they are doing several things in and around Nouméa. First, they have taken over Pan Am's seaplane base as a NATS station, just like they did for Canton and Fiji. Now they are putting the infrastructure together for hosting an armada of Navy ships for Admiral Ghormley, which means a lot of dredging, shore-based facilities and housing, and a couple of airstrips, which is where you could fit in.

"Lastly, they need to get the place ready for training some US Marine outfits, and that again means constructing a temporary camp with all the usual facilities, somewhere out in the boondocks—the countryside to you. Their government is Free French—or Fighting French, as they now call themselves—and they are ready to roll."

"I'll have to talk this over with Wendy later," said Peter. "As you can tell, she's not too pleased about my getting any more foreign or military entanglements. But what is the timing for Nouméa?"

"Yesterday, Peter, it's super urgent. Today is May 2nd, and the Japs are still on the move. They can pick and choose their next targets. You are a British reserve officer, which means if you'd stayed in Singapore you'd have already been called up months ago—assuming the place hadn't already been captured by then. Don't even imagine where you and the family might be by this time."

Bongo continued: "Look, Nimitz is going all out to stop the Jap advances, and there are some grandiose things about to pop. Eventually MacArthur will get his act together too, and this region will become a zoo of military activity. There's nowhere for a talented civilian to hide, so you might as well jump at the plums now, as wait and get dragged into something mediocre later on."

"I agree with you completely, Bongo, really I do. I just need to break it to Wendy carefully, as she is still under stress from what happened to Singapore, and then the trauma in Darwin. She really would prefer I find something here in Sydney, but let's meet somewhere tomorrow and you can tell me whom to contact."

"OK, sport, that's fine. Now for a pleasant dinner and chat about the world that was—not the world of Oz. By the way, where's the Geisha doll? Did it get here intact?"

Peter smiled wistfully: "Could you give it a decent home, if I bring it along tomorrow? Wendy thought I'd been fraternizing with the enemy."

"Ha, that's a good one. No wonder I got a frosty welcome; guilty by association!"

*** THE BATTLE OF THE CORAL SEA ***

Next day the radio news reported that a Japanese task force had occupied Tulagi, a small island recently abandoned by its British Resident and the commercial companies Lever Brothers and Burns-Philip, that had collectively used Tulagi to administer the vast Solomon Islands plantations. British and Chinese refugees had dispersed to Australia and Fiji on several inter-island ships.

"The IJN quickly established a seaplane base at Tulagi, and began scouting patrols toward New Guinea," Bongo told Peter when they met to discuss the situation.

"Several British government operatives stayed behind in the Solomons to form a coastwatcher organization, as in the Gilberts, which will no doubt prove invaluable in months ahead," Bongo added. "They hid themselves away with radio equipment on Guadalcanal, Malaita, New Georgia and other islands up the Solomon chain."

A few days later, after they had lunched near a dockside warehouse where the ONI had its temporary offices, Peter was reading some of the week's teletype messages about Tulagi, when Bongo interrupted.

"Listen to this one, old sport," Bongo said, perusing a long sheet from the machine. "It's an ONI report from yesterday: 'A large Japanese fleet rounded the eastern tip of New Guinea, and approached its capital, Port Moresby, with intentions to occupy it and threaten New Caledonia and Australia. American planes from Nouméa-based carriers, USS *Yorktown* and *Lexington,* attacked the Japanese transports independently, and succeeded in turning back the invasion force. *Yorktown* also attacked the new Tulagi seaplane base but was seriously damaged by other enemy planes and had to retire.'

"Tough action, eh? Now you can see how important the support base in Nouméa has become. Here, there's still more today: 'Later in the skirmishes, USS *Lexington* was bombed and torpedoed, set afire, and eventually scuttled, but the southern New Guinea invasion force was repelled. Had it not been, northeastern Australia, New Caledonia, New Hebrides, Fiji, and Samoa could have been next in line, according to Japanese war plan FS'."

Bongo then added: "This FS plan has apparently been put on hold, so our code-breaker guys say. Believe in miracles, Peter old thing?"

Peter was shocked at just how near the war had come to Australia, which for obvious reasons was not being told to the Australian public. The Japanese Navy was a formidable opponent.

Bongo continued: "So the Japs had an official plan to invade these southern islands, maybe even Oz. The last few days look like bad news and good news. *Lady Lex* is sunk, and *Yorktown* is a mess, but the Port Moresby invasion fleet from Truk has been stopped. Sounds like your friend Overwood might say 'Christians 5, Lions 5', something like that."

"Seems about right," Peter agreed.

Another ONI message quoted a famous New York commentator, who wrote to summarize the four-day battle: "This first-ever naval battle where opposing ships did not even see each other, is now officially known as *the Battle of the Coral Sea*; it may be a harbinger of things to come. The US lost a fleet carrier, and another was seriously damaged but able to retire. Japan lost a smaller carrier, and a large fleet carrier was probably put out of service for several months. Overall it was a slight tactical victory for Japan, but by blocking the enemy's New Guinea invasion force, it was a hard-won strategic victory for the Allies."

"I guess it's all in the eye of the beholder," said Bongo, "but thank goodness we stopped them from taking Port Moresby at any rate."

But then on May 6th some distressing news came over the evening wireless: "The American garrison on Corregidor in the Philippines has finally surrendered to the Japanese, after a long and heroic siege. The starving prisoners, led by General Wainwright, will soon face incarceration and—based on rumors coming from Bataan—brutality as well. Japan has probably now achieved all her original objectives in the Pacific, but the recent events of the Coral Sea are likely making the Emperor's war planners cautious about seeking more territory."

Peter and Bongo met a few more times in May, Peter having explained to Wendy that it was his duty to get involved in the war, even though they were not Australians nor Americans, and had only been in Australia a short while. She finally understood, and gave Peter her support, and even encouragement. Luckily, she was developing a good friendship with Doris across the road, and they could follow the war news together. John, meanwhile, attended school as if there were no war on at all, and seemed quite keen about the competitive sports for his age group—swimming and rounders. He had already excelled at the former in Singapore, and the latter was something like American softball, so they said—lots of fun and not too complicated.

The Rose Bay neighborhood was wonderful, and the family enjoyed taking walks together under shady eucalyptus trees, or strolling up to the Point, a slight rise jutting onto the bay, to watch the planes come and go.

John was always on the listen for his favorite laughing Kookaburra in an empty lot. The bird would dive down for garden snakes, and fly them back to a treetop, only to drop them again and again, until they were dead and edible. "Look, look!" the lad would insist.

A few days after celebrating John's seventh birthday, in which the boy was thrilled to be given a shiny new bicycle, Peter was finally asked by the US contracts office to join a New Caledonia engineering team, as a civilian consultant on water supply and treatment, which was no doubt the result of Bongo's diligent effort.

Peter was pleased but wondered whether he shouldn't instead offer his services on a military basis. He decided to consult Bongo at his temporary office, which Peter could reach by tram or bus.

Bongo chuckled and poured Peter a cup of coffee. "Look old pal, your previous military organization no longer exists, any more than Malayan dollars still exist. You may, in fact, be the world's only Singapore Reserve Engineer not yet in captivity. One would therefore presume that you could—with some effort—get yourself inducted into the military engineering services of the United States, Australia, New Zealand, or even Fighting France, but in all those cases you would doubtless be told to undertake orientation and training, which would be both humiliating at your age, and a grand waste of time. You might even have to learn the metric system, if you chose France, although those sexy kepis that they wear could make it worthwhile."

Peter hummed the opening bars of *La Marseillaise* and pantomimed putting on a French army hat in front of a little mirror.

Bongo laughed. "But let's get serious. You would make more money as a civilian expert; you would appear more like a gold-plated consultant than a grimy cog in the wheel; and you would be subject to far less crap on the part of higher military authority—which jealously guards its promotion channels—than you would have to endure otherwise."

Peter nodded thoughtfully in agreement, as Bongo continued: "Your civilian status would be somewhat like that of the coastwatchers, quasi-military, except you would be a civil engineering bloke instead of a wireless operator. You might suffer from loneliness on occasion, for lack of peer support, but you would always have old Bongo to fall back on, provided you could afford to ply him with Gimlets." Peter smiled.

"Besides," Bongo continued, "I rather fancy having you on board the ONI as a civilian operative in parallel with your engineering work, so that we 'spooks'—as the Dutch call members of our clandestine brotherhood—could see and hear a few things through your old-fashioned English eyes and ears, from time to time.

"We would continue to feed you lamb chops and mangoes, and relay secret messages to your family, all the while depositing some modest form of largess into a secret bank account, to defray future air travel after the damned war is over." Peter was quite surprised at the latter suggestion and refilled his coffee cup; Bongo passed his cup over as well, coming up for air.

"This has been a long speech for a Dartmouth man, but I'm urging you to consider the civilian job, period. They'll issue you some kind of uniform and work clothes, with a few non-descript brass badges, and no one in the world, except maybe Admiral Nimitz, will know whether you are a foot soldier or a general. You can spin your own mystique. End of sermon, my friend."

Peter was in awe, never having thought like an entrepreneur before, but gradually an intriguing future shone before his eyes. He was dying to explain all this to Wendy.

Bongo seemed to read his mind, for he added: "By the way, Peter, you are not to mention the ONI connection to anyone, anywhere, not even to your good lady wife. Understood, old sport?" Peter nodded, secretly relieved.

On the last day of May, just to keep Sydney on its toes perhaps, three Japanese mini submarines entered the harbor, having skillfully evaded the nets, and began launching torpedoes at moored ships and shore installations. There was scant damage and the intruders were soon dealt with, but it provided some local excitement, and made the war a bit more real to the people of Sydney than rationing had done. Those who thought about it more deeply, realized there must also be several full-size 'mother subs' off Australia's southeast coast, a sobering thought.

About this time, Bongo learned from Kiwi contacts in Fiji that the Overwoods had been released from hospital. Graham was now working as a mail censor, which must have been compensation for the stressful experience at sea, and probably his ongoing poor health. Bongo sent a teletype message to Michael Osborn, the NATS lieutenant in Fiji, asking that Graham be told about the *I-23* escapade if he didn't already know. When Osborn replied, he told Bongo that NZ Colonel McKee had personally visited the Overwoods after learning about the harrowing ordeal they had suffered.

*** THE BATTLE OF MIDWAY ***

Bongo told Peter about the Overwoods when they met again at the warehouse to sign an ONI contract, of which Peter was not given a copy even though he had insisted on not receiving any financial reward. "You'll just have to trust us, old worry wart."

It was June 4, 1942, and the first month of Aussie winter was already chilly. Bongo handed Peter a teletype message.

"Look at this, old man. The balloon's about to go up, as you Limeys like to say."

The message said Japanese planes had attacked the Aleutian Islands of Alaska yesterday, at which Peter scratched his head and handed it back to Bongo. "What's the point of their attacking Alaska?" asked Peter.

"Well exactly!" Bongo replied. "It's probably a ruse to try drawing our carriers away from the real target, Midway Island, a long way from Alaska. Our code guys have been listening to their chatter for several days, and they double-confirmed Midway was the main objective. Why don't you hang around here a while, and let's see what develops? Coffee?"

"Yes please." Peter prepared his cup as the teletype clattered again.

"When are you off to Nouméa?" Bongo asked.

"On Monday. There'll be three of us foreign civilians, apparently; one is a Dutchman and the other chap's a Kiwi. We haven't yet met each other. The Sydney contracts office says they still can't find any local talent in Australia."

"Hey, I told you, the Aussie engineers are all in Jap camps. Is Wendy OK with you going away in four days?"

"Yes, no more problems, now that she understands we all need to get involved in war work somehow. I think she and Doris plan to wrap bandages, or pack parachutes, something like that. At any rate, they've become great pals."

"Glad to hear it, old sport. I was afraid you would get derailed. By the way, I'll be in Nouméa in a couple of weeks to meet with Admiral Ghormley's advanced staff. My old boss is coming from Hawaii too; remember Captain Silvers? We used to call him 'Hi Yo Silver' behind his back, but decided it sounds too Japanese now. He's a good man."

"Certainly I remember him, at the CINCPAC building. He's the one who told me sneaky ONI spies like to hang out at the Moana Hotel."

"Oh did he now?" Bongo chuckled. "Well then, let's get together in Nouméa somehow so he can say hello to you again. Breakfast or lunch, whatever the Froggies do best. I'll find you."

The teletype clattered once more. Bongo tore off the messages. "Nothing much about a Midway assault yet, but apparently Marine planes on the island have flown off to attack the approaching Jap fleet. Alaska was definitely a diversion, see?

"This other message confirms that good old *Yamato* is the flagship, and Admiral Yamamoto himself is directing the fleet this time, sailing from Truk once again. Wish we had ringside seats; our people are lusting for blood. Sorry, but I'd better let you go, Peter; work to do now."

"Right, I'll be off then. Do come out for lunch on Sunday; Wendy's discovered a roast." Bongo smiled and nodded, reaching for a telephone.

By the time he appeared for Sunday lunch at the Perrys', there was still very little information on the public radio about the Alaska and Midway battles, except it was rumored that a huge Allied victory had been achieved.

108

Wendy welcomed Bongo at the door, and lost no time apologizing for her behavior during his previous visit to their home.

"I was very rude to you and am terribly ashamed of it. I remember you enjoy Gimlets, as do we, so please accept this one as a peace offering." She smiled, handing over a tinkling glass.

Bongo waved a hand in friendship: "Dear lady, there is no call for apologies, but a Gimlet is always very welcome. Now where is that rascal of a boy? I need instruction in the manly art of rounders. I suspect it is yet another amazing American invention that was plagiarized by the Aussies."

The afternoon passed in pleasantries, then Bongo offered some more insights into the recent naval battles.

"Folks we've received dozens of battle reports in the past few days, but it's very hard to summarize the Midway events with any clarity. I myself am still quite confused, which is perhaps my normal state, but suffice to say it was like a huge three-day shootout at the OK Corral. This time, though, the gunslingers were aircraft carriers, and their weapons were daring airmen with bombs and torpedoes. The sheriff's posse was the Marine fliers on Midway who led the first sortie against the outlaws, but unfortunately most of the posse has perished. After that, it was a free-for-all with incredible courage on both sides, and a clear victory to us for a change.

"The Japanese lost four large aircraft carriers, and some other ships as well. We lost one carrier, the unlucky *Yorktown* that had just returned home for repairs from the Coral Sea battle last month. She even sailed from Pearl for this Midway adventure with shipyard repairmen still on board! Imagine that! Well, both sides lost too many planes and people, but the Japs much more than us. It may not be a turning point in the war, but it probably has kept our unseemly opponents from pushing eastward toward Hawaii ever again."

"Midway atoll was an old Pan Am base. Is it intact and still in our hands then?" Peter asked.

Bongo nodded: "Yes indeed, Midway is safe, and *Yorktown's* crew and dock workers were evacuated before she went to the bottom. Strangely, though, the mighty *Yamato* never did appear, so we still have not had a close look at her. Apparently she withdrew after their carrier losses and is now hidden away somewhere like the famous Aussie swagman's lunch. Do you know the song? *Waltzing Matilda?*"

Peter said he had heard it once or twice but didn't understand it.

Bongo threw up his hands. "It's a great folk song, you stuffy Brit." Wendy laughed aloud and poured another round of coffee. Peter chuckled and threw his table napkin at Bongo.

Bongo grinned: "I love the way the white Aussies belt out the wonderful Abo words, like 'jumbuck', 'billabong', 'coolibah tree', though they don't give a crap for the poor Abos themselves. I also used to wonder why the tune wasn't really a waltz, then some fellow explained that 'waltzing' means 'wandering' in this context, and Matilda is the bundle of belongings, or 'swag', that the swagman takes with him. It's sort of like our homeless people in New York; you probably have them in London, too.

"The song has a sad ending; the swagman gets caught poaching and decides to drown himself rather than hand over the lamb that he pilfered." They sipped the coffee in silence.

"Anyway, we digress. So what was important about the Midway battle, one might ask? I guess the Japs were trying to lure the rest of our fleet out so they could destroy it. Well, they really screwed up this time."

The room grew very quiet, as the three of them contemplated the dramatic but tragic events in light of their own personal beliefs. Finally, Wendy broke the silence: "Why do people enjoy such beastly contests? They've always done it, haven't they? On the fields of battle in ancient England, or the horrible wars in Europe this century. Humans—especially men—must be born with an irresistible urge to smash each other. How can it be stopped?" She stared into space.

Quietly, Bongo thanked Wendy for the fine meal, and returned to his staff car and quarters. It had been a momentous week for the Allies.

*** NEW CALEDONIA ***

Next morning Peter flew to Nouméa, capital of New Caledonia, with two other civilian advisors among the mostly military passengers. The new colleagues were older than him and had that look about them of many years spent outdoors. Peter liked them both, and their polite introductions.

Pipe-smoker Hans Lazet was a recent Dutch refugee from Java and a bachelor, whose specialty was the building of docks and sea walls. He had helped enlarge the Dutch naval facilities at Surabaya in the Netherland

East Indies (NEI), from where he escaped to Australia early in the year after the Japanese approached.

The other slightly older man, a short wiry redhead, was originally from New Zealand but had an Australian family in Sydney. His name was Ralph-something—Peter didn't quite catch it—and his experience had to do with road building. Because of Ralph's wild Scottish appearance and his particular specialty, Peter immediately thought of him as Mister MacAdam, the presumed inventor of asphalt, which Americans often called 'tarmac' or 'blacktop'.

The RAAF seaplane that they rode in was a Short Sunderland like the one that brought Peter from Suva, except laid out for transporting more people. It even had an airman-steward who served beverages en route. As they winged out over the South Pacific, Peter learned a lot from his new companions about the US contracts office, as they had both worked for it already on short term projects in Australia. It seemed to be a respected and well-organized prime contract manager.

"And you enjoyed working with the Yanks on Canton Island, then?" Ralph asked Peter. "Where is that exactly?"

"Yes, very much; they usually get things done in a hurry. Canton's located between Fiji and Hawaii more or less," Peter replied. "No one here in Australia seems to know about that little atoll, probably because Pan Am never got this far with their seaplane service. But they did get to Nouméa for a year or so, on their Auckland route, so we might see some evidence of their former presence. The Navy is using Pan Am's Nouméa seaplane base now, so I hear."

Then Peter inquired of the Dutchman: "Are you from the Netherlands, Hans, or island born? I'm wondering where you got your specialized training."

"Peter, I did in Java grow up, but I study at University of Leiden in Holland. My Pa he did work for P&T Lands in Subang as a plantation manager. You know this company, perhaps? It is in West Java, near Bandung."

"No, I don't think so. What does it do?" Peter asked.

"Oh, P&T is wonderful big plantation owner, with interesting history. You come from Singapore, so you are knowing about Sir Stamford Raffles, correct? Well, before Raffles did discover Singapore, he was assistant governor of Java when Napoleon did occupy Holland."

"Really?" Peter exclaimed. "How could an Englishman be in charge of a Dutch colony, especially in the early 1800s?"

"For favors. Look, the French soldiers they did immediately occupy our Pacific colonies after Napoleon his defeat of the Netherlands, so our leaders and the British make a kind of deal. You British will chase away the French from our colonies, and we will do something nice for you some day in future. We do not know what that nice something could be, but Stamford Raffles he is soon having ideas.

"Raffles is finding our Java treasury without funds, so he did negotiate to sell huge part of Java to private English investors for plantation use, over two-hundred-thousand hectares! Very smart man; that piece of land it goes from Lembang in high mountains near Bandung, down to Java Sea coast in the north. Well, those first English investors they do sell their shares for profit in few years, then finally Dutch family Hofland they buy those shares, and start to grow everything—tea, coffee, rice, sugarcane, rubber, quinine, and so and so. But later this Peter Hofland he did lose control to banks, and banks they sell P&T to some more-smart English investors who can market all those good, um, commodities. This name 'P&T Lands' just stand for Dutch names of two places in the district, near the coast—*Pamanoekan en Tjiasemlanden*. Some people call it Anglo-Dutch Plantations now, the new name; more easy to remember."

"That's really amazing, Hans. I never heard people talk about this in Singapore. We all know about Raffles, of course, but evidently not his earlier achievements."

"No, of course not", Hans said. "Normally British and Dutch big competition, eh? This one time they make partners to fight Napoleon and French. Many British people, you know, they do work at this big plantation company on Java, up until this Japan war—engineers too, eh. But now Japanese they control this big plantation. Maybe they learn how to operate, but probably not succeed. I think nobody will help them."

Peter enjoyed the chat with both his new colleagues, and the time passed quickly. By mid-afternoon a large island was visible in the distance. "Do either of you know this place?" he asked. "What went on in New Caledonia before the war started?"

"Nickel mines, mainly," replied Ralph, the New Zealander, "By some accident of nature, New Caledonia is one of the world's largest producers, and Japan was a very big prewar customer. I imagine they planned to invade New Caledonia, but American Army troops were rushed here in March. I heard the governor was pro-Vichy, but the cabinet chased him off to Indochina back in '40. Some Australian commandos were here until the Americans replaced them."

"My word, what a surprise," Peter said. "Look Ralph, I'm terribly sorry but I didn't catch your surname when we first met. Mine is Perry, and yours is …?"

"It's MacAdam," the Kiwi replied, at which point Peter blinked and coughed. "Just think of the road surface inventor. People are always asking if we are related; I wish we were," he laughed.

Peter laughed too, a bit self-consciously. "You mean asphalt?" Peter asked.

"No, no, that came later," said Ralph. "Asphalt is tarred macadam, or 'tarmac'. Plain macadam was the discovery that small stones—compacted gravel, if you will—could make a road surface waterproof, if it was properly graded and maintained.

"Nevertheless, tarmac is my line of work today; I've put down a few thousand acres of it, here and there, probably. When my Aussie wife looks at my fingernails after a job, she tells our friends 'the tarred MacAdam is home again'."

Soon the plane splashed down onto a sheltered part of Nouméa harbor and motored over to the NATS seaplane ramp on a small islet in the bay. There were no signs of old Pan Am in the terminal building, but Peter spotted a telltale PANAIR launch at the jetty. Lots of Navy ships were at anchor all over the harbor, mostly gray or camouflaged, but a few in white—hospital ships, those, Peter assumed. *Gosh, another beautiful place*, he realized, excited to go exploring.

*** *A FLAGSHIP IN NOUMÉA* ***

When Bongo arrived from Sydney on May 17th, it was a Saturday, but everyone was still hard at work in Nouméa—the military, the civilian contractors, and even some of the locals. He commandeered a staff car

113

and driver as usual and managed to find Peter at a water treatment station. Bongo invited him to Sunday lunch with Captain Silvers aboard a Navy ship, as there was a great scarcity of weekend dining places in the town.

"Do you mind if I bring along two colleagues?" Peter asked. "I think you and the captain might find them interesting. They both have security clearances like mine—but like me, no formal clothes!"

"Great idea, old genius. Look, we'll send a launch for you informal experts, at the little commissary dock over there, OK? You know the one? Yes? 1100 hours sharp, and don't fall in the water." Peter smiled and waved his thanks.

At the appointed hour, a Navy launch took the three visitors out to the accommodation ladder of a rather undistinguished-looking Navy transport ship at anchor, the USS *Argonne* which, they were surprised to learn after boarding, was to become Vice Admiral Ghormley's Nouméa flagship in a few weeks. That explained the work crews painting the gray hull white. The admiral was still in New Zealand, as commander of the new SOPAC organization for Admiral Nimitz, but New Caledonia was now considered defensible and it was much closer to the enemy activities. SOPAC would therefore move north in a few weeks.

On the *Argonne's* deck, they were met by Bongo and another Navy officer, wearing khaki uniforms. The visitors, being civilians, did not salute the ship's flag, but simply shook hands with Bongo. Peter introduced Ralph MacAdam first, he being the eldest, then Hans Lazet.

"Friends, this is Commander Perkins, with whom I shared an adventure or two on the way over from Hawaii."

Bongo then presented the attentive Navy lieutenant at his side, in characteristic roundabout fashion: "Peter and good guests, eventually if one lives long enough in this man's navy, one has to face being made redundant. I have apparently reached that milestone, and upon my return to Sydney I shall be banished to Brisbane, Queensland, where the renowned Douglas MacArthur will shortly be moving his headquarters from Melbourne. To the best of my abilities, I am to become the official United States Navy liaison with the general's staff, where the war will no doubt pass me by and I shall grow bald and corpulent.

"My replacement in Sydney is this lucky rascal, Lieutenant McGowan, Robert F., USN-not-R, in other words an academy man of high caliber but dubious ambition as, unlike the present orator, he intends to make a career of the naval service."

Congratulations were acclaimed by all, who clearly saw that Bongo had received an important assignment, and each one wished Lt. McGowan the best of success. Bongo then led the party to the wardroom, where Captain Silvers from ONI Hawaii and the ship's captain, a Navy commander, were huddled together. The skipper excused himself and left the room to Captain Silvers.

"Well, well, we meet again Mr. Perry. What a pleasure!"

"Captain Silvers, the pleasure is mine, sir, and I remember with gratitude how kind you were to help a nervous Briton find his feet in Honolulu. Thank you for inviting the three of us to lunch."

The captain greeted the others then sat at the head of the wardroom table, motioning Peter to sit at his right and Bongo at his left. Two Filipino stewards asked the group for food and drink preferences, then Captain Silvers suggested Ralph and Hans summarize the problems they were facing in Nouméa to get their projects rolling, which mostly related to a lack of heavy equipment. After some serious discussion and note-taking, during which drinks arrived, Captain Silvers proposed a toast to the Allies. All rose with lifted glasses.

"Gentlemen we are thankful for the time and talent that people like yourselves share with us, and with each other, day after day, in the cause of defeating our common enemy, Japan. The Fighting French have welcomed us Americans to these lovely islands, in spite of fears that we may disfigure their beauty with all our coming and going. So we look to Allies like Peter from England, Ralph from New Zealand, and Hans from the Netherland Indies to help keep us mindful of our host's property. Let us toast the Allies."

"Hear, hear; the Allies!"

"Wonderful thoughts, Captain Silvers," Peter said; "Almost like a benediction."

"Thank you, Mr. Perry. This war will keep us all on edge for a great while. At its end, when we will surely have prevailed, we look to returning home with reputations intact, and many a lasting South Seas friendship.

"Now then, Lieutenant McGowan, will you kindly escort our guests, Ralph and Hans, for a quick tour of this fine old ship, while the rest of us discuss some unfinished business—say twenty minutes? By that time lunch should be ready and waiting. I would value some comments on the engine room, in particular."

"Aye, aye sir, with pleasure." The trio departed.

The captain then asked Peter, with a broad wink: "Mr. Perry, you have just heard that this rather slothful naval commander will soon leave Sydney for MacArthur's court in Brisbane. I wonder if you would care to comment in any way."

Peter chuckled: "Sir, I cannot comment on the wisdom of moving him from Sydney to Brisbane—that city being slightly closer to Nouméa where a certain Navy nurse has reportedly been transferred from Efaté (no one knows how or why)—but I do fear for a deterioration in Army–Navy relations if he is left in Brisbane for a great length of time."

"So you know of Nurse Ellie, eh?"

"Oh yes indeed, I actually met her on Efaté, and observed her speaking to the slothful commander while he lay wounded and helpless. I could not understand a single word of her strange dialect but was quite intrigued by her manner of delivery."

"That's an honest answer, and I thank you. We'll try not to let him disrupt MacArthur's goals for long, but while the errant commander is away in Brisbane, please help us to mold that young McGowan into someone who can think for himself. We see some potential in him, in spite of his association with the slothful commander of whom we were just speaking. As soon as he proves his worth, we'll send McGowan to Brisbane to patch up Army-Navy relations, and then award the offensive commander a more adventurous role in the war, which he has continuously requested. Meanwhile, the nurse can presumably fend for herself?"

"Of that I have no doubt, whatsoever," Peter laughed.

"You are a good friend of the ONI, Mr. Perry, which is why we are delighted to count you among our number. I was touched that you turned down our offer of financial compensation. And speaking of a certain nurse's strange dialect, I notice our slothful friend here has picked up a fair measure of fine English speech patterns while in your company, which— since imitation is the sincerest form of flattery—tells me you are a man we can trust." They shook hands, and Bongo stared at the overhead.

When the tour group returned and lunch was served, Captain Silvers seated himself between the other two engineers, while Lt. McGowan—wiping some grease from his fingers—joined Bongo and Peter. After Hans and Ralph offered fairly positive comments about the *Argonne's* engine room and other visible features, Captain Silvers remarked to Peter that the rather bulky old supply ship had come to Nouméa via Canton Island. *Argonne* had tried unsuccessfully to pull a chartered troop ship, SS *President Taylor,* off Canton's reef.

"When I reviewed the ship's log and saw those entries, I remembered your saying at CINCPAC that you had spent some time on Canton Island, Mr. Perry. It stuck in my memory because I had never heard of the place before. Were you there when this shipwreck happened?"

"No sir, I had apparently just left there for Enderbury and Hawaii," Peter replied, "but when Commander Perkins and I stopped at Canton on the way to Fiji, we saw the wreck in all its past glory. It must look to Jap submariners like we scored an 'own goal', I would imagine."

The group laughed, and so the pleasant afternoon progressed until it was time for the civilians to return ashore.

"What a fine man is that captain," Hans said aboard the launch. "He must go far in this Navy, I hope. And Peter, your friend the commander, he is a little crazy, eh? But a good man, too."

Ralph was semi-dozing in the launch but signaled his agreement. "Did I hear someone mention a nurse?"

*** *ABOARD THE SUPERBATTLESHIP* YAMATO ***

After the attempted June invasion of Midway Island turned sour and the Japanese fleet lost four large aircraft carriers, Admiral Yamamoto ordered a recall of his battered remnant, with the flagship *Yamato* and its consorts leading the way back to Truk in the Carolines, to lick their wounds.

The admiral had hardly slept for the past four days, his mind churning over and over the devastating loss of Japan's active carrier fleet and aircraft which, apart from two carriers undergoing repairs at home, had been all the large carriers that Japan possessed. He pondered the insane decision that an earlier fleet admiral had proposed, that of ordering the construction of four mammoth battleships, whose astronomical cost could instead have nearly duplicated the IJN's entire fleet of carriers and aviation inventory.

The IJN still deluded itself that there would soon be a 'decisive battle' with the American fleet, which Japan would win with the help of *Yamato* and her sister ships. *Did they expect the Americans to line up in a row for target practice by the IJN?* Admiral Yamamoto had no such illusions, but any further strategic plans on his part had just been scuppered at Midway, it appeared. There would be severe recriminations over the Midway losses, but he visualized an even worse scandal had he not held back *Yamato* from the battle zone, and US carrier planes had sunk the flagship as well! *The super-battleship, adored by the emperor personally, is highly vulnerable without a covering umbrella of defensive fighter planes, and where are those planes to come from now?*

The admiral resolved to send *Yamato* immediately back to Japan for an extensive upgrade to its anti-aircraft weaponry, and he would order the same for *Yamato's* sister ship *Musashi*, which was almost ready for sea trials.

And what about the other two monsters? Could those projects be canceled altogether? He had investigated and found the answer was 'yes and no'. The third sister's hull was taking shape and could not be canceled without wasting a fortune, so after consultation with his staff the admiral ordered the third one converted into an aircraft carrier, which would become the world's largest and would help Japan restore its ability to provide defensive air power, for Japan had clearly lost its offensive momentum at Midway. His staff recommended the name *Shinano* for the giant carrier-to-be, which with luck would be available in a year or so.

The fourth giant sister ship had only recently been started, so its keel could be scrapped and recycled as material for a trio of more conventional warships.

Admiral Yamamoto continued working on his top-secret report to the Emperor and the Imperial General Staff. He was unsure what to conclude from the enemy having discovered his fleet carriers in the first place. Obviously the Aleutian feint had not worked, and the Americans were instead waiting for him at Midway. Could there be a spy in his inner circle? He must assume so and take steps to purge the traitor or traitors; that is, if he was not forced to resign by the Imperial General Staff and the Emperor.

As the fleet slunk into the Truk lagoon, it was quite dark, appropriately.

*** THE NURSE AND THE GEISHA ***

Work on the Nouméa waterfront and surroundings proceeded apace for the rest of June and the month of July 1942. There was no harassment from the Japanese, surprisingly. Long-awaited dredges and pile-drivers arrived, and the dock areas were finally expanded and deepened.

Hans the Dutchman demonstrated his remarkable skills in working with the tides to position the pile-drivers and sink the massive logs even beyond their required depth. In spite of the initial delays, his assistants and the local labor force learned quickly, and produced an excellent result only slightly behind the original schedule.

The harbor meanwhile continued filling up with ships, while NATS seaplanes came and went with regularity. Bongo was among the passengers on the first RAAF direct flight from Brisbane to Nouméa, bypassing Sydney. It heralded a much-needed courier link between the two new headquarters of SOPAC and SWPA, both of which were nearly operational for Admiral Robert Ghormley and General MacArthur, respectively.

Bongo sought out Peter at his Army-run BOQ for civilians. "Peter, old laggard, I have come to buy you dinner tonight at a little French café. Apart from your delightful company I need you to witness a transaction. Are you familiar with the city center, or *centreville* as the Froggies say?"

"Somewhat," Peter acknowledged. "The old lags and I have done some Sunday walkabouts. Can't vouch for the food anywhere, however. It seems quite expensive, especially to my thrifty Scot and Dutch friends, and most places seem to be closed on weekends, when we are mostly available."

"Not to worry old sport. I have it on good authority that this little bistro has the best French food in the city, though not necessarily the most elegant décor. Do you by chance know the whereabouts of *Chez Louise?*"

"I think it's not far from the cathedral, is that the one?" Peter asked.

"Yes, that's it; *rue Frédéric Surleau.* Shall we say 1900 hours? I'll be in civvies."

"What on earth are civvies?" Peter asked.

"Civilian clothes, Neanderthal. It's a non-military evening." "Oh, you mean *mufti,*" Peter laughed. Bongo did as well.

"By the way," Bongo continued, "Guess who I saw at the NATS terminal today? Remember that flighty Ensign Culver on Canton, with the Hollywood salute? Well, he's now Lieutenant Junior Grade Culver, the assistant operations guy for NATS Nouméa. Still has his Hollywood salute. I asked him how things were going on Canton".

"And?"

"OK, for the most part. They've been bombed a few more times, but no big problems. I told him if he has a blocked toilet to call you."

"Very thoughtful of you," Peter said. "Until seven o'clock then."

The hilly old city of Nouméa in 1942 still held much Gallic charm, in spite of the multitude of foreigners steadily encircling it with their war machines and Quonset huts. The apparent reason was that Francophones and Anglophones tended to naturally stay apart within their own comfort zones—except for the notorious Pink House and its lovely hostesses. This establishment, amusingly, had been opened by military order, and was quite multi-cultural! Perhaps it was a strategy to keep *voulez-vous coucher?* off the city streets.

The hilly city was therefore not off-limits to the US Army and Navy, as so far it hadn't been necessary to invoke that restriction. A growing number of mostly-US servicemen could be seen walking about in the streets and parks, and a fairly steady stream of military traffic passed back and forth from the harbor onto the pre-war roads that passed for highways, resulting in a plethora of US military camps, warehouses, and hospitals out beyond Nouméa. French and New Zealand troops were also billeted in the countryside.

There were some nice parks in the flat lower part of the city center, in one of which—the long, rectangular *Place des Cocotiers* with its periphery of coconut palms—stood an elaborate bandstand from the previous century, built not long after New Caledonia ceased to be a French penal colony. The bandstand was a popular place for ducking out of Nouméa's fairly frequent rain showers. An adjacent park, *Place Courbet*, featured a large fountain of similar complexity and age as the bandstand. Beyond the parks, at the edge of the lovely harbor, was a passenger ship dock with its wrought iron sign, *Bienvenu à Nouméa*. Navy ships used this dock often, now that the war tempo was picking up.

Inland of the parks, up a fairly long flight of steep steps high above the Catholic Cathedral of Saint Joseph—itself predominant on a small rise—was a hill called *La Fol*. It was a popular lookout spot, up which

Peter and his colleagues had puffed several times to admire the magnificent views of Nouméa's harbor and port, and the nearby hills and islets. Peter had noticed from *La Fol* that Nouméa protruded into the harbor on a promontory, rather like Suva and Pearl City did into their respective anchorages.

Chez Louise was a modest wooden establishment, housed in a former residence down below the cathedral. The restaurant was set slightly back from *rue Surleau,* an old city street that eventually merged into the main road going up over a ridge to the new Navy airport at Magenta Bay.

Across from the restaurant was a small school, but the street was fairly quiet in the evening. Peter arrived a few minutes early and saw that Bongo was considerably earlier, judging by the half-full (or half-empty) bottle of *Veuve Clicquot* that stood between him and a pretty Navy nurse that Peter instantly recognized from Efaté. They both smiled and waved to him.

"Sweetie, this is my uncle Peter from across the sea; you may perhaps remember him from Efaté," was the predictable introduction from Bongo, as Peter shook hands with his bright-eyed companion.

Peter noticed at once that she did more than justice to the colorful summer frock she was filling, thereby erasing all memory of any naval uniforms he had ever seen. Could there perhaps be an absence of undergarments? He was too embarrassed to risk a second assessment, but the possibility would soon, no doubt, settle into his subconscious for the evening, thereby disrupting the normal protocol for eye control.

"Uncle Pete, say a big hello to nurse Ellie Norbush once again. You'll probably not understand each other's conversation, but please do your best."

"Miss Norbush, I am honored to, um, see you again," offered Peter, forcing his eyes to meet hers.

"Th' playzhuh is owl mahyun, suh," she responded in triphthongs, eyes a-flutter. Peter was completely at a loss for further comment.

"Some champagne, Uncle?"

The evening progressed famously, aided by another magnum after the *coq-au-vin,* and Peter marveled at Bongo's ability to comprehend the syrupy Southern drawl of his likely companion for the night. Peter also noted a constant flickering of discreet but appreciative bistro glances—both male and female—being cast toward the lovely Miss Norbush from around the floor, in concert with a steady hum of Gallic conversation that cried out for an overlay of background music. That soothing staple of café society was, alas, beyond the budget of *Monsieur Roger et Madame Louise*, so the level of conversation rose gradually but noticeably with the consumption of *vin du table*. It would be a profitable evening for the restaurant, Peter mused, smiling and nodding wisely at something Nurse Ellie had just said.

She spoke little during the meal, but when she did it was apparently with deep feeling. As dessert time approached, Ellie asked to be excused for a l'il ol' moment. This produced a deathly silence in the room, as she rose from the table with a furtive Gioconda smile. Peter took advantage of the break, to ask Bongo why on earth he had been invited.

"Stand easy, old man. I really did want to treat you to a decent meal, after what they say about Army cooking, but also hoped you would bear witness that I am about to complete a task you assigned to me several months ago in Sydney."

"Eh? What task could that possibly be?" Peter asked.

"All will be revealed—well, not exactly all, heh-heh—in just about two minutes."

They both stood as Ellie returned from the facilities, swishing sensuously across the main dining room floor to further appreciative glances by a fortunate cross-section of Noumean citizenry. When she was seated, smiling brightly, Bongo reached into a shoulder bag and brought out a nicely wrapped gift box, which he presented to her, saying: "Ellie dear, I hope you will accept this special present as a gift from a humble admirer. I was just lucky to find it on a secret trip into enemy territory, as Uncle Peter can attest."

Ellie carefully removed the fancy new wrapping, then she brought forth with a polite squeal of enthusiasm a (now familiar to her table companions) genuine Japanese ceramic doll, clad in a slightly tousled but elaborate Geisha kimono.

"Oh, yes, quite so, yes indeed," Peter managed to stutter, wondering whether to laugh out loud, or try for another sip of champagne.

Nurse Ellie was visibly delighted with the gift, which she vowed to keep locked up so it wouldn't get stolen by one of those unladylike new girls. She snuggled closer to Bongo to plant a juicy kiss on his cheek and managed to let her hand fall onto his thigh. An audible sigh filled the bistro.

"Well, Uncle Peter, I bet this collector's item is delighted to have a new home, as you instructed. Did you say you had an appointment after dinner?"

Peter made his excuses and departed for the entry door, pausing at the urging of his subconscious to steal a quick glance across the room below the tabletop as he waved goodbye. His earlier suspicions were still unconfirmed.

*** OLD FORT TEREKA ***

Peter's most recent letter from Wendy, which he had collected just that morning as he left the BOQ, informed him that their neighbors Doris and Fred had asked if they could give John a puppy from their part-Border Collie's litter. She wanted Peter's comments before making that commitment, but John clearly missed the Cocker Spaniel that they'd had to leave behind in Singapore. At seven, John was probably old enough for his own dog now, Wendy wrote. Peter thought so too and intended to write back as soon as he returned from the afternoon's outing with Ralph and Hans.

On that particular Sunday, Hans had arranged a launch to take the three consultants to *l'île Nou*, the small nearby islet that helped protect the Nouméa harbor entrance from severe weather damage, which was also the site of the NATS seaplane base that had formerly been Pan Am's. Peter scanned Wendy's letter again as they chugged across the harbor to the island's dock. A Navy ship repair group was billeted there in Quonset huts on an old parade ground that had been part of the French penal colony called Nouville in the late 1800s. Hans and his team had been enlarging the repair dock on that island.

The point of the Sunday outing was not, of course, to admire the Quonsets or the dock, but rather to climb to the ruins of an old French fort on a nearby hill. Hans had heard there were extraordinary views of the harbor mouth, that this fort had once protected with its cannon from hostile raiders.

The fort's long-ago garrison had been charged with maintaining order among the prison population down below, whose primary task over many decades was to construct Nouméa's government buildings and cathedral with local stone that they quarried on the little island, and eventually from the Noumean hills.

Taking a lead from England in the mid-1800s, which had decided to relieve her overcrowded prisons by shipping long-term offenders to American and Australian penal colonies, France decided to do the same with Devil's Island in the Caribbean and Nouville at Port-de-France, their original name for Nouméa.

After completing their sentences, released prisoners were offered land if they would stay on as New Caledonian settlers. Most chose to return to France, but the descendants of those Europeans who did stay became known as *caldoches*, now a significant voting bloc scattered about the main island of New Caledonia on farms and ranches. Some became country folk, or *broussards*, and married *kanaks*, the indigenous natives, another name for which was *niaouli* after a type of local tree. Still others found French or Pacific islanders to share their lives. Newer French arrivals to New Caledonia were known as *métros*.

The ocean and coastal views were indeed spectacular from old Fort Tereka, which still featured an impressive array of ancient cannons, pointing in seaward directions. Cannon balls were stacked at various locations near the guns, and one could easily imagine a gun crew's synchronized procedures of firing, reloading powder and ball, and firing again. It had been the post-Napoleonic age when this fort was constructed.

In spite of the impressive display of weaponry from the prior century, the outing that Hans had arranged was a peaceful contrast to the endless arrival of more ships and planes, and the resulting construction of still larger US facilities around modern Nouméa such as a huge motor pool for military vehicles. Even far beyond the capital, new facilities were being assembled at a hectic pace.

An example of the 'construction creep' was a huge new airfield at *La Tontouta,* situated some thirty miles north of Nouméa, from which Ralph had only just returned after a month of asphalting and dirty fingernails. It was built for the US Army to accommodate B-17 bombers, whereas the Navy's small Magenta airfield, just three miles from the city, could only accept light aircraft. Mountainous terrain dictated the size and location of those two new land-plane facilities, but of course NATS could handle seaplanes of any size in Nouméa harbor.

Standing on old Fort Tereka's retaining wall at the middle of July 1942, gazing thoughtfully out to sea, Peter supposed that Nouméa was about ready for anything. It had even received a new governor that August, a Monsieur Montchamp from the French colony of Chad in Africa, who redoubled the Fighting French efforts to welcome the Allied presence to New Caledonia.

*** NOUMÉA PHASE THREE ***

There in Nouméa, most people including Peter, Ralph, and Hans noticed a gradual up-tick in the rhythm of naval activity, such as an increased number of launches scurrying about the harbor, or seaplanes coming and going. Many more Americans crowded the streets of Nouméa, and its bistros and bars. The Pink House never closed, even on Sundays. It was clear that something big was happening out in the vast Pacific. Admiral Ghormley had arrived the week before and seemed never to leave his flagship *Argonne* thereafter, as he had many visitors at all hours.

One day, Peter was asked by the prime contractor's representative for Nouméa, whether he had experience in bridge construction. The man's name was Ronald Beamish, a retired Australian highway department finance manager.

"Oh certainly," Peter said. "I currently specialize in water engineering and sewerage treatment plants, but we all had to do bridge studies for our civil engineering articles, in other words for our certification. I had a few years' actual experience with bridges in England afterwards, before going to Singapore. Why do you ask?"

"I'm so glad to hear that," Beamish answered. "You see, our third and final phase of work in Nouméa is to prepare facilities for the arrival of some US Marines in about six months, which will include training a tank battalion. These are not the light tanks that Marines are presently using, but what the British have named the Sherman tank, which they have been receiving in the European Theater on lend-lease."

"When you say the British have named them, what do the Marines themselves call these new tanks?"

"Just M4 medium tanks, as far as I know. They are getting some from the Army in a few months and will be receiving their indoctrination in the dry climate of California. Admiral Ghormley said the Navy will want to know if these heavier tanks can be used effectively on the tropical islands of the Pacific, and especially which types of bridges can support their weight.

"They are far too heavy to be loaded aboard the typical old cargo ships that you see around here," Beamish went on, "so a new type of ship has been designed to take the tanks right up to the beach and let them drive ashore. Some of these new ships, called LSTs, may even be bringing the first medium tanks from San Diego to Nouméa—at least that's the plan at the moment."

"What a good idea, that ship design," Peter exclaimed. "Please let me know if I can help in any way. I'm due for leave this Friday and will be in Sydney for two weeks. If you like, Mr. Beamish, I could contact your Sydney office while I'm there. I know where it's located and have been to it already."

"Mr. Perry, that's a fine suggestion. I'll be in Sydney myself a week after you arrive. Why don't I telephone you, and then we can all get together at the office and plan something? Are your present assignments safe to leave, if the bridge project goes ahead?"

"I should think so," said Peter. "I have a good assistant who has worked with me at the camp sites all along, and who will cover for the next two weeks. If the bridge project is not too far from Nouméa, then I could keep an eye on the present work too, from time to time."

"Good, that's good. Until Sydney then." The two shook hands. Peter went to find Hans and Ralph to tell them the news. They would be staying at Nouméa while Peter was away on leave, since their Phase-Two projects were closer to completion. Peter promised to discuss their situations with the Sydney office, to see what other work was lined up for them.

He sent a cable to Wendy, confirming his arrival details, and saying he was looking forward to meeting John's new puppy.

Peter wondered about the Sherman tanks and where he might get some preliminary size and weight details. Bongo came to mind, or perhaps this was a chance to get better acquainted with Lt. McGowan at ONI Sydney.

*** ON LEAVE IN SYDNEY ***

Sitting comfortably in the NATS seaplane from Nouméa, Peter was determined to enjoy his two-week Sydney leave by spending most of it with Wendy and John, and of course the new puppy too, which he learned was named Digger. The name was neighbor Fred's suggestion, not to imply that the active young Border Collie was likely to uproot the rose bushes, but rather as a tribute to Australian soldiers, who were known as Diggers, just as US Marines were informally called Leathernecks. Digger-the-pup was a smart little fellow, who excelled at barking for his morning walk at exactly 6am, Wendy had reported.

It was mid-August, and the school year still had four more months to go before the long summer break over Christmas, curtailing any thoughts of mid-week excursions away from Sydney. *Just as well*, Peter thought, as he would need to be a bit flexible for meeting Ronald Beamish before the leave was over and looking in on Lt. McGowan of ONI as well.

It would be good in many ways to have another big project in Nouméa, and perhaps it might be possible to bring the family over for Christmas week, if such things were allowed. Doris and Fred would surely look after Digger. Peter made a note of this idea in his diary, but the plane vibrated so much that his handwriting was almost unreadable. He laughed to himself, thinking Wendy would accuse him of drinking on duty.

Wendy had also written Peter about a new project of her own, that really thrilled her. She had been invited by Government House—the Australian Governor-General's residence and offices—to propose a design for remodeling and decorating a suite of reception rooms. Apparently this came about when she had told Doris of a similar project she'd done in Malaya, and Doris spoke of this to the G-G's wife at a banking conference dinner. Wendy was now quite busy with plans and sketches for her proposal, which displayed a clever talent that she really hoped to develop more after the war. Doris enjoyed seeing the sketches as each was finished, and often told Wendy how she wished for a creative outlet, too.

There was also the mysterious telephone call from a Canadian businessman, that Wendy wrote Peter about. Whoever he was, he had arrived in Melbourne from Vancouver a few weeks ago and asked to see Peter in Sydney "at his convenience". What could that imply? The caller didn't clearly state his name but did tell Wendy he was an old acquaintance. Strange.

Well, first things first, Peter reckoned. Fred and Doris (whose surname was Smyth, he finally learned) had invited the Perrys to go swimming at Bondi Beach the coming Saturday morning. Bondi (pronounced 'bond-eye') was apparently a delightful beach for horizontal body surfing, which Peter was looking forward to trying. It didn't sound quite as exciting as the board surfing they did at Waikiki, but it would be pleasant to swim in the ocean again, which he hadn't had a chance to do in New Caledonia. But wasn't it still winter now? Could it possibly be warm enough to swim in Sydney?

And what was that exciting news Hans had just told him, about an invasion in the Solomon Islands by American Marines? It had something to do with Tulagi, which the Japanese had captured a few months ago during the Battle of the Coral Sea, and another island called Guadalcanal. Keeping track of the war was quite difficult, Peter thought, and Hans was sometimes difficult to understand. Perhaps a visit to Bongo's office would clarify that news.

As Peter's seaplane settled onto the calm waters of Sydney's Rose Bay, he peered from the little porthole trying to decide roughly where their cottage was located.

CHAPTER FOUR

★ ★ ★

Guadalcanal

First Marine Division Shoulder Patch

"Tell them what you're going to tell them;
Tell them;
"Tell them what you told them."
Marine Corps boot camp axiom

**** A SYDNEY SURPRISE ****

Peter felt wonderfully tired, but somewhat chilled after the winter morning at Bondi Beach with Fred and Doris Smyth, his immediate Rose Bay neighbors across Salisbury Road. Bondi was a long wide beach with such a gentle underwater slope that one could ride an air pillow for fifty yards or so after catching a wave. At the north, or left end of the beach looking out to sea, there was an area protected by a shark net some 200 yards offshore near a low cliff. That part of the beach was for young children and overly cautious adults.

At the opposite end of the long beach, jutting out from another low cliff, was a saltwater swimming pool of olympic dimensions, only slightly higher than the ocean at high tide. It was the club pool of the Bondi Icebergs, a fanatical group whose individual members were required to race there several times each winter, no matter the weather, or else forfeit their membership. This custom went on throughout the war years, for those not sent away to fight. The pool was quite crowded with Iceberg fanatics that chilly Saturday, whereas the public beach itself was scarcely populated. Fred was able to park the car right at the Bondi seawall.

In addition to the shark-netted area, the beach was also protected by famous teams of lifesavers, trained to march on the sand in tandem, and to launch surf boats in aid of swimmers in trouble for whatever reason. These sturdy men wore full-body skin-tight suits in bright colors, and their high-stepping practice drills were a unique spectacle to watch.

Occasional low-flying single-engine planes patrolled beyond the Bondi surf, equipped with loudspeakers to hail swimmers if sharks were spotted. Sometimes they were, but not often enough to deter enthusiastic but compliant bathers, who would move briskly out of the water if ever there was a sighting alarm.

According to Fred Smyth, Bondi surf quality could be quite variable, depending mostly on wind conditions. It ranged from gentle to dangerous.

Fred rated this day's surf as moderate, which was typical for the month of August when winds were still more northeasterly than southeasterly, and the beachfront was partly sheltered. Since it was the last month of winter and Sydney was in the temperate zone south of the tropics, the air was chilly—and more than invigorating in Peter's opinion. Luckily, it was also sunny. Doris and Fred were in the water far more often than Peter, who hadn't been exposed to winter weather for several years. He mostly sat on the beach with a towel around his shoulders or strode briskly on the sand to stay warm. Wendy was smart to stay at home, he concluded, shivering. It was a far cry from Singapore or Canton Island which were both near the equator.

Geographically, Bondi Beach was not far from the seaplane base at Rose Bay that lay in a sheltered part of Sydney Harbor, facing northwest, with a pleasant view of the city's handsome new bridge. Bondi, by contrast, was a long sandy cove on the open ocean, facing southeast. The two waterfronts were thus diagonally back-to-back, just a few miles apart on either side of the promontory that formed the south headland of the harbor entrance.

Wendy had stayed home with young John because of an optional school sports event, and because she didn't relish being at a beach in the winter chill. Doris, however, was accustomed to the mild winter weather of Sydney and loved the outdoors, so she went along with the men while Wendy walked John and his energetic Digger-the-Pup to the school grounds. The Border Collie would need serious training before long, Wendy noted, or he would soon be difficult to handle.

After leasing the Rose Bay cottage, Wendy and Peter had decided to enroll John in the Cranbrook School, an Anglican day and boarding school for boys of various ages. It reminded Peter very much of the Monmouth School in Wales, of which he had many fond memories. Conveniently, there was a Cranbrook junior school right in the Perrys' Rose Bay neighborhood, and the senior school was just half a mile away (in case they were still living in Sydney when John turned thirteen, in five more years).

The main competitive sports at the junior school were rugby, cricket, and swimming, but that Saturday's event was just a series of sprints and relay races on the outdoor track. John managed to cop a second-place ribbon among all the arms and legs of his age group—the youngest in the school—while Digger barked encouragement, his black-and-white fur fluffed out with the winter chill.

Wendy invited the Smyths to lunch after the Bondi swim, but they begged off from weariness and the need of freshwater baths to remove the salt. As they said their goodbyes, Wendy heard her telephone ringing and ran back into the house. A few moments later she beckoned Peter, who was tossing an old tennis ball back and forth to John, which Digger rushed to intercept at each throw.

"Darling, it was the Canadian chap who telephoned last week. Again, I couldn't catch his name, but he asked if he could visit this evening. Apparently he is staying in a hotel and will use a taxi, so I gave him our address. It really is strange, but he seems to know you from somewhere."

"Good grief," Peter responded, letting Digger catch the ball that time, "what on earth can this fellow be after? I don't know any Canadians, do I? When will he be arriving? We'd better get cleaned up, starting with John-O. Should we eat supper first, or wait and include the visitor? What do you think, dear?"

"I should imagine we'd better wait and include him," Wendy replied. "It's only two-something now. I'll think about what to prepare while you and John get yourselves cleaned up. Did you enjoy the swim? It must have been cold out there in the wind, but then you had lovely Doris to cheer you up. She must be quite something in a swimming suit."

Peter mumbled unintelligibly as he went inside with John, leaving Digger with Wendy.

It was nearly six o'clock when the doorbell rang. Wendy, who was in the kitchen, asked Peter to answer the door. She chuckled upon overhearing his response.

"Good god, what in blazes are you doing in Sydney?" Peter barked at the visitor—who was none other than his younger brother Edgar, more often known as Ned.

"May I come inside?" laughed Ned, who was wearing a ratty old Monmouth School prefect's blazer.

"Yes of course." Peter recovered and shook hands. "This is the smallest world I can ever remember. How are you, wretched boy? Still dressed in rags, I see. And by Jove he's grown a mustache!"

"None of that old nonsense, if you please. You're not head boy at school any longer." Ned, standing three inches taller than Peter, threatened to pick him up. Just then Wendy joined them, holding John by the hand.

"Hello, Wendy dear. And this must be John." Ned gave them each a kiss. "Thanks for going along with this silly surprise. I think my big bro is speechless, for once in his life." Wendy explained to John that this was his Uncle Ned from Canada.

Peter had meanwhile disappeared, but the sound of an ice block being chipped, and wardrobe doors banging, betrayed his whereabouts. Soon he reappeared with three Gimlets on a tray, wearing his own equally tatty Monmouth blazer. Wendy went to fetch some cheese and biscuits.

*** KELLOGG'S CORNFLAKES ***

At supper, Ned explained that he had recently arrived at Melbourne with his wife, Marjorie, and two-year-old son, Barrett. They traveled from Vancouver on a Swedish passenger-freighter, MV *Mirrabooka*, with other families, including some from the Canadian Air Force. Their July voyage had taken four long weeks instead of the peacetime two, because the ship had intentionally avoided normal sea lanes and Jap submarines by sailing far down the coast of South America, before turning west across the Pacific. It also made a stop in Auckland, New Zealand.

The captain knew well that his neutral Swedish flag might not spare them from a torpedo, so he chose the long southern route despite stormy winter weather. The deck cargo of Canadian lumber and railroad engines was well lashed down. They reached Melbourne several weeks after the Jap mini-submarine raid on Sydney Harbor, and saw one of the captured subs on display at the Melbourne docks with a big hole in its side, being taken on a War Bond fund-raising tour of Australian cities.

Peter had scarcely seen Ned since the latter finished his schooling at Monmouth in 1928, leaving soon afterwards for Canada at age eighteen to attend McGill University in Montreal. Four years later, Ned joined the W.K. Kellogg Company, purveyor of breakfast foods, as a manufacturing engineer in Ontario and was still working for that firm a decade later, with several innovative cost-savings projects to his credit. The brothers had written each other from time to time over those fifteen years, but not often, especially once they each had new families and lived in different countries.

Their father, a banker, had died of a heart attack in England while both were still in boarding school. Being the oldest male among the siblings of two boys and four girls, Peter became legal head of the family even while he still had a year to go in school, and even though he was younger than his sisters, and his mother was still alive. That was the British way, known as primogeniture. Born in 1910, Ned was youngest of the children, five years behind Peter.

Funnily enough, it was Ned who had first met Wendy on a school trip to Ipswich, where she was teaching, and afterwards introduced her to his elder brother. It was a good introduction; Peter and Wendy were soon engaged, being teased by their friends as Peter Pan and Wendy after the classic boys' adventure tale. Later in 1928, Ned disappeared to Canada for university and Peter went off to work in Singapore, returning on his first home leave three years later to marry Wendy in London. Ned married Marjorie Barrett, a Canadian, six years after that.

There was a lot of catching up to do that evening, assisted by a goodly number of Gimlets and the occasional Foster's lager. Wendy gave up after some while, suggesting Ned spend the night rather than return to his hotel. Before she turned in, she put sheets and a blanket on the couch.

The brothers carried on. Ned explained that Kellogg's had sent him to Australia as plant manager for their factory in Botany Bay, essentially because so many Australian men were either away in Europe or were prisoners in Singapore. There was a tremendous shortage of local technical management (just as Bongo had pointed out before, Peter remembered).

Ned explained further: "Kellogg's had to get permission from the Canadian government to release me, as I was a private in the Army reserves like nearly everyone else. They only decided to offer me this job after the Midway battle in June, when parts of the Pacific seemed a bit safer for travel. Marjorie and I still thought it over quite carefully."

"It's really amazing that we're both in Sydney; I still can't believe it," Peter said for the third or fourth time. "By the way, why did you go off to Canada anyway?"

"To get away from you! The Canadian Army was nothing like being subordinate to a bossy elder brother. Even after you left Monmouth I was still getting your orders all the time."

"Cripes, sorry about that," Peter said. Ned chuckled, and rolled himself a cigarette with some odd-looking hand-held gadget. "Not to worry," he said. "You're forgiven."

"My word. What now; where will you live in Sydney? You said Marjorie is still in Melbourne, correct?"

"Yes, she is," Ned replied, "but she'll be here mid-week. Kellogg's found us a partly furnished house in North Sydney on a year-to-year basis for the duration of the war. It's in the Cremourne district. I'll commute across the Harbour Bridge every day, then pass not far from here on the way to Botany Bay. I've been doing that from the hotel already".

"No housing available around here then?" said Peter. "We're certainly a lot closer to Botany Bay than you will be in North Sydney. So how exactly will you commute back and forth then, by tram?"

"In that vaguely respectable Ford outside, that's how." Ned laughed. "You thought I came by taxi today, right? But no, that's why Wendy didn't want me driving back tonight after all your delicious Gimlets."

"Dammit!" said Peter, "my snotty little brother shows up on the doorstep, and he even has a car to drive. There's no justice in the world for Singapore refugees! Here, roll me one of those fags on your funny little machine, and I'll fetch some more beer."

*** THE GUADALCANAL SCOUTS ***

On August 7, 1942, US Marines led by Major General Archer Vandegrift invaded Guadalcanal and Tulagi in the Solomon Islands, which were British possessions that Japan had recently seized. The Marines had to fight hard for Tulagi and its little islets but landed with surprising ease on Guadalcanal to capture a nearly completed Japanese airfield that they named Henderson Field. They set up a defensive perimeter of five square miles to guard the vital airfield and were soon busy dodging artillery barrages and fighting off Japanese troops that were being landed nightly at both ends of the big island.

While Marine Corps engineers rushed to complete the Japanese airfield for their own use, their D2 (division intelligence officer), Lt. Col. Frank Goettge, led a patrol to attempt capturing some Japanese personnel for questioning. Tragically, the patrol was ambushed and Goettge and most of his party were killed.

A few days afterwards, when Henderson Field was declared ready for use, Admiral John McCain sent over his personal PBY Catalina from Efaté. Among those aboard the McCat was Commander Elmer Perkins, better known to his friends as Bongo. His job was to assess the remaining intelligence capabilities of the Marine division and give a quick 'how-to' course to a kindly lieutenant colonel of artillery who had agreed to take on the D2 job for Gen. Vandegrift until a qualified replacement could be supplied by the ONI.

During those early days on Guadalcanal, the Marines received another surprise. One morning, as the completed airstrip was being tidied up, two long files of fuzzy-haired native militia appeared, led by an Englishman in khaki shorts and shirt with an Aussie bush hat. He introduced himself as Army Captain Martin Clemens.

He was a former district officer, who had stayed behind on Guadalcanal with a few colleagues. It was Clemens, in fact, who had first alerted the Allies by radio to the Japanese capture of Tulagi in May, and the airfield construction on Guadalcanal not long afterwards. Hiding out in the mountainous interior of the large island, Clemens was, in a manner of speaking, the author of the US Marine involvement in Guadalcanal and Tulagi. He received a hearty welcome from General Vandegrift as a result.

The saronged and often shirtless natives were to be a boon to the Marines for the rest of the long campaign. Bongo promised to ship over additional weapons and clothing for these men, whom Captain Clemens planned to disperse into five zones around the island to keep watch on the Japs.

Before Bongo's departure on the PBY, a distinguished-looking middle-aged native joined the group. Clemens introduced Sergeant Major Jacob Vouza, a no-nonsense former police officer.

"Aftanum, nem blong mi Vouza. Wanem nao nem blong iu?" said Vouza, smiling.

"What the heck did he say?" Bongo asked.

"That's local Pidgin," Clemens replied. "He was asking what your name is."

"Oh, of course," Bongo smiled back, shaking Vouza's strong rough hand. "Me Bongo," he replied, pointing at his chest.

"Mi hapi tumas fo mitim iu," the sergeant-major answered. "Me Bongo," said Bongo once again, not knowing what else to reply, as Vouza laughed and laughed, and Clemens clapped him on the back.

"I guess it's beginning to sound like a Tarzan film, right?" Bongo chuckled.

*** NEWS OF GUADALCANAL IN SYDNEY ***

After helping Ned get Marjorie and Barrett settled into their nice Cremourne house across the bridge and having them over to Rose Bay for an afternoon, Peter still had a few days' leave before he would return to Nouméa. Ronald Beamish, the contractor's representative, telephoned as promised, and Peter had an afternoon appointment with him the Thursday before his leave ended. He managed to catch Bongo in town the same day and was invited to lunch with him and Lt. McGowan, to whom Peter had spoken on a few occasions while Bongo was up in Brisbane with General MacArthur's staff.

Sydney's excellent tram system once again took Peter close to the wharf area that he had visited previously, below Observatory Park near the city-end of the Sydney Harbor Bridge. A change of trams could take him on across the great bridge to the Cremourne district of North Sydney where Ned was now living, Peter had already discovered.

The Navy warehouse looked a little less temporary this time, and there were two US frigates moored at adjacent piers, with a Navy guard shack and a heavy wire fence near the wharf intersections.

"Hey, remember this is MacArthur-land," Bongo admonished, after Peter commented on the small warships. "We can't really bring larger ships to Oz, not for fear of the Japs but in case MacArthur would appropriate them! I got to know him a little bit in Brisbane, not that a peasant like me could ever get close to him or Jean, but I'm still not sure how to read that old warrior's tea leaves. Time will tell, I suppose. He is a very persuasive person, I can say that, and supposedly a brilliant strategist."

"There isn't much about him in the Sydney newspapers, according to Doris and Wendy", Peter said, "But probably you Americans are much more visible in Brisbane."

"We certainly are," Bongo replied. "Meanwhile you've heard about Guadalcanal, I assume? I made a brief visit there from Nouméa the other day. Things are about to get pretty hot for our Marine brethren. The late-for-lunch Roberto there"—pointing to Lt. McGowan's empty desk— "is going over to 'the Canal' tomorrow for a week or so, with a Marine light-colonel who will replace the D2 that General Vandegrift recently lost in a bizarre ambush, or rather this one will replace a temporary volunteer. McGowan will thereafter be the new man's *alter ego* in Oz for anything that might be needed in the way of special equipment and will keep him apprised of devilish Japanese tricks that might affect the Solomons.

"McGowan will also help support an interesting countryman of yours called Martin Clemens, a sort of super-coastwatcher assigned to our Marines. This is even though the coastwatchers have their own organization under a mad-dog Aussie naval commander named Eric Feldt, a man I very much hope to meet one day if I can find time to pop up to Townsville in northern Queensland. His *Operation Ferdinand* has set up over sixty coastwatching stations in New Guinea and the Solomons, can you believe? Those fellows are mostly former colonial officials or planters, quite courageous. You can imagine what the Japs do to them if they are caught."

"Cripes, when can I go to Guadalcanal then?" Peter asked seriously. "I'll be talking to Beamish the contractor this afternoon about a new assignment to build bridges on Nouméa and Guadalcanal for some heavy Marine tanks that will be out here soon."

"Peter, I have good news and bad news, old sport. First the bad news: you won't be allowed on Guadalcanal for several months, because you are a civilian and the battle zone is about to erupt."

"And the good news?" Peter asked, suspiciously.

"It's the same as the bad news. Now here comes an apologetic McGowan; let's go to lunch—what we do best."

Peter laughed and nodded.

*** *ESPIRITU SANTO ECLIPSES NOUMÉA* ***

Having enjoyed his two-week break in Sydney with the family, Peter Perry was excited to be back in Nouméa again, as September 1942 was likely to be a busy month. He contacted Hans Lazet and Ralph MacAdam as soon as he arrived, to tell them there would definitely be projects for both of them very soon, but on a New Hebrides island rather than Brisbane, Australia. The New Hebrides group, east of New Caledonia, was also more northerly, and therefore closer to the Solomons where the Marine Corps was in urgent need of air support.

Espiritu Santo, code-named BUTTON, was by far the largest island of the New Hebrides, located some 400 miles north of Port Vila, the colonial capital on Efaté.

'Santo' was also more primitive than Efaté, but had flat land available for several airfields, and excellent sheltered waters for a seaport to relieve the congestion of Nouméa Harbor. Best of all, from an aviation standpoint, Admiral McCain's first Navy airfield on Santo would be nearly 800 air miles closer to Guadalcanal than Nouméa's *La Tontouta*, which had been built for Army B-17s with their longer range.

There was suddenly a big push to add more Navy runways on Santo for bombing the Japanese and helping the Marines, and to construct a large seaport where troops could be brought 'in bulk' from the States aboard Liberty Ships, then reshuffled and reloaded with their specific weaponry into various sorts of landing craft for invading other islands in the Solomons.

This new seaport was where a long-standing problem of 'stevedores versus soldiers' would finally get resolved. At Santo, the classically loaded Liberty ships, with big heavy items stowed down in the holds for ballast, could be discharged into warehouses in an orderly manner. Then, their cargo would be reloaded onto remarkable new flat-bottomed invasion ships according to the fighting man's priorities—regardless of ballast considerations. Many of the new ships, such as LSTs and LSDs were creative British design concepts being built in American shipyards.

"Peter, why the Americans did not build up Espiritu Santo first then?" Hans asked, logically.

"That's an excellent question, Hans," Peter answered. "Beamish the contractor thinks it may have been a political thing. The development on Santo is concentrated near a town called Luganville, at the island's southeast corner. That region is under French administration, so he suspects some political tie-in with the French in New Caledonia. The British zone on north Santo at Hog Harbor is even closer to Guadalcanal than Luganville, but it doesn't have flat ground for airfields and year-round sheltered water for docks and seaplanes.

"So the real question is not why the Americans chose the French zone over the British zone on Santo," Peter went on. "That was just an issue of suitable geography. Rather, the question is why the Americans didn't choose the New Hebrides over New Caledonia in the very beginning, right?"

"Or at least why they didn't choose Espiritu Santo over Efaté," Ralph chimed in. "Efaté will probably be obsolete once Santo gets rolling. It's a good thing the Americans have lots of money."

"That it is, but I think probably all the recent changes had more to do with the Japs' sudden appearance on Tulagi and Guadalcanal," Peter said. "That is a campaign the Americans hadn't planned for. To support twenty thousand pairs of combat boots on the ground requires at least twice that many people behind the scenes, which in turn calls for more facilities such as we are helping to build, and more ships to move the people around. I suppose several Pacific islands will inherit some amazing infrastructure after the war, which they'll wonder what on earth to do with."

The three men were sitting near the Nouméa seaplane boat dock, having just finished a typical lunch of lima beans, mashed potatoes and fried spam at their civilian mess hall, after which they strolled to the waterfront to watch the daily panoply of motion that was Nouméa Harbor. The actual seaplane landing ramp, built originally by Pan Am, was at *l'île Nou*, but NATS also took over Pan Am's boat dock on the Nouméa shorefront, where pre-war passengers had bought tickets and checked in their luggage before being taken out to the departure island. A pair of venerable PANAIR launches still ran back and forth to the old penal colony island and its sheltered waters.

Admiral Ghormley's USS *Argonne* lay at anchor some two hundred yards offshore, Peter noticed, and farther out was a more handsome vessel, the seaplane tender USS *Curtis,* commandeered by Admiral John McCain. Both flagships were painted white like the hospital ships, but without the big red crosses, of course.

Hans broke out his pipe, and Peter took up the conversation again. "I doubt Admiral Nimitz felt comfortable with using either the New Hebrides or New Caledonia as support bases right after Pearl Harbor, since the Japanese were then invading everything in sight. Remember, it was only a month ago, after the Coral Sea and Midway battles, that the Americans started moving their SOPAC support up this way from New Zealand, and then the magnitude of the Solomons fighting caught everyone by surprise. So, I don't think this new construction on Santo is political as much as an inevitable muddle."

Peter also told them that he would probably be staying behind in New Caledonia for the next few months because of the forthcoming bridge projects, once his present water and sewer installations were completed.

"But you never know," he added. "Things can change from week to week. It wasn't all that long ago that they planned to send you two up to Brisbane, remember? Perhaps I'll end up joining you on Santo eventually."

Hans nodded, and knocked out his pipe ash. "Well, one o'clock; back to the nose-grinder wheel, isn't it?"

"That's close, you crazy Dutchman" laughed Ralph. "Shall we go?"

*** *BONGO'S BAD NEWS* ***

Peter waved to Lt. (jg) Culver as they passed the NATS boat dock office. They had chatted with Culver a few times since the trio started eating together at the BOQ cafeteria and taking their short walks to the harbor. He must remember to tell Bongo that Culver was bustling about as always, still striving for the top of the heap. Peter had expected Bongo to put in another Nouméa appearance by then, but it was nearly two more weeks before his friend dropped off a note at the Quonset: "*P, let's do* Chez Louise *in civvies again for a serious pow-wow tonight; 1800 this time, lots to tell you. Call the Big White Whale if you can't make it,*" referring to Ghormley's flagship.

Peter hurried to get cleaned up. When he arrived at the familiar little bistro, Bongo had another man with him at a table, who was just getting up to leave, dressed like Bongo in casual civilian clothes.

"Meet my Brit friend, Peter Perry," Bongo said to his guest. "Peter, this is Lt. Commander Robert Quackenbush, Uncle Sam's Navy. He does photography. Sort of an unforgettable name, eh?"

Peter and the photography officer laughed and shook hands. "Not as unforgettable as Bongo the Brash. Very pleased to meet you, sir."

"My pleasure as well sir," said Quackenbush. "Sorry I have to run. Thanks for the coffee, Commander." Bongo waved a thumbs-up.

"Peter, I'm really glad you're here," Bongo began as a waiter cleared the table. "Couple of lousy things to tell you, old friend, then let's get caught up on all your family news. First, our lovely Ellie the nurse was assaulted by some drunken bastard doctor right there at the MOB-5 hospital a few days ago and was beat up badly when she fought back. She's now at Pearl with a broken arm, broken nose and two missing teeth, and the bastard doctor is here in the brig under the care of some burly Marine guards, awaiting court martial."

"That's terrible news," Peter said. "I remember our nice meal here at this very table. She was a very special girl. I'm so sorry."

"Yeah, and she still is," Bongo sighed dejectedly. "You'd think doctors would have enough sense not to mess with the staff. I guess this jerk must have been bottom of his class in med school. I won't tell you his name, but I damn sure won't forget it myself."

"You're quite enamored of Ellie, then," Peter observed. "She is a lovely girl, but I just could not understand her southern dialect, I'm sorry to say. That left me little to judge her by, other than being, well, a lovely girl."

"OK, silly Brit, no one said you were cut out to be a linguist. Yes, I am quite fond of Miss Ellie. She is a sweet and intelligent friend who just happens to possess a fabulous bod, a beautiful face, and a charming southern accent. So what, no one's perfect."

Peter laughed. "Will your parents be able to understand her?"

"Well, I sure hope so," Bongo said. "Anyway, there's more; it's been a shitty couple of weeks. McGowan was wounded on his little trip to Guadalcanal, and the ONI-vetted light colonel he was traveling with was killed. Looks like Vandegrift's volunteer D2 will keep the job now, and he's coming along fairly well anyway."

"Good heavens!" Peter was quite shocked, "What happened?"

"Jap *Zero* snuck in on them as their Cat was touching down on Henderson. Both pilots dead, too. In fact, everyone bought it but McGowan and the blister gunner who got them both out. The PBY flipped and caught fire. Remember our trip from Pearl to Canton on one of those babies? Great little planes for land or water, but this time just unlucky. And the sneaky Jap pilot got clean away, what's more."

"Well, I can see why you didn't want me visiting the Canal just yet," said Peter. "Will McGowan be alright?"

"Presumably so," Bongo replied. "He wasn't burned, just shot up. Crap, let's order and then talk about photography. I wanted you to know about Quackenbush; he's a focused one-man show who theoretically works for McCain, but a little bit for me as well. We're apparently way behind the Nips on photographic interpretation—or photographic anything—but Quackenbush is going to change all that and build up a professional Navy and Marine organization."

"Nips? What are Nips?" Peter interrupted.

"Japs, Nips—same thing. It comes from *Dai Nippon*, the name for Great Japan in their language. *Comprenez?*" Peter nodded.

"Anyway, USS *Curtis* has a photo lab on board, which is why Quackenbush opted to join McCain's staff, even though he was hired by Ghormley. Flagship *Curtis* will be moved to Santo very soon, perhaps tomorrow, since they now have a fighter strip ready over there. McCain's Marine and Navy fliers are still at Efaté for the moment but will probably move to Santo in a few days too. I must say he has an impressive fleet of aircraft, including the biggest collection of Dumbos in the South Pacific."

"What on earth are Dumbos?" Peter asked, chuckling at the image of Walt Disney's cartoon flying elephant that the world had come to love in 1941.

"Ha, not what you're probably thinking. Dumbo is what people out here now call my favorite airplane, the PBY Catalina; like the Cat we were just talking about that nearly killed McGowan. I don't know how Dumbo got started; maybe because it's such a versatile icon these days; you know, 'the little airplane that could.'"

"You'd think the ubiquitous Jeep would claim a similar honor," Peter suggested, "and Jeep for GP—General Purpose—is simple enough to remember. This rotten war has certainly spawned some amazing inventions."

"Too true," Bongo agreed. "By the way, old man, speaking of war-related inventions, *Yamato's* first sister ship has joined the IJN Combined Fleet now. The new monster's name is *Musashi*. We think those fearsome twins are both together at Truk or the home waters. Quackenbush is going to try for some photos, then we'll send a big raid if either one is found. Keep it to yourself, OK? Captain Silvers sends his best."

Bongo closed his menu. "Know what you want?" Peter nodded, and Bongo signaled the waiter: *"Encore, s'il vous plaît."*

*** CHANGE OF SOPAC COMMAND ***

On October 18, 1942, Vice Admiral William Halsey—known to the press as both Bill and Bull—arrived in Nouméa to replace his tired and frustrated friend of 40 years, Vice Admiral Robert Ghormley. Halsey had actually been Nimitz's first choice as COMSOPAC but was confined to hospital with a serious skin ailment at the time the new job was created. Ghormley, who was a brilliant analytical staff Admiral before, jumped into the breach willingly and gave it his best shot, but he was criticized for never once visiting the battle zone of Guadalcanal, and for his perceived lack of aggressiveness toward the enemy.

At first Halsey followed Ghormley's choice of flagship USS *Argonne* but found the venerable old transport quite limited in terms of space for staff and visitors. He soon moved his flag ashore to a multi-story building in the attractive Anse Vata beach section of Nouméa, which was part of the Army complex that locals called 'The Pentagon.'

Admiral McCain had by then already left with USS *Curtis* for Espiritu Santo, for more effective control of his fighters and scout planes—and perhaps also to distance himself from Halsey. Quackenbush went with McCain, his eye on duplicating the *Curtis* photo lab ashore at some forward base, with a squadron of his own camera-equipped planes.

Bongo had alerted Peter to the pending change of command when they last dined at *Chez Louise*. Peter was fascinated to watch the new activity in Nouméa's harbor, as some ships left for Espiritu Santo or the Solomons and others arrived to supplement Halsey's headquarters. New

Caledonia seemed to take on a quicker tempo and personality overall, and in Nouméa there were hospital ships coming and going as well, with wounded Marines. Peter remembered what Bongo had told him about McGowan's PBY being jumped. He tried to imagine Guadalcanal on a large scale.

One of the first things Admiral Halsey did was fly General Vandegrift to Nouméa for an important conference on the Guadalcanal situation. The crucial meeting included General Holcomb, Commandant of the Marine Corps, who had flown out from Washington. Assured by Vandegrift that his Marines could hold the island if they received more support, Halsey promised Vandegrift 'everything he had'. For the moment, he didn't have a lot to offer, though, apart from two squadrons of Marine warplanes that Admiral McCain had assured him were *en route* from Hawaii to Henderson Field on Guadalcanal.

*** *RUGBY AND BOOMERANGS* ***

Back in Sydney, with Peter off in in Nouméa again, there was not as much opportunity for Wendy and John to get away from the house on weekends. Wendy had submitted her proposal to Government House for the guest suite remodeling and was waiting eagerly for a response. She often dreamed of her creation and collected boxes full of random sketches and magazine clippings.

Now and then the Smyths would invite them for outings, or they could catch a tram across the Sydney Harbor Bridge to Cremourne Junction, where they could walk just three blocks to Ned and Marjorie's new home that overlooked a pretty little harbor inlet where people enjoyed sailing small boats. But mostly they stayed at home in Rose Bay, where John could play with Digger to his heart's content.

The handsome pup was nearly full size now, and close to six months old. Fortunately, he seemed to be house-trained at last. Wendy, John, and Digger were a familiar early morning sight in the neighborhood, where many people knew them by name, and the other dogs barked eagerly as they strolled by.

With the arrival of springtime, Ned invited Wendy and John to watch a Sunday afternoon rugby match between two leading clubs at Sydney's

Trumper Park, which was not far from Rose Bay. Ned came by himself to collect them in the Ford, explaining that Marjorie was not a great fan of sports. John was beside himself with excitement, never having seen grownup teams before. People were still streaming into the park as the match got under way, and the Perrys managed to find some seats with a reasonably good view. Next time Ned would bring them earlier, he promised.

At the half time interval, they were delighted to see an exhibition of boomerang throwing by some Aborigine experts. It was fascinating to see how the curved wooden 'flying wings' could be expertly flung, spinning, in a big circular path that more or less brought them, still twirling, back to the thrower. The clever aerodynamic design's purpose was to not lose the somewhat heavy and carefully crafted weapon if it failed to connect with a targeted animal. Instead, it would return to the thrower.

The highlight of the demonstrations was an older man who could fling a twirling boomerang so precisely that it not only completed a twenty-yard circle back to his location, but then as its momentum abated it would spin a few times above his head before dropping right into his hands. It was like magic, and John talked about it endlessly.

The rugby match was energetic, and surprisingly fast. Although many of the famous club players had been called up into military service, there seemed to be a constant roster of servicemen from different parts of Australia showing up to play on weekends. Public sporting events had only just been approved for Sundays in order to accommodate more of these weekend-only experts, and the crowds of spectators grew to record levels. Wendy enjoyed being outdoors to join in the cheering and the lovely October spring weather, which helped her forget about wartime rationing.

"Can we please bring our neighbors Doris and Fred the next time?" she asked Ned.

Australians, like the British, were mad about rugby football. It was a bruising amateur team sport that men could play if their jobs afforded them enough time for practice. Ned had enjoyed rugby at Monmouth School, but the real expert in the family was Peter, who had gone on to play for Lancashire's county team in his early UK engineering days, and later captained a rugby club in Singapore.

Wendy wished Peter could have been with them to enjoy that afternoon or, better yet, could have been out on the pitch with the action. She missed his constant presence that had been their way of life in Singapore. Ever since he was called to Canton Island, their relationship seemed to be one of separations.

Next week she had promised to help Doris with spring cleaning, which they had agreed to do together at both homes alternately, during some mornings while John was in school. Fred seemed to be away more and more often on banking business, which gave the two women ample time to arrange their own schedules as they wished. They seldom failed to meet for morning coffee, with a hug and kiss on the cheek.

*** THERE GOES THE NEIGHBORHOOD ***

In mid-October 1942, Hans and Ralph were reassigned to Espiritu Santo, to help the Seabees plan an expansion of a rudimentary harbor and hospital complex near Luganville. Peter stayed behind in Nouméa, to work on the Marine training camp and the bridges needed for their heavy tanks.

Before the first Navy survey team had come to Santo at the end of June, Luganville was a sleepy trading port at the mouth of the Sarakata River, with a population of ten thousand or so French, English, Australian, Chinese, Tonkinese, Javanese, Kanak, and various people mixtures there-between. The town was rather plain, and even ramshackle in places, with a few sallow bars near the waterfront. It contained three little churches for people of European backgrounds—Roman Catholic, Presbyterian, and Anglican—but most Kanak natives were not Christians.

Several ranchers kept homes in a nicer end of town for their wives and children while they were away, which helped support a fairly respectable elementary school system. There was a local produce market on Saturdays, and some Chinese stores carried rudimentary imported provisions. The official languages were French and English, with French predominant, but many other ones could be heard on the streets.

Government people were required to know both English and French because of the Anglo-French Condominium that had been in existence since 1900. Occasionally, some sea captain or other visitor would ask why the town was called Luganville, but no one seemed to remember. *[Perhaps originally spelled Louganville, or else misspelled Lougainville after French explorer Louis Antoine de Bougainville, who came ashore on Santo in the 1700s.–Ed.]*

Beginning in August '42, an initial battalion of Seabees and a US Army platoon of Negro troops had been heavily involved with construction of three airfields on Santo for Guadalcanal support, two for bombers and one for fighters. Those completed projects had been handed over to Admiral McCain's staff, so they could move their aircraft up to Santo from Efaté. Now in October, while the planes flew several missions each day, it was critically urgent for civil engineering work to focus on the docks and port facilities, so that a growing number of replacement personnel could be redistributed to various front-line units and ships.

Ralph MacAdam, in the role of his famous namesake, was helping a team of Seabees create the first thirty miles of a hundred-mile road network around the southeast corner of the island, extending in both directions from Luganville so that all the American facilities would eventually be reachable regardless of weather conditions. Rain was a constant companion most of the year, so it was Ralph's job to see that the new roads were designed with adequate drainage and had waterproof surfaces. This involved close coordination with the Seabees, who provided most of the coral-blasting teams and road-building equipment.

A couple of hastily finished airfields on Santo were already in need of reworking due to the rains and flooding. A newly arrived battalion of Seabees would begin on that, soon after they finished a third bomber field on Penda Point, east of the town, for which Ralph would also be consulting. The cheerful New Zealander theoretically lived at a BOQ in Luganville but was often away for days at a time after the road work was started, sleeping in tents and swatting flies with the Seabees.

Ralph was very pleased with someone's foresight in widening the main road bypassing Luganville to four lanes, otherwise the traffic would have been a constant chaos. There was no real dry season in Luganville, but people said with a touch of sarcasm that October would soon bring an end to the less-wet season. There was no need to ask the Seabees to hurry up; they were working flat out already!

Ralph's colleague, Hans Lazet, was meanwhile a key contributor to the dock and pier development in the wonderfully sheltered Segond Channel.

Three large dock complexes were needed for unloading Liberty ships and other deep draft vessels and warehousing their cargo. Rather than dredging the natural channel along its coral shoreline, the engineering committee decided to construct the docks out into deep water, using hardwood pilings to support the connecting piers. Luckily, the daily tidal changes at Santo were not great.

Each such complex was constructed in the form of a 'T', with the top of the T being the main offshore ship-docking area, and the stem being a connecting pier from shore to dock, which itself provided sheltered unloading for smaller vessels. When completed, the system would be able to handle six large and a dozen medium ships at a time, which put the Port of Nouméa to shame. It could also reload a like number of modern LSTs, via ramps along the shoreline.

Construction work proceeded ten hours a day, with huge pilings for the piers and seawalls being procured for the Seabees by the US contractor's office, but work had to cease at night because of concern that lights might attract shelling from Japanese submarines, as they had previously. *[The whole of Luganville would be blacked out at night until mid-1944–Ed.]*.

Local labor was sometimes engaged to supplement the Seabees, directed by supervisors who could speak Bishama, the local Pidgin dialect of Santo. The friendly Melanesian natives also spoke one of over a hundred distinct tribal languages of their own but used Bishama to communicate with each other and with people from other lands. Some supervisors were lent by French plantation owners, who also provided local-type meals to their crews. In late 1942, the Luganville vicinity was a beehive of activity rarely seen on the planet Earth.

*** *UNEXPECTED SYDNEY LIAISON* ***

Unbeknownst to Fred and Peter, who were habitually away from Sydney for short or long durations, their wives became 'special friends' one fine spring morning in October 1942. It happened accidentally but spontaneously, when John was at school and Wendy was visiting Doris to help with her spring cleaning, a big chore for each household that they had agreed to share together. Doris was standing on a wobbly little step ladder in the kitchen, dusting the tops of the cabinets. Alarmed, Wendy moved over to steady the ladder, surprisingly aroused by the sight of Doris' fine legs just inches before her face, disappearing up into a short blue sun dress. Trying to recover her composure, she bumped the ladder and Doris fell, knocking them both to the floor where they lay together for a moment, breathless.

"Are you alright, darling?" Doris whispered, kissing Wendy on the cheek.

"Oh yes," Wendy murmured, turning to kiss Doris on the lips. They embraced where they lay, then their hands flew, groping, caressing.

"Oh God, what are we doing?" Wendy began, but then Doris kissed her again and they rose to walk hand in hand into the bedroom.

"I suppose it's because of the war, as they always say," Doris chuckled afterwards. Then they both shrieked with laughter and hugged each other once more.

*** THE LOCALS ON SANTO ***

During all the frantic American projects of those days, which appeared to the local Melanesian Kanaks like a series of incredible miracles as the Land of Plenty bedeviled their imaginations, a small pre-existing religious cult grew rapidly around a mythological figure known as John Frum, who was supposed to possess the power to replicate the magic of American 'cargo' acquisitions. John Frum, it was believed, could lavish an endless supply of luxury goods upon his worshipers, given the appropriate incentive of ritual and prayer.

The cult became especially strong on the fairly remote condominium island of Tanna *[where John Frum Day is still celebrated every February 15th – Ed.]*, but its ritual and lore were clearly derived from Santo, because that is where most of the daily American miracles were actually taking place.

Hans was quite intrigued by the cargo cult phenomenon and succeeded in befriending a Luganville official who spoke English, French, and Bishama, and who shared an equal curiosity about the developing beliefs of the Kanaks.

In time, Hans was invited to a Luganville council meeting as an observer, on a day that did not involve the regular weekly banter with Navy planners. There he was introduced to other civic leaders, one of whom kindly invited him to a Monday family outing in the mountain foothills, since October twenty-sixth was a special school holiday that year. Hans arranged to be off that day too, even though it was a workday for the Seabees.

The new acquaintance's name was Philippe Orly, a distinguished middle-aged Euronesian originally from Efaté. The group of about thirty young and old Orly cousins, and Hans, made its way toward the foothills on horseback, for which Hans was fortunately quite proficient. Riding mostly in silence for some twenty miles, sometimes at a canter when the field or path was well clear of obstacles, otherwise at a cautious walk, Hans enjoyed seeing the beautiful trees and flowers of this large island, so similar yet subtly different from his colonial Java. Santo lacked the conical volcanoes of his homeland, and the large fields of sugarcane, yet the warm, moist tropical climate was familiar and quite agreeable.

He felt almost at home that balmy October morning, which made him recall how surprised he had been to see occasional Javanese men and women in the streets of Luganville, wearing colorful batik sarongs. He had spoken to one or two, but found they did not understand colonial Dutch, only the Bishama of Santo or their own *lingua franca* from Java, known as Bahasa Melayu. He wondered whether they were still Muslim, after being in the Hebrides for some time, perhaps generations. Until that moment on the horseback outing he had forgotten about those encounters, but now wondered anew what had brought native people from Java to work in the Hebrides islands. He must remember to ask.

It was late Monday morning when the riders reached a lovely fenced meadow, by way of several cattle barriers and gates. Some rustic rain shelters stood near a sort of corral, where everyone dismounted and unsaddled the horses. Water and fodder were plentiful, and the animals showed no sign of wandering away. Some older boys prodded the youngsters into grooming the mounts after they cooled down. A nearby patch of paw-paws (papayas) grew with abandon, and children harvested the large, luscious yellow fruit for their families, followed enthusiastically by two or three dogs that had accompanied the riders all the way from Luganville.

Philippe beckoned to Hans, and they strolled up a slight rise that let them see over the treetops to the distant town and ocean, a fabulous land-and-seascape that included part of the Segond Channel and several offshore islets.

151

"Hans, are you American?" Philippe inquired as they sat cross-legged under a tree, admiring the beautiful view. Tiny American planes could be seen leaving in batches from faraway airfields near the coast, and what looked like a large ocean liner was slowly approaching the Segond Channel entrance from the east. "Your accent seems different from the others."

"No, Philippe, I am Dutchman from Java," Hans explained. "I did escape to Australia just before the Japanese they invade my country. What of yourself? You are from here?" Some handsome girls and boys brought them wooden bowls with various interesting vegetable dishes and fish, then ran happily back to their mothers.

"Yes, but I think I mentioned when we met that I am not originally from Luganville. After I studied the geography of these islands in my school days on Efaté, I wanted very much to see Santo and become a peanut farmer, or planter as we are called, and my father bought me a few hectares of cheap land down there in the flat wet area near the coast, that nobody wanted. Well, predictably, I had constant trouble draining the land, but these days—praise the Lord—my land is part of the new American airfields, so what I do now is help the Navy grow their own vegetables. In reality, I have some Tonkinese contract workers doing most of the work. Those people are from French Indochina, you know, so they can legally work here or in New Caledonia. They are excellent vegetable farmers."

"How very clever. So you are French, then?" Hans asked.

"Well, yes and no. My great grandpa was a French prison guard at Fort Tereka, off Nouméa, and after that he stayed in New Caledonia to marry with a local-born French girl, whose father had also been a guard, I think. Their son, my grandpa, he attended the French *lycée* in Nouméa, then went to sea—you know, local ships around here, New Hebrides, Fiji, New Zealand. He worked like that all his life, and eventually became a ship captain. On one voyage he married a Polynesian girl from Tahiti, and she would travel with him on the ships; eventually so did their children, one of whom was my father. Pa decided to move over to the New Hebrides from Nouméa when I was six or seven and became a businessman on Efaté."

Hans told Philippe about his visit to the Fort Tereka ruins at Nouville.

"Yes, Hans, my great grandpa was on that little island for twenty years. The convicts worked every day in the granite quarry, then most went back to France after they were released. A few stayed in New Caledonia, though, because of a free land offer, and they married Kanak or maybe half-Kanak, or sometimes French girls. Now we call those ex-Nouville descendants *Caldoches,* meaning old-time Caledonians from Europe. Most of them live on *Grande Terre,* the big island, but not in Nouméa city usually."

"Why not Nouméa?" asked Hans.

"Nouméa has so many recent people from France itself—they are called *Métros*—so I suppose the *Caldoches* still don't like the French-French for sending their ancestors to prison out here. Or perhaps they still feel guilt and shame about it, in a strange sort of way. Shall we stroll some more?" They stood and stretched.

Hans told Philippe that he would be astounded by the changes at *l'île Nou.* "And there is also a Navy seaplane service on the island. Nouville, it is full with Quonset huts and sailors, just like you do see here at Santo."

"That's amazing, Hans, but with people now coming to these islands from all over the world, nothing is really that surprising any longer. By the way, did you hear the news last week that a plane carrying Captain Eddie Rickenbacker has disappeared at sea? They say he is a famous American flier from the First War, and now the chairman of some big airline. We just heard about it this morning."

"Where did this plane go down, then?" asked Hans.

"Apparently near a little island called Canton that they were trying to find, somewhere near Hawaii I think. I just thought you might have heard of him— isn't Rickenbacker a Dutch name? They are still searching for survivors."

Hans shook his head. "No, I don't know that name, but my English friend, Peter Perry, did work on Canton Island. He said it is a fairly small atoll and difficult to find in the big ocean without good navigation skill. But he also said that a troopship was wrecked on the reef, so the island should be easier to see than before. I guess Mr. Rickenbacker must have been very far off course."

After another glance at far-off Luganville where the liner—which they agreed must be a troopship—was about to enter the east end of the curved channel, the two men wandered back down the little hill to some sheltered tables where a dozen or more women and children were gathered and settled themselves on a nearby rustic wooden bench. Some youngsters came over to speak courteously to Philippe in French, addressing him as *mon oncle.*

"Now Stéphanie, André, Raymond, mind your manners," Philippe scolded mildly. "Practice your English with this fine gentleman who is our guest today. Go on."

Hans stood smiling to shake hands with the confused trio, who looked to be ten or eleven years old. "Hello, I am old man Hans from Java. I speak English and Dutch. Please tell me a story about your family." He sat down again, seeing he was making them nervous.

The children whispered together for a moment, then Stéphanie, the eldest perhaps, stood up straight and harrumphed in slow cadence: "Good day, meestair. *Mon* nem eez Stéphanie Bardot. I um zee doughtair uff Madame Yvonne Bardot, *là-bas*"—pointing to a flustered woman who was trying to organize some games for the other youngsters—"ahnd I um *aussi* zee browzair—*non*—zee seestair from zeez bad boys. Sank you."

Hans clapped enthusiastically and Stephanie, red-faced, quickly sat next to her uncle, leaving the two boys standing sullenly alone. "Ah em André" muttered one; "Ah em Raymond," whispered the sibling.

"Can you say something more?" urged Uncle Philippe. The boys shook their heads stubbornly, looking at the ground. "All right you two, go and fetch your mother."

With intense relief showing on their faces, the boys ran laughing to the nearby table and tugged on their mother's arm, pointing up at the bench.

"Hans, she who is coming is my dear sister Yvonne. Her husband was drowned two years ago when the inter-island ferry sank near Efaté. The loss has been hard on her and the three children, but she is a strong woman and we have been helping her get back to normal. These days she is teaching at the Luganville School." The men stood as she started toward them.

Yvonne waved as she drew near. She kissed Philippe and extended a hand to Hans, who thought her quite attractive. Like the other women in the group she was wearing a long, split skirt and leather boots for riding.

"*Bonjour m'sieur, comment allez-vous* ? », she asked of Hans

"*Seulement anglais s'il t'plaît, ma chère Yvonne* » Philippe murmured. « *Ce m'sieur Lazet est hollandais, et je ne crois pas qu'il parle français* ».

"Hans, this is my sister, Madame Yvonne Bardot... formerly Orly," Philippe hastened to add. Stéphanie giggled.

"Oh I am so sorry, Mr. Lazet! Please forgive my mistake," Yvonne smiled guiltily at Hans, who bowed slightly, embarrassed as well. "You are

Dutch, my brother says. How very interesting. I don't remember meeting any Dutch people here before. You must hate this tropical heat and all the rain, *non*? Please, do sit down."

They sat together on the bench, and Yvonne shooed Stéphanie away with a smile. Hans guessed Yvonne to be in her late thirties, about a decade younger than himself. He explained quietly:

"Yes, I am Dutch, but I am Java-*geborn,* so the tropic weather most of time for me is good. I am grateful so much to you and your brother Philippe for invite me to your family outing today. Here is such a beautiful place, and I am happy to be away from engineers and contractors."

"Oh, what are you doing on Santo then?" asked Yvonne. "I'm sure it must have something to do with the Americans, *non*?" She glanced at Philippe for approval, who shrugged.

Hans laughed: "Yes, of course it does. I try to help them make the seafront construction, you know, the docks and piers. The first big dock project, it is almost complete, then we are building two more like that, almost so big. In Java I did work at the Dutch navy base, Surabaya. Santo does remind me so much of home, especially here today in these hills."

Philippe asked whether Hans' family was elsewhere in the New Hebrides, or perhaps Australia.

"Oh, I have no family, Philippe, now my parents they are gone. I seem a life-long bachelor, working all the time."

He reached nervously for his pipe, then replaced it.

"Oh please smoke if you wish, M'sieur Lazet," Yvonne quickly invited, pronouncing his name Lah-zay instead of Lahzet. "I must get the children organized now, as we should all return to Luganville in an hour or so, to arrive before dark. Thankfully, today is not a rainy day, but if we go riding next month, we will be drenched! *Au revoir, Monsieur.*" Yvonne rose and shook his hand, casting a backward smile as she started toward the tables and noisy children.

*** *LOSS OF A LUXURY LINER* ***

In spite of the children's noisy games, the adults could make out a muffled explosion far away but paid it scant attention. Then there was another, and yet another. "Come Hans, back up the hill! That sounded like Luganville

155

or an airfield. Perhaps it is a Japanese raid!" The pair ran up to their former viewing point.

"*Mijn God*!" Hans heard himself say, for there in the upper Segond Channel they could clearly see the fancy troopship listing to port and heading straight at the shore. "Is that ship torpedoed?"

"More likely they did not see the minefield! What a disaster," shouted Philippe. "Look, they are going to run into the bank! This will be like your friend's Canton Island!"

There was no seawall in the channel that far from the seaplane base. As the men watched, fascinated and anxious, the ship suddenly veered to port while the momentum carried it broadside onto the reef shore. There was an abrupt shudder, which they could almost imagine hearing as the ship was nearly uprighted from the shock of collision, but it quickly returned to the list angle again, away from the shore. They could look right down the eastern channel to see tiny figures milling about on the shoreward side, apparently jumping or sliding down ropes. Emergency vehicles were struggling along the bumpy ground at the shore, where there was no proper roadway.

"We should get our group moving!" Philippe said. "So much could happen in the two hours before we can get back home. I must help with the shipwreck soldiers!"

"Have you a wish to go fast ahead?" Hans asked. "Those older boys and me"—pointing to some young Orly men who were saddling the horses—"we could bring more slowly the ladies and children."

"Yes, *oui, merci* Hans; I must rush now," and Philippe shouted for his horse, stopping to give instructions to Yvonne. Then he was away at a gallop.

*** *MORE NEWS OF GUADALCANAL* ***

There were always rumors about Guadalcanal on BUTTON, the code name for Espiritu Santo, due to the continual air sorties and some talkative pilots. In spite of the remoteness of their airfield from Luganville, news and rumors of Guadalcanal seemed to reach Luganville almost daily from the Marine pilots after they returned from a raid.

Among the air fleets stationed at BUTTON were two Marine fighter squadrons, VMF-213 and 214, based at Turtle Bay Field, quite some distance up the east coast of Santo from Luganville. Those squadrons were in the early process of converting from the F4F Wildcat to the F4U Corsair, a fast gull-wing fighter plane that should finally match the Jap Zero for maneuverability and speed. But they had no Corsairs yet in 1942, just preliminary manuals and drawings, and their Wildcats were often outclassed by the Zeros.

Occasionally one of the Marine pilots would not return from a 400-mile sortie to CACTUS, but perhaps he might be spotted later by search planes, floating in the sea—or perhaps not.

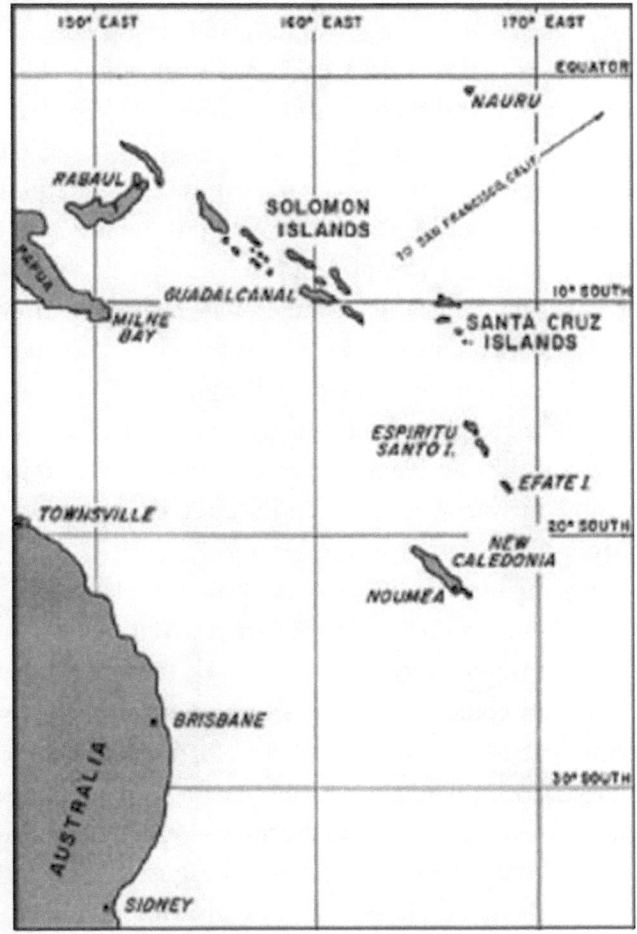

The Coral Sea
(https://www.carlisle.army.mil/ahec/index.cfm)

With this 'Russian Roulette' existence, life was stressful for the aviators, who tended to drink too much and sleep too little. At first light they would be away again, sometimes just one squadron, often both, sometimes a second sortie at mid-day to escort Army bombers from Nouméa across the Coral Sea. Often, the Marines would fly on up the Slot beyond CACTUS to tangle with the Japs. One of their aces, "Pappy" Boyington, had flown with the Flying Tigers in China before the US entered the war.

Occasionally a shot-up fighter from BUTTON would have to land on CACTUS—Henderson Field—for repairs, or for its pilot to leave his wreck and catch a ride back to Santo in something else the next day, perhaps a Dumbo or an R4D (DC3, C47). Meanwhile the BUTTON pilot could trade scuttlebutt and share a drink or three with counterparts from VMF-223 and 224, the CACTUS-based Marine squadrons. They were a brave fraternity that lived for today, not tomorrow. Through this grapevine one mid-October day, word reached Rear Admiral Aubrey Fitch on Santo, who had recently taken over from Admiral McCain, that CACTUS had been plastered heavily by nearly a thousand 14-inch shells from two Jap battleships for nearly an entire night, not just the usual one-hour pasting from cruisers or destroyers with their smaller guns.

Fuel dumps had exploded, several Marines and pilots were killed, and most of the American planes were destroyed on the ground. A few poor lads went temporarily insane from the endless, screaming shells and heaving ground.

A US Army regiment had just arrived on the island too, the 164th Infantry from Nouméa, to reinforce the battered Marines. They got a real baptism under fire when scarcely dug in.

Dante Alighieri could conceive nothing worse than this inferno, as the two enemy battleships cruised back and forth off Lunga point, with their heavy barrages no doubt being directed by Jap spotters on Mount Austen, radioing back corrections to the ships—except it was nighttime, and thankfully the view from Mt Austen was vague and dim. Clearly the Japs intended to obliterate Henderson Field this night, and they almost succeeded. Those on CACTUS who survived the vicious bombardment would relive the horror in their ongoing nightmares, perhaps even for the rest of their lives.

But the Allies always did the same to Japanese defenders before invading a Pacific Island, sometimes for days in a row. It was called 'softening up the landing zone.' War is Hell!

In Brisbane, when Bongo heard about this particular bombardment on Guadalcanal, he immediately thought of *Yamato* and *Musashi*, but got confirmation from Vandegrift's D2 that the raiders were a pair of older battleships, *Kongo* and *Haruna,* and the shells were definitely 14-inchers— some duds had not exploded.

So brutal was the Henderson Field bombardment that word of it was spread far and wide throughout the Pacific theater and would eventually reach even Hans at a Navy social event on Santo. The base commander for BUTTON had invited civilian contractors to a Thanksgiving dinner at the O-Club, in honor of Seabee officers and the fine progress made at the docks. The invitation was for "Mr. Hans Lazet and Companion", so Hans lost no time inviting Madame Yvonne Bardot to be his guest.

Hans and Yvonne, by then on a first name basis, had enjoyed a pleasant chat on the way back to Luganville from the Orly family horseback outing, the day the chartered luxury liner SS *President Coolidge* was wrecked and sunk by mines. A few weeks later Hans had spotted Yvonne in town, and she had time for a coffee. "Where is Philippe today?" he asked.

Yvonne paused before answering. "Oh, probably checking on the vegetable farm or else arguing with the Navy," she replied vaguely. "That is mostly what he does now that... now that his wife has gone away to Nouméa."

Hans looked puzzled, and Yvonne continued: "I'm sorry, I didn't mean to confuse you. You see, Philippe and his wife Anne are divorced. They have no children. She left him over a year ago, for a *Caldoche* of all things." Yvonne looked away, hiding her eyes.

Hans sighed. "I am much sorry, Yvonne. Such a fine man is Philippe. Just this other day he did tell me something about the *Caldoche* community of New Caledonia, which was so interesting. I remember he said they did not like to live in Nouméa."

"Anne's new man is an exception," Yvonne almost hissed. "He is a scoundrel politician, very notorious. They are not even married yet. Well, shall we speak of other things? Do you miss your Java and the Dutch community? I have read that the Netherland East Indies has been a Dutch colony for several centuries already."

Hans told Yvonne about his father and mother, and his time in Holland at university. "I did almost stay in Leiden to work, because I did love a professor his daughter. But then, I was too shy to talk with her father the professor, and his daughter found another man better than me. I was sad a lot, so I come back to Java to help my parents."

"And you never fell in love again, ever?" Yvonne teased. Hans sipped his coffee, thinking what to say.

"Yvonne, I was for some time a Dutch Army man there on Java, the KNIL it is called. I was in secret branch, civilian clothes, supposed to investigate the Indisch—the Eurasian people. Dutch always they are checking such things. I meet a very nice Indisch girl and we are crazy for each other. I am supposed to spy on her father, who is international businessman, but I make false reports that he is OK and no risk—because of the girl, of course. But her father, he is supporter of Sukarno, actually he is probably financier for Sukarno."

Hans stood up to get more coffee. "Sukarno is native pro-independence leader, very smart and popular. The Dutch administration they hate him. He was in jail then for subversion, and there was breakout attempt. The girl her father was, um, implicated. They arrest him, and he is shot, just like that. The nice girl thought I turn him in, and she did try to kill me ... but she is killed instead by KNIL. I am under suspicion for having affair with her, which was true of course, and those KNIL spies they kick me out of the Army. I guess they could maybe kill me too, for—how to say—duty derelicting, or at least lock me away. But my father he did know the KNIL colonel in Bandung and did get me free. So I move away to Surabaya, you see?" Yvonne nodded, not wanting to interrupt his story.

"It was sad time, around ten years ago, so I dedicate myself to my parents for the rest of their lives. But they are both gone now. My Pa he was a plantation manager at P&T Lands, which is big Anglo-Dutch company near Bandung in West Java. When he did retire, I bring my parents to Surabaya where I am working. That is East Java, Dutch Navy base. There is where I learn dock construction."

Yvonne was attentive, particularly about the Indisch girl. "Hans, you can see that Philippe and I are Euronesians. Out here in the French islands it doesn't mean anything, except perhaps to some British or Americans … and I have been wondering about the Dutch. You are a white man—though much sunburned! Tell me about Dutch attitudes."

Hans laughed. "To honestly say, Yvonne, I think Dutch prejudice is more about economics, not, um, race, so could be we are like the French that way. Many Dutch, usually men, marry Indisch women, sometimes even native women, and their children they are accepted in Holland or Java. You say "Euronesian"; this maybe is better word than Eurasian or Indisch. My Pa he did bring Ma from Holland, but many friends of family they marry with local brides and have all kinds mixed children. But in Dutch society there sure is a, um, order pecking; but it is for wealth or power. Who is caring about that?"

Yvonne patted his hand and smiled. "Hans that is the most I have heard you say since we first met. We must talk again, but I have to leave now, sorry. See you soon, OK? *Au revoir.*" She left the table but turned and waved from the café doorway.

Two weeks later Yvonne happily accepted the invitation from Hans to the Navy Thanksgiving *soirée,* which he hand-delivered to her home in Old Luganville.

"Can you help me find something for wearing?" he asked her. "I have only working clothes out here in Santo!"

"Of course! You and Philippe are nearly the same size, so I will raid his wardrobe. His home is close by. Philippe received an invitation too, by the way, so he can drive us. Good, eh?" She laughed and called the children. "Boys, Stéph, come. Your Dutch uncle is here!"

The Thanksgiving dinner was a fine affair and a great success. Somehow the Navy had acquired turkey-flavored spam, cranberry sauce and a big variety of local vegetables, plus cases of good French wine that one of the planters had provided for a hefty fee. For dessert, there were canned peaches, pears, and apricots, and fresh papaya and mango, with wonderful mountain coffee from Santo itself—and vanilla ice cream! Two dozen large round tables were filled with Marine, Navy, and Seabee officers, some of them escorting Navy or Red Cross nurses or civilian women—plus two whole tables for the Luganville and other civilian invitees. A Navy swing band played dance tunes, and a few couples took to the floor.

Rear Admiral Fitch and senior staff came ashore from USS *Curtis* before dinner was served. The admiral made a rousing speech about the certainty of an Allied victory, and his enormous gratitude for the Seabee construction and the joint Seabee-civilian engineering work. An experienced aviator and carrier admiral, who had provided able leadership in the Battle of the Coral Sea, Admiral Fitch was a good speaker.

In closing, he dispatched his handful of staff members to each join a table in the room, there to "lift a glass to the best Naval Base in the South Pacific", and to then carve and serve the Spam 'roast turkey' for those tables. It was a nice gesture. The admiral dined at a smaller table with the base commander, the *Curtis* skipper, and some visiting French officers from Nouméa.

Hans and Yvonne sat with Philippe. They were joined by Ralph, the tarred MacAdam, who had lots of amusing stories to tell about the road work crew. Philippe beckoned to some other council members with their wives to join them.

Everyone at the two civilian tables stood to toast the admiral's designated staff member. He was Lt. Commander Robert Quackenbush, whom nobody knew, but he was a good conversationalist and quickly got some lively discussion started. His short toast was quite well done, ending with: "It would have been absolutely impossible to accomplish what we did without the individual sacrifice and commitment from each and every one of you ladies and gentlemen here tonight. Thank you on behalf of the United States of America!"

It was in the chit-chat that followed, that Ralph and the others heard from Commander Quackenbush about the brutal IJN bombardment of Guadalcanal the prior month. "The Marines, Soldiers, and Seabees there are battered, but still hitting the Japs where it hurts. They know we are here and supporting them, and amazingly they are also enjoying a Thanksgiving dinner today, possibly their first full meal in months. I doubt the Japs are so lucky."

CHAPTER FIVE

Turning the Tide

Second Marine Division Shoulder Patch

Nous Essayons Quand Même
–We Strive Regardless

*** *A NEW YEAR DAWNS IN NOUMÉA* ***

Christmas Day 1942 had not been one to remember, Peter Perry thought as he wandered through the city parks of Nouméa a week later, on New Year's morning 1943. Among other things, the city was strangely quiet, almost lifeless. Gone were the noisy military vehicles, trying to move partly assembled aircraft through the streets, and gone were the pretty French secretaries with their bicycles, competing for space with hordes of pedestrians. Instead, the streets were now almost deserted just as they had been on Christmas Day, so he opted for the city parks this time instead of the USO Club.

Admittedly, though, the USO Club was doing its best to create a homey atmosphere for the many Allied personnel who were stuck in New Caledonia for the holidays. Red Cross nurses pitched in as well, to help serve drinks and provide music for the occasion, but they were just as depressed as the men at being far, far away from home on the most special family holiday season of the year.

Peter had stopped in at the USO with his guest ID card on Christmas Day but didn't see anyone he recognized. A mournful hymn was being played on a distant upright piano in need of tuning, with a few voices trying their best to follow it. From another corner came the sound of a lethargic ping-pong match. Peter had stood at the counter long enough to quaff a cold drink, then ambled back into the quiet streets for the long walk back to his quarters.

When he took his two-week leave to Sydney the past October—to which he was entitled each three months in return for being on the job six days per week, ten hours per day—he had hoped it might be possible to bring Wendy and John over to Nouméa for Christmas and New Year's, both to see where he was working and to experience a Francophone environment. But it turned out that 'non-essential' civilian travel by air, even with the offer of paying for it, was out of the question due to wartime regulations.

They could have made the visit by ship, but that would have used up too much of John's school holiday (and perhaps risked a Japanese torpedo), so they decided to forget about the idea and just get together in Australia at the end of January, when Peter's next leave would be available. Wendy and John would spend Christmas Day with the other Perrys—Ned and Marjorie—meanwhile, and some time with neighbors Doris and Fred. There would doubtless be lots of bike-and-dog walks.

So, Peter didn't bother with the USO on New Year's Day, because he knew it would be the same again—depressing.

He missed the daily banter with his colleagues, Hans and Ralph, who were still involved with Espiritu Santo, so far as he knew. Bongo Perkins hadn't appeared for nearly six weeks either, he realized, but remembered Bongo had left for Pearl Harbor to be with Ellie the nurse. She had been released from the naval hospital but was still recuperating from her assault.

Peter's life was thereby irretrievably boring. He had made no friends among the French-speaking population of Nouméa, and wished he had Bongo's fluency with the language. As he strolled along in thought on New Year's morning, a quick rain squall blew inland from the harbor.

Drat! Peter said to himself as he ran to take refuge with several others inside the old bandstand at *Place des Cocotiers*, deciding he might as well go back to the Quonset BOQ and write another letter to Wendy.

Just then, a young man who looked vaguely familiar dashed into the bandstand, with a slightly older woman who was shaking the rain out of her hair. As both were in civilian clothes, Peter failed to recognize Lieutenant (jg) Culver, with whom he had often chatted at the NATS boat dock, so he started to pass them by as he strode toward an exit when the rain began to taper off.

"Mr. Perry!" came a cheery hail from Culver, who added: "Won't you stay a moment? I'd like to introduce my sister, Abby."

"Lieutenant Winthrop Culver, by Jove; Happy New Year! I'm so sorry to not recognize you out of uniform. Please forgive me." Peter shook hands with them both, and said; "Please call me Peter, you two. I'm so pleased to meet you, Miss Culver."

"It's a pleasure for me as well, Peter. I'm 'Abby the Widow' Culver-Hobbs, and Abby is short for Abigail. You already seem to know my precocious little brother—but don't call him Winthrop; he prefers his middle name, Andrew. Unfortunately, the little rascal outranks me; I'm still just an ensign, Navy Nurse Corps."

"That's enough, Abby, you'll give away all our family secrets," Andrew Culver chuckled. "Isn't she a talker, Mr. Perry, er, Peter? Always been that way."

"What a pleasure to run into you two," said Peter. "It's been a rather dull holiday week, don't you think? What are your plans for the day? And come to think of it, Andrew, I haven't seen you at the NATS boat dock recently."

"That's true," replied Culver, "they've rotated me over to *l'île Nou,* at the seaplane landing ramp. Now I have more responsibilities, which I'm happy about, and I'll have a new boss in a few days, from NATS Fiji."

"Today we're just catching up with each other's news," added Abby, "and looking for some place that might be open for lunch on a holiday. Care to join our ramblings?"

"Why certainly; that would be wonderful," Peter beamed. "I do know a little bistro-type restaurant close by, as a matter of fact, but have no idea whether it's open today. Shall we go and look?"

"Lead on, lead on," Abby smiled to the men, linking her arms through theirs as they dodged the puddles, grateful for the sunshine that would soon dry the water away. "Isn't this the most delightful climate on earth?" she remarked, giving Peter's arm a gentle squeeze. "I've only been here a month, but I adore the place already!"

The trio chatted happily on their way to *rue Frédéric Surleau,* and were ecstatic that *Chez Louise* was indeed open, and decked out with faded holiday streamers. A large rain-streaked sign over the door proclaimed **Bonne Année et Bonne Santé**, having apparently been used for the past several New Years.

M'sieur Roger, the husband of Madame Louise, recognized Peter and held up three fingers, questioningly.

"Um, *oui,*" mumbled Peter, nodding and trying to recall what else Bongo had said before. "*Oui oui*, er, *merci.*" Chuckling with relief, Peter motioned the others to proceed. "Gad, can either of you handle this charming language? I'm more or less lost," he asked after they were seated.

"I speak some French, Peter. Shall I order for us?"

Abby's cheerful announcement flooded Peter with relief. "Oh, of course," he almost applauded. "Are you proficient too, Andrew?"

166

"Sorry, Peter, not me. Abby is the talker in our family, in whatever tongue. Just sit back and watch her go. She's five years my senior, so my head has always rung with the sound of her bossy voice, like a hereditary ear worm."

"Andrew, please shut up or I'll swat you one, outranked or not!"

After their plates arrived with the bistro's special New Year meal, 'house wine and gratuity included', their conversation turned to the war. Andrew was more up to date than the others.

"The Army is now in charge of fighting the Japs on Guadalcanal," he announced. "You've probably heard about the Americal Division that was formed and trained here in New Caledonia by General Patch." Peter nodded, but Abby looked blank.

"Americal relieved the First Marine Division early December," Andrew continued, "which is now raising Cain in Melbourne—a miraculous recovery, no disrespect intended. Wine, women, and song seem to be the universal cure."

"Andrew, please. That's not at all nice." Abby glowered at her brother, prompting Peter to say that the Marines were probably just glad to be alive after the hell of the past few months.

To change the subject, Peter asked if the others had yet heard the new Christmas ballad by Irving Berlin, *White Christmas*."

"By Bing Crosby, you mean," Abby gushed. "What a voice! I think he and Bob Hope will be doing a USO show here in Nouméa, or is it Espiritu Santo? I can't remember what the girls said."

"Well, let's have a toast to the new year, then," Peter suggested. "To the troops everywhere who are on the front lines today; here in the Pacific and over in Europe; and all the sailors at sea." They sipped thoughtfully.

"And the prisoners of war too, and the families of the dead and wounded," Andrew suddenly added, self-consciously.

"Why Andrew, that was very thoughtful," Abby smiled. "There's hope for you yet."

Culver coughed self-consciously, and Peter changed the subject again. "Andrew, did you say your new boss is coming here from Fiji? Would it be Lieutenant Mike Osborn by any chance?"

"Why, the very same, except he's a lieutenant commander," Culver said in surprise. "How in the world did you know his name?"

167

"Commander Perkins and I made his acquaintance at the NATS station near Suva, after bidding you farewell on Canton Island nearly a year ago. I look forward to seeing him again, here in Nouméa, and getting some news of my friend, the former British administrator for Canton Island, as a matter of fact. What a small world."

"Indeed, it is," said Culver. "By the way, Peter, speaking of Canton Island, did you hear that Captain Weaver was transferred to Bora-Bora, to oversee the fuel supply operation there? I guess he was overqualified for a NATS unit. I imagine he'll have no trouble finding a Bridge foursome now. I hear Bora-Bora is a very popular place to be stationed, though I can't imagine why. It's about as far from the war zone as Kansas or Iowa."

"I heard it had something to do with hormones," Peter said, then blushed. "Oh, sorry Abby, I didn't mean to say that in your presence. Please excuse me."

"Why, Peter," she answered coquettishly, "I didn't realize the English knew about hormones."

*** DIGGERS BACK FROM NEW GUINEA ***

Peter's first leave of 1943 finally arrived. He went to Sydney by seaplane on January 30th, a Saturday, and was surprised but pleased to see his brother Ned at the Rose Bay airport, rather than Wendy and John, and guessed there was a transportation problem of some sort.

"How are you, Lord Kellogg," he joked as they shook hands; "I'm mightily pleased to be back in Sydney again, after the boring holidays in Nouméa. Is everything all right at home?"

"At my home, yes," Ned replied, "but I'm not so sure about yours. I don't know if Wendy told you about your neighbors, Fred and Doris, splitting up, but apparently Fred is divorcing her. And he's naming you as a correspondent in the case, what's more!"

"What on earth!" Peter exclaimed. "Why, I hardly know Doris. Come, let's have a beer in the lounge so I can sit down and digest this."

They moved to a table in the airport pub and ordered two half-pint drafts of Australian bitters.

"Ned, what is going on, do you have any idea?" Peter asked as they clinked their glasses.

"Not really, though one could speculate. You see, Fred has moved out and left the house to Doris. It seems the breakup wasn't totally unexpected, as he had been away more and more often—all this according to my Marjorie, mind you, who got it from Wendy."

"Fine, but where do I fit in, for heaven's sake? I haven't even been here. If this wasn't January, I'd think you were having me on for an April Fool. I don't think I've spoken a dozen words to Doris since we first met, and that was when I was shivering on Bondi Beach at the end of last winter."

"Quite so, I agree. Apparently, Fred and Doris had a big row about his carrying on with someone in the City, and pretending to be away on business a lot, but Fred wouldn't admit to anything. Doris finally told him to get the hell out, or words to that effect, and that she was in love with their neighbor across the road anyway, so there."

"But how did you come by all these details? Have you been lurking in their rose garden?"

"Hardly, but Wendy let this slip out on the telephone, when she told Marjorie that she and John would be moving in with Doris to keep each other company. That was two weeks ago. Then she asked Marjorie if I could collect you at the airport today, since it was a Saturday and I'd be off work."

Peter drained his glass of beer and ordered refills from the waitress. "Let's have the other half then," he said. "I can't quite fit all this together. It probably does make sense for the ladies to bunk up together, since Fred and I are mostly away; and it probably makes sense for Fred and Doris to split up if they don't care for each other, but I still don't understand why Doris told Fred she was in love with me—although I suppose I should be somewhat flattered. Perhaps her solicitor has thought up some cunning plan."

The refills arrived, and they clinked another toast, momentarily fascinated by the sight of Peter's seaplane taking off again. It had slowly edged out into the harbor, then turned and roared back toward them to get a lift from the southeasterly breeze. Conversation was impossible, as the large British Sunderland roared overhead.

"It's going back to Nouméa I suppose, or on up to Brisbane," Peter said when the noise had abated. "Well, hopefully Wendy will fill me in when we get home. Thanks ever so much for coming to collect me. How about some fish and chips while we're here?" Ned nodded, and Peter waved to the waitress.

"Ned, are things going well at the Kellogg factory?" Peter asked, at which Ned gave a big smile and thumbs-up sign.

"Oh yes, I absolutely love the job. I have around two hundred people, many of them women, and they are a fine team. I've almost learned to understand their funny Aussie dialect! You must come for a tour one day and bring John along." Peter nodded his agreement, enthusiastically.

"So, what's the war news then?" Ned asked, "You probably get more of it, being around the military people in Nouméa."

"They say Guadalcanal is about over, thank goodness," Peter answered, "and the Yanks have taken over some smaller islands nearby, called the Russells. I met two PT boat skippers on leave in Nouméa last week, who said some of their squadron is moving to the Russells from Tulagi. It must be exciting up there. Bongo told me—oh, you haven't met him yet, he's a Yank Navy friend—he said I could probably get over to Guadalcanal to help build up a new supply base, soon after it's secure. I'll probably be doing some bridge-building, actually."

Ned and Peter chatted a bit more, enjoying the savory codfish with the dregs of their Aussie beer, then decided to head over to the Rose Bay cottage. But just then a dark green C-47 flew in at the landing field outside. It had Red Cross markings, so they decided to watch a bit longer.

The landing field was at an inland edge of the terminal building, perpendicular to the bay but visible from the lounge where the brothers had lunched. They hadn't noticed the ambulances before, but there were five or six of them parked just off the tarmac, awaiting the plane. The drivers and orderlies wore Australian uniforms, and there were a couple of American Red Cross nurses standing with them.

The iconic workhorse C-47 *Dakota* motored over near the waiting ambulances, then cut both engines as the rear door was opened. A small ramp was rolled up to the cargo door, and a crusty-looking Aussie sergeant emerged, to hand out a clipboard to the medical orderly who had mounted the ramp. The orderly waved to the ambulance crews, who queued up at the plane and then slowly four at a time climbed the ramp to enter the sloping fuselage.

The first stretchers appeared and were carefully eased down the steps and over to the nearest vehicle. It soon became obvious that these were serious casualties, mostly with head wounds, too critical to return home on a hospital ship. Each ambulance left once it was loaded with six stretchers, klaxon blaring.

More spectators crowded into the end of the lounge near the Perrys. "Look at the poor blighters, will you? Who are they, then?"

Another man answered: "Seventh AIF Division, back from Papua, some sodding place called Buna. My mate's one of the ambulance drivers; asked me and the missus to come and see this. They don't have the skills to treat the head wounds in Brisbane, so they have to fly the poor lads all the way here from New Guinea. It's a wonder they're still alive."

"These Diggers gave a good account of themselves, so I hear. There'll probably be nothing in the papers about the wounded though. General Blamey isn't keen about publicity that could upset the public."

"Three more plane loads coming this evening,"

"Good on these lads!" someone shouted; "Kept the bloody Nips from getting to Australia, they did." The lounge erupted in applause.

Peter tugged Ned away. "Well, there's the real war news. Damned shame for those chaps, but I need to get to the cottage and see what Wendy has to say about the neighbors. Shall we go?"

*** OBFUSCATION ***

It was the third day of his Sydney leave, and Peter was still somewhat confused about Wendy's behavior. Although she had moved her personal things—and John's—across the street, to keep Doris company during the latter's acrimonious divorce proceedings, Wendy and John had settled back into the cottage for the duration of Peter's leave, and Wendy's reception had been sincerely amorous.

But she was adamant about returning to live with Doris as soon as Peter's leave was over. In fact, she strongly suggested to Peter that they give up the cottage all together and save the rental expense, as she and John could live rent-free across the street. Besides, with the new rules for civilians working at Allied bases in the Pacific, home leave was being changed to one month out of every six, instead of the previous two weeks out of every three months, as the war momentum picked up. This meant Peter would not be back for another half year.

"We could perhaps spend that month traveling Australia," Wendy suggested, "and still not need our own place in Sydney."

"Except," Peter reminded her, "that would be August again, and the schools would still be in session."

"Perhaps Ned and his family would even be interested in taking the cottage," Wendy went on, "which would save Ned the long daily commute from North Sydney to the Kellogg's factory at Botany Bay. Finding a replacement tenant for the landlord would also enable us to recover our security deposit, which we might otherwise forfeit."

It all made sense, Peter told himself—and he promised Wendy to discuss her suggestion with Ned—but he was still uneasy about being named a correspondent in Fred's divorce action against Doris.

Doris had come over to the cottage to apologize for that misleading action on her part, saying she was in love with their neighbor was just something that popped into her head in the heat of the moment, to annoy Fred and get him to leave her alone.

"For simplicity's sake, I promised Fred not to contest his accusation, in return for him signing the house ownership over to me, in lieu of any alimony or support income."

When Wendy took up the same discussion again with Peter that evening, she said that Doris had a small inheritance to live on. "And I would, of course, contribute to the upkeep too."

Like most women in Australia, Peter realized, Doris and Wendy were being pressured to take on some war work activities, which they were actually both looking forward to doing during the time of day that John was in school. They agreed with many of their friends that it was about time women were valued for their contributions to society.

"But what about after the war, Wendy?" Peter had asked. Her reply was part of what unsettled him.

"Doris and I will go into business for ourselves; not manufacturing, but some sort of post-war shop or boutique—or perhaps a design firm. I love Sydney, Peter, and don't ever want to leave here. The climate is divine, the lifestyle is free and open compared to stuffy Singapore and England, and Doris is my very dearest friend. John is growing up nicely and seems to enjoy becoming an Aussie."

Peter knew better than to continue arguing about something as abstract as what to do after the war was over; that point in time seemed years away. Instead, he took John and Digger for a walk down to the bay. He wanted to see some planes coming and going, to get his mind off the present dilemmas. This in turn brought back the image of those poor soldiers being unloaded on stretchers a few days ago. *Compared to them, what do I really have to complain about?*

*** *THE ONI BECKONS* ***

Peter decided to visit Lt. Robert McGowan at the ONI compound, and telephoned to see if it was convenient for him to drop by for a visit.

"Peter, how nice to hear from you! I just finished speaking to Commander Perkins in Queensland, who said I should contact you one of these days to see what you were up to. He thought you must be back in Sydney around this time."

They settled on the next day for Peter's visit, and McGowan promised to 'keep the decks clear' so they could chat.

When Peter arrived at the docks the two frigates were gone, but in their place was a strange-looking large ship with a wide ramp at the stern. Robert McGowan seemed fully recovered from the near fatality in Guadalcanal, when his PBY was jumped by an enemy plane.

"I was extremely lucky, you know, Peter, as almost everyone else aboard was killed. It still gives me nightmares. I haven't told my parents yet, and maybe never will. I was really sorry about the Marine colonel I was riding with, as he was going to take over D2 division intelligence for General Vandegrift. ONI had a lot invested in that poor fellah."

Picking up on McGowan's clipped accent, Peter asked: "Where do you hail from then, Robert? I've never thought to ask you before. Are your parents retired yet?" Peter gratefully accepted the proffered coffee cup, the lifeblood of the ONI, apparently.

"I'm from the east coast, like Commander Perkins, though in my case it's not Boston but a tiny town called Bath, in a tiny state called Maine that you've probably never heard of. We build ships there for the Navy and others, and my dad is a foreman at the Bath Iron Works, nowhere near retirement. I couldn't conceive of going anywhere else to college than the

Naval Academy, and Dad luckily got an appointment for me from our state congressman."

"Yes, I remember Bongo mentioning you were at the academy, when we met in Nouméa aboard that old flagship of Admiral Ghormley's. That's quite interesting, as I learned quite a bit about the Coast Guard Academy at New London, Connecticut, when I was sailing to Hawaii aboard one of their ships. They must offer similar educations, I suppose."

"Well yes, but somewhat different maritime traditions. We train for war and they train for peace, in a manner of speaking. There's also a Merchant Marine Academy up east, at Kings Point, New York, which teaches a lot of naval tradition too. All three institutions require congressional appointments, just as the Army does for its West Point Academy in New York."

"What about the Marines then? Do they attend West Point with the Army? They seem to fight the same sort of battles."

"Oh, heavens no!" McGowan replied in mock horror. "Marines go through the Naval Academy, of course. How else could we communicate with them? Isn't it the same way in Britain with the Royal Marines?" Peter confessed that he didn't know that answer but would investigate.

The telephone rang on McGowan's desk. He answered it smartly, then passed the receiver to Peter. "It's for you, Peter. He says it's your nephew calling."

Bongo was brief, and hardly allowed Peter more than a grunt in reply. Peter alternatively smiled or rolled his eyes until the conversation ended, then passed the phone back to McGowan, grinning.

"He says you're to invite me to lunch and tell me about something called *Cartwheel*. Also, he's coming to Nouméa a week after I get back there, and—oh yes—I'm to stay the hell away from nurse Ellie. Good grief, I didn't know she was back in Nouméa, but I do know another nurse who can fill me in about her."

"OK then, Peter, we'd better talk privately about *Operation Cartwheel* here in the shop, before we go outside for lunch," McGowan said. "It's a really big hush-hush program to push the Japs completely out of New Guinea and the Solomons, shut down Rabaul, and then roll clear on through the Marianas and Philippines. Could take 18 months. Your favorite nephew is one of the planning links between General MacArthur and Admiral Halsey, and he was with them both at a meeting last week in Brisbane. Here, let me show you some maps."

*** *BUILDING BRIDGES WITH ABBY* ***

Peter's two-week leave came to an end, not smoothly and quickly like the first one, but somewhat bedraggled this time.

John had been in school most days, so except for one Saturday at Bondi Beach, there was no real opportunity to get away with the family and do anything special during the balmy summer weather. He dreaded the thought of another holiday like that—especially twice as lengthy—when he returned in August.

Everyone else would be occupied; Wendy and little John, Ned and his family, and of course the ONI. What was the point of a month off like that? And actually, he was also growing bored with the civil engineering work he was doing for the Seabees and the construction office. Peter wanted some excitement for a change, something to remind him of the scintillating days when he had first come out from England to Singapore via Suez, Aden, and Penang to see the Far East firsthand.

His thoughts turned to Bongo, who had revealed similarly adventurous longings after he got the appointment as MacArthur's naval liaison in Brisbane. They needed to talk!

In spite of his frustrations, the flight from Sydney back to Nouméa was fine. Peter was fascinated to see, from the seaplane porthole, the southern part of the main Caledonian island, *Grande Terre*, come slowly into view, with its enchanting coastline and mountainous interior. He could pick out some familiar spots around Nouméa this time, as the plane settled down onto the calm harbor and chugged over to the ramp at *l'île Nou*.

Andrew Culver was there, greeting the passengers with a cheery smile. Adding a sly wink, he passed a small envelope to Peter, which turned out to be a brief note from Abby inviting him to visit her at the nurses' lounge one evening soon.

Peter warmed to the suggestion, as the stalwart old PANAIR launch took the passengers over to the pontoon boat dock at Nouméa's shore. *This is such a charming city*, Peter thought to himself. *If only I could manage to learn French*. Three days later, Peter had the answer, or thought he did.

"Peter, are you listening? Did you hear what I said?" Ensign Abby Culver Hobbs of Fall River, Massachusetts, tugged at the sleeve of visiting Englishman, Peter Perry of Bolton, Lancashire, lately of Singapore and Canton Island, who sat staring at nothing, with a silly smile on his face.

"Peter, please, are you interested or not? We could take the French course together in the evenings at the USO—Tuesdays and Thursdays. A few of the other girls are interested too. Peter, are you there? Hello?"

Abby's voice finally penetrated Peter's semi-somnambulant state.

"Oh sorry, my mind must have wandered, Abby," Peter finally said. "What a brilliant idea! Yes, let us sign up immediately. Absolutely brilliant. I just hope I can cope with the class, as I don't seem to have an ear for languages."

"Well, I'll help you learn, you can be sure of that," Abby said in a soft voice, holding Peter's hand. We could even practice after class."

Peter's silly smile returned, and just then a familiar face moved into his peripheral vision at their little corner table in the lounge. Peter stood up at once, recognizing the lovely features and lilting accents of Nurse Ellie Norbush.

"Whah Peetuh, whut a playzuh tuh see yuh heah agayun. Ah'm souw glayad tuh bee bahyak in Nooomeeyah. Ah gayuss yuh know thet Bongow wiyell bee heah ohn Sunday, rahyat?"

"Oh Ellie, how wonderful to see you again. I heard you were back here and did so look forward to seeing you. Yes, Bongo told me he would be here on the weekend to see you, but I'll be unable to catch him this time. You do know Miss Culver, I presume? We're about to take a French course together."

"Shooah ah doo know Abby. How ahr yuh, shoogah?" Abby stood, and they gave each other a cursory hug.

"Good heavens," Peter exclaimed, "I just realized that I understood everything you said, Ellie!"

The girls laughed, and Ellie added: "Weyul Peetuh, yoo jes maht payus thuh Frayunch coorse ayftuh awl."

Peter blushed, and Abby glowered at her colleague as Ellie departed. "Peter, you'd best keep away from that silly Southern show-off!"

Peter basked in the unaccustomed attention he was receiving that evening. On his way to the BOQ from the nurses' quarters, he vowed again that he would master the French language. It couldn't be all that hard. After all, he had mastered mathematics, hadn't he?

*** *A BRIDGE TOO FAR* ***

After getting approval from Ronald Beamish to sign over his completed sewage project to the advance Marine liaison party, Peter plunged into his new work at their camp with gusto. He had a working party of Marines and civilians to assist him. The hilly site, crossed by numerous ravines, was not far to the north of Nouméa—about halfway to the big new army airfield at Tontouta—and was ideal for training the expected Sherman tank companies that would be arriving soon from California.

The plan was for half a dozen beam-type wooden bridges to be constructed, so the tanks could cross the steep valleys at the campsite, and maneuver into the hinterlands. Several different bridge variations were to be evaluated, to see which would be best for the forward campaign areas on other islands in terms of available materials, soil conditions, and speed of construction. After evaluation by the tankers in Nouméa, the results would be sent to the Seabees for their guidance in the upper Solomons.

The first such beam bridge, a deck truss design, would span a small gorge of twenty meters width and fifty meters depth. It was likely to encounter a maximum load of about one hundred tons, in the event that three 34-ton Sherman tanks were stalled out on the span for whatever reason. Peter therefore designed the bridge to support five hundred tons, following the usual four-to-one safety factor, including the weight of the span itself.

With procurement of the specified timber beams, construction of this initial span took five weeks. Peter realized that was far too long to be practical in a war zone, but he reckoned the assembly could be shortened to two weeks, or even less, if cutting and lifting equipment, and all materials—including tempered fasteners—were available in advance, and if the construction crew had sufficient training.

The first little bridge, when completed, built with stained hardwood from the local forests, looked quite handsome and utilitarian with its under-deck truss and a pedestrian handrail. It was crossed over repeatedly by the camp's six-ton trucks, often with a driver's wave to Peter if he happened to be standing nearby. Peter felt proud to be part of the training team for the Marines, and he was amused at some of the earthy vocabulary and raw jokes that he had acquired from them. He began to feel content again, and glad he was finished with the monotonous sewage and water treatment projects.

He was working on a second beam-type bridge design in a field office tent at the Marine camp, this time a through-truss version for greater span length, when an orderly brought a TWX message from Ronald Beamish, directing Peter to the contractor's office right away. Curious, he carefully put away his drafting instruments and reference books and checked out a jeep for the run into Nouméa.

Down at the harbor, near the NATS boat dock that he had often visited when Hans and Ralph were still around, Peter parked at the busy warehouse that served as the contractor's depot. He was quite unprepared for the surprise announcement that Beamish made.

"Mr. Perry, we've just had a set-back to our plans for the Marine camp development. I'm afraid there'll be no more wooden bridges, apart from the first one that you so admirably completed."

"But why?" Peter said, crestfallen.

"Lack of funds, primarily," was the reply. "With the crash programs on Espiritu Santo, and soon the development of an advanced base on Guadalcanal, we and the Seabees have outrun—hopefully temporarily—the funding that the American congress has authorized.

"The tanks will be arriving here in August, as scheduled, but will simply be parked at the campsite until they are needed elsewhere, with no live firing or maneuvers at all on New Caledonia. But don't worry, Mr. Perry, you'll get your bridges eventually—on Guadalcanal in about four or five months, before any M4 tanks arrive there!"

"Oh, I see, well that's somewhere I'd been hoping to visit anyway," Peter said. "although I suppose the weather will be a bit warmer than Nouméa."

"That is probably an understatement, and there is a lot of malaria in the Solomons, so do be very careful about mosquitos."

"I shall," Peter promised. "But what now? What should I do for the next four or five months? And another question: who are the Marines that are now moving into the camp? I see a lot of older officers among them."

Beamish chuckled and lit a pipe. "The tankers won't be very happy when they arrive, but they have been usurped and will be banished to a former Raider camp, miles away in the interior, with even more hilly country. They shall have to leave their beloved tanks behind, however, parked at your present campsite, which is about to become the HQ for a new organization known as IMAC, to which the tankers belong although they probably don't know it yet.

"It must be your exquisite plumbing and water treatment facilities that lured the IMAC brass to this particular site, that is so convenient to Nouméa and Admiral Halsey's headquarters."

Beamish chuckled again, then shrugged. "Mr. Perry, I think we'd like you to visit Espiritu Santo for a while. How would you feel about that?"

There goes my French class, there goes Nouméa, and worse than that, there goes Abby, Peter realized. "Right, Mr. Beamish, when would I need to leave?"

*** *SANTO AFTER ALL* ***

As Peter walked thoughtfully back to the parking area, he heard a car horn being tooted nearby, and looked up to see if it was meant for him. It was. He broke into a grin briefly as he saw the Navy staff car blocking his way, an unflappable Bongo seated in the rear, looking pointedly at his watch. Peter sauntered over to the car, trying his best to look bored. Bongo lowered the window.

"None of that, now, Limey plumber. You've already wasted half my morning after I finally found out where you were hiding. Your friends inside must be quite talkative. How are you, pal? Hop in, I'll give you a lift to your Quonset."

"Kind of you, but I have to return that jeep," Peter answered, pointing across the parking zone. "Look, why don't you let me drive you around and show you what I've been up to? Then I can extend the jeep checkout, and drop you at your secret skullduggery center later, wherever that is. We could even eat at the camp if you don't mind Marine Corps food—chow, I think it's called."

"Well, why not; it's a nice day." Bongo spoke to the driver, who hopped out and opened his door. Bongo was wearing khakis and no tie, not

179

quite the Aloha Class-C of yesteryear but suitable enough for Nouméa. He returned the yeoman's salute, and then joined Peter in the jeep. As Peter swung the vehicle north onto the airport road, Bongo lost no time updating him.

"Look, Limey pal, first things first—rugby! Some Aussies and Kiwis are getting up a game this Saturday—or a match, as you call it. It will be way the heck up north, past Tontouta, but we can get there in about an hour and a half. It starts at ten, so I could pick you up around eight at your mess hall, then we can go by for the girls. How about it?"

"The girls? What girls?" Peter laughed, gearing the jeep down as an MP waved the traffic around a broken-down bus.

"Don't give me that crap, Mister Engineer. Girls, they are those soft round things you dream about sometimes. And I happen to know from Miss Ellie that you have been seen in the nurses' lounge on several occasions. Hmmm?"

"Well, yes, that's true," Peter confessed, bringing the jeep back up toward highway speed. "You see, I was about to start taking French lessons in a class with one of the nurses, who by the way is Lieutenant Culver's elder sister, that's all." Peter concentrated on his driving as Bongo laughed, holding onto his hat as the jeep gained speed.

Peter shouted against the wind: "Actually I'm supposed to work on Saturdays, but as I've just been fired, more or less, I suppose I do have this Saturday off, not to mention all the other days that follow. So, alright, let's watch the rugby match. I assume you'll organize 'the girls'?"

"You bet; and a picnic lunch too. Uncle Sam's Navy is famous for exquisite cuisine, as you probably know. Anyway, what's this about you being fired? How the hell did you manage that?"

Peter slowed the jeep and turned off at the road to the Marine camp. "Bongo, this hilly area is where I've been working since well before my last leave in Sydney. It was supposed to be the camp for a Marine tank battalion that is coming in a few months. I put in the water treatment system last year and was getting ready to build half a dozen bridges among the hills so the tankers could wander about with their Shermans and fire away in the hinterland, and meanwhile test out the bridges to see which types best lend themselves to kitting up for Guadalcanal and other islands." Peter paused at the security gate, as the sentry saluted Bongo and waved them in.

"Actually, I did complete one small bridge already; I'll show it to you. Well, they seem to have run out of money for more bridges, and meanwhile some organization called IMAC has commandeered the camp as its headquarters. No more money, no more bridges, and no more work for me in Nouméa. They want to send me to Santo for a while, then perhaps the Canal. Long story, eh?" Peter drove on while Bongo mulled over the news.

"Here you are then, secret agent," said Peter. "The first and last tank bridge in Nouméa." They drove halfway across and looked down at the ravine.

"Well, crap," Bongo finally uttered, peering at the truss below. "A nice construction job, Peter, but a crappy outcome. Sorry about that. No one's fault, I guess. It's not even a genuine snafu, just the breaks of the game. What will they have you do on Santo?"

"No earthly idea," Peter answered. "Could be any number of things, I suppose. I'm sorry to lose the chance to learn French, though, not that I'd have gone far with it, but I was really getting to like Nouméa."

"And the nurses' quarters too," Bongo smiled. "Well, Luganville on Santo is a frenchy town too, y'know, though a much more primitive place."

Another jeep stopped off the road behind, with a beep of the horn. Peter put his in gear and started forward, but the other one beeped again, longer and louder. The driver waved at Peter to back up. When the two vehicles were side by side, the other driver, a Marine corporal, dismounted and said:

"Beg pardon Mr. Perry, and Commander," saluting Bongo, "Colonel Twining's compliments, sir. I'm his orderly. The colonel would like to invite both gentlemen to his office for some Irish coffee and a short discussion, if that would be convenient, sir."

Peter glanced at Bongo, who smiled his agreement. "Thank you, Corporal, that would be a pleasure. Please lead the way and we shall follow you," Peter confirmed.

Trailing behind the lead jeep, and coughing along some dusty tracks leading toward a faraway side of the camp, they parked together in front of a large camouflaged tent, where a handsome red sign with gold lettering and the Marine Corps crest proclaimed:

Headquarters Commanding General
First Marine Amphibious Corps

A trim lieutenant colonel in Marine dungarees stepped out of the tent, dismissing his orderly with a respectful nod, and shaking hands with Bongo and Peter in turn as they climbed out of their vehicle.

"Merrill Twining, gentlemen. C3 Operations for IMAC. Generals Vogel and Brewster are in town with Admiral Halsey at the moment, so I was hoping we could chat together while time permits. Sergeant-of-the-Guard reported a naval person aboard, with a civilian driver."

"That's us, colonel," Bongo responded. "My name is Perkins, and this here Englishman is Peter Perry, lately of Singapore, who was showing me his new bridge design for the Marine Corps."

"And Commander, what is your naval occupation, may I ask?" There was no doubting the expectation of an honest reply from Bongo, whose rank was equivalent to the Marine lieutenant colonel, but whose unannounced presence on a semi-secret Marine Corps facility bordered on trespass. It would do no good to blame it all on Peter, Bongo knew, who apparently didn't realize he had erred. Nonetheless, Bongo didn't want to reveal his role with MacArthur's staff, or especially with the ONI, so his opening gambit was to test the waters.

"Well sir, I'm sort of a roaming troubleshooter from Pearl," Bongo tried on for size. "Just making sure our civilian contractors are working out to everyone's satisfaction. Have only just arrived. Sorry not to have called in advance, but I'm very glad to make your acquaintance now that we're here."

"Bullshit, Commander, what a load of crap. I've seen Mr. Perry around here for the past several weeks, but because he is held in high esteem by our Marines I'm not going to write up this little breach of protocol on his and your part. But I'm sure you Pearl Harbor Navy fellows know there's a war on, and security is what keeps us safe, even here in the rear echelons. OK, step into my office and you'll get your reward for not hassling my orderly when he brought you."

*** *NATS TO YOU, MISTER* ***

A week later, Peter talked Bongo into riding the PANAIR launch over to *l'île Nou* with him, both to see him off to Espiritu Santo, and also to greet Lt. Commander Mike Osborn, who had been their companion during the wild Fiji evening with Kiwi Colonel McKee back at Lauthala Bay, another lifetime ago.

Osborn was now in charge of NATS Nouméa. His assistant, Andrew Culver, was also in evidence, with his famous Hollywood salute, as Bongo and Peter stepped onto the boat dock.

"Well done, former-Ensign Culver," Bongo growled, "you're staying in shape I see. Well, it seems everyone has come up in the world since we first knew each other a year ago, myself included. Ha, only civilians fall behind in wartime, eh Mr. Perry?"

Peter nodded vigorously. "Glad someone understands at last!"

Mike Osborn appeared just then, beaming at seeing his old companions. "You're probably wondering about the Overwoods, correct? Come inside and I'll bring you up to date. Lieutenant, will you watch the counter please?" Culver delivered a snappy salute; Bongo rolled his eyes.

"The Overwoods appear to be in fairly good shape now," Osborn related, "after their bad experience with the Jap submarine. Graham especially is looking and feeling quite fit, but Lois less so. She seems to have some lingering debilitation, but nevertheless they are both working in Suva and only visit *Zanzibar* on occasion, having left the ketch on a mooring buoy off Nukulau's settlement.

"One thing they really long for," Osborn continued, "is for you both to return and spend some time with them, especially Peter who shared their life on Canton Island. I used to see them probably once a month, and that is what they always said. Graham hoped I might find you here in Nouméa one day; he gave me this for you, Peter, in case that should happen."

He handed Peter a small brown envelope of the sort that stamp collectors use. Inside was a little slip of paper with one word scrawled on it; *Naburo?* Peter passed the note to Bongo, who nodded.

"So how come you were transferred to Nouméa, Osborn?" Bongo asked, to change the subject. "Did you get bored with that fine old hotel?"

"And the surly Tamil staff, you mean. They kept thinking there'd be a Jap invasion any day, and they would have the chance to help kick out the whites from Fiji. Well, the US Army has just taken over Fiji security from the Kiwis—it's the Americal Division that wrapped up Guadalcanal—and they won't put up with the Tamil crap for long. The regiment in charge of the Suva region is the famous 164th that was on Guadalcanal the longest; they even have a regimental band." That brought a smile from Bongo, the sometime musician.

"But the reason I'm here is that I got a promotion, and supposedly outgrew the Fiji job. It's considered a notch below Nouméa because there's less traffic, and therefore less to worry about—apart from the Tamils that is! Gee, it's good to see you two again; what a great part of the world, eh? I wouldn't mind returning here to Nouméa after the war."

The inbound seaplane from Sydney splashed down on the harbor and nosed over to the ramp, so Peter prepared to depart while the plane was being refueled. Before saying goodbye to Bongo and Mike, he strolled to where Lt. Culver was preparing the onward manifest for Luganville, and sailors were loading a launch with passenger bags.

"Andrew, thanks for everything. Look, please tell Abby I'll miss her and will write soon. We had a lovely conversation last Saturday at a rugby-and-picnic day up the coast. I'm very sorry about my sudden change of plans, as I was quite looking forward to learning a bit of French with her kind assistance and getting to know her better. Your sister is a fine person."

"We understand, Peter; not to worry. Just take care of yourself on Santo. Abby and I will both miss you." The special Culver salute pleased Peter immensely.

*** OFF TO LUGANVILLE ***

The NATS flight to Luganville crossed the parallel central spines of New Caledonia's mountains, flying northeast. Then there was a long patch of open sea, during which Peter half dozed while running the events of the past week through his mind. He was excited about his recent private discussion with Bongo, who would be visiting Eric Feldt—the coastwatcher chief—at long last. Bongo would look for something temporary to do in that line of work, not only for himself but perhaps for Peter too if the civilian status was not a problem. Peter was ready for some excitement, and apparently Bongo was also. He had mentioned several times that Lt. Robert McGowan was about ready to take over his administrative liaison duties in Brisbane.

Then there was Abby. During the picnic last weekend, she had revealed her recent history of being widowed when her husband, a merchant mariner, was lost on Atlantic convoy duty. He had been a high school sweetheart, and nearly lifelong friend since elementary school. Abby had kept her grief bottled up inside, until Andrew gradually persuaded her to join the Navy as a nurse, knowing she could still—at that point in time—specify where she would like to be assigned, such as one of the Nouméa mobile hospitals.

Abby was very grateful to Andrew for his thoughtfulness, since he instinctively knew that an intriguing foreign environment like New Caledonia would appeal to her love of languages. She was fairly steady in French from high school, she told Peter, but even before that she had picked up a working knowledge of street Portuguese from her mother's cook.

Fall River, Massachusetts, a two-hour drive from Boston, contained a large Portuguese population and fishing colony that was also involved with running an ocean ferry service to Long Island. This efficient service provided an alternative way for people to travel between Boston and New York, that many preferred over the railroad, and of course air travel was only for the very wealthy. The Culver hometown was therefore more international than many other places along the East Coast, apart from New York City. Abby was eager to learn more about the world—including the personal interests of polite English engineers around her age, even though one in particular would be leaving for Espiritu Santo shortly.

Peter had promised to write Abby after settling into Luganville, he reminded himself as he watched the changing view from his starboard-side porthole. A large green landscape gradually appeared below the aircraft, then disappeared again as the plane nosed down to settle amongst a collection of anchored Navy ships and smaller islands. He realized, for next time, that the other side of the plane would be better for a view of Luganville town.

Much to his delight, Peter discovered the flight was being met by Hans Lazet, who was standing near the ramp with an attractive woman whose light brown coloring identified her as a Euronesian from somewhere else. Hans was attired in his usual, but cleanest set of work clothes, and his pretty companion wore a colorful flowered skirt with a white, short-sleeved blouse. The climate was noticeably warmer than Nouméa, but not uncomfortable.

"Peter, welcome to Luganville. I wish to introduce my fiancée, *Madame* Yvonne Bardot. Yvonne, this Englishman is Peter Perry, an old colleague from Nouméa."

"Well what a pleasure, *Madame*; and Hans, what a surprise to learn you're going to be married! Congratulations to you both. When is the big date?"

"Ha!" exclaimed Yvonne before Hans could reply. "If we live that long, it will not be until the war is over, just in case something happens to one of us in the meantime. I am happy to meet you, Mister Englishman. You are a good man in the eyes of my Dutchman husband-to-be, and that is very important. Please call me Yvonne and consider yourself part of our international family."

"Yes, Peter," Hans added, "and I am wishing you could act the best man for this wedding. That is, if you can appear in Luganville after the war. I myself am not ever going to leave this place. When my contract work is over, I will start a construction and maintenance company for Espiritu Santo, with Philippe—the brother of Yvonne—as partner, and stay here forever. We will be having plenty of business. You must please come for dinner tomorrow, for meeting this brother and the nice children of Yvonne who will become my stepchildren. We are all happy with this plan, except the young ones they say I must hurry and learn French and Bishama. They are quite correct."

"Bravo Hans and Yvonne, I would love to visit tomorrow, provided they don't intend to send me to some remote worksite right away. I will have to check with our local contract office in the morning, assuming you know where it is and where I'll be sleeping tonight. I too was going to start taking a French course in Nouméa, by the way, but this sudden transfer to Santo of course scuttled that idea."

"Then, my good friend, you must come to the class I joined only two weeks ago. It is teaching basic French. There are also students from the American Navy, and the instructor she is very good,"—smiling at Yvonne, who was clearly the instructor—"and the price it is very reasonable!"

"Spoken like a true Dutchman," Peter laughed. "Well, that sounds like a perfect plan. How about Ralph; is he still around?"

"Oh yes, but he temporary is away to Efaté. When they did learn about his tarmac-knowing, they want him to teach how to make good roads at Port Vila, the capital. But you will see Ralph soon. He must return here in some few weeks, then go to Australia on leave again. He was there in November, a month after you. Now the rule is every six months, no longer three months, do you know?"

Peter nodded that he knew about the change: "Well, Hans, can you please show me where my quarters are?"

*** THE GRAND TOUR ***

Peter was astonished the following day at the immensity of the development on Espiritu Santo, in what Hans said had been less than a year's time. The little francophone village of Luganville was completely dwarfed by Allied military activity. Hans took him for an extensive tour, including some of Ralph's new roads, most of the airfields, and the harbor facilities. There were four Seabee battalions hard at work, and two more coming soon, Hans explained.

It was late May 1943, and the New Georgia campaign had just begun in the Solomons, aiming to push the Japs back up the Slot. There were many daily bomber and fighter sorties from Santo, and a steady movement of ships in the Segond Channel. Like Nouméa, there seemed to be huge tank farms and hundreds of the curved Quonset huts everywhere. What a clever invention, Peter thought; if already assembled, they could even be nested for transportation.

Peter was also shown the big site—still under construction—for Base Hospital Three, which was planned as much to deal with the growing level of tropical diseases as to treat the actual wounded. Santo itself was not malaria free either, so its hospitals would have to be carefully controlled. In the meanwhile, early casualties from New Georgia were being taken to Nouméa by ship, until Santo was ready to take on its big share. Peter imagined Abby was keeping busy.

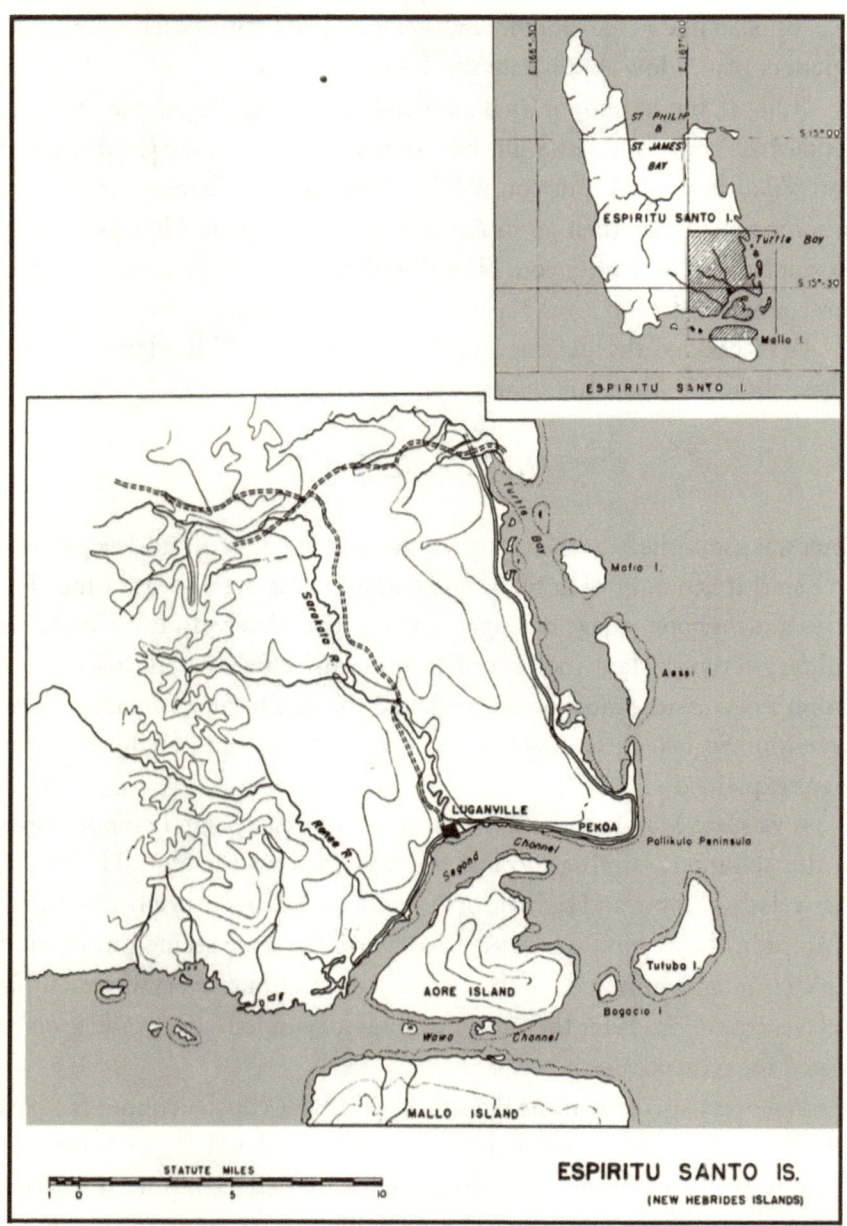

(https://www.ibiblio.org/hyperwar/USN/Building
Bases/maps/bases2-p229.jpg)

Whoever had told him that Luganville was more primitive than Nouméa—perhaps Bongo—was guilty of a gross understatement. Luganville was a ramshackle, though colorful place, like an old Caribbean town. It had a small rudimentary dock for exporting copra, the chief product of the large island.

Cotton growing had been tried for a while, too, but failed. Then cattle ranching was started successfully before the war broke out, but now the Navy commandeered one hundred percent of all available beef, so there was still little need to expand the civilian dock. Other commercial businesses included coffee, cacao, and hardwoods, but again, the Navy was basically the only customer that counted. A few new developments, like Philippe Orly's vegetable farms for the Navy, became additional captive suppliers.

"We are not really using Old Luganville for anything, do you see?" Hans told Peter during their jeep tour. "It is too much cramped and disorganized, so we more or less are building this new command post and civic center for the Navy their base, with a wide highway in the middle, and Old Luganville it is left alone. We are expecting a population maybe fifty thousand for working on the base, and probably ten times more as patients, front line troops, or replacements.

"See the big docks we are building. This is where I do my work," Hans said proudly. "Look, there is one Liberty ship from yesterday, and more of them in the channel. And over there we have the floating dry dock, even so large for repairing a heavy cruiser."

He drove on by the docks and finally turned eastward past the seaplane base and PT Boats, then further along the Segond Channel shore toward what he said would become the newest airfield, called Pekoa. Almost in view of the open sea, Hans turned carefully down from the 'tarred MacAdam' road, onto a bumpy track that led toward the channel shore and reef, displaying a few illegible yellow and black signs.

"Peter, in Nouméa were you hearing about the SS *President Coolidge*?" Peter shook his head. "No, I don't think so, Hans. What about it?"

"Not the good story, more like some disaster. The USA they charter this big luxury liner *President Coolidge*, really nice, to use for troopship. It did take some Army troops to Australia last year March, then it did come to Santo this October from San Francisco, with five thousand more troops, and did try to enter the channel right there"—pointing toward the ocean—"but the ship her captain he is not told by Navy that they did place a minefield outside the channel, so the ship she strike some mines—BOOM—and start to sink. I myself did see this happen from far away in hills with Yvonne and Philippe their family."

"My word, that certainly was a disaster. Then what happened?" "Peter, that ship captain, he is very good man. He is bringing the sinking ship right over here to this reef shore where we are now, so everyone they can get off safe, but the heavy ship she is not stable on reef. Soon she does slide under water, and still she is down there now. Beside soldiers, this big ship did carry many vehicles, heavy weapons, ammo, machinery, supplies, and the people all their personal things. Everything is lost." Hans parked the jeep right at the channel's edge.

"Admiral Halsey, he very angry and call for inquiry. Navy does try blame ship captain, instead to thank him for life saving, but he is found innocent and Navy is found guilty. Some Navy people here they are sent away, but nobody is punished, I think. What you call a big SNOWFOW, no?"

Peter laughed and corrected his friend: "SNAFU, Hans, SNAFU, and certainly one of the biggest I've heard of so far! I must ask Commander Perkins what he knows about this. Remember him from Nouméa? Certainly, the ship's captain should get a medal."

*** NEGRO TROOPS ON SANTO ***

Peter soon learned that the US Army Corps of Engineers was helping to develop Santo on a temporary basis, in conjunction with the Seabees. A couple of weeks after his delightful welcome dinner with Yvonne and the others at Philippe Orly's home, Peter told Hans that he had been assigned to work with the Army Engineers on a large water treatment plant, which Hans was pleased to hear.

"There's certainly no shortage of fresh water here," said Peter, referring to the rivers and almost daily rains, "but we need to start collecting it for the large population that Santo is starting to see."

His Army liaison for the water projects was Major Elias Crighton of Flagstaff, Arizona, with whom Peter got on very well and soon developed

190

an after-hours friendship. One day when work was over, Peter and "El", as the major liked to be called, were downing a few cold beers in the O-Club. Peter decided to put forth a question that he had been holding back out of politeness.

"Elias ... El, I noticed driving over to one of the airfields that the Army has negro troops working here. Um, isn't that somewhat unusual? Are the troops from America? I don't mean to be rude; am just curious. You remember, I told you about my working with Army Engineers on Canton Island, but I saw no negroes in their group."

"That's a very good question, Peter, and by the way I understand they now prefer to be called 'colored people' rather than negroes—and certainly never that other word that starts with 'n.' But, yes, it is quite unusual to come across colored people in the Army, and I suppose it's very strange to see them here in a foreign place. You know I come from Arizona, right? It was not one of the Civil War states, so people there don't carry the deep prejudice that those unfortunate people face in some other parts of the United States, where they are called pretty awful names. But I can tell you, they are looked down upon all over our fair land, although more so in the south than anywhere else."

Peter listened intently as El continued: "I don't know why it is, but we just grew up with the idea that they are inferior by birth, and therefore they should be segregated in everything they do. Maybe they *are* inferior, like people say, 'cause the few that I've met don't seem too bright. Anyway, they live in separate barracks here on Santo, and likewise back in New Caledonia where this Company B of the 810th Engineers came from.

"They have their own mess hall too, and until this week they always had white officers to look after them. Now there are two black lieutenants, the first such in their entire battalion, so I'm told. If you like, I'll introduce you one day. I know their company commander, a white man of course, who says the new officers are OK guys, and so are the troops for that matter. They are helping the Seabees to build airfields."

"Oh, that might be quite interesting. Yes, I would like to meet the new arrivals, if you would be so kind. Another beer before we dine?"

"No thanks, Peter. I'm pretty hungry already. But OK then, I'll see what I can set up in the way of a meeting. I imagine the new officers would rather meet in town than here at the club. That OK with you?"

"Certainly," Peter replied. "There's actually a fairly decent eatery in Old Luganville that a Dutch friend showed me. It's called *Le Petit Palais*, if you can understand my bad pronunciation. I was invited to join a French class but decided not to, because I'll only be here a few months."

Elias laughed at that: "I should take a class myself; we all should. By the way, I'm enjoying working on the treatment plant with you, Peter. If we don't quite finish by the time you go on leave, then my guys can certainly wrap it up soon after."

*** HOSPITAL SHIPS ***

Peter, who was of course writing regularly to Wendy, was also keeping in touch with Abby in Nouméa as he had promised. Abby's recent letter mentioned a hospital ship, from the New Georgia campaign in the Solomons, having arrived at Nouméa, bringing a few hundred wounded men to the MOB hospital tents. They were unloaded down at the old city passenger pier, many on stretchers, not far from the park where she and Andrew had met Peter on New Year's Day. Abby had been among the nurses who helped get them into ambulances, and later she met some of the men during her hospital rounds.

Apparently, this group of wounded had been cursorily examined and more or less stabilized, at either Banika Island in the Russells or else Guadalcanal, which still had only a rudimentary field hospital and first aid station. In only a few cases had there been sufficient debridement—the removal of dead tissue—before the men were released for the ocean voyage, and as a result their healing process was longer than it should have been. A few of the wounded were Marine Raiders or Navy, but most were Army.

Then a few days later in June, Peter received Wendy's weekly letter on a similar, though even more disheartening topic. A northbound Australian hospital ship, the *Centaur*, was torpedoed and sunk off the coast of Queensland the night of May fourteenth, and the news had been suppressed by the Australian government for more than a week. Wendy included a recent newspaper clipping. People were enraged by Japan's uncivilized act of sinking a fully illuminated hospital ship, and further annoyed by the Curtin government's decision to hold back the bad news as long as possible.

When the *Centaur*'s S.O.S. was received, several ships had converged at the site, including a destroyer searching with asdic (British sonar) for the submarine, but 268 people had died including 11 of 12 nurses aboard. The *Centaur* was bound for Port Moresby to bring back wounded from the Papua campaign. Recruitment posters all over Australia shouted AVENGE THE NURSES, Wendy had added.

Those two letters heightened Peter's awareness of the risks that unarmed hospital ships faced, and the bravery of the crews that manned them and the medical staff who accompanied them. He imagined the anxieties that immobilized and half-dead patients underwent before, during, and after a perilous voyage. Peter knew the first big hospital on Santo would be opening next month, so there would no doubt be hospital ships in the Segond Channel as the Central Solomons campaign heated up—*Operation Cartwheel*, he remembered.

Before Peter left Nouméa, Bongo had added further details to what Lt. McGowan said about *Cartwheel* in Sydney. The gist was that the New Georgia campaign was under Admiral Halsey's overall command, with the objective of stabilizing the Central Solomons. The main objective was the large island of New Georgia, where a Japanese airfield had been discovered at Munda Point, the plantation site of a former Roman Catholic mission.

The airfield had been cunningly developed underneath the cutaway leafy tops of coconut palms suspended from cables, and was almost completed when an alert photo-analyst on Guadalcanal noticed the build-up of coral tailings, and the change in shadows from one day to the next.

Bongo said capturing Munda was essential to eliminate more Japanese bombing of Guadalcanal so that civilians could be brought there to work, Peter included. Taking Munda would not only clear the way for Guadalcanal to become a major new support base, but the captured, clandestine airfield would be most useful for stifling enemy resistance to a northward Allied incursion into Bougainville, which was the key to neutralizing Rabaul.

"Ground forces for this stage of *Cartwheel* were commanded by the IMAC organization that had commandeered the Marine camp near Nouméa, that you helped develop," Bongo reminded Peter. "Remember

Colonel Twining's Irish coffee that funny day in May? I imagine he had a good hand in the Munda planning."

But time dragged on in the New Georgia campaign. The 4th of July 1943 came and went—with lots of baseball and picnics around the South Pacific—but the Munda airfield was not captured until August.

Even to reach that point, there had been much heavy fighting with unexpected losses. Numerous bombardments, and almost continuous Allied raids by day (Marines and Navy) and by night (NZ 'Black Cats') had been needed to support two incompletely trained Army divisions of the XIV Corps in their slow jungle advances. Before it was over, the neighboring island of Rendova was captured by the Allies as a springboard, and Marines were still waiting for transportation to take Vella Lavella and cut off Japanese reinforcements. Two steps forward; one step back.

By this time, newly promoted Lt. General Vandegrift, hero of Guadalcanal, was slated to become Commandant of the Marine Corps in January '44. He had temporarily stood in for Lt. Gen. Vogel at Halsey's insistence, to breathe some life into IMAC's erratic progress. Now on Guadalcanal, New Zealand forces began to take over operations of the expanding new support base from the US military.

*** *A NIGHT IN LUGANVILLE* ***

Over on Santo around that time, Peter and Elias collected one of the negro second lieutenants, Thaddeus Jones, for a meal at *Le Petit Palais*, but Jones' colleague didn't want to come along. Peter had also arranged for Hans and Yvonne to meet at the bistro, to help create a friendly atmosphere for the discussion. It worked out well, and the evening was mostly relaxed and enjoyable.

Yvonne, herself part Polynesian, was particularly interested in talking to an American negro, whom she was no doubt evaluating with regard to the indigenous dark-skinned Melanesians of Santo. Everyone had lots of questions for Thad, the name by which he introduced himself, once the initial awkward greetings were past and the obvious topic was broached. Some good food and wine helped shed collective inhibitions.

"Yes, we colored folks feel downtrodden at home in the States," was the gist of Thad's thesis, "and in some ways even more so here in the Army—sorry for saying that, Major."

El smiled and waved a hand for Thad to carry on freely, in confidence. "We're off duty, Jones, no problem. Speak your mind."

"Well, we are called lazy and stupid wherever we go, but few white people seem willing to help us train for better jobs or get a decent education. That's where the problem lies. Most of the brothers and sisters are poor and illiterate, and the whites seem to prefer us that way—so they can look down on us always.

"I myself was lucky to get a scholarship to university, but not a great university. My pa is a preacher, so I got me a good moral upbringing from that fine man, but I'm a big exception to th' rule. I try hard to speak like a white man, but I know my accent pegs me as a black boy, a negro, a nigra, a nigger, a darkie, a coon, a jig, a splib—I see you folks wince when I say these words, so imagine how bad they hurt when the whiteys call us such names." Thad struggled to cool his emotions.

Yvonne raised her hand, as Thad calmed down and nodded to her. "Yes'm?" he invited.

"Thad, why then did you join the Army if it feels worse than at home? I think we are all wondering that, no?" She glanced around the table, and everyone nodded.

"Well ma'am, we're all here because we want to defend our country jes, er, just like the other soldiers do. By fightin' the Japs we hope to lift ourselves up in the eyes of the whites, but they hardly give us a chance. They keep us hidden out of sight and away from the front lines like … like … convicts almost, though some of the brothers they have seen combat kind of accidentally."

"And those Army engineers proved themselves to be fine soldiers," Elias-the-major added. "There were some great examples recently on New Guinea—at Port Moresby and Buna. Some of those men even delivered tanks ashore." Thad's eyes glistened with gratitude.

"What part of America do you come from then, Thad," asked Peter.

"Birmingham. It's in Alabama, the deep south, imagine it!" Thad laughed for a change. "Why, every judge and lawyer and policeman, they buy so many extra bed-sheets for their Ku-Klux-Klan meetings that Alabama is one of JC Penney's most profitable locations! Lord have mercy!"

He waved his hands in the air in mock supplication. "And the Australians don't want us neither. Damn! They kicked out the rest of my battalion to Nouméa."

"Thad, I am Hans the Dutchman. I did grow up on Java where there are many races, but the white people in Holland they run the show. I am what you can see is a white guy, but I have nice experience living in mixing-race society, so I am going to settle here on Santo with my lady wife-to-be. I love it here, but I think the local, er, colored people, the Melanesian Kanaks, they keep separate from the rest of us by choice. Am I right? Have you had a chance to study that? I guess it's a different situation from yours, because the Kanaks were here first and have right to be aloof."

"You mean like the Indians were in America first?" asked El, chuckling. That broke up the party, and everyone left in a good humor, promising to get together again.

"I may have to miss the next one," said Peter, "as it's almost August fifteenth when I'll be going to Sydney on leave, then probably to Guadalcanal to work for the Marines. But Thad, best of luck to you and the brothers and sisters. Keep your spirits up, and surely things will get better after the war is over and the world needs rebuilding. I feel honored to have met you, and to feel your trust tonight. Thank you so very much."

Peter failed to clarify that he was going to Brisbane to meet Bongo, instead of to Sydney and his family, although Wendy knew that was the case, and had agreed it would be better to postpone his home leave for another four months, to catch the long year-end summer holidays in mid-December. Until Peter was certain he could fit in with the Coastwatchers, he had better keep the pending interview with Commander Feldt to himself.

*** THE COASTWATCHERS ***

Having bid his friends goodbye the evening before, Peter departed Santo on August 15th via NATS seaplane to Nouméa, ostensibly to connect with a Sydney-bound flight the next morning. In reality, however, he was met in Nouméa by Bongo, and they flew on to Brisbane that same Sunday afternoon after a quick coffee with Mike Osborn. Although Peter was still writing regularly to Abby, he had not told her he would be coming through Nouméa, thus he was relieved to see that brother Andrew had the Sunday off. He wanted to see Abby again, but not for a rushed half hour at the crowded NATS dock. Nor did he want to appear rude by sneaking through Nouméa in secret. He was glad when the flight for Brisbane was finally in the air, though he would have to endure Bongo's snoring for a few hours.

The long Queensland coastline finally appeared, which excited Peter at the thought of a new place to explore. The NATS terminal for Brisbane lay inland on the bank of its namesake river, at a place called Colmslie, where they learned that Admiral Halsey and a few senior staff had come over from Nouméa to meet with General MacArthur just the week before. The 'buzz' was that Halsey and MacArthur got on quite well together, much to everyone's amazement.

For the past year, MacArthur's offices and quarters had been in the city's business district at a handsome ten-story former insurance building on the corner of Queen and Edward Streets. Conversely, the NATS terminal on the river was not all that near to the city, being actually part of a rather modest US Naval Station Brisbane, where Bongo maintained his official office.

RAN Commander Feldt, the coastwatcher-in-chief, had suffered a heart attack while visiting Guadalcanal some months earlier, so now he had his office in Brisbane too. Fortunately, it was no longer necessary to visit Feldt in Townsville, a nearly 24-hour additional journey to northern Queensland by train or bus. Another Australian naval officer had taken over the bulk of Feldt's daily communication routine with the coastwatchers, at the limits of their wireless equipment's transmission range.

The commander was delighted at the dinner invitation. Bongo treated the trio to some good Australian beef at a city restaurant, where much of the clientele wore Allied uniforms of various sorts. Downing their second pints as the meal was being prepared, Peter had a fleeting thought that both his companions were in naval intelligence but forced himself to avoid making any silly oxymoron puns for the moment.

"Mr. Perry, are you certain you'd fancy an assignment in our *Ferdinand* network? And Commander Perkins, I should ask you the same thing, sir. You realize there could be some physical danger?"

It was Bongo who replied first: "What sort of assignment might that be, Commander Feldt? We are both reasonably fit, I think, and not terribly ancient yet."

"Unlike myself," Feldt chuckled, who had been in the First World War, then in civilian life until he was called back up for the present emergency. Between the wars he was a government official in Papua and Rabaul, traveling extensively throughout the Solomons, Bougainville, and Efaté in the New Hebrides. In those travels, he developed the impressive roster that became his coastwatcher network, known as *Ferdinand*.

In those glory days, he had also acquired the fine purple vocabulary for which he was notorious, that had perhaps hastened his banishment to (that ar'sole plice) Townsville.

Addressing Peter then, Feldt observed: "Yes, I do realize you are a civilian, Mr. Perry, though a reserve officer as well, but nearly half of *Ferdinand's* complement are unpaid civilian volunteers too. You would just need to sign the necessary waivers—that is, if the assignment appeals to you."

"Did you say 'unpaid'?" Peter asked. "Ah, then do you have any short assignments?"

Bongo chuckled, and Feldt burst out laughing, nearly spilling his drink.

"Mr. Perry, that's certainly being honest. Most of the ruddy sods I deal with either give me a frigging speech about king and country, then disappear, or else are genuinely rich and don't really care a fig about money at all. Ha-ha, short assignments, I must remember that one!" Luckily the food arrived at that moment or there would certainly have been another round of lager.

Soon the happy threesome was on a first-name basis, as they tucked into delicious steaks—possibly purloined by the restaurant from a US or Australian commissary, washed down by passable Oz-wine in any case.

"Look, Eric," Bongo said through mouthfuls of beef and gravy, "Perry here is a civil engineer in thrall to the US contracts office, that coddles his every waking moment. He was, and still is, due to transfer from Santo to the Canal in another four weeks, to build fancy wooden bridges for the Gyrenes. If we could do something for you in the Solomons as you implied, why don't we let Peter go ahead with his bridge assignment so that he has an income, and I will meanwhile get myself detached from the ONI over here and reassigned short-term to the IMAC staff on Guadal. My boss in Hawaii has already agreed. Then, when it's time for whatever you need us to do, we'll both wangle time off to accomplish the dirty deed. People on the Canal are coming and going all the time, so it's a wonder the personnel people keep track of anybody. Also, the Kiwis have started to take over Guadalcanal operations, which adds another modicum of confusion. I'm frankly surprised we don't have a Jap colonel running operations this month. Weren't there one or two of them left behind recently?"

"Wouldn't sodding surprise me at all," Feldt replied. "Alright then, Yank-Limey team, here's what needs to happen, and why I can't trust the present *Ferdinand* network to pull it off. But can't you hang around in Brisbane for a couple of weeks, now that you're here? We need to get a lot of squishy stuff into your heads, like codes and protocols, and though you say you're both in shape, I've seen better specimens, frankly. A few daily hours on the rugger pitch with the Aussie fifteens will get you both tuned up."

Peter and Bongo smiled at that invitation and listened attentively to Commander Feldt's 'State of the Coastwatchers' overview.

*** *NEW LIFE FOR GUADALCANAL* ***

So it was that Peter and Bongo found themselves on Guadalcanal in mid-September '43, more 'splendidly fit' than they had deemed possible, and still displaying a few bruises from the 'splendidly serious' rugby workouts.

Bongo, who had briefly visited the Canal a year before, thought the place was utterly transformed, whereas Peter, whose first trip this was, thought the large island was hot, primitive, wet, noisy, and chaotic. Fleets of trucks threatened to destroy the new gravel roads, bringing supplies and equipment to various inland warehouses from ships unloading at dilapidated pontoon docks; while planes of all shapes and sizes came and went from the four or five airfields, including the much fought-over Henderson Field. Two more airfields were still under construction!

Across the Slot and Iron Bottom Sound, dozens of ships were anchored in the sheltered lee between Tulagi and larger Florida Island. Many of the remaining PT boats had moved further up north one night, probably to Rendova, someone said.

In the not-too-distant hills of Guadalcanal, one heard weapons large and small being test-fired, and always there was the constant background hum of a thousand voices shouting at one another. An occasional Dumbo splashed down at Tulagi, which had become a small naval communications station that still suffered the occasional Japanese bombing raid.

General Vandegrift was back on the Canal for a while, this time in charge of reorganizing IMAC, whose Marine commander, General Vogel he had recently replaced for the forthcoming Bougainville assault. Soon to become Marine Corps Commandant in Washington, Vandegrift was at the same time preparing to hand IMAC over to Lt. General Charles Barrett, recently of the Third Marine Division, who had been promoted to take over and direct the complex corps-sized Allied assaults that were key to *Cartwheel*'s success.

Senior Marine officers capable of handling multiple infantry divisions were by definition scarce, as none had been trained for that level of command responsibility before. Vogel had failed the test; Vandegrift was qualified but otherwise committed to go stateside; how would Barrett shape up? Halsey and Vandegrift were crossing their fingers, though Barrett had done a fine job with the Third Marine Division when he was a major general.

Busy Colonel Twining was there too, with new eagles on his collar— Bongo told Peter—and had nodded politely in the staff mess. Bongo, being Navy, was not expected to be a permanent part of the IMAC staff but would assist the C2 people with fleet traffic and interpretation of CINCPAC dispatches. It was a busy environment.

By bizarre coincidence, President Roosevelt's wife, Eleanor, was making an extensive goodwill tour of the Pacific Area support facilities around that time, looking in at Guadalcanal overnight on the 18th. Hastily erected screens around the heads (latrines) and mess tents testified to a flurry of activity on her behalf. It was expected that the First Lady would also visit Santo, Nouméa, and Efaté to see the actual hospitals where the boys were being sent.

Her visit was tremendously much appreciated by the wounded young men who were still coming back in dribs and drabs from New Georgia for the next hospital ship evacuation, but she was not as much appreciated by the top brass at the camps, who had to clean up and look smart.

Peter somehow missed Eleanor's visit. While waiting for special equipment to arrive from Commander Feldt in Australia, he got right to work on his first bridge design for Guadalcanal and did not even see Bongo all that often. He was once again teamed up with the Army Corps of Engineers rather than the Seabees, and found there was a sawmill in the vicinity, being operated by a New Zealand crew. This surprising discovery would greatly facilitate the preparation of local timber for the bridge, scheduled to span the fast-flowing Lunga River.

At long last, the M4 tanks of IMAC Company-D were carried from Nouméa to Guadalcanal and deposited by LST-446 at a beach across the Matanikau River from the original 1942 Marine perimeter, next to a wrecked Japanese troopship, *Kinugawa Maru*. The LST then hurried away to its next series of loading assignments prior to Bougainville.

Peter made a point of visiting Marine Captain Lou Aronson, the tank company commander, at the beach right away, to discuss priorities for the tank maneuvers. While his men erected tents among the coconut trees or bathed in the surf, Aronson and his driver asked Peter to jump in and guide them on a tour of the principal roads and trails, to see what looked passable for the heavy Shermans.

Peter obliged, after which they tried some off-road sorties with the headquarters tank *Diablo* crossing the sandbar at the mouth of the Matanikau. Finally, they led the attention-getting machine across Peter's new bridge that had just been completed over the Lunga.

"Well, this one sure is strong enough, sir," the captain's driver opined after *Diablo* had crossed successfully, he having apparently once worked for the Texas Highway Department, "but I'm sure glad we didn't try the pre-fab Army bridge over that other river." Peter smiled his thanks.

"Yes, Corporal," the captain responded. "now let's get Mr. Perry back to his important work, or we will be spending the rest of the war stuck on that beach with the Jap freighter."

"Will you be joining the Bougainville show then, Captain?" Peter asked.

"Supposedly," replied Aronson, "but so far they can't schedule another LST to take us there. Those new wonder-boats are all committed for hauling other stuff as of now. We are the first of four medium tank companies to ship out of Nouméa, and now we are part of the Third

Marine Division. Maybe the division can get this resolved somehow." Peter shook hands at the beach, then took his jeep back to the Army Engineering area.

*** *THIS IS A COASTWATCHER WATCHING YOU* ***

On October 1st, a small but heavy wooden crate arrived at Henderson Field from Commander Feldt, via some priority naval routing or other that had not prevented *KILROY WAS HERE* from being stenciled onto the surface.

Inside was the prototype of a new teleradio (transmitter-receiver) design, in the use of which Peter and Bongo had recently been trained when they were in Brisbane. It was one of the commander's only two samples, which he would not even trust to be hand-carried from Brisbane to Guadalcanal by the very team that was going to evaluate and introduce it to the coastwatching community.

Most of *Ferdinand's* surviving coastwatchers, still hidden in the dense island jungles of nearby islands, were using large and cumbersome pre-war teleradios made by a company in Australia. Although these sets worked reliably for the most part, they had a limited voice range of about 400 miles, and with their awkward multiple modules and 200-pound overall weight, they required a team of at least six people to move them effectively—and twice that many if the movement was very far. This was one reason the coastwatchers needed the services of so many loyal natives, in order to stay ahead of the Japanese who often detected their transmissions and searched high and low for them, occasionally with dogs. If caught, a coastwatcher invariably faced torture and execution.

Commander Feldt was quite happy with the new teleradio that had one-third the bulk and weight, and supposedly three times the range of the older models, apart from the fact that it was American made and the promising device had not yet been tested under jungle conditions by civilized people, meaning Australians or, failing that, Kiwis or Poms.

To rectify this deficiency, Bongo and Peter were kindly requested to deliver the prototype to reinstated district officer and former coastwatcher Martin Clemens—now back on Guadalcanal from leave in Sydney—for his personal evaluation, explaining to him how it worked and was serviced, etc., so he could in turn broadcast his testimony in code to other coastwatchers of the network. Failing such a blue-ribbon testimonial, Commander Feldt knew it would be a waste of time trying to get the network to give up its rather ancient gear, even if the new sets were delivered free of charge by a normally parsimonious Royal Australian Navy.

When Peter, Bongo, and Martin Clemens helped the six (rather than twelve) natives tote the new teleradio up to the high central mountains of Guadalcanal, where Clemens had stored his old equipment and battery the year before, the rain came down quite heavily, and Peter gained a great appreciation for the typical coastwatcher's miserable life on the islands.

There were still pockets of half-starved Japanese on Guadalcanal as well, remnants of those left to fight a rear-guard action last February so their comrades could escape. Clemens and the little party were therefore armed, just in case of trouble. They were thoroughly soaked, cold and dirty when finally reaching a rudimentary little shelter by a muddy jungle trail, high above the airfields and Sealark Channel. They were higher by far than Mt Austen, which appeared from above 'like a grassy knoll.'

"Should be a good spot to give 'er a go," Clemens announced, unwrapping his moldy old equipment that had been left in the shelter under a tarp for a year.

"Right, there are nine of us. Thirty minutes each on the bicycle to bring up the batteries should give us enough 'oomph' for a good test in the morning. You first, Mr. Perry, please, so the boys can get some food started while the rest of us clean out the cabin. It's remarkably dry inside, don't you think? And I see the bedding is still here—might need shaking out a bit." Peter grimaced and mounted the rusted bike-charger after wiping off the seat with a rag.

Amazingly, they discovered upon waking in the damp frigid dawn at four thousand feet, that the pair of old six-volt car batteries had accepted and held a charge and could successfully power the new radio they had taken turns back-packing up the mountain. Making a voice transmission on a special crystal-controlled frequency not normally used in the islands, they were able to raise Eric Feldt in far-away Brisbane. He had apparently been sitting by his other sample radio each morning for a week.

"Blimey, it's about time," he growled (with mild traces of enthusiasm). "Been taking a holiday, have you?"

The team of nine on Guadalcanal grinned from ear to ear, even the taciturn natives, for the commander's way with words was well known.

"I make it about 1,350 miles, point-to-point; not bad for a voice contact," he continued, "which means it would do at least 2,000 miles with the Morse Code key." And finally, as an afterthought: "Everyone all right, I trust?" Without waiting for a reply he signed off 'ten-four', and that was it.

The adventurous coastwatcher assignment is nearly over, Peter thought to himself, pleased once more to have chosen engineering as a profession instead of, say, farming ... or coast-watching.

Before they packed up the valuable prototype to bring it back down the mountain, they decided to scan the airwaves for any useful news. It was October tenth, and they learned on one mundane channel that it was National Day in China, but on another channel they were shocked to hear an announcement that a Marine general named Charles Barrett had recently died from an accident in Nouméa.

"Must have been visiting Halsey," Bongo said. "Cripes, that'll screw up the IMAC schedule again. What could have happened? I wonder if Twining was with him; they were in the process of moving IMAC headquarters here to CACTUS."

The little group moved as carefully and quickly as possible back down the mountain, to the sprawling camp below.

Three weeks later, Peter installed a second small wooden bridge, with help again from the Kiwi-run sawmill and the Army Corps of Engineers. A third, much more complex project was in the works too, a very long causeway to cross a wide inland area of the Matanikau River that was subject to flooding.

Meanwhile, the M4 Sherman tanks were finding it hard going in the uneven jungles that had never been cleared for coconut planting. Huge hardwoods blocked their way, and soggy ground from constant rains caused them to sink alarmingly.

"Not really good tank country, sir," the captain's driver observed wryly, "even with better bridges."

He received no comment from Captain Aronson, other than "thank you, Corporal".

Bongo had meanwhile returned to Brisbane, to confer with Cdr. Feldt about the logistics of replacing the old coastwatcher wireless equipment.

The brief test transmission from Guadalcanal had been such a success that there was hardly any reason not to proceed. But then, practicality set in one evening over a beer; the war was moving northward too fast. Both men had learned through their respective organizations that Bougainville and Rabaul would probably be neutralized within another few months, which would render the remaining coastwatchers redundant. "That means I'm probably redundant as well," intoned the crusty Australian, whose blood, sweat and tears had held the organization together since 1939. "Well, we had a damned good innings. Cheers, Bongo."

*** ANOTHER JAB AT JAPAN ***

Suddenly, across the Pacific Ocean to the east, more trouble was brewing for Japan, following two weeks of B-17 bombardment from Canton Island (at last!) and other nearby airfields. On November twentieth, not all that long after a surprise IMAC landing at Empress Augusta Bay on Bougainville, the Second Marine Division went ashore on Betio from inside the Tarawa lagoon of the Gilbert Islands, in a fiercely contested three-day horror that almost tipped in Japan's favor at first, causing tremendous casualties for both sides.

Fourteen Company-C Sherman tanks from Nouméa were delivered by USS *Ashland* and went into combat for the first time, but it still took brute force and individual sacrifice for the Marine infantry to gain the upper hand. Fittingly, the former RCS *Viti*, now HMS *Viti*, was part of the vast Allied flotilla at Tarawa, commanded by an Australian naval officer. Sir Harry Luke was doubtless proud to hear of it—from retirement.

Meanwhile, on Butaritari Island where Marine Raiders had stirred up a hornet's nest the year before, Army soldiers recaptured the Makin lagoon, and completed the liberation of the British Gilberts.

A few days later, Admiral Nimitz flew out from Hawaii to inspect the little island of Betio, where denuded palm tree stumps, wrecked equipment, and 3,400 Marine casualties testified to the brutality and stout defense that a determined Japanese admiral had brought about.

Nimitz and his advisors were unaware that Admiral Shibasaki's staff photography expert, Hawaiian-born IJN Lieutenant Naburo, lay among the mangled dead that were being bulldozed into mass graves, to help rid the island of the dreadful stench of rotting corpses.

Desperate to find an opportunity of somehow surrendering to US forces, Naburo had volunteered to return to Betio from Truk. During the year of frantic construction that followed his arrival, he often recalled his brief meeting with Graham and Lois Overwood, in the peaceful sleepy days before war reached the Pacific Ocean. He'd had no news of the Overwoods since then, nor of his parents in Honolulu, and supposed they had all forgotten him.

While evacuating the Japanese command post on Betio with the admiral and his staff on the first afternoon of the horrendous battle, so that the indestructible bunker could be converted into a hospital for Japanese wounded, Naburo had spotted the bold American destroyer turning close by, inside the lagoon. He reached out to caution the admiral, just as the first 5-inch naval shell screamed down to kill them all.

Hidden away somewhere westward, toward the protected center of their mandated islands beyond the Marshalls, the mighty battleships *Yamato* and *Musashi* were still crouched in expectation of a textbook 'decisive battle' with the American fleet, a battle that so far hadn't materialized. One of the very few captured Japanese petty officers at Tarawa had snidely referred to the senior battleship as 'the Yamato Hotel', which said it all.

The IJN seemed at a loss what to do with its expensive super-ships, now that Admiral Yamamoto was no longer at the helm. The fleet admiral's plane had been recently gunned down by USAAF P-38s while he was on an inspection tour near Rabaul.

CHAPTER SIX

The Middle Game

Third Marine Division Shoulder Patch

"If the Table Moves, Move with It"
Sakaue

*** *A BIGGER SYDNEY SURPRISE* ***

Peter Perry finally managed to get six weeks of leave in Sydney when school was out for the long summer holidays, mid-December 1943 to the end of January 1944. He accomplished this by postponing his leave entitlement for work performed in Nouméa and Santo and tacking on another entitlement for Guadalcanal.

As he and Wendy had often discussed since first arriving in Sydney, they made plans by way of their weekly letters to take John to visit other parts of the southeast, including Melbourne, Adelaide, and Canberra. At first, Wendy seemed reluctant to make the bookings but finally she did, agreeing they would travel by rail, bus, and the occasional taxi, staying at city boarding houses or country inns.

It should be a grand occasion, Peter felt, as he hadn't been home for almost a year. The Pacific war made it quite difficult for people to get together, but whenever Peter felt unlucky and despondent about it, he invariably thought of his Singapore friends who were dead or imprisoned. Then he felt at peace again.

When he left for Sydney this time, Guadalcanal was not yet an official NATS stopover, but it had some civilian-option seats allocated on military aircraft. Peter caught a lift on one of the available seaplanes from Tulagi.

The 7pm splash-down at Rose Bay caused him to relax from the tension of the prior few months; he almost dozed off as the plane motored over to the ramp. Wendy, John, and Doris were there to meet him, as they had been on his very first arrival in Sydney, but this time the ladies wore tennis attire while John was in his pajamas and dressing gown. From the Smyth divorce settlement, it appeared that Fred had donated Doris the black Ford as well as the house, Peter noted thankfully. Hugs were exchanged all around.

As before, John sat in the back seat with Peter's luggage, and Peter was squeezed up front between the women. He was conscious of the short tennis skirts and nicely tanned legs as they hopped in close to him on either side. He could smell their perfume too, and was beguiled by their throaty chatter to each other, while they were getting everyone arranged.

"Peter, after we get John to bed at Doris' place, let's invite her to dine with us at the cottage. It will be fun to celebrate your long overdue arrival in Sydney. I laid in a nice supply of grog for the occasion."

"Certainly dear," Peter replied cheerfully. "It's wonderful to be back in Rose Bay again, although I do wish you could have come over to see Nouméa last Christmas."

"Not to worry, darling, I may get there one day. I'm so happy that you like your work, and I hope the French lessons are going well too." A momentary image of Abby flashed through Peter's mind.

"Well, here we are," Wendy announced as the car pulled into Doris' driveway. "Come along with Mummy, John, and we'll put you to bed. Then we'll drive Daddy and his luggage across the street and help him unpack."

John hopped out with Wendy, and said cheerily, "Good night, Pops; let's take Digger for a walk tomorrow, please."

Peter smiled and nodded as they went inside. He started to slide away from Doris, so they could converse more easily, but was surprised when she placed a hand on his leg to keep him where he was.

"Oh, there's no need to move, Peter. Wendy will be right back," Doris smiled.

Peter stayed where he was as the front door closed behind Wendy and John. He reached for his cigarette case to offer Doris a smoke. Suddenly he was surprised again, as lovely Doris turned toward him and kissed him full on the lips.

"Welcome home, neighbor," she whispered. "I hope we'll have a chance to get better acquainted."

"I say, what's this then?" Peter was blushing and stuttering. "No cause for alarm," Doris whispered, "Wendy and I wanted to give you a nice homecoming, that's all." Peter, stunned, let Doris kiss him again. She still didn't remove her hand, even as Wendy returned and joined them, though she soon had to shift gears to get the Ford across the road. Peter's heart was already beating quickly as he felt Wendy's strong hug and heard Doris whisper "All aboard for Paradise!"

*** THE WIZZIES OF OZ ***

Peter awoke next morning to the sound of a dog barking. His head was throbbing. He lay naked under a sheet on their bed, his and Wendy's bed, except that it had been his and Wendy's and Doris' bed last night. He couldn't remember everything, but what he did recall included Gimlets, several glasses of champagne, and some wonderful steaks, quaffed and grilled by two fanciful chefs, alternatively dancing slowly with him to sentimental ballads on the gramophone, alternatively stumbling to the bedroom with him, then …. falling asleep.

The startling thing, he realized as he slowly emerged into fuller consciousness, was how the women had displayed the same level of intimacy and tenderness toward each other as they did to him. But where were they now, those vixens? How much had been a dream? The answer soon came in the form of a Hawaiian song playing faintly on the gramophone in the parlor.

Peter recognized the tune as *Pearly Shells*, that had been constant background music aboard the ex-Coast Guard cutter *Taney* as he approached Honolulu in another lifetime. As he was contemplating that old memory, the bedroom door opened to admit a louder volume of music and his two smiling companions of the prior evening, attired in grass skirts and floral leis and apparently little else. They danced a passable hula and undulated over to the bed. Peter gathered the sheet around him.

"G'day sport," intoned Doris. "Nice to see you awake at last. We've been up for hours after walking young John to school.

"But Doris, Wendy, what does all this mean? What are you doing, I mean why are you …? Wendy, you're my wife, how can this, er, I must be dreaming…."

"No, Peter dear, I'm very sorry to startle you but I'm not your wife any longer, except on paper; Doris and I are a couple now. I am her spouse and she is mine, I mean not legally of course, but that is our precious relationship. When she blurted out to Fred that she was in love with her neighbor across the road, she meant me, not you, but being self-centered men, it was clear that neither of you would figure it out. And I am in love with Doris, completely, eternally. I suppose I was from the day we first met, but it took us both some time to realize we had this, um, special tendency."

Peter was quite taken aback at the unconventional talk. "How long has, er, you know…," he began.

"Over a year, darling. Doris and I declared our love for each other about the time you were trying to get John and me a passage to Nouméa for Christmas '42. I'm terribly sorry that I couldn't find a way since then to tell you in writing. Please forgive me." She professed a downcast look.

"But what about John?" Peter asked. "Doesn't he know what's going on? My god, the poor lad must be very confused."

"All is fine with John, don't worry. To him we are Mummy and Auntie. He has his room and we have ours, and both require a knock on the door. He doesn't think anything of us women sleeping in the double bed, and we always wear our nighties.

"I hear Doris running your bath," Wendy continued, "So let me just say something else. It's about the one gift we can't give to each other, she and I. Doris wants to bear a child for us to bring up, Peter, and that's where you come in. Perhaps she'll already be pregnant now, perhaps not; but in case not, she wants to double her chances while you are still in her clutches, understand?

"Now be a good boy and cooperate. If it didn't work last night, then you might reconvene with her after our tour of Australia with John. That'll give you something special to think about during the trip, but please understand that you and I have just had our last such liaison."

She kissed Peter somewhat tenderly. "That's for old times' sake, darling. Now you can see why I adore Sydney over Singapore."

*** NATIVE ARTS AND CRAFTS ***

When passions had cooled, and they had all taken John and Digger for a walk to the bay after school, Peter felt relaxed again and almost cheerful, although he sensed in his subconscious that events were overtaking him and he was losing some control of his life. He must somehow get Wendy alone for a serious talk, but how? She and Doris were rarely apart.

When they returned to the Perry cottage and were sipping tea on the terrace—knowing John wouldn't catch the point of the conversation—Peter asked the ladies how they had come by the grass skirts, and the hula lessons for that matter.

Wendy explained: "You know that Doris and I both work at an aircraft assembly plant, right? We asked for time off while you were home—an extended weekend for Doris and a month for me, and it was granted. Well there are hundreds of women working at the plant, of all ages and sizes, since there is a lot of government pressure now for women to aid the war effort."

"And we love it!" Doris interjected. "We build fighter planes from kits, and the planes are flown to the war zone just as fast as they are assembled and tested."

Wendy picked up the conversation: "We also chat and gossip with the other girls, of course. One of them brought a grass skirt to show us that her beau had sent over from Espiritu Santo, where he said the local women were as ugly as sin, but they went around barefoot with only the skirt on."

"It's the same in the Solomons," Peter interrupted, "and they are just as ugly as on Santo. Right, so why do you two happen to have those grass skirts then? Do you have a beau in Santo?" he teased, hoping the answer would be no.

"Of course not, Peter," Doris answered. "It turned out that another woman at our factory had acquired several of the skirts somehow, somewhere. She was selling them for twenty Australian pounds apiece, so we bought these two as part of our grand plan for entertaining you. Looks like they work fairly well for such occasions, eh?" Doris winked, and Wendy giggled.

"Uh, so they do, so they do," Peter mumbled, "but twenty pounds is an outrage. That's eighty American dollars, and you can buy these skirts on Santo for around four dollars, so Hans told me. We noticed a hideous Tonkinese woman selling them by the beach—to think I almost bought you one, Wendy! Well, if you add, say, another dollar apiece to ship them to Oz, then that woman at your factory made a four-to-one, or four hundred percent markup when she sold them to you for twenty dollars, gosh, that's very interesting!"

"No, Peter, you daft engineer, they sell for twenty *pounds* over here—that's *eighty* dollars, remember?" Doris jumped out of her chair. "That's … what? … one thousand six hundred percent markup, isn't it? Yes, four hundred times four."

The others nodded. "Good lord, how large is the market then?" Peter asked.

"Let's find out!" Wendy jumped up as well. "Peter, can you write to Hans before we leave tomorrow, to rush a big box of them to us—say, fifty skirts—so we can test the market? Will he trust you for the money? Our risk will be two hundred dollars plus shipping, and a little bit more for an advertisement in the Sydney papers, but we might be able to make four thousand dollars in sales, and perhaps even set up agents for the other cities if we can buy enough of the skirts. Do you think there will be Customs duties here, being arts and crafts and no local production?"

"Peter and Wendy," Doris added, "the quality must be first rate, even for rustic things like this. One or both of you must get to Santo somehow after your holiday—or even during it—to organize the supply side and see what else could be bought there, such as seashells, perhaps. Our prosperity depends on this. I'll look after John if Wendy is away, and hopefully I'll be knitting little booties soon, anyway. If not...."

She gave Peter a come-hither glance that made him shift in his chair. Wendy roared with laughter.

Peter blushed, and rattled his teacup. "Well, Doris, I might be able to get back to Santo fairly soon, but there's probably no way Wendy and I can get there together and then get her back to Sydney. Let's think about that crucial point, though. Perhaps we'll have to involve Hans the Dutchman for a share of the profits. He would fully understand about quality control."

*** SEEING MELBOURNE ***

A few days later, with the subject of their marriage still hanging over them, Wendy and Peter set forth with John on their month-long rail journey through three adjacent southern states and the federal district of Canberra, the national capital. They knew there would be very difficult parts to their conversations. Peter felt great anxiety, knowing that Wendy would be reluctant to let John out of sight, as a barrier to frank dialogue.

It turned out there were equally difficult parts to the journey itself because of Australia's peculiar changes in rail gauges between the various states, a situation that had arisen in the last century. This historical blunder added to Peter's frustrations, and he began to wish they had not undertaken the holiday trip after all. How could a British colony have been allowed to do such idiotic things? And how could his wife have been so idiotic as well? The two competing problems kept Peter awake on their first night in the little railway cabin that Wendy had booked. He couldn't concentrate on the more personal problem of Wendy and Doris, while his engineering nature was challenged by the incredible cock-up that had befallen Australia's railways.

Although individual Australian states had indeed been advised by British engineers to standardize on a single railway gauge, few of them heeded the advice. Instead, the gauges were chosen by each state with an eye to economy of investment or ongoing maintenance—or simply the availability of any rolling stock at all to meet emergency transportation demands, such as the Australian gold rush in 1851, soon after the dramatic one in California.

In due course, Victoria and South Australia—the only adjacent states in the entire nation that had any commonality—adopted the 'Irish broad gauge' of five feet three inches, whereas New South Wales adopted the 'British standard gauge' of four feet, eight-and-a-half inches. Later on, frugal Queensland—seeking lower costs for rolling stock—adopted what became known as the 'Australian narrow gauge' of three feet six inches, which was subsequently adopted by Tasmania and Western Australia, neither of which were adjacent to Queensland. It was a bizarre outcome, from a lack of central control.

Crossing from one state to another created bewildering difficulty, therefore, as General MacArthur must have learned the hard way when he decided to move his headquarters northward from Melbourne to Brisbane, to be closer to the war theater. The US army would have had to load, unload, and reload its stash of equipment onto different gauges of rolling stock in order to pass from Victoria through New South Wales, and then repeat the wasteful exercise once again to access Queensland. Even the Japanese couldn't have thought up a cleverer plan to slow down the Allied war machine.

It didn't just affect cargo, of course. People traveling by rail from one Australian state to another had to disembark from their original train system and re-board another, at special 'break-of-gauge' stations near the state borders. This was only a minor inconvenience if both trains happened to arrive at the same time, but such was not always the case. Curiously, even at the border of Victoria with South Australia, the re-boarding exercise was still carried out in spite of those two states having both adopted the Irish broad gauge, simply because neither state was willing to lend rolling stock to its neighbor!

The Perrys had chosen the state of Victoria as their first destination, which was separated from New South Wales by the Murray River. Having made the requisite train-gauge change at Albury NSW on the river's north bank, they planned for a full week of holiday, including Christmas Day, at Victoria's capital, Melbourne. Peter remembered hearing from Andrew Culver that Melbourne had been the post-Guadalcanal recuperation site for the First Marine Division, before Nimitz reluctantly lent the battered warriors to MacArthur for some future SWPA operation. While Peter, Wendy, and John were settling into a comfortable Melbourne boarding house, Peter learned that one of the Marine regiments had even been camped at the Melbourne Cricket Ground, while the division's other regiments were billeted at nearby towns like Ballarat.

After recovering from wounds and malaria, and undergoing training for half a year, the veteran Marines—brought back up to strength with new replacements—were sent off to join General MacArthur's forces, just as Nimitz had pledged. They would become part of *Operation Cartwheel,* the complex Allied plan to neutralize the Japanese naval base at Rabaul.

But the Marines were very much missed in Melbourne now, Peter and Wendy noticed. People still talked about their former presence, as it was only a month or two before the Perrys arrived that the last Leathernecks had departed.

After breakfast at the boarding house, the Perrys—for that's what they still were, legally—lingered in the dining room over maps and guidebooks. Mrs. Belfast, the owner, asked if she could help with their holiday planning, in the run-up to Christmas.

"Oh yes, please," Wendy said. "We would love to see Melbourne's sights, and perhaps some events as well, if there are any scheduled prior to Christmas."

"Well dear, I suggest you go to Port Phillip first—you know, the big harbor—to get an idea of the city's size. There are beautiful views from the shore. You could catch the tram right here and get off at the docks near the mouth of the Yarra, and afterwards walk along the Esplanade to see our many interesting memorials and buildings. I would be happy to pack a lunch for the outing, if you wish. When you're tired, just come back and John can have a nap while you two carry on somewhere else. I'll keep an eye on the lad, so you can enjoy your holiday."

Peter appreciated the offer, as he was desperate to get Wendy alone to talk about their marital dilemma.

"We would much enjoy seeing the docks," he said to Mrs. Belfast. "That's always a fascinating thing to do. Well, we're off, then. Please don't bother about the lunch, but you are wonderful to suggest it, and to watch after John later on. Thank you again for your kindness."

Melbourne's excellent tram system took them right to the docks. East of the old city, the huge body of water known as Port Phillip was far bigger than they imagined, almost like a huge saltwater lake, and they could scarcely make out the far-off passage into the Tasman Sea. Near to where they stood, several cargo ships were berthed at the freight wharves, so they walked along to show John the large steamers, such as none of them had seen up close since leaving Singapore a long while ago.

"Look for the different flags, John-O," Peter coaxed. "You can tell from the flags which countries the ships come from."

Peter explained that the flag of a merchant ship's registry flies at the back, the stern, whereas other ones on the ship could be the courtesy flag of Australia that foreign vessels fly at the yard arm, or perhaps the house flag of the ship's owners at the peak of the mast. John caught on quickly. "Oh look, Pops, there's the Union Jack on a red flag." John pointed to the ship they had just reached. "What does that mean?"

"If it's just plain red with the Union Jack in a corner, then it's a British merchant ship, but if it's a red version of the usual blue Australian flag, with the five Southern Cross stars and that other big star, then it's an Aussie merchant ship. If you ever see a white version of either flag instead of a blue or red one, then it would be either a British or Australian warship," Peter added. "Those Navy flags are called the White Ensign". John got the idea faster than Wendy, but still didn't know all the answers.

"Look Pops, there's a funny one. Light blue with a yellow cross."

He pointed to a large ship tied up ahead of the British freighter that they were passing. The other ship's stern, with the strange flag, was pointing toward them.

216

"Gosh, I don't know," Peter confessed. "Let's see what the name is. A ship's name is usually shown on the stern, with its home port name underneath."

They walked onward. "Hmm, *Mirrabooka* is the ship's name, which sounds Australian, and the home port is Gothenburg, wherever that is. Could it be in Queensland perhaps? Wait a minute, wasn't *Mirrabooka* the name of the ship that Uncle Ned came to Melbourne on last year? Wendy, do you remember?"

"I think you're right; yes, that was it," Wendy confirmed.

"Then this flag is Swedish! And Gothenburg is in Sweden, of course; don't you recall from school geography? I remember thinking, when Ned told us about his trip from Canada, what was a Swedish ship doing with an Abo name? I wonder what *Mirrabooka* means."

As they were chatting aloud about this interesting discovery, two of the ship's officers, who were passing nearby toward the gangway, overheard Peter's question. One of them had four stripes on his jacket sleeves and was probably the ship's captain. He stopped to look at the trio, while his companion nodded and went aboard the ship.

"Oh hello there," the captain said in a nice sing-song accent. "Excuse me for overhearing, but you may like to know that *Mirrabooka* means 'Southern Cross', which are those five stars on your Australian flag! Are you surprised?"

Seeing that they were indeed surprised, he continued, looking mostly at John: "I am Captain Axelsson, the former captain of this fine ship. Now I am the company representative in San Francisco, but I had to bring the ship to Australia this time so the new captain could take his annual leave. What is your name then, young man?" he asked John, "and can you please introduce me to these older people you are with?"

"Yes sir!" John almost shouted with enthusiasm. "This is my father, and this is my mum!"

"But what are their names, young man, what are their names? And what is your name, please?"

"Oh, I am John Perry. They are Father Perry and Mother Perry." Everyone laughed, and John looked a bit forlorn, but the captain shook hands and John recovered his sparkle.

"Well I can hear that you are not Australians," Captain Axelsson said to Peter. "Will you be traveling on this ship with us the day after Christmas? We will go up to Brisbane, then back down to Sydney to collect more cargo and passengers, then we shall sail from Sydney to America."

"No sir, regretfully we shan't be joining you, but we do know this is a passenger-freighter because my brother and his family came to Melbourne from Vancouver on the *Mirrabooka* in July '42. He is Edgar Perry."

"Then you must come and see the ship for yourselves and stay for a little lunch. Do you have time? *Ja*? Good. I am sorry not have met your brother, but I was in California all last year. I can tell you, however, that the ship's owners were quite worried about that particular voyage, as it was our first one during the Pacific war, soon after the Battle of Midway, and there were in June some Japanese submarines working along the US northwest coast, near Vancouver. *Ja*, we felt there was still some risk in July, but the Canadian government was quite eager that we take some of the Air Force families with their household things to Australia. I suppose your brother was one of them."

"No sir, he is a civilian, but his employer wanted him in Australia as soon as possible. He told me your ships don't normally call at Vancouver, is that correct?"

"That is right, Mr. Perry; only occasionally. We normally load passengers and freight at San Pedro or San Francisco in California, after passing through the Panama Canal from Europe. Most of our voyages used to go completely around the world, you see, but no longer. Well, shall we go aboard? Madam Perry, would you care to lead us?"

*** *A SPY STORY* ***

After lunch in the handsomely paneled passenger dining room, and then a quick tour of the bridge and a handful of cabins and other accommodations, the three visitors sat in the passenger lounge with the captain.

"I must say this is a very comfortable ship, Captain Axelsson. Sitting inside here, it's hard to believe this is really a freighter. I wish we were going somewhere with you," Wendy offered, sipping an aromatic cup of coffee. "I suppose that is not a sensible idea in wartime, though. You must be concerned about passenger safety these days."

"We are indeed, madam, and our own safety too," he smiled. "Even though Sweden is a neutral country, we have already lost several ships to torpedoes in Europe, and therefore we do not trust the Japanese and Germans to completely respect our neutrality. So we sail well away from the battle zones, and hopefully away from prowling submarines too. It is no longer realistic for us to cross the Atlantic, even in a convoy, so now we—and our sister ship *Parrakoola*—just wander back and forth between the South Pacific and California, avoiding the traditional shipping lanes."

"Does the South Pacific schedule include Nouméa or Espiritu Santo, by any chance?" Peter asked.

"What a clever question, Mr. Perry. You must be a spy!" The captain then laughed apologetically: "Forgive me, that was not intended to be an insult," he continued, seeing Peter's defensive expression. "It just caught me by surprise, as motor vessel *Mirrabooka* will shortly be calling on both those ports for the very first time ever, in place of our usual stopover at Auckland, New Zealand. How on earth did you know? This change has not been publicized yet."

"I didn't know, believe me," Peter hastened to assure, "but if I really was a spy I wouldn't have asked the question, since I would already have the answer! And if Mrs. Perry was also a spy, she would have kicked me hard in the ankle."

"*Ja, ja*, very good! Well, we did once have a Japanese spy aboard this ship, you know. It was our Captain Malmgren in charge of *Mirrabooka* during those July days of 1937, soon after the notorious Marco Polo Bridge Incident in China.

"Captain Malmgren received a request to take aboard a Japanese passenger and companion here in Melbourne and deliver them to the Japanese embassy in London. This our captain agreed to do, as the gentleman in question had a receipt for passage paid directly to our office in Sweden, for two adjacent cabins. His name was Watanabe, as I recall, supposedly a professional photographer in Melbourne. Of course we did not know it when he sailed with us, but this clever man left behind a network of agents that did not come to light until after the war began in Europe." Wendy nudged Peter at the mention of a Japanese photographer.

The captain continued: "An interesting note that Captain Malmgren recorded in his logbook, was about Watanabe's female traveling companion.

She was described as an attractive woman, said to be the daughter of the former Spanish Consul-General in Australia. Her father, a vocal supporter of General Franco in the Spanish Civil War, had resigned his consular position and returned to Spain earlier in 1937, and doubtless helped Franco come to power two years later. The German Nazis and Italian Fascists helped Franco fight the Spanish Republicans, as we all know. Apparently, the consul's daughter also decided to leave Australia in '37 and although she was not married to Watanabe she accompanied him, rather than her father."

"I see," Wendy observed, "so Watanabe had more stature than a mere photographer would, it seems. We knew a Japanese photographer in Singapore, as a matter of fact, that Peter here approved of, but I did not care for that man at all." Peter stared glumly at his cup.

Just then another ship's officer came into the lounge for a coffee. "*Hej*, Jurgen," the captain waved. "I know you are very busy, but could you possibly escort this young midshipman named John on a brief tour of the ship?" Peter and Wendy smiled their consent, and Jurgen the bosun did not seem the slightest bit annoyed to be assigned the task.

"*Ja*, of course captain. I would like to ask his opinion about the deck cargo and the engine room. Come along, young sailor." John was absolutely thrilled and leapt from his seat.

Captain Axelsson pressed ahead with the spy story. "Now, the peculiar thing is that the Australian authorities somehow failed to identify Watanabe as a spy,"—Peter pouted, while Wendy gestured in sneering triumph to an invisible government functionary—"and they instead focused on a Japanese professor Seita, who arrived in 1938, several months after Watanabe had departed. By early 1938, there was shocking news coming out of China about Japanese aggression and destruction in Shanghai and Nanking, so the Australian security service at last decided to keep an eye out for Japanese agents over here." Wendy raised her hands in mock applause.

Captain Axelsson smiled: "Well, because Professor Seita had suddenly appeared, he became a suspect by default. Then as Watanabe's spy ring was gradually closed down, they simply assumed the ringleader was Seita. He was arrested after Pearl Harbor and repatriated along with Japanese consular staff.

"Professor Seita was quite a dignified gentleman," the captain added, "who most likely had an assignment to mingle with upper class Australians and promote Japan as a friendly nation and reliable business partner, more or less a lost cause as time went by. I vaguely remember him, as I was by 1938 the regular *Mirrabooka* captain. We used to say hello at a few Melbourne events, whenever the ship was here in port for a few days."

"This is very interesting, Captain, but how did it come to light that Watanabe-san was a spy? Perhaps he really was just a photographer," Peter ventured, his thoughts wandering off to the one in Singapore who had taken his and Wendy's wedding photographs in 1931. Wendy sniffed.

"It was the woman," Captain Axelsson answered. "After this ship was a few days at sea, she came running to the captain's quarters one evening, saying that Watanabe had jumped overboard! She begged the captain for asylum, saying she did not want to debark in England, because the Japanese would probably kill her over what she knew about Watanabe's affairs in Melbourne."

"My word," Peter interrupted. "What became of her?"

"Well, Captain Malmgren and his officers debated the matter, but did not want to radio our home office for instructions in case the Japanese would intercept the message and take action against our ship. In the end, the ship's officers took collective responsibility to offer the woman asylum and deliver her to Swedish immigration at the end of the voyage. That is the Swedish way, you see, consensus. The woman was very relieved and grateful. She told Captain Malmgren that she had been cajoled by her father into traveling with Watanabe to London, to spy on the Japanese for General Franco, of all things!"

"What a strange story. My goodness, what did the Australian government say about Watanabe's role and his suicide?" Wendy asked the obvious question.

"Oh nothing; they didn't ask us, and we didn't like to get involved if we could avoid it, so we did not volunteer this information to them. The woman became a Swedish citizen eventually and is now married to a diplomat. I must not tell you their names, of course, but we think she influenced her father to advise Franco not to join the Germans in this current war. Perhaps that is some small achievement for us Swedes, eh, helping to keep Spain neutral like Sweden."

*** CHANGE OF PLANS ***

After their goodbyes on the *Mirrabooka*, the Perrys took a long stroll away from the docks and along the Esplanade, then back toward the city center. It was sad to see how many shops were closed in Melbourne, no doubt because of the war—young men off to fight, and women doing industrial work. Wendy said she had noticed the same thing in Sydney. Although some distance away from the combat zones now, Australia nevertheless suffered considerably at home because of her small population and vast commitments.

It must be the same in New Zealand, Peter thought, *and of course even worse in Britain because of German bombs and rockets. Hard to realize what chaos has been caused by those egotistical madmen Hitler, Mussolini, and Tojo. If a civilian's house gets blown up in a war, who's to help him rebuild it? Probably not the warring parties.*

Early in the afternoon, they caught a tram and took John back to the boarding house. The excited boy kept up an incessant chatter about what he had seen of the ship, and what the bosun had said about this, that, and the other, including the fact that the bosun was Danish, not Swedish.

Peter and Wendy were so pleased to see John interested in something new that they scarcely paid attention to the various Melbourne sights along the way. When they got off the tram at the boarding house, they were too tired to go anywhere else that afternoon, so they too decided to lie down for a while and then go out for a drink somewhere in the evening, leaving John in the care of Mrs. Belfast.

She recommended they walk to the lounge of a nearby small hotel, which she said was supposedly fairly quiet—"unlike the Old Vic in the city where the Marines used to go".

They took her suggestion, and found the hotel's décor cozy, and the little lounge almost deserted. Peter automatically ordered Gimlets.

"Wendy, hasn't it been fun making this trip together with young John?" Peter tried his opening gambit, setting down the drinks. "It's just wonderful to be back together again. I apologize for being such an absentee husband, and for causing your change of, um, orientation."

Wendy laughed aloud: "You didn't cause anything, silly man. I just never realized I had been waiting all my life for someone like Doris to come along. I simply suppressed those thoughts and did my best to be a good wife for you, as well as a good friend. I don't think I'll ever stop being the latter, unless you keep on hounding me about Doris, that is."

"Hounding you? That isn't fair. This is really the first chance we've had to talk privately about things between us. Surely it's not unreasonable for me to want our marriage restored to good health, don't you agree?"

"Well, I suppose that's logical, but Peter, please understand that it is a complete waste of time to carry on with this topic. Look, both Doris and I dallied with you the other evening. It wasn't really a pleasure for either of us, I'm sorry to say, but we pretended it was. I had promised Doris to help arouse you to get her pregnant, that's all. There's nothing more to talk about on that score. It either worked or it didn't."

Peter ordered another round of drinks. "Wendy, this isn't natural, or normal, or whatever you call it. People are designed to be compatible male to female, don't you think? If otherwise, there must be some sort of disorder at work. Darling, look, would you at least agree to speak privately to a psychiatrist at my expense?"

Wendy had been on the verge of tears over Peter's anguish, but at his latest comment she lost her temper and slapped him hard across the face. "How dare you pontificate to me, Peter Perry? What makes you think you understand what is normal and what is not? Damn you! I want a divorce, and the sooner the better!"

Wendy stood up abruptly and started for the door. Halfway there, she paused and glared at him: "I'm going back to the lodgings. You can stay here and get drunk, or whatever men do when they can't get their own way. Just remember what I said: 'the sooner the better'. I think our holiday trip just ended."

Peter sat there, stunned, watching Wendy stride out the swinging doors. *What's gotten into her? She isn't herself any longer. Getting drunk sounds like a promising idea, but then what about tomorrow?* Jumbled thoughts raced through his mind. After another Gimlet and some light supper, he called for a taxi and asked the driver to take him to the docks, alongside MV *Mirrabooka*. Captain Axelsson welcomed Peter back aboard.

***

The telephone rang at the boarding house the following morning. Peter asked to speak to Wendy, who warily said hello.

"Look, Wen, I'm sorry to have spoiled your holiday, and particularly John's, but I agree it would be uncomfortable for us to carry on with the original travel plan. I have a suggestion instead. Last night I stayed on the *Mirrabooka* and asked Captain Axelsson if we could travel with him to Sydney in a few days. The ship will leave Melbourne the day after Christmas—Boxing Day—and proceed far up north to Brisbane for a couple of days before coming back south to Sydney, by when it should be January third or fourth. There are no other passengers at this stage, but several will likely board at Sydney for California, and perhaps Nouméa or Santo. What do you think of taking John for a coastal cruise back to Sydney on *Mirrabooka*, and forget about the rubbish railways? It should be a treat for all of us, I imagine."

"But can we afford this? Surely it will be quite expensive." Wendy sounded embarrassed and subdued after the prior evening's blow-up.

"Not a problem, dear. Because the ship doesn't normally carry passengers while loading at various ports, the captain offered to take the three of us all that way to Sydney for just thirty-five pounds, room and board, nine days at sea or in port—or twelve days if we want to board now for our last three days in Melbourne, same price. We'll save more than thirty-five pounds by canceling the rest of our month in Adelaide and Canberra."

"Gosh, that's true, it's costing us about five pounds a day for room and board now, and we would save the ongoing rail fare too. We haven't been to sea since home leave in England, when John was a baby. Alright then, let's do it, but whether we move aboard the ship now or later, I think we should pay Mrs. Belfast through Christmas, as it's not her fault if we cancel early. Meanwhile we could use her telephone for canceling the other reservations. Where are you calling from, by the way?"

"From a busy kiosk on the dock, but it's not very suitable as there is already someone waiting for me to finish. Right, then, I'll confirm with the ship, and then come to the boarding house for lunch."

He hung up, and gave the thumbs-up to the bosun, who nodded and waved back from the ship's railing. Peter then strode along the dock toward the center of the city.

With the arrangement that he had made for the *Mirrabooka* to bring his family aboard for up to twelve days at a rate of thirty-five pounds, and Wendy's honorable decision to pay Mrs. Belfast through Christmas Day regardless, the Perrys found themselves in a flexible situation where they effectively had two short-term 'homes' available for several days. They opted to enjoy both but had not yet decided whether to celebrate Christmas Day on the ship, or ashore.

Peter still wanted to see the Melbourne Cricket Ground, where some of the First Marine Division had been billeted, so he could take a few snapshots for Bongo and Lt. Culver. To the Marines, it was most certainly a home away from home. Much remodeling had been done to provide semi-private but windy sleeping quarters up among the spectator seating.

In the end, after two more days of sightseeing, and in case they couldn't find a taxi for their luggage on Christmas Day, the Perrys decided to move aboard *Mirrabooka* on Christmas Eve. They settled their bill at the guesthouse, bid a grateful farewell to Mrs. Belfast, and went off to the docks.

John was almost speechless with excitement as they crossed the wooden gangway, where his friend the Danish bosun solemnly piped them aboard.

*** *ALL AT SEA* ***

Each of the ship's twelve passenger cabins contained a pair of over-and-under bunks, so they chose two adjacent cabins in the middle of the array. John and Wendy would occupy one of them, and Peter would once again sleep alone.

It was customary in Australia for Father Christmas (Santa Claus) to arrive just after the tree was decorated on Christmas Eve, to fill the children's stockings. While Wendy was settling John down early for his first night in the top bunk, which thrilled him to pieces, she asked Peter to adjust the cabin ventilation.

"It feels awfully stuffy in here, and I can't seem to get the grille to open more. Do have a go, before we accept the captain's eggnog invitation and help decorate the tree."

Peter pushed on the grille lever but saw that it was jammed in the almost-closed position and could not be further opened. "Ruddy thing must be rusted," he told Wendy. "Half a mo, I'll borrow a screwdriver from someone and take the grille off."

John went along with him, wearing pajamas and slippers. Conveniently, Jurgen the bosun was in the lounge, setting the tree up in a metal base. He passed a screwdriver to Peter and exchanged a naval salute with John. Peter told John he could stay and help the bosun until the screwdriver was returned.

Back in the cabin, Peter used the desk chair to stand on, and with surprising ease removed two rusty old screws from the ventilation grille. "Ah, here's the problem, Wen," he said, removing a dirty-looking wrapped object that had somehow jammed itself under the dusty grille lever. "I wonder what this is; why don't you open it while I put back the grille?"

Wendy was equally curious, and carefully untied a brown shoelace that encircled an old oilskin wrapping.

"Peter! Look at these!" Wendy was aghast at the package's contents which, she breathlessly told Peter, included a Luger-like pistol, an apparent Japanese code book, a thin sealed envelope, and a thicker one with possibly a lot of money inside, because its outside was marked in pencil: £5,000.

"Good lord," Peter whispered, "Five thousand pounds; that's a fortune. It must be that fellow Watanabe's stash, I should think. Let me run and get the captain. I think we need to open those envelopes in front of him, don't you?"

Wendy nodded: "Yes, of course. And perhaps John should stay out there with the bosun for a while longer." She rinsed her hands in the little bathroom.

Walking briskly, Peter returned in a few minutes with a visibly puzzled Captain Axelsson. Peter explained where the package had been found, and that they had only untied the outer wrapper. "If this collection belonged to Watanabe-san, as it would seem, then perhaps he was pushed overboard! Otherwise why would he leave all this money hidden, instead of giving it to his lady friend?"

"Who can say?" the captain shrugged, "Let us see what the envelopes contain, please, then I will take this pistol to the ship's armory in any case"

Peter was startled to find that the thin envelope contained a detailed sketch map of Melbourne's harbor area, with Japanese notations here and there. A smaller inset sketch showed the headlands near the sea, and the location of military gun emplacements. By now, the 1937 details were surely not of much military value to anyone, but they certainly were intriguing. If nothing else, the map fairly well confirmed Watanabe's suspected espionage role, assuming it was he who hid the bundle in the ventilator.

Then the money was inspected. It turned out that the pencil notation was exactly accurate. Each person counted out a stack of one-hundred-pound notes—which were British pounds, not Australian, and therefore twenty percent more valuable—then they re-counted each other's tallies. There were exactly fifty of the pre-war £100 bills in the envelope—five thousand pounds sterling, the equivalent of six thousand Australian pounds, or twenty-five thousand American dollars!

"Mr. and Mrs. Perry," the captain intoned solemnly, "it is impossible to say whom this money really belonged to before, but it certainly was not the *Mirrabooka* or her crew. It may have been the unfortunate Mr. Watanabe, who alas is no longer among the living, and surely it was not his lady companion or else the money would have moved on with her. If I hand over these British pound notes to my company, they will effectively vanish. I myself do not aspire to any share of them, therefore I am officially— but unofficially—giving these funds to the two of you who made the discovery. This is more or less the law of the sea. So, congratulations! If you were to ask my suggestion for how the money should be spent, however, I would propose using it to put John through university when the time comes. Would that be a reasonable request?"

"Good heavens, yes!" Peter stuttered. "Wendy, are you agreed?" She nodded silently.

"Very good, then," Captain Axelsson smiled. "When I write in the logbook, there will be no mention of any money being in the packet, only the pistol, the code book, and the map. That will be enough to intrigue our company directors anyway."

They laughed, and Peter shook Captain Axelsson's hand with enthusiasm. The captain added: "Just be certain to hide the money very carefully now. No banks will be open before we sail for Brisbane the day after tomorrow."

"Should I hide it in the ventilator then?" They laughed again, and the captain said he would keep it for them in the ship's safe.

227

*** *IN MACARTHUR'S SHADOW* ***

MV *Mirrabooka*, of six thousand registered and nine thousand gross tons, and of four-hundred-fifty feet length, traveled from Melbourne to Brisbane in a small convoy under the protection of an old RAN destroyer. Two Australian-flagged freighters made up the rest of the convoy, each slightly larger and slower than the Swedish passenger-freighter. The speed of the slowest, around twelve knots, determined the transit time of the group, which was effectively reduced to ten knots because of zigzagging in case of submarines.

When, four days and nights later—during which they had passed Sydney well out to sea—the convoy finally reached the mouth of the Brisbane River at Moreton Bay, having followed the destroyer carefully though a defensive minefield and anti-submarine boom, the three commercial vessels were each told by their escort to heave to and await a pilot, for the wharves were a fair distance inland and there was considerable river traffic, primarily naval and military.

A few days earlier, when they were already out to sea from Melbourne, Captain Axelsson had given Peter the news of another Allied landing, this time at Cape Gloucester on New Britain. Peter was relieved to hear it, for he had been wondering whether the ship would be safe from submarine attacks along the Australian coast, but now he agreed with Captain Axelsson that Japan would doubtless muster all its nearby resources to defend New Britain and Rabaul.

It was the First Marine Division again, that went ashore at Cape Gloucester in MacArthur's sphere of operations. *That news will electrify the many brides and mothers-to-be in Melbourne when it is released*, Peter chuckled silently.

Now that Brisbane was at hand, Peter learned that *Mirrabooka* had been chartered by the Australian Navy twice in recent months, to bring crated kits of American fighter planes from Melbourne to MacArthur's air forces, thus Captain Axelsson's first mate knew the Brisbane River's twists and turns fairly well.

Furthermore, the Swedish ship was powered by twin diesel engines rather than a single oil-fired steam-driven shaft and was therefore much more maneuverable than the two conventional freighters. These attributes exempted the Swedes from having to engage a tugboat to navigate the river, but a pilot with up-to-date information about the tidal river's ever-changing depth was still a requirement.

Mirrabooka reached the Howard Smith Wharves at sundown on New Year's Eve 1944, beneath the new and much-admired Story Bridge that spanned the wide river at an abrupt bend near the central business district. Before docking, the ship was carefully turned around to face back down the river. The local agents, Howard Smith Ltd., advised that *Mirrabooka* would be in port for four days rather than two, because no stevedores would work on the New Year holiday, not even for overtime pay.

On this trip, the ship would be loading repairable aircraft engines for USASOS—the US Army Service of Supply—before sailing back south to Sydney, her last Australian port before leaving for New Caledonia and the New Hebrides, and on beyond to California.

The Perrys were looking forward to stretching their legs ashore, and particularly to finding a Barclays Bank branch so they could deposit the large stash of English pounds. Because of the New Year holiday on Saturday, their banking would have to wait until Monday.

Peter was also curious to learn whether Lt. McGowan was still at the US Navy facility up-river, where Peter and Bongo had met with Commander Feldt last year. Peter also yearned for some in-depth war news, to help him decide what to do once his leave was over, but he was fairly certain no one would be at the naval station until Monday except for Marine guards.

The Perrys would have to wander the city for two days, therefore. This hearkened Peter back to a quiet New Year's weekend in Nouméa the year before, except then he had been with Abby, and Wendy had been with Doris. *How strange the ways of fate,* he thought to himself.

During the slow northward trip from Melbourne, he and Wendy had spoken often about their relationship, after John was asleep, but Wendy was adamant that she would be staying with Doris 'forever'.

"What will people say if Doris is pregnant?" Peter wanted to know.

Wendy reckoned it was no one's business, and nowadays there could be any number of reasons because of the war. Melbourne, for example, seemed full of pregnant single girls fathered by Marines or Aussie troops. People will probably assume Doris had a similar liaison, she imagined, but it didn't really matter as no one was likely to ask. Besides, it would be good cover for the relationship between Doris and herself; perhaps that was why Doris wanted to have a child, though Wendy wasn't certain.

They had talked on about the future as they sailed north toward Brisbane in the small convoy, with occasional glimpses of faraway Australian mountains through the haze, and the destroyer's periodic change of position providing some break to the monotony. It was during those chats that Wendy asked Peter to provide half of his income to her for raising John (they eventually settled for one third), and she insisted Peter must promise to visit from time to time. Above all, Wendy was adamant that they should legally divorce, to give them each complete freedom.

"Are you certain it's wise to bring up John without a father?" Peter had asked. "I am really very concerned about his future." This question had been at the back of his mind ever since Melbourne, when Wendy first asked for the divorce.

"Peter, I truly do not know, but it has to be. There are lots of single mothers now—widows, divorcées, non-marrieds—so John will not be the odd one out at school, without a doubt. I honestly believe that Doris and I can bring him up to be a responsible citizen. But please don't disappear, Peter. You are still, and always will be John's father."

"I see," said Peter, although he didn't quite.

"By the way, John will be attending a different school this year," Wendy advised. "I meant to tell you sooner, but it slipped my mind with all the emotional business. It's a wonderful thing for him, an advance placement test that he passed for Fort Street School, over near the Sydney Harbor Bridge where you used to meet Bongo. This school brings together the brightest children from all over Sydney for their last three years of elementary. And he can easily get there on his own, by tram."

"Oh, that *is* splendid," said Peter. "I must congratulate him in the morning. I shall try my best to visit you and John several times a year, war regulations permitting. Damn the war, anyhow. Look what it's done to our family."

"And there's more about John," Wendy went on, relaxed now that their tense discussions seemed to be at an end. "John will be joining the Cub Scouts this year as well, and I'll be one of the pack leaders for our neighborhood. I'm really happy about having that outside activity, which will take place at John's old school."

"It sounds like you and John, and Doris, will have a good year then. That's very nice. I don't quite know what I shall do in the future, as I'm still in shock about all this divorce business, but it will probably have something to do with the endless war. Speaking of which, I'll need to talk to Lt. McGowan on Monday after we do our banking here. I feel very out of touch without current news. The lack of it almost lulls one to sleep, but certainly there must be a lot going on with the Japs. Brisbane appears to be a very busy place, for example, which must mean something big is happening out there. At any rate, perhaps you and John can do some more sightseeing while I visit McGowan, if you don't mind." Wendy smiled and nodded, glad to be helping Peter get his bearings.

"And by the way, I have some undelivered news for you, too," Peter added, "that I also forgot. Ned said Marjorie doesn't want to take over our cottage, even though it would cut Ned's daily commute in half. It's partly because she wants to stay in the fancier Cremourne neighborhood, and partly because of the constant airport noise that is causing concerns in Rose Bay, as you have also mentioned. So we might as well give notice to the landlord if you're certain you want to give up the cottage altogether."

Wendy nodded again: "I'm so sorry, Peter, I truly am. I hope I haven't caused you too much pain."

Well," Peter replied, "on a lighter note, Ned and his neighbors have started to make home brew on weekends, so he is probably just as glad to stay where he is in spite of the long daily drive."

*** *IS ANYONE HOME?* ***

At the US naval station near Colmslie on the Brisbane River, Peter Perry was delighted to find not only Lt. Robert McGowan on board, but also the elusive Cdr. Bongo Perkins, Peter's on-again off-again companion in Pacific Theater adventure. With typical straight-faced nonchalance, Bongo opened the conversation with a long complex story about having become bored with Guadalcanal, bored with the Navy, and being on the verge of resigning his commission to take up residence in China as an attaché to Generalissimo Chiang Kai-Shek.

McGowan laughed aloud, and Peter rolled his eyes, having heard many a Bongo utterance of similar structure in the past.

"No, I'm serious, ugly Brit. Look, I'm studying Chinese now and have mastered at least 500 words—well, more or less. Listen up: *Ni hao ma? Ni jiao shenma minzi? Wode jongguo minzi shr 'Ban Guo'. Hen hao ting, dui-bu-dui?* Well, what do you think, Limey pal? Want to come with me to China?"

"Good grief. How long has this mad scheme been brewing? What on earth tickled your fancy about China? And why are you here in Brisbane instead of the Canal?"

"Well, what audacity! Mister McGowan," Bongo addressed the junior officer, "we might well ask this nosy person the same question, right?" Lt. McGowan nodded vigorously, pushing Peter into an empty chair and setting down a succulently brewed cup of Queensland coffee beside him.

"Right, Commander, let me worm it out of him; you are far too lenient with your English friend, as far as I can see."

Facing Peter, McGowan donned his sunglasses and took out of his desk drawer a leather riding crop with which he alternatively slapped his leg and hand—*slap, slap*.

"Now Mr. Perry, you have exactly one minute to answer the following questions: number one—*slap*—why are you frequenting an American naval facility in Brisbane? Two—*slap, slap*—how did you arrive in said City of Brisbane without a naval permit or deployment order issued by the ONI? And three—*slap, slap, slap*—why have you abandoned your family in Sydney to make this clandestine journey? Well? Hurry up, English spy, you have only 45 seconds left!" *Slap, slap*, went the riding crop.

"May I please telephone my solicitor?" Peter pleaded through clenched teeth, the coffee burning his palate. "You see; I am just a lowly salesman for Scottish whiskey. I am certainly no spy, oh no, oh no indeed. I have come here at considerable expense just to ask whether any honorable American gentlemen might wish to purchase a case of my unworthy product; very special low price for American naval officer. I can even offer a free sample now, if the gentlemen will but release me from harm,"

Peter groveled, pulling a bottle of Johnny Walker Red from his attaché case on the floor. "Beyond that, I know nothing, nothing at all, honorable and kind sirs. You must believe me. I am an honest man; I have many irrational international references, you see."

"Ah, that throws a different light on the matter," Bongo hastened to say. "Well done, Mister McGowan, well done. You have broken the case, so to speak. You may ask the firing squad to stand down."

Slap, slap went the riding crop: "Aye, aye sir." A sweet aroma of whiskey and coffee filled the room, and the sun broke through the clouds as if the very Gabriel had blown his horn and stopped by for a sample of Navy elixir.

*** *WAR PLANS FOR 1944* ***

Over some more carefully-laced cups of coffee, and a tray of spam sandwiches delivered from the mess hall—the other choice being mutton sandwiches which Americans seemed to loath—Peter absorbed the exciting news that Lt. McGowan presented, along with maps and photographs. He learned much more about the campaign at Cape Gloucester, and the First Marine Division which had dispatched its regiments from Melbourne to Townsville during September and October, then sneaked them around the eastern tip of New Guinea to a small island called—amusingly—Goodenough.

From there, the division executed a beach landing on nearby Cape Gloucester, New Britain, where they were still heavily engaged. Along with them went a company of old M4A1 medium tanks, donated by the US Army after use on Bougainville.

"My word," Peter commented, "the Marines went ashore the same day as I sailed from Melbourne to get here. They must still be in the middle of their fight, as you said."

"Yes they are," McGowan replied, "but they have captured the Japanese airfield, and our Seabees are making steady progress with it in spite of the rain and mud. You can see here on the chart that Rabaul lies at the opposite end of New Britain from where our forces are now fighting. Rabaul is Japan's heavily defended naval base and command center for the southern region.

"New Britain lies along MacArthur's *Cartwheel* track, while Bougainville is on the Nimitz track. Rabaul will soon be history, once MacArthur's Australians clean out the rest of New Guinea's north coast airfields. We don't actually plan to attack Rabaul, only to isolate its garrison."

Peter also learned of the Navy's pending actions in the Marshall and Caroline Islands, which would be following on the heels of the bloody Tarawa invasion last November.

"This will be a sort of third cartwheel track, then?" He asked McGowan.

"That's right, Peter, but I can't tell you much more than that at the moment. They are all important steppingstones, however."

"So now what?" Bongo asked. "Tell us what you're up to, OK? How is the family doing? I forgot you must be on leave still."

Peter recounted the highlights of his family holiday trip to Melbourne, and their change of plans when coming across the Swedish ship in Melbourne harbor. He left out any mention of the big problem with Wendy. He also had a niggling hunch that he should inform Bongo or McGowan about the Japanese map of Melbourne, and particularly the old code book, both now locked away in the ship's safe. The quandary was doing this without letting on to the ship's captain or Wendy that he, Peter, was a part-time ONI operative.

"Look, would the two of you care to come aboard the *Mirrabooka* for a drink tomorrow evening around six? Wendy and John would be delighted, and I'm sure the captain would enjoy meeting you, provided Bongo doesn't start speaking Chinese."

"Good plan, Limey tourist. I can make it," said Bongo," but McGowan has to deliver a report to General MacArthur's ADC on Sunday evening, don't you Lieutenant?" Lt. McGowan nodded, looking relieved.

*** *OF SPAIN AND FRANCO* ***

The Sunday evening was very enjoyable. Young John recognized Bongo immediately he came aboard and shook hands formally. Wendy welcomed him warmly with a hug. Captain Axelsson gave Bongo a quick tour of the ship, then settled with him and the Perrys in the lounge, where John was engrossed in a pile of comic books that the bosun had discovered.

Over chilled champagne from the ship's stores, they toasted the Old and New Year, and wished each other good health and fortune in 1944. Talk inevitably turned to the story of Watanabe the spy and his hidden documents, and of course the mysterious Spanish woman with her involvement in keeping General Franco from joining forces with Hitler. Bongo picked up on that one, but not before Wendy excused herself and took John to the cabin.

"Night-night, all," she said. "I've heard enough about this Spanish woman already." John sleepily saluted the captain.

"Look, folks," Bongo said to the men after Wendy and John had departed, "I can tell you another story about that same subject: Mr. Churchill had been after Franco for years to stay out of the war, and even bribed some Spanish generals to use their influence on the Generalissimo. The final intervention, which seemed to put an end to the dithering, was a—shall we say—generous donation of three million pounds sterling, a considerable sum, I think you'll agree." The other three men were all ears, as Bongo fed them the story.

"These funds were duly handed over in cash at the Hotel Grande Bretagne in Athens, in the early '40s. A briefcase was delivered in the hotel bar to Franco's representative, by an MI5 courier named Ian Fleming. My boss, Captain Silvers, had the pleasure of meeting Fleming in London last year, by the way, so you see, the mysterious Spanish lady didn't accomplish all this on her own, but certainly, by persuading her father to suggest neutrality to Franco, she must have helped Churchill in the end. That's one less country we have to fight in. So, Captain Axelsson, might I borrow the Watanabe documents for a few days?"

"Bravo, Commander, I shall remember that story for our directors," Captain Axelsson vowed, "but unfortunately I cannot lend you the map and code book that we found in Watanabe's cabin, as we are strictly neutral in Sweden. But would you care to stay aboard for dinner? We shall have some fine Australian mutton tonight."

"Er, thank you very much for the kind invitation, skipper, but I'd better hit the sack now. Lt. McGowan and I have a very early and busy Monday morning, then I must fly back to Guadalcanal at noon. But next time perhaps, with thanks in advance. Meanwhile, I wish you smooth sailing." And upon Wendy's reappearance in the lounge, Bongo added: "Adios, Perrys, hope to see you again soon. Peter, do stay in touch, OK?"

Mirrabooka was in Sydney by Friday morning, docked at Pier Five in Walsh Bay, near the foot of the Sydney Harbor Bridge where the ONI had once leased the warehouse that Peter visited several times in 1942. Wendy was excited to point out that John's new school was just a short climb from the docks to Upper Fort Street and Observatory Park.

"What a coincidence!" she exclaimed, "We're almost home. I'd better telephone Doris and tell her we're back. She can come get us, which will save on a taxi." She placed the call to Doris from the dock, then told Peter to hurry and pack, as the car would arrive within the hour.

"Wendy, I'll come visit you and Doris tomorrow afternoon for a drink, that's all. If our relationship is final, as you stated, then there's not much point prolonging my part in it, is there? I've paid Captain Axelsson to keep my cabin for me as far as Santo. Before we sail, I'd like to spend a day in Sydney with Ned, too. When I get to Santo, I'll still have two more weeks of leave available, so I'll go spend some of it with Hans and get the grass skirt supply set up for you ladies to develop. Hans and his fiancée Yvonne could be your business partners if you like. They are most reliable, as you will see."

"Oh Peter, I'm so sorry, but I think you're right. Since we decided to put John's education money into war bonds under his name, instead of in our bank, then we might as well get started with the divorce paperwork soon, do you agree?"

Peter reluctantly confirmed his agreement, and watched John and Wendy leave the wharf with Doris an hour later. He waved from the ship's railing.

When he called on them in Rose Bay the next day, Peter learned that Doris was pregnant, which resulted in a round of champagne. With John out of earshot, Doris jokingly suggested renting Peter out for stud fees, and Wendy laughingly agreed. Peter blushed, and another round of champagne followed. He asked why Doris had no children with Fred. She explained, downcast:

"We tried now and then, but Fred had a fancy for young boys, unfortunately, which I hadn't realized before we married. I lived with it for twelve years, and perhaps that may have somehow tilted me toward Wendy, not sure. I'm happy now that I'll have a child, thanks to you Peter, as I'm thirty-five and getting near the practical limit. Yes, I'm three years younger than Wendy, and five younger than you, Peter. Oh, and by the way, the sample grass skirts have arrived from Santo, and I already sold half of them at the £20 target price!" Wendy clapped her hands.

On that note, Peter bid the ladies farewell and went outside to find John, who was combing Digger's matted coat.

"John-O, I have to go back to work across the sea. Take good care of Mummy and Auntie Doris, and I'll be back again one day soon. Would you like to ride your bike with me to the tram stop?"

*** BACK TO NOUMÉA AND SANTO ***

The lovely south coast of New Caledonia slowly materialized in the morning light, far off the port bow. *Mirrabooka* was the only commercial ship in the small convoy of naval vessels this time, trailing behind an armed Liberty ship and a tanker, under escort by a USN frigate.

The ships approached the immense barrier reef that Captain Axelsson said was the world's second longest, and which in turn formed the world's largest lagoon that surrounded the main island of *Grande Terre*. A pilot boat came toward the lead ship from an offshore islet on which a remarkable white lighthouse was standing, marking the approximate position of the *Passe Boulari* (Boulari Passage) into the lagoon near Nouméa's harbor.

"Is it not an amazing sight? I have read about it, but this is the first time for me to actually see the Amédée Light," the captain said, standing with Peter at one end of the wheelhouse as the first mate steered the ship.

"Our sailing guidebook says this lighthouse was prefabricated in Paris in the 1860s and assembled there to verify stability. Two years later it was disassembled, packed into hundreds of crates and shipped to New Caledonia for reassembly! That must have been soon after the penal colony got started.

"Here is more: 'The structure was named *Phare Amédée* after the little island on which it stands. An inner wrought-iron skeleton is protected by a skin of riveted metal plates, which has enabled the lighthouse to withstand the tropical climate for such a long time. It is a similar concept to the Statue of Liberty in New York Harbor, which is also a French creation.' Amazing, eh?"

As the ships drew closer, and the pilot for Nouméa boarded the Liberty ship, Peter fully agreed that the lighthouse was a work of exquisite engineering. Soon the column of ships left it behind and slowed at the approach to the Nouméa headland. Peter pointed to another island that was partly blocking the harbor mouth. "Look there, Captain Axelsson, you can see the ruins of old Fort Tereka on *l'île Nou*. I went there with some friends. It was guarding the penal colony in the old days."

"The fort seems the same era as the lighthouse," the captain said, "but they have looked after the lighthouse much better."

As the convoy entered the harbor itself, they were astounded to see the large number of ships at anchor. "Good heavens," Peter said, "what are the chances of us getting to a wharf for unloading?"

"Not this evening, I'm afraid. We shall have to anchor now," said Captain Axelsson, "but I know you are eager to get ashore while we are in port. After we anchor, I will try to get permission for you to go in by launch."

He went to the radio room to contact the harbormaster's office, which was of course under Navy control. Peter went down to the lounge to join the few other passengers who had come aboard in Sydney. Three middle-aged men, whose nationality he had not yet determined, were huddled at one of the tables, and two younger Australian couples with small children were seated on facing couches.

One of the huddled trio stood to ask Peter how he was able to get up on the bridge while the ship was coming through the reef.

"Oh, just a courtesy from Captain Axelsson," Peter answered. "I've been aboard as the only passenger for the last several ports, and he has taken pity on me. Are you going on to California? I'm certain there will be lots of time aloft for everyone. Perry is my name, gentlemen."

"Carstens here," the speaker said, "please do join us for a drink before dinner. These are my colleagues, Rivens and Forrester." Peter nodded to the others, who seemed vaguely antisocial.

"You're not Australians then?" Peter asked.

"No indeed, we're not," said Carstens. "Each of us hails from the island of Efaté in the Hebrides. Have you heard of it?"

"I certainly have," Peter replied, smiling. "I was there for a day to drop off someone at the Navy hospital, then we went to Port Vila by boat for dinner. Months later, I spent a little time on Santo with the Americans and met some French planters who came from Efaté originally. It is a very pretty island."

"A paradise, Mr. Perry, a paradise, but this war will leave all these islands changed in many ways. We like to think the changes will be for the better, but that may not be so. Hopefully the Anglo-French condominium will manage to survive, for one thing."

Just then a new steward entered the lounge, who had joined the ship in Sydney. He was playing a little tune on the small musical chimes that normally announce when meals are being served, only it wasn't quite mealtime. "Paging Mr. Perry," the steward said quietly as he walked discreetly past the guests in the lounge, tapping on the little xylophone that hung from his neck. "Paging Mr. Perry."

"I am he," said Peter.

"Please follow me to the wireless room, sir," the steward said politely.

"Well gentlemen, excuse me. I look forward very much to continuing our conversation another time." The three Anglo-Hebrideans nodded to Peter, then resumed their huddled conversation at the table.

The captain awaited Peter in the 'wireless shack', as it was more commonly known. "I have a surprise for you," he announced. "It seems someone ashore wants to see you and is sending a boat over. How lucky you are."

"Good heavens, who can that be? Someone from the Navy?" "Didn't sound like it. When I requested permission from the harbormaster for a Mr. Peter Perry of British nationality to come ashore, I was told that the American contractor's office had been trying to find you on Guadalcanal and Australia for some time. It is they who are sending the launch. Please let me know if you need to stay in Nouméa for some while, and I'll have your things sent ashore. You will get a partial refund, of course."

"Well, I hope I don't need to stay. I did want a day ashore here but really need to go on to Santo too. I'll be in touch tomorrow, Captain Axelsson. And thank you, as always."

The second surprise of the afternoon came when the launch turned out to be one of the PANAIR boats from the seaplane base.

"Hello there, Peter," called a cheery voice. "We just got a request from the harbormaster to collect a passenger named Perry from a Swedish freighter. I figured it might be you, but your form of transportation seemed a bit unusual."

"Andrew! What a delightful surprise! How in the world are you? And how is Abby? I haven't written her since Guadalcanal a month ago and was hoping to find her here to apologize."

"I left her a message at the nurses' quarters before I came to get you," Andrew Culver said. "I'm sure she's expecting you by now. By the way, the Contracts Office just closed for the day, but they want you there at 0830 in the morning. Now let's get you ashore at the NATS boat dock."

"Gosh, this is wonderfully kind of you. But where can I stay tonight, then? It may be hard to get back to the ship after dark."

"Perhaps Abby will have some suggestions," Andrew chuckled. "Why don't you ask her?"

*** *PLUS ÇA CHANGE …* ***

Basking in the delight of his reunion with Abby, Peter left the hotel room without waking her, in order to attend his 0830 meeting at the contracts office. He managed a quick breakfast at the pleasant dining room of the *Grand Hôtel du Pacifique* and noticed from the local headlines that a murderer from Java was to be guillotined today at *l'île Nou*, which the public was invited to watch! That didn't sound like a pleasant way to spend the afternoon with Abby. Back to reality!

As the hotel had also been the former residence of Army General Patch and was still partly commandeered by Army brass, the room was beginning to fill up with a variety of high-ranking Allied uniforms by the time he had looked for a taxi. Peter and Abby had agreed that she would wait at the hotel until he returned, and for this she had arranged a day off from her hospital duties.

It had been a month of odd surprises for Peter, both bad and good, but one of the better ones awaited him at the US contracts office when he arrived and asked the receptionist for Mr. Beamish. "I'm sorry, sir, but Mr. Beamish has been retired from his duties, and has returned to Sydney. I'm afraid he has suffered a serious heart attack, you see."

"Oh dear, I'm very sorry to hear that. I'm Peter Perry, and I was asked to be here at half past eight this morning."

"Oh yes, sir. Mr. MacDougall, the managing director, is here from Sydney, standing in for Mr. Beamish. I'll just ring and say you're here."

Peter remembered Hamish MacDougall from his visit to the Sydney office when he was first hired by Beamish to work in Nouméa. As he followed the receptionist back to the offices, he wondered whether he was about to lose his employment again, for the third time after Singapore and Canton Island.

"Ah Mr. Perry, do sit down. We have been chasing after you for a couple of weeks now, up and down the Australian coast. Imagine our surprise when you suddenly appeared right here in Nouméa. Cigarette?"

"Thank you, no sir. I've been on leave from Guadalcanal and still am, so I apologize for leading the firm on a wild chase."

"Well, I think the receptionist told you about poor old Beamish. He had a bad heart attack three weeks ago but lived through it in a feeble sort of way. We've had to pension him off, I'm afraid, but he did recommend that we consider you for his replacement out here in the islands. Would that be something that might interest you? Guadalcanal will become the new center of activities for us, with Nouméa and Santo remaining as satellites. Then there would be new construction beyond Guadalcanal as the Allies move further toward Japan. As you know, we follow in with a more permanent infrastructure after the Seabees have blazed a trail."

"Why yes sir, it certainly would be of interest to me! I'm honored to be considered," Peter tried hard not to grin with delight.

"Well, it's not quite certain yet, Mr. Perry, but we needed to know about your interest. There is one other candidate on his way here from Fiji to see me, an Englishman like yourself, but I don't think he has your depth of experience. Still, I've told the Americans that we'll take a look at him. It seems someone named Overwood from the colonial office recommended this chap to the Americans when they were looking for a helping hand at the seaplane base on Suva."

"Overwood? Is that Graham Overwood by any chance?" Peter asked. The director shuffled through the papers. "Yes ... yes, it is, Graham Overwood, do you know him?"

"I do indeed," Peter replied. "A good man; he was the British representative on Canton Island when I was there. He got banged up by the Japs on his way to Fiji, and we met again when he was going into hospital. May I ask who he is recommending to you?"

"Mm, apparently it is a cousin of Mrs. Overwood, though it is the Americans on Fiji who have suggested the chap to us, not the Overwoods themselves. But we're always leery of nepotism, though that's just a general statement. We don't know this chap's name yet. Look, where can we contact you, Mr. Perry, around a week from now?"

"Well sir, I was planning to stay with the freighter and get off at Santo for my last two weeks of leave, and fly back to Guadalcanal from there, but if you'd like me to stay here for that time, I'll be happy to do so." Peter had a pleasant vision of a week or two with Abby in Nouméa, although she told him last night that she had signed up two weeks ago as a volunteer for the new hospital on Guadalcanal. Either way, Abby would be part of his life soon enough.

"No, I think your plan is fine, Mr. Perry. We'll have decided by then and will let you know on Santo what the decision is. You're familiar with our little office over there, I assume. Just let them know where to find you when we send a message. I am personally very pleased that you would be happy to take on the new assignment."

*** ... PLUS C'EST LA MÊME CHOSE ***

On the way to Santo aboard MV *Mirrabooka*, a thirty-four-hour voyage this time in the company of two armed LSTs but no destroyer or frigate escort, Peter got better acquainted with Bruno Carstens, the more vocal of the Efaté trio that kept to themselves in the ship's lounge. The other two—Charles Rivens and Jean-Marc Forrester—turned out to be somewhat awkward socially, rather than hostile as Peter had first thought. They were all third-generation islanders, where the custom was, even for the English on Efaté, to give their children French forenames. All three were completely bilingual and often spoke in the island's *patois* when trying to make a point. Peter was quite fascinated.

The gist of their conversation revolved around the future of the islands after the war with Japan was over, which by 1944 appeared to be just a matter of time. Both the English and French communities of the New Hebrides were concerned about agitation among the Kanaks for postwar independence, should the winds of change blow across the Pacific region. The Japanese sham 'Greater East Asia Co-Prosperity Sphere' was fanning the flames of anti-colonialism among indigenous people everywhere, and some military units from British India had even deserted and joined Japan as mercenaries!

The mission of the three men aboard the *Mirrabooka* was to acquire arms; arms with which to defend the European communities in case of rebellion among the islands. Unfortunately, they had failed to gain support from the military in Australia, which was too preoccupied at the moment with wresting New Guinea back from the Japanese. The Americans might see things differently, they were told, so they were going to Santo to speak to the American admiral in charge. Could Peter lend some weight to their cause, perhaps?

"Well, I'm not certain but I'll ask around while you have your meeting with the admiral. I have heard that the US bases will probably not ship their war material back to the US, but that could be a rumor. How will you get back to Efaté from Santo, by the way? Perhaps we could have a meeting before you leave."

*** *A BRIEF TIME ON SANTO* ***

Peter found Hans, Yvonne, and the three children living at her home outside Old Luganville. It was a happy family that welcomed him to their table. Stéphanie still seemed the best organized of the children and functioned as a sort of major-domo for the household, organizing the shopping, schooling, and banking for everyone. Hans was living like a king, it was clear.

Peter paid Hans for the sample shipment of grass skirts and asked if he and Yvonne (and perhaps Stéph too) would like to work with two women friends in Sydney, to develop a bigger market for the Kanak arts and crafts. He explained the economics to them, which aroused their interest and a strong commitment.

Peter left an extra one thousand US dollars as a pledge, and they matched the figure themselves. This would be their working capital. It would allow them to buy and ship 400 grass skirts, and they would include samples of other things like shells and wood carvings for comments by Wendy and Doris. They would ship by sea whenever cargo ships came though Santo, otherwise by air when non-military space was available.

That being settled, Peter, who was staying with Yvonne's brother, asked Philippe what he thought about buying arms for a possible future emergency.

"Oh certainly," Philippe replied. "I know those men from Efaté that you mentioned. Let us meet them tomorrow and see what they learned from the Navy. I, too, fear an uprising when the Americans leave, who—more than Japan—are becoming the inspiration for independence and democracy here and elsewhere in the Pacific. When they leave, the Melanesians, driven by their strange ideas of the John Frum cult, are likely to riot and try to kill the colonial Europeans, and people like us who are Euronesians. With guns and vehicles, we can probably contain a rebellion, but it will be disruptive and dangerous. I don't think independence will be good for these islands, at least not in the near term."

So the civilians met secretly in Luganville with the three visitors. Hans and Yvonne joined Peter and Philippe in representing Santo at the meeting. Bruno reported on the admiral's comments: "The admiral said he thought the United States has far too much invested in Santo for the base to close down in the near future. He said the base would remain here long after the war, perhaps for a decade or more, and therefore it would probably deter any uprisings by the natives. He said the war would go on for several more years, culminating in a long and bloody invasion of the Japanese home islands, and much more matériel would be arriving throughout the Pacific to support a million combat troops for the big push ahead. He doubted if anything would be for sale in the way of weaponry here but said if there was any surplus then he would make it known to us before a public disclosure."

"Hmm, that's not what I've been hearing up in Guadalcanal, which is growing into a big base like Santo," Peter commented. "There the talk is all about bringing the Americans home the minute the war ends, although they too say it will take several more years to defeat Japan. Already the Kiwis are starting to run the Canal, to free up Americans for duty elsewhere. I say, Bruno, do you have funds to buy weapons if they become available?"

"Yes, but probably not as much as we will need for a multi-island militia," Bruno replied. "Officially, our condominium government will not offer to buy anything, as they think the US would leave it all behind anyway, but we civilians think that is a foolish position to take. We need not only weapons, but transportation as well—jeeps, trucks, small boats, and so on—even a few scout planes."

At Philippe's home there was a message for Peter to telephone the Contracts Office, whereupon he learned that he was now officially in charge of the US South Pacific contracts business, based on Guadalcanal. The promotion somehow seemed anti-climactic, as it was a substantial change in responsibility, more than in pay. A private message was included: *'Congratulations Perry. Overwood's man not even close! MacDougall'*. Tomorrow he would see what air transportation was available to get him up to the Canal. *The more things change, the more they stay the same*, Peter mused.

*** PHOTOGRAPHIC INTERPRETATION ***

When Bongo hurriedly departed from Brisbane, after toasting the 1944 New Year with Peter on MV *Mirrabooka,* it was to meet with a Marine major on Guadalcanal, named Charles Cox, who had replaced Commander Robert Quackenbush in September 1943 as senior photo intelligence officer for the South Pacific. Supplying daily photos for the major's Canal-based interpreters was a squadron of modified PB4Y-1 (B-24) aircraft known as VMD-154, which among other achievements was credited with discovering the secret Japanese airfield at Munda on New Georgia Island that was later captured and used by the Allies in their push to Bougainville.

Now in late January, the Fifth Fleet's invasion of the Marshall Islands was just a week away, with Marines assigned to attack the islands of Roi and Namur and the Army assigned to capture Kwajalein. VMD-154 was extremely busy supporting that operation, and its successor VMD-254 would remain so for a successive push into the Carolines. At that point, the Marine photo squadrons were due to be replaced by a new Navy organization, VD-1, so Bongo wanted to be certain that historical photo records dating back to Quackenbush's time were properly documented for VD-1.

The leader of VD-1, Commander Howell Dyson USN, would be bringing a squadron of eight PB4Y-1P bombers, especially modified for photographic reconnaissance with higher-powered cameras. Unlike the Marine squadrons that had been based on Espiritu Santo's Elrod Field, the Navy squadron would call Guadalcanal's Carney Field its home.

VD-1's aircraft had new Fairchild cameras that produced 9 x 18-inch high-resolution negatives. Their films would be developed, analyzed, and printed on special 10 x 19-inch photographic paper by Interpron-1, an equally new companion photo interpretation unit.

VD-1, which operated the aircraft, would become part of the umbrella organization for Navy aircraft squadrons in the Pacific, whereas Interpron-1 would be part of Naval Intelligence. This division of responsibilities represented a major change from the more informal procedures of past years.

Of interest to Navy planners was, as always, a day-to-day view of Japanese defenses, shipping, manpower, airfields, and such things, on the various islands of the Pacific that might or might not be selected as invasion targets in the march toward Japan. But also, of invaluable local use in the Solomons and beyond, was the accurate water depth estimates that the photo squadrons were able to provide for naval charts, and for PT boat squadrons that dashed about in the Solomon waters over coral heads and reefs. Bongo's other task was to insure there was no loss of continuity for this, in the handover from the Marines to the Navy in a few more weeks.

*** BACK TO THE CANAL ***

The day after his promotion, Peter was allocated a seat on a twin-engined Navy R4D leaving Santo at 0800 hours for Guadalcanal. Aboard were five other passengers and a large cargo of fresh fruits and vegetables from the farms that Philippe Orly operated on the Navy's behalf. The aircraft and its crew of four had come down from Guadalcanal the previous afternoon. Known to many as a *Dakota*, the Douglas aircraft's civilian nomenclature was DC-3; for the Army it was a C-47.

When the noisy plane took off, it climbed southeast into the trade winds then circled back around over the Segond Channel toward the interior of Espiritu Santo Island, heading northwest to the Solomons. Peter was fascinated to see the substantial number of ships in the channel and at the docks, and the acres of Quonset Huts ashore. Guadalcanal could become like this, he imagined.

He realized it was almost two months since he had left there for Sydney, and so much had happened in that brief time. The situation with Wendy still bothered him, or at least it bothered his ego. *Well, she's made her bed, so to speak, and kicked me out of it. Now to find another one. I still worry about John, though.*

Soon the plane was out over the ocean, with no land in sight that Peter could see. The pilot announced that they were flying at ten thousand feet. Peter was thankful for the cooler temperature, which reminded him that the Canal would be quite a bit warmer than Santo. A few hours passed in dozing daydreams.

Suddenly a shudder and bang awakened everyone. The starboard engine—Peter's side—was trailing smoke, and the propeller was locked fast.

"Sorry folks, we've just lost an engine." A series of individual gulps greeted the announcement. "We'll drop down to four thousand feet just in case of more problems, but these babies can fly just fine on one engine, though slower of course." It was around five hours since they had left Luganville.

One of the portside passengers said to no one in particular: "Hey, I can see land way off to the left. Let's hope it's Guadal." The plane seemed to be vibrating and the working engine was making irregular noises, not very encouraging. The pilot came back on:

"I guess you can feel the problem folks. The second engine is misbehaving, so I'm going to ease it off a bit and kind of glide us over toward that big island out there to port. I wish I could tell you it's Guadalcanal, but it isn't. That's San Cristobal, about 150 miles southeast of Henderson Field. I've sent an SOS to Tulagi that we might need a boat to pick us up. Please belt up in case we need to ditch. There's no airfield on this island, unfortunately, so we'll have to come down on the water, unless this engine starts behaving again."

The two sailor crew members in the cabin moved slowly along the inward-facing bench seats, helping the six passengers prepare for a water landing. Peter and the others just stared at each other, grim-faced. Those on the port side craned their heads to squint out portholes.

"The island's looking a lot bigger now. Seems like we can get that far at least." That was vaguely encouraging, but the thought of crash landing in the ocean didn't cheer Peter at all.

The pilot again: "We're going to come down soon. The engine is almost useless, so I'm not going to try for Guadal in case we end up in the water far from anywhere. A PT boat is on the way from Tulagi but will take about four hours to get to us. There's a Dumbo out here somewhere close, that they they're trying to contact; maybe that plane can beat the PT boat if they can alert it. The other ones on patrol are too far away. We're going to ditch just outside the surf on the north shore. There are natives on this island, and they've helped other plane crews before. Hopefully, their canoes will come for us."

The pilot broke off for a radio message. "OK, that was Henderson Field. They concur with our plan. Now listen up: we have two ten-person inflatable rafts on board. Theoretically we'd only need one of them, as we're exactly ten people, but we'll inflate them both once we're in the water and the door is open. You'll have to leave your personal gear behind in case this machine sinks like a stone, but it should float for a while. Maybe we can collect some small bags once we're in the boats, OK? So, don't panic, we're trained for this kind of emergency. Just relax and follow the crew's instructions. Single file out the door as soon as it's open. The cargo in the back will be blocked from us by the netting. Talk to you later."

Oh splendid, Peter thought, *there go all my clothes and books.* He tried to see past the people at the portside windows, and guessed they were still about four hundred feet high. The pilot banked the plane around to bring it into the wind, and to attract the attention of the natives. Down they came, slower now.

A crew member came on the speaker: "You folks are sitting side by side. Be sure you're belted up good, then try to hold onto those straps that we just dropped down. My buddy and I will each be at the head of a file to help keep you from sliding off the seats. To keep the nose up so we don't flip over, we'll have to land at about 80 miles an hour; there'll be some bumping, but it won't last long. Skipper will try to skim the wave tops to slow us, before he lets her down. Brace yourselves now." He sat down at the head of Peter's row. Peter admired the sailor's calm manner and tried to stay calm himself.

The first wave tops slammed at the belly of the plane, and the remaining engine sputtered out as the waves stopped the prop. More blows could be heard and felt below their feet, and the short files of people lurched toward the front of the plane. Something cracked loudly, back in the tail section. They stopped moving over the waves and went down into a trough with a violent lurch that shoved the people together and squeezed one of them forward toward the center of the cabin; but the belts held as they came to an abrupt stop, pitching and yawing with the waves.

The other crewman latched open the door and pushed out one of the boats. It automatically inflated and was already bobbing in the water as the second one went out the door.

"OK gents, one at a time now, behind Billy. I'll try to hold a boat close to the door, but if you have to jump in the water please kick off your shoes, then Billy Boy here will pull you aboard the raft."

Seaman Billy jumped into the closest boat and beckoned the first passenger to follow. It was an Army captain, who practically stepped right into the boat. That meant the plane was sinking fairly fast. The pilots came into the main cabin. One had a gash over his eye that he was trying to staunch.

"Is everyone OK? Any injuries?" A cheer went up from the remaining passengers, who were still unbelting themselves and helping the next one out the door.

"You'll have to move faster," the pilot said, "we're sinking now. Please, everyone out the door quickly and into the water if you can't reach the boat from the door. Let's go; move, move."

The next three people jumped into the water and swam clear of the fuselage. They managed to catch the other raft and climb into it. Next it was Peter's turn; he left his shoes on the plane and dove headfirst alongside the second boat. The others one at a time went into the water, some diving, some jumping, and the pilots left last.

"Pull everyone into the boats and cast off, then row clear of the plane so we don't get tangled!"

Someone else shouted: "Be sure the boats are not tied to the plane!" The water level was about a third of the way up the open door.

"Take a head count, quick." There were only nine in the boats. "Pull clear of the plane; pull clear, now! Look around all sides of the boats; there's still someone in the water!"

"Crap, how could that happen? You guys were doing so well. Did we have a non-swimmer? He should have said something."

Then someone pointed at the plane's open door, where a man could be seen waving and shouting. The water was almost up to his head. "Get out of the plane! Get into the water! Push away! Swim!" went a dozen suggestions together." The plane gave a sudden lurch and nosed down further into the sea; the door and the face disappeared as the tail lifted into the air. There was a shocked silence in the boats.

"Pull away, people. We can't help him now. Anyone know his name?" Two men pulled on the little oars in each boat.

"Wasn't he the fat guy sitting near the door, that other civilian? He was helping people get past him into the water, I remember now."

The rowers pulled harder, as the tail section of the plane slid under. Then the boats were alone outside the surf line.

"Yeah, that's who it was", someone answered. "He was helping all of us, but I guess he didn't want to jump. Jesus, poor guy."

CHAPTER SEVEN

★ ★ ★

Cartwheels Converging

PB4Y-1P photo recon VD-1 (WA Clark Jr collection)

From three little maids take one away; Two little maids remain, and they Won't have to wait very long, they say; Three little maids from school.
From Gilbert & Sullivan: *The Mikado*

First little maid is a bride, Saipan, With her attendant, Tinian; Guam is the third little maid who can Show what she learned in school.
The Marianas Campaign

*** *GUADALCANAL HOSPITAL* ***

"What the hell are you doing here, crazy Brit?" Bongo had not yet heard about the San Cristobal plane crash and PT boat rescue but had stopped by the MOB-8 hospital tent camp hoping to find out which of the Navy nurses had come up from Nouméa. He didn't off-hand recognize any, so he decided to inquire at the duty desk if a nurse named Ellie Norbush was among them.

"Oh no sir, Ellie has resigned her Navy commission and has probably left Nouméa already for the States. I know her quite well," the lieutenant (jg) duty nurse said.

"Well, darn, she told me she would be coming up here with someone named Abby," Bongo pouted.

"I'm Abby," the nurse replied, smiling, "and I can assure you she isn't here and won't be coming either. She heard that a former beau in South Carolina got elected state senator, so she decided to leave the Navy and follow that other trail."

Seeing Bongo's downcast face, Abby added: "I'm so sorry if that is unwelcome news, Commander. Ellie and I were roommates recently; she sort of blows with the wind, I would say. Is she someone special to you?"

"No, not really," Bongo lied. "No, not at all, in fact I can't even remember what she looks like. No problem, nurse."

"Aren't you called Bongo?" Abby asked the visibly upset commander. "Don't you remember me from Nouméa? The rugby weekend with Peter Perry?" Bongo nodded slightly, still looking crestfallen, and now also embarrassed.

"Oh, then I really am sorry, sir. I didn't make the connection, this being Guadalcanal and all, and you in uniform. We only just got here yesterday. Look, Ellie gave me a note and gift for you before I left Nouméa. I'll run get them after I check the wards one more time. My relief will be here in half an hour. Would you like to make the rounds with me and help cheer up the fellows? Some were just admitted an hour ago and I haven't seen them yet. They are plane crash survivors. Shall we go?"

"Well OK," Bongo said meekly. And that is how both he and Abby happened to find that Peter had arrived on Guadalcanal after all. The discovery amazed them both.

Grasping Abby's hand, Peter gave Bongo a brief overview of the San Cristobal plane crash, and the situation with Wendy.

Bongo then blurted out that Nurse Ellie had left him and the Navy "for a damned politician, would you believe."

*** LOOKING AHEAD ***

By April 1944, the capture of the Marshall Islands had been successful, providing the Allies with large atolls as new anchorages for the mighty Pacific Fleet at Majuro and Eniwetok. The Eastern Carolines were being assaulted as well.

Guadalcanal also continued to grow apace, with Quonset huts delivered by the boatload to replace the old tent camps—except for the hospital, which Peter was pleased to have assigned to a NZ construction company for a proper building with vertical walls.

But most tent camp replacements were Quonsets, the very first one on Guadalcanal having been sequestered by long-departed Commander Quackenbush in late 1942 for his photo intelligence people. It was still in use as such, while Quonset hut G387 was claimed by Mr. Peter Perry for the US contracts office, of which he was the new overseer. Like much urban blight on Guadalcanal, his Quonset was located in a commercial zone at Point Cruz, near the flood plain of the Matanikau River.

Peter began to meet Abby in the evenings at the rustic facilities that passed for a naval officers' club, hastily built by Peter's predecessor. Abby talked of her hometown Fall River, Massachusetts, and showed him letters and photos from her mother. Trying to describe the beautiful autumns of New England when the leaves turn red and gold, Abby told Peter: "Even in summer the weather is never hot like Guadalcanal, but I think that's true of most places."

One evening they were hailed at an outdoor table by Bongo, who had two other Navy officers in tow.

"Good friends, let me introduce these newly-arrived specialists from Houston in the great state of Texas. Abby and Peter, this is Lt. Commander Frank Evans, CO of a brilliant ONI concept called Interpron-1. The other Texan is Lt. Bill Clark, XO—that's Executive Officer to you, ugly Brit. Make way, if you please."

Peter and Abby squeezed over, so the trio could join their table. Bongo went in search of more cold beer, the life-staple of Canal living. He was soon back with chilled bottles of Foster's, an Australian brew for which most everyone on the island had developed a special fondness. A gentle breeze blew in off the water not far away, which flickered the candles on the tables. Most tables were occupied now by thirsty colleagues, and the noise level gradually rose. Several other Navy nurses were present, besides Abby.

"Frank and Bill, this lovely nurse, Abby Culver, has somehow developed a fancy for English gentlemen, in particular the one at her side who hails from their former colony of Singapore. Peter Perry was once a captain of army engineers until the Japs disbanded his organization. Cheers, all." The newcomers nodded to Peter, smiled at Abby, and drank thirstily.

Bongo continued: "Peter is now here as 'Inspector-in-Chief' of the Solomons Inspectorate, or Protectorate, something like that. Confidentially, it means keeping an eye on us Yanks so we don't steal any of the Lever Brothers coconuts."

"Sounds like a complicated job, Peter," said Bill Clark. "Let us know if you need any help."

They shook hands all around, glancing approvingly at Abby from time to time. Feeling somewhat outnumbered, she decided to call it a night. The others stood to offer her a safe walk to her quarters.

"Oh, they're not quite that close, but over at the new hospital. Anyway, I've got a jeep; so please give my British Protector a lift home, OK? Good night all."

"Well, that's a switch in protocol," said Evans. "Wish I had her as my XO instead of this old duffer. Besides, I've known Bill far too long already, way back before the war started when I taught him to hunt ducks on the bayou. He never did learn very much, though."

The conversation turned to more practical matters. Bongo explained that the Texas specialists were geologists from Houston, Texas, in civilian life, but their Navy job was photographic interpretation for the ONI and others—hence the funny name Interpron-1.

He also told Peter that he and the Texans were going to Tulagi in the morning, to talk to the PT boat people about mapping the coastal water depths for them far beyond Bougainville, which the stereoscopic cameras in the B-24 planes were able to do remarkably well. The Marine photo group before them, VMD-254, had done this job as far up as Rendova and the Shortlands, but soon the boat squadrons would be working close to shore around New Britain, and needed new mappings to help them stay clear of the inevitable reefs.

"Peter, I've told these gents that you have an ONI security clearance like theirs, so I wondered if you might like to join the meeting on Tulagi? A lot of the islands up near New Guinea are British or Australian, so I'd feel better if we had someone like you along to correct our spelling and pronunciation."

Peter laughed: "That's probably a hopeless task, but I'd love to see Tulagi in more detail than when I took a seaplane from there to Sydney a few months ago. Tulagi was the pre-war British Residency for the entire Solomons, you know. Colonel Noel, the new British resident commissioner, was even considering setting up his office over there like the old days, but you Yanks convinced him to choose Guadal instead, in spite of the mosquitos."

"Correct; we met with Colonel Noel again yesterday, as a matter of fact. It seems your Colonial Office is eager to get the islands back under control again."

*** THE TULAGI VISIT ***

A lovely song called *"You and I"*, released by Bing Crosby in late 1941, finally caught everyone's fancy on the Pacific bases by mid-1944, Peter and Abby being no exceptions.

> *Darling, you and I know the reason why a summer sky is blue*
> *And we know why birds in the trees sing melodies too,*
> *And why love will grow from the first "Hello"*
> *Until the last "Goodbye."*

255

Peter couldn't stop humming it to himself as he returned from Tulagi on a Coast Guard shuttle boat with Bongo and the two American geologists, having toured the hilly little island and its bombed-out homes, then having met the PT boat skippers at their base near an old Chinese village. They were also given a quick tour of the Tanambogo and Gavutu islets—which the sailors called 'Bogo' and 'U2'—learning that some of the heaviest fighting had taken place there on August 7, 1942, when the Marines first arrived.

But now the battles had moved elsewhere, well beyond the Solomons. During June and July 1944, a series of invasions began north of the equator, that wrested control of the Mariana Islands—Saipan, Tinian, and Guam—from well-entrenched Japanese defenders. Planes from Fifth Fleet carriers destroyed most of the Japanese land-based air defense ahead of the invasions, then the VAC—Fifth Amphibious Corps—rolled ashore on Saipan with both Marine and Army M4 medium tanks. These new campaigns affected Guadalcanal in that virtually all available US combat troops were required for the Marianas, causing New Zealand to expedite some land, air and sea resources to the Solomons to take over the Allied base operations. Britain likewise brought resources to take on the administration of native populations and restart the plantation economy.

As civil stability returned to Guadalcanal and the lower Solomons, many former coastwatchers, gold miners, missionaries, and functionaries came out of exile or hiding. Iron Bottom Sound between Tulagi and Guadalcanal took on a contrasting character from the brutal battle days not so long past, although everyone still 'sensed' the dozens of ships, large and small, Japanese and Allied, that lay on the bottom of the wide channel, many with entombed sailors still at their battle stations.

Although Marines and GIs had suffered heavy casualties from combat and disease during the six-month land campaign, the US Navy actually lost twice as many personnel while protecting the seas around the lower Solomons and trying to block Japanese reinforcements and heavy weapons.

Now with a clean-up campaign in full swing, Peter was glad to note that mosquito control was one of the new priorities, in an attempt to eradicate, or at least mediate the terrible scourge of malaria. Much to everyone's delight, the natives took the lead with this effort, trying to make stagnant rivers such as the Ilu flow freely again by opening up their sand barriers to the sea.

On went the song in Peter's brain. The late afternoon's fading tropical sun, glinting from the water near Tulagi, contrasted with the northern beaches of Guadalcanal that they were approaching, which were already in shadow. Peter half dozed as the small craft's engine droned on, and then he thought about Wendy and John, who seemed a million miles away. He still felt guilt about the way things had turned out with Wendy, tending to blame himself whenever he tried to make sense of things.

As for little John, he was obviously a lost soul now as far as Peter was concerned. Although Wendy had stressed that Peter should visit them often, he realized that it was highly unlikely ever to happen unless by accident. *No*, he thought, *she wanted me out of there, so that's what she gets—me out of there.*

Besides, he was growing quite fond of Abby—*there's that song again*—and the first set of Wendy's divorce papers had reached him several weeks ago. He had signed and returned them promptly.

Bongo, pontificating as always, was deep in conversation with the geologists most of the way back across the channel. They looked up when Peter called attention to an interesting old sailing craft that was making its way westward along the Guadalcanal coast near Point Taivu, perpendicular to their present course but still far away.

"Probably it's the weekly shuttle from Aola Bay, which was the location of Martin Clemens' administrative post before the war," Peter explained.

Peter remembered Clemens talking about the fleet of old wooden sailing ships that had plied the Solomon Islands before the war, most of which had managed to get hidden away in mangrove swamps from the Japanese. Those ships, known as Auxiliary Vessels (A/V), were put back into service once the islands were secured.

The one he pointed out now to his companions—although barely visible as it approached from the east—was a two-masted ketch whose keel was probably laid down in the early years of the century. It still displayed a rakish line here and there under sail, but a somewhat hogged waterline gave proof that it had seen better days.

"That is certainly an old timer, Limey shipmate; classic Somerset Maugham in fact," Bongo observed. "Thinking of making them an offer, are you?"

The two Texans laughed at that remark; Bill Clark added: "Listen Peter, Frank and I know a guy in Louisiana with a sister ship that's for sale. Bet we could get it cheap and have the Navy bring it over here for your fleet."

"Awfully thoughtful of you, Bill. I'd take up your offer, except we'd never get the navy to bring one of those old work boats all the way from America to Guadalcanal."

"Oh, sure we would. Now that my big brother's an admiral, he can get anything done. He would probably show it on the paperwork as an admiral's gig, and it could be here in four to six weeks, together with the next batch of Higgins PT boats from New Orleans. So OK then, how much would you pay to own a boat more or less like that one?"

Feeling somewhat trapped, Peter nonetheless pushed on with the game. "All right then, I'd pay one hundred US dollars for a seaworthy 50-foot two-master, with a decent diesel engine. That's what Clemens said was the size of this one, which used to be his official workboat for Guadalcanal when he was the DO here. This boat's name is *Ramada*, by the way, after little Ramada Island near New Georgia."

"Yeah? How can you tell which boat it is?" Bill asked, "I thought there were half a dozen of these old schooners back in use here, more or less all the same size and vintage."

"That's just it. Everyone, including Martin, calls them 'the schooners' but *Ramada* is really a ketch. They may all have two masts, but *Ramada*'s foremast is taller than her aftermast, which makes her a ketch not a schooner. Here, it's getting a bit dark but look through the glasses and you'll see what I mean." Peter handed the binoculars to Bill, who squinted carefully through them and passed them on to Frank Evans.

"*Ramada*, eh? Heck, that's a good Mexican name as well," Frank chimed in. "Means something like 'bower house' in Spanish, you know, a rain shelter built from tree branches. We could rename the Louisiana boat *Ramada II*. Or *Ramada tee double-oh* if you prefer. I think it's called *Boudreau Shrimper V* at the moment."

"How very thoughtful," Peter observed. "Well, all right then, clever ducks, I'll call your bluff. You get the other boat delivered here to Lunga or

Point Cruz and I'll pay you one hundred American dollars for it, assuming it floats, has a full set of sails and a working diesel engine."

"Not so fast, Limey pal, not so fast," Bongo jumped in before the others could answer. "Look, someone trustworthy—myself for example—has to be banker for this transaction, and we have to encourage side bets from others too, otherwise what's the point, eh? So, Peter, you need to cough up one hundred bucks in advance for the boat, and fifty bucks more for transaction fees and commissions. And you Texans need to put up fifty bucks between you for your fees and commissions too." The others looked at each other with a mixture of consternation and amusement, as Bongo continued.

"OK, then we'll have two hundred bucks seed money in the kitty, being one hundred for the boat, fifty for unforeseen expenses, and fifty for bank commissions. This here Limey engineer's share is probably a month's salary, I reckon, but the balance—at fifty cents a drink—is probably just a month's bar bill for you two overpaid Texans."

Their Coast Guard launch droned on toward Point Cruz. The ancient A/V *Ramada* could still be seen creeping along the darkening coastline under sail, but clearly would not reach the dock before nightfall.

"Well, I don't know, Commander," Frank Evans smiled, "that's a lot of bread to leave in the hands of a Navy spy, if you ask me."

"Trust me, my boss works for CINCPAC," Bongo said, holding high an open palm, "and Peter here knows my boss real well." Peter nodded.

"All right, so what about the side bets then?" Evans asked.

"OK, I'll explain, but first of all let's ask this Limey mariner why in the world he would want to buy an old workboat anyway, apart from maybe living on board to avoid the mosquitos, hmm?" They all leaned toward Peter to hear his reply over the engine noise.

"Well actually, chaps, I didn't think of this until Bill mentioned the other boat being for sale. It sounded like a perfect addition to the Solomon Island fleet, which as you may know has lost a couple of its former vessels. Martin said in particular that coastwatcher Charles Kennedy's *Wai Ai* on Ysabel was similar to old *Ramada*, but someone told the Japs where it was hidden, and they burned it to the waterline. I thought it might be nice to provide those good people with a replacement."

Bongo laughed. "That's what I thought, you old do-gooder. I couldn't see you restoring an old shrimp boat for your personal use. So now I propose that all four of us kick in equally on the shrimper and the fees—50 bucks apiece in other words—then raise a lot more money as a team through the side bets, to give the locals a kitty for overhauling their fleet and making it seaworthy again. No point having someone drown between the islands, especially after all of the fighter pilots that these boats have rescued for us. 'What say, chaps', if I can borrow this quaint Limey expression?"

"Great idea."

"Absolutely."

And they patted Peter on the shoulder.

"But what about the betting? How will that work?" Evans still wanted to know.

"Well, there's the dock," Bongo pointed out as the launch slowed down. "Let's go have a beer and figure it all out."

*** AN OFFICER-MESSENGER ***

So it happened—with Bongo's help at the ONI—that Lt. Bill Clark managed to get himself designated two months later as an 'Officer Messenger' to Rear Admiral Joseph "Jocko" Clark, his elder brother, who would by then be refueling his carriers and support ships at Eniwetok Atoll in the Marshall Islands. To help justify his visit there, Bill would bring along some secret photo intelligence to Jocko aboard his flagship, the new USS *Hornet* (CV-12), that would greatly influence the next campaign of the US fast carriers.

Jocko commanded the four fast carriers of Task Group 58.1, one of four such groups in Task Force 58 under Vice Admiral Mitscher that in total comprised 15 carriers and an astonishing armada of support ships.

TF58 was in turn part of the Fifth Fleet under Vice Admiral Spruance, which had laid on the pre-invasion bombardments, landed the invasion forces, and was later active in protecting the Marines and Army on the various Mariana islands from air attacks during the past June and July. In so doing, Mitscher's TF58 destroyed nearly four hundred Japanese carrier-based planes in what came to be called *The Great Marianas Turkey Shoot*, or more formally *The Battle of the Philippine Sea*.

Those downed enemy planes were flown off Japanese fleet carriers that had emerged from and then retreated back to the Philippines after their futile attempt to reinforce the Marianas. It was clear that the US had just taken a giant leap forward in terms of resources and technology.

Admiral Nimitz especially, who had been somewhat reluctant to take on the Marianas so quickly, was amazed at the successes of TF58 and the fast carriers, and the brilliant offensive and defensive tactics that had been developed by Marc Mitscher and Jocko Clark.

But there was one shortcoming: although the enemy planes were mostly destroyed, TF 58 had been unable to catch up with the retreating Jap fleet itself, because Admiral Spruance held them back too long for protection of the landing forces, in Jocko's opinion.

Sulking a bit, Jocko charged off with TF58.1 to the Bonin Islands, closer to Japan, with Admiral Mitscher's blessing, to soften up the Chichi, Iwo, and Haha Jimas. *[Jocko lost a few planes over Chichi Jima that time, some pilots of which were captured ashore and later beheaded, while others were picked up by an attending US submarine. One of the lucky ones was future US President George H.W. Bush. —Ed.]*

Soon Admirals Spruance and Mitscher would hand over the Fifth Fleet and its formidable carriers to Admirals Halsey and McCain for six months (to be renamed the Third Fleet and TF38, leading the Japanese to think the US had two such terrorizing armadas available), and go back to Hawaii to plan the next major campaigns. Nimitz could see now that the fleet would carry on with its brilliant achievements under the new management.

Japan, its vaunted 'Greater East Asia Co-Prosperity Sphere' in shambles, must have seen the handwriting on the wall at this stage. Any of the US Pacific Fleet's four fast carrier task groups, with their superior planes and pilots, was practically a match for the entire remaining Japanese Navy. And MacArthur's Admiral Kinkaid had the US Seventh Fleet, which was almost as robust, poised to help the Army take back the Philippines.

Gone was Japan's chance for a negotiated settlement to the Pacific War, but a few crusty die-hard admirals in Tokyo still trumpeted the secret weapon of sister ships *Yamato* and *Musashi* that were as yet undamaged.

They are also untested, the generals replied, but the emperor himself was enamored of the giant battleships and the nearly completed super aircraft carrier *Shinano*, that was set to undergo sea trials.

Never mind that there are no experienced pilots left in the Imperial Navy, the generals pointed out in vain. So the war went on, as the emperor apparently wished.

*** TRAGEDY ON SAIPAN ***

Long before Bill went off to meet Admiral Clark on Eniwetok at the end of August, word had filtered down to Bongo on Guadalcanal that a terrible tragedy had happened on Saipan, to the civilians who were living there.

Both Saipan and Tinian had significant populations of ethnic Taiwanese and Okinawan farmers, who had been encouraged to emigrate when Japan acquired those substantial Mariana islands from Germany after the First World War. By 1944, some of those expatriate civilians had lived on Saipan nearly thirty years and had grown-up children and grand babies. There were, of course, many Chamorro natives as well, and even some islanders from the Carolines, all of whom were loyal to Japan by definition.

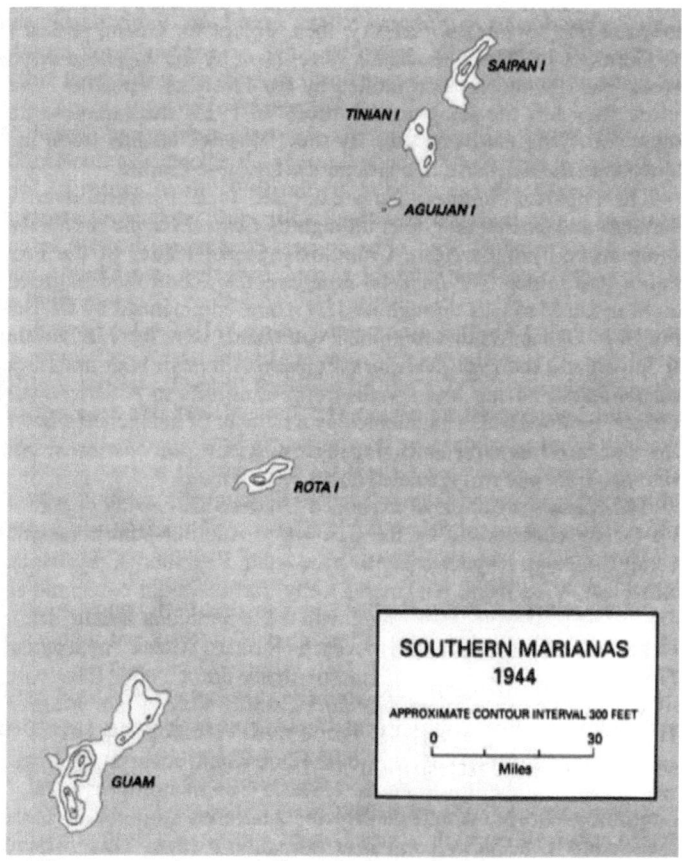

The Southern Marianas
(https://www.ibiblio.org/hyperwar/ USMC/III/USMC-III-IV-1.html)

Saipan was the first of the Marianas to be attacked by the US. It was a tough fight, for which the Japanese had plenty of time to get prepared. Although their land planes had been severely decimated by the fast carriers of TF58, some thirty thousand Japanese troops were well deployed and armed. They still had substantial artillery and dozens of tanks—medium tanks—on hand, to help destroy the hated Americans.

But the Americans pushed the Japanese from the landing beaches toward the north end of the island, where terrified civilians were also gathered, freshly agitated by anti-American propaganda *[and by some alleged official instructions from Tokyo urging suicide over capture for both military and civilians –Ed.]*

As the Americans grew closer, having obliterated nearly all the defending troops—including 4,000 who died in a final sake-fueled Banzai charge, the largest one of the Pacific War—the civilians apparently believed it was their fate to be tortured to death. In a mass panic some began hurling themselves from the cliffs onto the rocks and sea below, in spite of broadcasted entreaties to stop.

Mothers dashed their babies' heads against stone walls or leapt to their deaths with infants clutched to their chests. It is thought that a thousand civilians died in this manner, jumping off the high cliffs at Saipan's Marpi Point.

Tinian and Guam were captured next, but fortunately the civilian mass suicide horrors were not significantly repeated. A fourth nearby island, Rota, was bypassed, being too hilly for airfields and therefore of no military value. Its Japanese garrison was left to fend for itself.

Bongo explained all this to Peter and the Texans one Guadalcanal afternoon, when they went swimming at a north shore beach, not far from the wrecked freighter *Kinugawa Maru* where Marine M4 tanks had been dropped off by an LST the year before.

Peter well remembered his conversations with the tank commander and a loquacious jeep driver from the Texas Highway Department. *Those fellows must have gone off to Saipan, I wonder how many are still alive.*

"The Japs sure are fanatical," ventured Frank Evans. "Can you imagine people at home doing something like that if, say, FDR told them to commit suicide for the sake of the country? Heck, they'd go and impeach him, chop-chop. What about Britain, Peter? Could the monarch have that much influence over his subjects, like the Jap emperor?"

"Of course not," Peter replied forcefully, "but I daresay King George does exert more influence over our people, in general, than the president does over Americans, don't you think?"

"Heck, I don't have any idea," Bill Clark said. "Peter, what would be an example of King George's unusual influence over you Brits?"

Peter blushed, unused to such repartee. "Oh, er, I don't really know; well perhaps, um, good manners, that sort of thing." The Americans laughed, as Peter tried to extricate himself.

"You know, we respect the royal family more than we respect our national flag, the Union Jack, but you Yanks are the opposite; it's your flag that brings out the emotion. Your leaders change all the time, whereas we see our king as head of a family to which we all belong, in some small way." Peter coughed, hoping to change the subject.

Bongo chuckled: "Good grief, he sounds like a Jap emperor-worshipper. Let's throw him into the sea!" And they did just that, splashing each other vigorously as they sought to upend Peter.

When the horseplay ended, Bongo grew serious: "Guys, you're probably thinking that this suicide business will shock our people back home, and reflect badly on our Marines and GIs, right? Well, guess what else happened while Saipan was being captured, something even more important."

"What?" they all said together. Bongo grinned: "One cold beer from each of you?" Three heads nodded as one.

"Well, this is already old news in the free world, but here on the Canal we don't get updates very often. So listen up: we amazing Yanks and our noble British allies have invaded France! The biggest invasion force ever seen on this planet crossed the English Channel and is now pushing the Krauts back toward Paris! That's why there won't be much in the news about Saipan and the Marianas, I'll wager." The others began to laugh and shout, but Bongo interrupted them.

"Oh, and one more thing. We learned from our code snoopers that Tojo has resigned in Japan. I guess he bet the farm on Saipan being defensible. He's the evil bastard who pushed the emperor into all this in the first place, with his war on China in the '30s. I hope we get to hang them both after the war. Now let's go and enjoy those beers, for which I thank you in advance."

*** KIWIS INVADE THE CANAL ***

New Zealand was gradually taking on responsibility for Guadalcanal military matters during the first half of 1944, but after the Marianas campaign had virtually cleaned out most Americans from the island, the Kiwis were asked to take complete control of the land, sea and air operations as a step toward handing the Solomon Island Protectorate back to full British sovereignty.

The first telltale hint had come in July, when vehicles were required by military order to drive on the left side of the roads. Much ado was made of this unusual rule that had taken effect at 2am on a particular Sunday. A growing crisis was noticed some days afterwards, when traffic accidents began repopulating the recently completed Navy hospital that had been steadily discharging those Marianas wounded who were recovered enough to be shipped back to the US, or to their old units. Abby brought the 'Traffic Rule News' to the club one evening, having just assisted a Navy doctor with the amputation of an American arm and a New Zealand leg.

"I don't see how advanced nations can differ in something as basic and fundamental to civilization as which side of the road to drive on," she expounded to the men, in frustration.

"Ha, here's a good one for you then, Abby," Bongo responded. "Do you know that cars drive on the left in Japan too? It must be a peculiar phobia of insular nations like Japan and England, and Australia and New Zealand, and even Singapore, don't you think? Clearly such island nations cannot be as civilized as—for example—the United States and Canada, not to mention China, that drive on the right."

Abby smiled, but Peter couldn't let that one go by. He spoke up quickly: "And what about the Germans then? How do all those countries drive in Europe? On the right side, correct? Are the nasty old Huns so civilized after all?"

"Well, they're not insular at least. That must be the key to it," Bongo carried on. "And here we are stuck on another island while the Kiwis try to convert us to 'World Island Rules'. Soon they'll have to bring in a whole team of their doctors to keep up with the traffic accidents, at least until all the civilized Americans are dead or gone."

"I suppose the next thing will be cricket," Bill Clark observed. "Well, Frank and I got our marching orders today."

"Yep," Frank Evans nodded. "We have to close down the photo intelligence business at the end of August. That'll probably be the end of VD-1 and Interpron-1."

"But I heard there'll be photo ops on Guam," said Bongo. "Isn't that where you'll go from here?"

"You're right about the Guam photo ops," Frank replied, "but those will be new units, VD-2 and Interpron-2. They'll arrive there next week from Pearl to take over the Pacific role from us. Our units are being shut down, and we'll go back to Hawaii for a while to train new people, then maybe back home for good. 'Maybe' depends on whether we're needed somewhere else later on."

"What about you then, Abby?" Frank asked. "Will you be transferred to the Marianas? I suppose Peter knows that answer already."

"Peter doesn't know, and I don't know either," Abby replied, "but there are rumors that the American medical staff will stay here on Guadalcanal until the end of November at least, because New Zealand doesn't have a surplus of nurses and doctors at the moment, nor does Australia. We could well be here beyond Christmas, apparently."

Then Bongo asked Peter for his forecast of events, who replied: "There should be a lot of post-Seabee construction on Guam and Saipan soon—particularly for rebuilding Guam—but obviously I would like to stay here or go onward with Abby whenever possible, as we plan to marry as soon as the opportunity presents itself, but...."

Bongo stood up: "No 'buts', Limey pal; no 'ifs' or 'ands' either. This calls for a celebration, and I don't mean with more of this delightful Aussie beer, life-enhancing though it be. What do people from England and New England usually drink for engagement parties?"

"Why, champagne would be very nice, if such a thing exists out here," Abby said, hopefully.

"Be right back," Bongo muttered, and headed to the club office.

Frank changed the subject: "While he's checking things out, Peter, what do you think we should do about the old workboat in Louisiana? My

Cajun cousin did determine that Boudreau is willing to sell it, and that it's apparently seaworthy. Why would he sell? Because half of his former customers are over here or in Europe, and his other two boats are all he needs for the near future.

"Boudreau will accept a hundred bucks for it too, but one of us needs to take a closer look at the boat, and Bill still needs to negotiate with his brother, the admiral, to get it shipped out here somehow, before we pay Boudreau the money. Ideas, anyone? With Bill and me leaving here soon, and most likely Bongo too, I would imagine, how can we organize the betting and so forth, to raise up that extra pot of cash for the 'great white fleet'? Or should we just forget about the whole idea?"

Abby spoke up: "I think it was a fine idea, and still is. Peter and I—or I and some other nurses if Peter is gone—could look after the betting, sell tickets, whatever it takes, if the boat could be here by, say, mid-November. Peter was planning to organize a race across the channel to Tulagi and back, against *Ramada* and whichever other old workboats they still have available, weren't you dear?"

"Yes indeed," Peter smiled, "and even if I've been transferred to Guam I could probably get back here for a few days to help organize the race, though it would certainly be good if Abby and her friends could sell tickets in advance. Look, today is July twenty-fifth. When could you go and talk to your brother then, Bill?"

Bongo returned and overheard Peter's remarks. He said: "I've been thinking about this too, fellow schemers. Here's an idea, for what it's worth. If Interpron-1 is being closed at the end of August, and you Texans are going to Hawaii, why doesn't Bill go to Hawaii via wherever the admiral will be at the end of August, so they can talk face to face? I could authorize that travel routing if, for example, Bill could be an ONI courier of some important photo intelligence for the admiral and the Pacific fleet. What do you think, Frank and Bill?"

"Sure thing; that would work. Let's just hope my brother's not at sea when it comes time for me to leave here. Clever idea, anyway. So how did you make out on the champagne, Bongo?"

Bongo waved to the bartender: "Watch this, my friends." A small procession headed toward their table with a bottle in an ice bucket, five

267

glasses and mugs of various shapes and sizes, and a bucket of vanilla ice cream.

"Tah-dah," exclaimed Bongo, leading the singing. Abby clapped her hands and laughed aloud.

Peter was overcome. "My word, what a touching moment", he stuttered. "You know, it's quite wonderful for Abby and me to share this exciting time together in the Pacific islands. We'll always have these memories as we grow older. I'm, well, awfully grateful to you chaps, you know that."

Bongo laughed and gave them both a hug.

A few days later, on July twenty-ninth, a big party took place at the club to jointly celebrate Peter and Abby's engagement, and to acknowledge the New Zealand role in administration of Guadalcanal. It was an event of several hundred people, including all the Navy and Army nurses, and some nurses from the Red Cross too.

A respectable dance band had materialized like magic from among the assorted services, and after the speeches that evening came a clever satire of the left-hand driving rule, that everyone toasted with great solemnity.

*** RED RIGHT RETURNING ***

A few days later, the next Kiwi befuddlement was proclaimed—new navigation rules for ships. For some inexplicable reason, US rules of the road for coastal waters followed a system commonly referred to as 'Red, Right, Returning,' which meant that ships approaching (returning to) a coastal channel marked by navigational buoys would keep red buoys to their right side, and therefore green buoys would stay to their left. They would negotiate the channel marked by those buoys, confident that 'Red, Right, Returning' would keep them out of trouble.

Pacific Island ports under US administration, such as Guadalcanal and Espiritu Santo (but not Efaté or Nouméa) were made to observe this RRR rule, and soon got used to it. But the rest of the world followed international rules, which were exactly the opposite, the logic in that case being that red buoys should be kept to the left, or port side of a ship, because red is the color assigned the world over to port, while the color for starboard is green.

[Why does it matter which system? Think about it: buoys are used for marking a safe channel into a harbor or river mouth; on one side of a buoy the water is deep enough for safe entry, while on the other side the water is shallower and perhaps reef infested. –Ed.]

Finally, the day came for a complete official handover to New Zealand of all remaining base functions in the Solomons. The outgoing and incoming base commanders—a US Navy captain and a New Zealand Army colonel—decided on a grandiose change-of-command ceremony to mark the occasion, involving practically everyone who could manage to march in step to a brass band.

The review took place along the main road of the principal Guadalcanal military base, which had recently been named Honiara and designated as the Solomon Island's eventual new capital city. In the parade marched US sailors, nurses, seabees, soldiers and airmen (there being no Marines left on the island), followed by their counterparts, where available, from New Zealand. At the end of the procession came a long file of native scouts, who had served so well in the dark days of Guadalcanal's liberation, and who received a rousing applause from the spectators. Sergeant-Major Vouza marched proudly at their head, wearing a Marine Corps dress blue blouse with his chevrons and medals, and a sarong 'below deck.'

British Colonel Noel, in pith helmet and civilian clothes as the territory's new resident commissioner, warranted a front row place on the reviewing stand with the two commanders. In the rear rows Peter, Bongo, Frank, and Bill stood among several other honored civilian and naval guests, and two withered-looking bishops who had somehow survived the Japanese occupation, one a Roman Catholic and the other an Anglican. Crowds of watchers lined the road for several hundred yards on either side of the stand, including islanders and local clergy. Several happy dogs wandered about the road, their eyes keenly alert for hand movements in the crowd that might indicate a treat for the occasion.

Band music was provided by the Royal New Zealand Army Corps, sited in a small redoubt across from the reviewing stand, which after some discordant warm-ups dutifully rendered the national anthems of the United States and Great Britain to polite applause. Then they issued a great drum roll, signifying the commencement of marching feet, though not their own, as they had chosen to remain in place for the occasion.

The band launched into a panoply of martial compositions from each nation, including several by John Philip Souza. When Souza's *Semper Fidelis* was rendered, the anthem of the United States Marine Corps, the well-trained crowd erupted in unfettered cheering and waving.

Midway through the procession the band switched over to some popular Gilbert & Sullivan marches, which lent a cheerful air to the festivities that followed. It was a splendid afternoon, particularly since the rain held off until four o'clock.

As they descended from the platform, Peter nudged Bongo: "Look there, the new base commander is Colonel McKee from Fiji; don't you recognize the mustaches?"

"No, I missed that," Bongo replied, "because we were directly behind him and he didn't move a muscle for the entire event, except to salute. Good, we'll have to look him up one of these days. But do you know who else was on the platform with us? I learned this earlier but still don't know what he looks like—the Australian managing director of Lever Brothers, that's who. They say he's probably here to count the damaged coconut palms so he can put in an early claim for compensation. Perhaps we can get some decent soap again if they get this plantation restarted."

"Soap?" Peter queried, "What on earth do palm trees have to do with soap?"

"Well goodness, don't you know, Mister Engineer, that dried coconut meat is called copra, which yields coconut oil, which is used for making soap and other things that keep our smelly bodies clean? Copra is the basis of the economy in these here islands, clever Brit, and Lever Brothers Ltd. makes several distinct brands of soap—Lifebuoy, for example."

"Oh I see. No, I didn't understand about copra; thanks for opening my eyes. But I think the company is called Unilever now, is it not?"

*** *ENEMY ON THE RUN* ***

Two weeks later, after they watched a clever USO show by Bob Hope, Frances Langford, and Jerry Colonna on Guadalcanal, Bongo informed the others that he would soon be transferred to Guam, to help prepare a new headquarters for Admiral Nimitz and staff.

"Yep, CINCPAC will move over from Hawaii for the end game with Japan, now that we can reach Tokyo from Saipan with these amazing new B-29 bombers. The Army Air Corps is about to enter the world stage."

"Where will they put the admiral's offices then? Aren't all those islands more or less in ruins?" Peter asked, hoping for some new business for his contractors, who were slowly disappearing back to their home countries.

"It'll be at some temporary place first, from the sound of it, like a bunch of Quonset huts and tents, or the admiral may even decide to use one of the old battleships for CINCPAC. After all, he doesn't want to stay there forever. You'll be needed on Guam too, Peter old worry wart, more than Saipan or Tinian after the Seabees get through cleaning up the mess from our bombardments. Guam was ours before the war, if you remember, and will be afterwards too. Needs to look nice and prosperous for post-war elections."

Peter was still skeptical. "I hope you're right, but so far I haven't heard a thing from our directors in Sydney about any projects for the Marianas. They're as puzzled as I am, and since it's no longer the Americans' job to rebuild Guadalcanal, our US contracts office is fast running out of work here. There's nothing for Santo or Nouméa any longer either. Hans has resigned, and Ralph is working back in Australia for the Aussie government. Our former little office on Santo is a Red Cross information center now."

"Yeah, well times are changing. Just imagine what things will be like when peace really breaks out all over," Bongo laughed. "All those Aussie warriors will be home looking for work and kicking the women out of their old jobs. Their government will hardly have enough money for paying both the women and the men. It'll be the same situation in the States, most likely, but even worse in Europe where those bombed out countries will need complete rebuilding; zillions of homes needed, for example, in England and France, not to mention Germany and the rest. Where will the money come from, one wonders?"

"Where indeed?" Peter asked, a guilty memory of Wendy and Doris flitting across his mind because of their work at the aircraft assembly plant. *Well, they are survivors*, he told himself.

"Listen, old buddy," Bongo went on, "I heard something interesting the other day that will apply to Europe, but probably not the Pacific region. Our General Marshall, who is the Army's chief honcho—the theoretical boss of MacArthur and Eisenhower—is working on a plan with FDR for rebuilding Europe, in order to avoid another uprising by some idiot like Hitler. This will mostly take place in Germany. Since you like international adventure, you and Abby might want to look into this and think about volunteering for it early on—not really volunteering gratis, of course, since they'll be shelling out reams of US dollars. You have a good reputation from your work for the US over here. Your boss in Sydney should know how to get you into the loop, and if he doesn't then Captain Silvers (who's up for rear admiral soon, by the way) could probably help. Talk to Abby, is my advice, and start learning German, not French!"

"Then what will you do after the war, since we're on the subject?" Peter asked his friend.

"Heck, I don't know, but it'll probably have something to do with intelligence work, which I really enjoy. The other day, Captain Silvers met with an interesting and highly decorated Army colonel from the First World War, named 'Wild Bill' Donovan, who is also a famous lawyer and a friend of FDR. Silvers told me FDR liked the colonel's ideas about centralized intelligence for the US, which at present is not the case. I may throw in my hat with these people, especially since Hoover hates Donovan, so they say, and I'm not an admirer of Hoover after the way he treated the Hawaiians."

"Do you have an eye open for Europe too?" Peter asked. "It would be great to continue seeing each other after the war."

"Yes, I certainly agree with that, but probably I'll end up staying in the Far East, old pal. I'm getting pretty good with Chinese now and have scratched the surface with Thai and Japanese. The Ruskies are sort of our allies at the moment, just to help put Hitler down, but as soon as he's in a box then Stalin will start making mischief everywhere on the planet. He already has a rebel named Mao in his pocket for China, and one of the many Kims for Korea. I kind of fancy staying out here in the East, maybe to work for MacArthur for a while in Japan if he gets to run it, or else for Donovan in Thailand. It should get exciting."

"Well, that's a pity, actually. I very much like your suggestion about Europe but hope we can meet somewhere from time to time, somehow," Peter said earnestly. "But look, there's Bill Clark wandering around without

Frank. That's unusual." They both waved until Bill spotted them through the cigarette haze and came over to their table.

"What's going on, Bill?" Bongo asked. "Where's your fearless leader tonight?"

"Frank suddenly had to go back to Texas for a family emergency, and here I am scheduled to go see my big bro in Eniwetok this weekend. Darn, that means I'll have to come right back here to supervise the roll-up, after I courier some important documents for Jocko to Hawaii. That's a hell of a lot of traveling for an old Louisiana shrimp boat, Peter and Bongo. I hope this makes me famous somehow."

"Of course it will, never fear," Bongo answered with a grin. "I'm sure our government has a medal for virtuous deeds, but in any case, the Brits will have one for sure."

"Oh joy," Bill sighed. "Say, Peter, where is Abby this evening? Is she sick or something?"

"No, no, she has the duty tonight at the hospital. That's why I got started early with Bongo. We're sitting here making forecasts for the post-war world. What do you plan to do then, Bill?"

"Shoot, I'll just stay in Texas and go back to work. Right now I'm on leave from Slumber-J, being the first US geologist for that French company, but no one's out looking for oil now, though they ought to be. I reckon it'll be a stampede after the war; I may take the plunge and start my own business."

"Good idea. Is Frank a partner then?" Bongo asked.

"Naw, he's a competitor if anything. We've known each other for some time, but he's already in his own business as an oil producer. I think I could do that too if I can find some backers. What about you two, Peter and Bongo? What do y'all have your sights set on after this is over?" Bill asked, signaling for another round of Fosters.

Peter glanced at Bongo, then answered for both of them. "The Pacific war is a long way from over, so they say, but having taken the Marianas means there's no doubt now about the outcome. Bongo plans to stay out here in the Orient afterwards, whereas I hope to try Europe if Abby agrees. Haven't asked her yet."

"Oh, I see, hot new ideas then. I guess neither plan is for me; I'm a real homebody. You know, my pa is part Cherokee Indian from Oklahoma, which means I'm one too, more or less, and so is my big brother. Jocko is the first Cherokee admiral in the US Navy in fact, or any other navy for that matter. The press calls him Big Chief and says he's on the warpath in the Pacific. He's a pretty wild character."

"I'd enjoy meeting an admiral like that," Bongo said. "My boss will be an admiral in another week, by the way, but he's pretty calm and collected. I like him anyway!" The others laughed and made to head back to their quarters.

"Wait a sec," Bongo murmured. "Let me give you some scoop that just came over the wire today. This'll help you sleep well tonight, and you're free to spread the word tomorrow."

"OK, Commander, I'll get some more beer. I know a hint when I hear one."

"No, no, Bill, we can use the dregs for this. The good news tonight is that Paris was liberated yesterday. They say Hitler ordered it put to the torch, but his garrison commander refused. Lucky for that guy he's our prisoner now, or Hitler would have his balls. Cheers, one and all; *bonne soirée*.

"And Bill, have a safe trip to Eniwetok as Interpron's first-ever officer-courier," Bongo added. "I'll probably be gone when you get back here afterwards."

*** *PELELIU* ***

Soon after Bill Clark left by air for Eniwetok Atoll, the daily R4D medical flight arrived at Henderson Field from Banika Island in the nearby Russells, where another US Navy hospital—MOB-10—was still operating. The pilot, a jaunty Navy lieutenant who was one of several on call for shuttle flights, jumped on a bus for the new Guadalcanal hospital that used to be MOB-8, to shoot the breeze with the nurses while his plane was being fueled and loaded with medical supplies for Banika. Abby spotted him as he came through the front door.

"Hi Joey. Say, did you bring us any people today, or are you just collecting supplies?" she asked the salty-looking flier.

"No people this time, sweetie, but I brought you some hot scoop. You know that Pavuvu Island is right next to Banika, right? Well there are a

LOT of ships anchored off Pavuvu today, loading up the First Marine Division. I remember in November when they did that before and took 'em to Cape Gloucester. This looks like another big operation. How's that for scoop? Good for a coffee? What else you got for a morning snack?"

"Sure, that's good news," Abby responded, remembering the conversation in Nouméa with her brother and Peter when the First Marine Division was in Melbourne. *Goodness, that would have been New Year's Day 1943*, she thought, *and here it is almost 1945*.

"Joey, thanks. Help yourself to anything in the mess hall. Some of the girls may be there to chat with you. Sorry I'm on duty now. Will you be flying back here tomorrow again?"

"Very early tomorrow Abby, but not for hospital business. I have to take someone up to Guam in the morning. Anyway, looks like we medical people are pretty much the only Americans left around here, except for those sailors on Tulagi. See you later."

Joey Foster was known to be a smuggler, though how he managed it no one was sure. He always seemed to have an ample supply of food, drink and smokes on hand for any occasion, and Abby knew from experience that he kept the Navy officers club well stocked too, such as the bottle of champagne that Bongo bought. To keep the brass off his trail, Joey kept them supplied with welcome gifts of Bourbon whiskey and Cuban cigars. He usually brought presents to the Guadalcanal nurses too, since Joey was known to be especially fond of a particular one, Ensign Ethel Smith, a striking brunette of enticing proportions from a small town in Iowa. One of the jokes about Joey, when no one could find him, was 'Oh he's probably out pumping Ethel', the homophone Ethyl being a slang name for AVGAS, aviation gasoline.

That evening Abby told Peter about the Marines' departure from Pavuvu. She also told him about the directive that arrived later in the day, to staff up the Navy hospitals on Guadalcanal, Banika, Nouméa and Santo, and insure they were well stocked with medications and other supplies.

"Oh my; it looks like we'll be getting some wounded Marines again soon, and we just cleared the last of the Marianas casualties off to the States. I wonder where the boys are going this time. I'm really grateful that

275

your contractors finished the new hospital building last month, Peter. We have a lot more room now. Perhaps we'll need it all."

Bongo showed up late at the club, as he was due to fly out in the morning with Joey Foster for Guam. When asked about the Marines' new destination, he said vaguely: "It's in the western Carolines, that's all I can say. They call it *Operation Stalemate II*."

"This is the next big thing, then?" Abby asked.

"Well, maybe" Bongo replied, "it's supposed to be an easy one, but you never know. I keep remembering Tarawa."

Meanwhile Admiral Halsey, now back in charge of the Pacific fleet—renamed the Third Fleet, with its fast carriers under McCain now designated TF38—realized that Japanese resistance was beginning to crumble in the Pacific, and the timetables could be pulled forward.

Halsey promptly recommended to Nimitz and MacArthur that *Stalemate II* be cancelled, as it was no longer necessary to capture Palau and protect MacArthur's flank for an invasion at Mindanao in the Philippines, since the Philippine island of Leyte, further north, was far more lightly defended.

MacArthur happily accepted Halsey's recommendation for a landing at Leyte instead of Mindanao. Nimitz contacted the Joint Chiefs for final approval, who were then attending the Second Quebec Conference with FDR and Churchill.

The Chiefs also concurred with the Leyte proposal, but Nimitz unfortunately added a condition that the Palau attack should still go forward as planned. The transports and gunnery ships were already at sea, making it difficult to bring everything to a halt before D-Day, two days hence on September fifteenth.

So the invasion went ahead in the Palau Atoll, which the Japanese fleet had recently abandoned as an anchorage in favor of Singapore's roadstead and Brunei on Borneo, where fuel was more readily available.

Like Betio in the Tarawa Atoll, the objective for *Stalemate II* was to capture a still-active airfield on an island thought to be lightly defended, and where the terrain was presumed to be flat. But it was none of those things. Like Tarawa, it would turn out that the enemy strength was severely underestimated, and the pre-invasion naval gunnery was ineffective. The terrain was anything but flat.

The island's name was Peleliu, and it was even bigger and rougher than Betio. Short of water to drink and stultified by one hundred-fifteen-degree heat, elements of the First Marine Division suffered sixty to seventy percent dead and wounded, before its hapless regiments were relieved after a month by the Army's 81st Division. Had his staff been better informed, Nimitz would doubtless have canceled Peleliu, but as it was, he apparently felt it would be a simple event that could give the task force—already at sea—some realistic training.

Hospital ships offshore at Peleliu departed with capacity cargoes of maimed Marines, bound for the hospitals that a clairvoyant medical commander had made ready, just in case.

Peleliu was a blood bath of over-reaching horror but, like Tarawa and the Marianas, it was consigned to the back pages of most American newspapers, as headlines captivated the public with General Douglas MacArthur's dramatic return to the Philippines, and General Patton's exciting achievements in France. It was good news, not bad, that sold newspapers in the 1940s.

Abby's hunch was right. The Guadalcanal hospital would be filled to capacity; many men from the First Marine Division would never return to Pavuvu for R&R. She had been unable to meet Peter for several days because of the huge influx of wounded, and the need to work double shifts. Kiwi Colonel McKee made a point of visiting the wards at least once daily. He ran into Peter waiting outside the hospital for Abby one evening.

"Mr. Perry, I must say I am overwhelmed with the courage of these young Marines. The hospital ship's captain who brought them here told us about the battle for Peleliu. With all their newfangled technology it is hard to believe that the Yanks knew so little about the island before the invasion. How can it be? What does your friend Commander Perkins have to say about this disaster?"

Peter replied: "He was transferred to Guam a few weeks ago, before the battle started. Knowing him, he will dig out the facts. I also have some American friends who handled photo-analysis here, and I know they are very thorough. They must have scrutinized the Peleliu photos, I'm certain of that, but it seems clear that there just weren't enough of them taken. And they were replaced by a new photography group on Guam around then, which was probably bad timing."

"It's a ruddy shame, that's what it is. Come by for a drink one evening, Mr. Perry, would you? We haven't had a nice chat since those good old days in Fiji."

"With pleasure, Colonel McKee. My fiancée is an American nurse in this hospital. May I bring her also?"

"But of course. I assume she has more sense than some of the Yank planners. Good evening, Perry."

*** *AT THE COMBINED FLEET ANCHORAGES* ***

Waiting for the next shoe to fall, the Japanese warships that had evacuated Truk and Palau, and slunk back without their planes after a futile attempt to reinforce the Marianas, were at anchor off Brunei and Singapore. They could still get oil at this stage but were beginning to run short of ammunition from Japan, and of course aircraft and pilots too.

In anticipation of various possible Allied scenarios in future, the chief of the Combined Fleet, Admiral Toyoda, devised four complicated plans for repelling whichever of those Allied attacks might next materialize. At first it seemed the Allies would invade Formosa, but when MacArthur landed on Leyte in the Philippines, practically the entire remaining Japanese naval arsenal went off to do battle, including *Yamato* and *Musashi*.

*** *HE HAS RETURNED* ***

News was coming into Guadalcanal about the US Army landings on Leyte, which appeared to be a great success. General MacArthur was even photographed wading ashore with his staff from a landing craft, a tremendous PR coup if ever there was one. He announced at once to the Filipinos the news of his return and asked for their support; this news was broadcast to the whole world as well. Although Admiral Nimitz had gone on record with the Joint Chiefs to say the Philippine invasion was probably unnecessary, he had to admit that the spectacular MacArthur publicity was quite helpful to the cause of the Pacific war.

The invasion must also have seriously demoralized the Japs, as Tokyo Rose was quite subdued in her evening broadcasts for a while. Halsey, who respected MacArthur a great deal, was instrumental in convincing Nimitz to go along with the Philippines plan. Little mention was made of Peleliu to the US press corps.

Then there was news of an immense three-day naval battle in the Philippines, centered on Leyte Gulf, as the Japanese sought to intercept and destroy the US landing forces under Admiral Toyoda's 'Plan 1'.

Colonel McKee told Peter afterwards that he thought the Jap fleet was finished, in spite of a few missteps by Halsey: "It looks like a home run, Perry, as the Yanks would say."

*** *THE LOUISIANA SHRIMP BOAT* ***

Peter and Abby appeared at the New Zealand regimental officers club the Saturday following Colonel McKee's invitation. He made them very welcome, and in fact broadcast their arrival in fine fashion, mustaches a-twirling.

"Right, you lot, put your shoes back on and straighten your tunics, for tonight we have in our midst a fine example of ecumenism in action. I wish to present—glancing at a slip of paper in his hand—US Navy *Left*enant junior-in-grade-but-senior-in-charm, the lovely Miss Abigail Culver, and her Pom fiancé, Captain Peter Perry of the Royal Singapore Army Engineers. Please make them welcome by avoiding any customary off-color remarks and so forth. Some of you may remember Captain Perry from Fiji."

At the table, Peter and Abby learned that the colonel's regiment had been part of IMAC in the Central Solomons and had gallantly led the way in the capture of the Treasury Islands as part of the subterfuge that enabled the main invasion force to get ashore unscathed at Empress Augusta Bay on Bougainville in late 1943.

"I developed a liking for the Yank Marines then, as they were always there when we needed them. It's where I developed a respect for ecumenism, to borrow a churchy word; you know, inter-service cooperation, that sort of thing."

During the pleasant evening, in which Abby was asked to dance by at least half the regimental officers, Peter unveiled the 'great plan' for donating an old Louisiana workboat to the Solomons government and shipping it out to Guadalcanal by quasi-official means.

"It should arrive here in a month or so by mid-November, and if we allow, say, another month for getting it in shape, then the plan is—with your kind permission as military commander—to organize a New Year's race with the other old workboats, across to Tulagi and back, selling tickets—and bets—far and wide to raise funds for the little fleet's ongoing maintenance. I should probably speak to Colonel Noel as well, he being the civil authority. At any rate, may we have your blessing for this event?" Peter asked.

"By all means," the Kiwi colonel responded. "I have a few lads who were bookies at the racetracks before the war, and I'm certain they can be persuaded to lend some, ah, technical expertise to the betting. I think one of them is in the stockade just now, but that can be adjusted. Do have a word soon with Colonel Noel, as you suggested. I'm confident he will also help get this thing going."

"Yes sir, I shall," Peter promised, "and in case I get moved to Guam, which is a fair possibility, then I'll make a point of getting back here for race week. Meanwhile, Miss Culver will get her fellow nurses to help with ticket sales. May we put you and your staff down for a few books?"

"Good show, Perry, that's the spirit. Yes, of course, my office will purchase some blocks of tickets. Now please enjoy yourselves this evening. I must dash off to check on the wharf situation, as we are expecting another hospital ship from Peleliu tomorrow. This time there will also be some Yank soldiers among the wounded."

*** THE GUADALCANAL CEMETARY ***

A sad day dawned a week later in October, when five of the new casualties died overnight at the base hospital, adding to the cumulative dozen who had already succumbed since the wounded from Peleliu began arriving on Guadalcanal several weeks before. The original twelve, already buried at the Guadalcanal cemetery, were from the First Marine Division, but the new deaths were all 81st Infantry Division. A funeral and memorial service was held for the seventeen fallen warriors together, at which Colonel McKee and three chaplains spoke from the heart to the large gathering of solemn witnesses outside the chapel. Peter and Abby were among those attending the dismal occasion, standing respectfully as the rifle volleys were fired.

"Oh Peter, I'm so sad that these poor lads couldn't be saved. They were in such horrible condition when they arrived, but without this new Penicillin wonder drug there would doubtless have been more of them. Let's get away from Guadalcanal somehow, please; I'm tired of the heat and the depressing reality of the war." Abby was crying as she spoke, and Peter was depressed as well.

"Abby dear, I've been thinking about this too. Our next postings are likely to be on Guam, where my contractors are finally building a new hospital to take over from the temporary one there. You'll probably be asked to work in that hospital by the time the CINCPAC staff arrive in January, whereas I'll likely have to move to Guam at the end of this month, ahead of you. But on Guam we can't escape the war either; if anything, it will likely get worse as our troops get closer and closer to Japan. I think what we need is some time together on leave, to get away somewhere else for a week or two, where we can relax and ... get married! Would that make sense?"

"Oh yes, Peter, it most definitely would! But how can we get married without my having the Navy's approval? You are in the clear since your divorce was finalized, but I still need to wait for the green light. You know there is a ban on women marrying in the US services."

"Ah yes, but I think we can win that battle on a technicality. You see, Colonel McKee is the top military authority on this island now that the Americans have handed over. I've spoken to him, and he wasn't at first certain his authority could be applied to personal matters of the US forces, though his legal counsel is certain that it could. You saw the colonel call me away for a moment after the funeral service; he had spoken to your head doctor to say that he, as commandant, would grant your request for marriage to a British subject, if the doctor will kindly forward him your papers. And apparently the ban will be lifted by the US in a month or so anyway, therefore he isn't worried about having his decision overturned."

"Oh Peter, that's wonderful news! When can we be married then?"

"Soon, I think, though there's another obstacle. I thought all along that one of the chaplains here could marry us, but apparently not. In the US and Britain, a clergyman is also a representative of the state and therefore has a civil license to marry people, as does a civilian ship's captain in international waters, for example, but here on land in a war zone the civil license is not available to these service chaplains. The law of the land in the Solomons was British before the war, but then the Japs invaded, and British civil law was suspended. Colonel Noel, to whom I also spoke, thinks that British civil law has not yet been fully restored, being as there is a military presence here as well, exercising martial law and so on, you see?"

"Yes, I see," Abby replied, paying close attention. "Look Peter, in that case wouldn't it mean that Colonel McKee, rather than Colonel Noel, would have the authority to delegate this power to the chaplains?"

"I would have thought so, but his legal chap says that the colonel clearly has the right to grant you permission to marry, but not necessarily the authority to actually marry us. Therein lies the problem, I'm told. Bit of a Gilbert and Sullivan muddle, what?"

So what do we do then?" Abby asked, becoming somewhat agitated. "Run away to sea on one of those copra freighters, so its captain can do the job for us?"

"Ha, what a good idea. I may have a better one, though. Look, what would you think of going to Espiritu Santo on leave and getting married there?"

"Well, uh, sure, why not. But why Santo, Peter? Why would that be better than Guadalcanal?" Abby asked.

"Because the New Hebrides Islands were not invaded, hence their civil law has not been interrupted, you see? Any Anglican priest there could marry us under British law, or likewise a French priest could do so under French law. Take your choice. And no worries about there being an American base on Santo; it's just a guest facility, that's all, with no powers of martial law."

"Darling, you're a genius. Of course let us get married on Santo—at once!"

"Abby, I have another reason for suggesting Santo, as we could just as well have picked, say, New Caledonia or Australia instead. You haven't met my good friends on Santo yet, but I've spoken of them to you several times. Hans and Yvonne are engaged to be married also, but they are planning to wait until the war was over to 'tie the knot', as you Americans say. Hans already asked me to be his best man, in fact. I think I could persuade them to get married now if we were to do the same thing.

"Yvonne would doubtless want to have the ceremony there in Luganville, in French, so I assume that would be agreeable to you, and you could teach me how to say 'I do' and other responses in French, before we arrive. They are wonderful people, Abby, and I do so want you to meet them. Well, what do you say? Shall we do something completely different?"

*** THE GREAT RACE ***

Slightly ahead of schedule, a cargo ship arrived at Tulagi on November 12, 1944, and, one by one, lifted over her side a set of five splendid new Higgins PT boats for sea trials and fit-out by the Tulagi base, and onward delivery to Vella Lavella, where they would join a new RON that was being formed up at Emirau to patrol Rabaul. These boats would help make certain no besieged Japanese could escape from their encircled former naval base.

A sixth boat, presumed to be an admiral's gig according to its manifest, followed the PTs over the side and settled gently into the water. It did not look nearly as splendid as the PT Boats, but nonetheless bore a fresh coat of white paint above the waterline and had two sturdy masts lashed to the deck.

A crusty-looking chief petty officer scratched his head, and commented to the Tulagi harbormaster standing by his side, a young Navy lieutenant with a wise and knowing air: "Which admiral would this one be for then, Mister Jones, if I may ask?"

"Never you mind, Chief. This is a wartime experiment of some secrecy, so if I were you I wouldn't go around telling your lads about it. Just be sure this fine old boat is floated into that empty shed, until I get hold of the ONI and let you know what else to do. Clear, Chief?"

"Oh, aye, aye sir, clear as a muddy river. I hope the old girl don't sink on me before we get her into dry-dock."

"Chief, if this boat sinks then so do your seventeen years in the US Navy. How would it feel to be a plain old seaman once again?"

***

Still enjoying their Santo honeymoon, Peter and Abby were awakened early one morning by the desk clerk at their cozy little hotel on Aore Island, across the Segond Channel from Luganville. Peter shook himself from sleep and put on his robe to answer the door.

"Beg you pardon mistair," the attractive Tonkinese girl said. "This telegram come for you now." She handed Peter the message, which stated: ADM GIG HERE STOP PLS ADVISE SOONEST STOP JONES LT USN HARBORMASTER TULAGI.

"Thank you, Miss Liat," Peter said, glancing at her name tag. "May I send a reply from here? No? Then how soon can you get us over to Luganville? We must leave this lovely hotel three days early, I'm afraid."

Later in the day, back on Santo, as Peter strolled down the wide Navy dock with Hans, they chatted about the wedding ceremony that had gone off without a hitch the previous week, in spite of Peter's nervousness.

"Your French speaking it was not so bad, though some more teaching would help," Hans opined. "But Abby, she is quite, er, well. Yes, she is very more well than me, I do think."

"Yes, she *does* quite well," Peter chuckled. "And your dear Yvonne can speak English just as well as French. I'm really amazed. But now I shall have to learn German, I'm told, if I want to work in Europe after the war. I have applied for a job with the pending reconstruction agency. What about you? Are you still planning to stay on Santo, now that you've given up being a Navy contractor?"

"Oh yes," Hans replied, "Philippe and myself we have the local contractor business now going good. Santo is for me the paradise place."

"Well, that's good, Hans. Abby and I shall come back to visit again one day. Santo, Efaté and Nouméa are about the only places in the South Pacific that one can still call paradise. Most other islands have been ruined, I think. And there's still more to come.

"The Japanese can't seem to realize that the war is over. Their emperor keeps telling them to die for him, or so I've heard."

"That is so, I have heard it too" said Hans. "Look here at these big communities here on Santo. They are full now with soldiers mostly, waiting to go on next big battle, or they come here to recover from last one. Hospital always full. Well, everybody is eating nice vegetables from Philippe his farms!"

They laughed at that truism. Peter shook hands and smiled at his friend. "Best of luck, Hans, to you, to Yvonne, and to the fine children.

My goodness, they are growing up fast. But now we must part. Abby said she would be on board the frigate already. Because of her, we were very lucky to get a ride to the Solomons with this Navy ship, as there are no seats available by air for several days. We will get back faster than if we had waited for our confirmed seats on the Friday plane, and frankly, after my last trip to Guadalcanal from Santo, I think I'd prefer to go by ship anyway." Hans nodded vigorously at that statement.

"Just one more thing, old friend," Peter continued somewhat reluctantly: "Hans, what is the situation with the grass skirts, and so forth now? Are Wendy and Doris managing all right?"

"Oh certain they are. Business it is still very good. Yvonne and me we are sharing profit with those ladies 50/50. We and they each make sixty-five thousand dollars so far. They are very good in selling, and we are getting the best quality skirts and carvings. That is how we can afford to buy the little hotel where you stay on Aore. We buy half for cash and Philippe he finance other half for us. Slowly we will make some more, er, improving-ments."

"Thank you for telling me this, Hans. It is a relief to know they are doing so well, and great that you and Yvonne are doing alright too.

"Oh we are very happy also. Miss Abby does she show you the envelope yet? Possible you not see her after Yvonne bring her to ship this morning. Envelope is for you both. It is two thousand US dollar money order for repay one thousand that you lend us to start this business. Wendy, she make this suggestion, and say it is for wedding present."

"Oh my goodness, I am quite touched. What a wonderful surprise." They shook hands again, Peter's eyes glistening.

"Well, stay on feel," Hans said sincerely, making Peter laugh again. "You mean 'stay in touch', I think. Farewell, old Dutchman."

***

Back on Tulagi a week later, Peter and Abby thanked Lt. Jones the harbormaster and his crew for putting the sailboat in dry-dock, so the bottom could be inspected and painted, and the masts stepped and rigged.

"Oh, it's no problem at all, Mr. Perry, we're not all that busy anymore, now that most of the PT boats are up north. A year ago—even six months ago—things were very different. We used to run the dry-dock 24 hours a day at times.

"So OK, we'll check the caulking, give her a good two coats of anti-fouling paint and pull her around the back, out of sight. Her diesel seems OK; the Chief here ran it after she arrived, so I reckon you might have a winner for this race of yours. When will that be?"

Before Peter could reply, the Chief elbowed in: "And what about her name, Mr. Perry? Surely a name like *Boudreau Shrimper V* isn't going to attract many supporters, now will it, ma'am," he said, turning to look at Abby for support. "Even *Good Queen Madruga* would be better than that."

"I completely agree, Chief Machinist Mate," Abby smiled and nodded. "What name would you suggest, then? Hopefully not *Queen Madruga*."

"Why, I hadn't really thought of one, ma'am, but how about your birth date sign, seeing as you'll be the lady sponsor. Would that be all right?"

"Great idea, Chief", said the harbormaster. "So, Lieutenant (jg) Culver, what is your birth month, please?"

Abby laughed: "Actually it's Lieutenant (jg) Perry now, sir, and I was born in May. I won't tell you which year."

And so it was that the challenger was rechristened *Taurus V*, and a nice stern plaque was hand cut and lettered by the chief machinist mate, who had a not-so-secret fondness for sailboats and Navy nurses.

TAURUS V
TULAGI, BSIP

Somehow, in all the excitement, Peter had managed to blurt out to one and all: "December sixteenth will be the race day; it's a Saturday, a month from now, and a month sooner than we expected."

***

Three days before Race Day, Bongo and Peter arrived back on Tulagi with a NATS flight from Guam. As the Dumbo swept in from across the Slot, they could see a pair of masts sticking up from the landward end of the PT boat dock. "There she lies, old pal," Bongo pointed out to Peter.

After they had deplaned and gone ashore from the NATS dock, they walked over to PT Country for a closer look.

"So our Good Ship Lollipop is a ketch like *Ramada*," Bongo remarked to Peter, remembering the lesson in mast-manship.

"That's correct," said Peter, and she looks pretty good for an old workboat, don't you think?"

Bongo nodded: "Sure does; let's get aboard; I'm dying to see below the deck. Still smells a bit 'shrimpy', if you ask me."

"I agree, but no big problem. There are three competitors in the race," Peter said, as they climbed onto the deck, "A 95-foot schooner A/V *Tulagi* from Malaita, a 40-foot sloop from San Cristobal—I've forgotten the name, and the 48-foor ketch A/V *Ramada* from Guadalcanal. *Ramada* is the closest in size to our *Taurus*. In theory the big schooner should take it, but you never know. I think they have the lowest betting odds at the moment and we probably have the highest."

Just then the harbormaster and the chief jumped aboard to join them, with handshakes all around. Peter made the introductions:

"Friends, this is Commander Perkins from Guam, an old friend and fellow investor in this boat. He and I will be the crew for this race, and we are most grateful that Lieutenant Jones has agreed to be skipper."

"Mister Jones, let me echo those sentiments," Bongo said, "and Chief, thank you for all the hard work you've put in to get our challenger shipshape and Bristol-smart."

"Aye sir, and it was a pleasure to be on the team," the chief expounded as Lt. Jones nodded. "But may I say in all sincerity sir, that a workboat this size needs more than three people to sail her, especially as we'll be allowed to use the engine as well as the sails, whenever we wish. When I painted the new name *Taurus* I left the 'V' from the old name, thinking it meant five people in the crew, as that's exactly the minimum that this sort of boat should have. Don't you agree sir?" the chief solemnly asked the harbormaster.

"I do agree one hundred percent, Chief," said Lt. Jones, "and thank you for bringing this up. I would have, myself."

"Then where could we find two more crew members at this late date?" Peter asked.

"Sir, if I may be so bold," the chief chimed in again, "your dear wife said she loves to sail, and she will be over here from Guadal tomorrow morning to see if we, er, if you need any help. Well sir, Miss Abby would be a fine crewmember I'd wager, and perhaps you would consider my unworthy self to be your engine room and pumping man."

"That's enough, Chief; no need to grovel," Skipper Jones said, stifling a smile. "Chief Lubinski was in China Station before the war; he does have a way with words. But I agree with him that we'll need a couple more hands. Mr. Perry, if your wife has experience with sailing then she's most welcome. And of course, how could we possibly go to sea without the old chief."

"That is completely up to my wife," said Peter, "But I just wonder how we are going to function as a team without a trial run, sea trials, or shakedown, whatever it's called in the US Navy."

Lt. Jones answered: "It will be a little difficult, Mr. Perry, I admit, but your wife wanted us to keep the *Taurus* out of sight until the day before the race, to raise the betting totals at the last minute. I think she has some professional bookies on her team. The first planned appearance for *Taurus V* will be as we sail from Tulagi over to Guadal the afternoon before the race starts the day after tomorrow. That thirty miles should give us a good shakedown, I would imagine."

***

The cheerful crew left A/V *Taurus V* under armed guard at the Guadalcanal docks the evening of December fifteenth, feeling quite content with the teamwork on board once the tasks had been balanced out, and savoring the fast and glorious sail over from Tulagi on a beam reach. Chief Lubinski stayed on board with a loaded shotgun that night, just in case of competitive sabotage, while the others commandeered a jeep to visit the Navy O-Club and talk about the race some more.

"It's like old times, being back here," said Bongo, "but I wish Bill and Frank were with us to watch the race."

"Who are they?" Lt. Jones inquired.

Abby answered: "Two nice reserve officers from Texas who invested in this project with us. I don't know whether we'll win the race tomorrow—it really doesn't matter—but the Texans will love to hear how we did."

"Yes, they certainly will," Peter said. "And Abby dear, we're so pleased about the nurses helping you build up the amazing pot of money. How on earth did you get them to work so hard?"

"I've been wondering about that too," said Bongo. "This gal is super talented."

"Do you really want to know, gentlemen? Well, I was a bit naughty," Abby replied, causing several eyebrows to raise uncontrollably. "No, you oafs, nothing like that! Commander ... Bongo, if I may ... do you remember when we met at the hospital right after I arrived here? About your nurse-friend Ellie Norbush?" Bongo nodded, feeling embarrassed and sad once again.

"I told you Ellie had left a note and gift for you, remember? Well, I gave you the note, but you didn't seem interested in the gift, so I kept it. I haven't even shown it to Peter, but it's a beautiful Japanese Geisha doll, a real collector's item. I decided to award it to the nurse who brings in the most cash from her betting sales. We also have several clever Kiwis helping us, that Colonel McKee introduced. They seem a rather shady bunch, but those fellows really know how to run a betting house. Wait till you see the numbers afterwards, net of their commissions! ... But what's the matter with you two?"

Peter and Bongo left the table, laughing uncontrollably.

***

Saturday morning, December sixteenth, held much promise for an enjoyable day at the races. Most of the spectators drifting down to the shore were New Zealanders and local islanders, the latter with many family members in tow. There were a few Aussies and Americans among the crowd too, more interested in getting to know each other than anything else. In the background, some brass instruments were warming up. Palm trees overhanging the beach lent a paradisiacal background for those who had cameras.

The *Taurus V* crewmembers were dressed in identical short-sleeved navy-blue jump suits and white tennis shoes. They waved to the crowd as the committee boat took them out to the former shrimper on its mooring, where the chief had stayed on board. The other ships' crews looked more irregular.

Colonels McKee and Noel arrived together at exactly 0858, two minutes before the start. It was beginning to get warm as the four old workboats jockeyed back and forth offshore, sails flapping and diesel exhausts emitting grey-to-black puffs of smoke, while their skippers sought favorable positions at the starting line for the up-wind leg to Point Taivu. The committee boat, a well-cared for 1942 landing craft, seemed to drift indifferently into the shade of a passing cloud, oblivious to the tensions that enveloped Guadalcanal's Saturday early-risers.

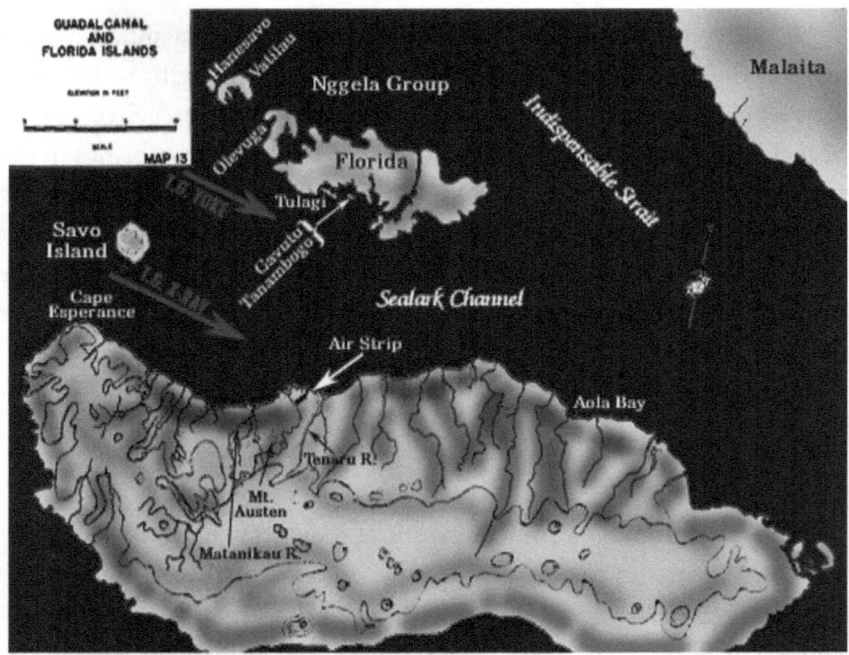

Old invasion map of Guadalcanal and Tulagi. Point Taivu is the promontory just below the letters '<u>Ch</u>' in Sealark <u>Ch</u>annel.
(Perry-Castaneda Library, U. Texas)

Suddenly there was a 'pop' from the starting gun, and the four old workboats hauled in their sails and headed into the wind, seeming to come alive, shaking off their rheumatism and ancient memories, aware only of two thousand pairs of eyes that stared judgmentally, urging them onwards toward Point Taivu in the direction of Aola Bay, where a large red buoy had been anchored in the channel by obliging Kiwi frogmen.

The four old ladies would round that buoy, and then run back across and up the wide channel—once called 'the Slot' by long-dead Marines and Sailors—heading for Tulagi. The old girls on that downwind run would find it easier and more relaxing. They might even shut down the engines that had helped get them to the first buoy, but perhaps not. Anything was acceptable in this race, that allowed them to replicate their workboat routines.

But they had never worked like this before, so hard, so fast and so excitedly. *Who is the strange one in the race*, the local boats thought to themselves? *American*, they had heard. *No, French*, said one. Didn't matter; a Solomons boat would win the race because they had practiced for decades, had hidden in the mangroves, had cursed the dry rot and wet rot and insects and, oh, cursed the roaring birds with red-dotted wings that searched for them. Yes, the Solomons would win. *Here comes the moment: here it comes....*

As *Taurus V* rounded the large red buoy near Point Taivu and started her second leg towards Tulagi, in the middle of the pack behind the big schooner, an odd sound came from her hull deep in the water, sort of a groan and a soft bang. The chief heard it, but he was busy idling the engine to cool it down and let the sails do the downwind work. Up on deck, people were letting the sails out for the long run that they would have for twenty miles or more. They fiddled and faddled to set out the mainsail and mizzen on opposite sides of the boat, and the jib to fit in wherever there was space.

"Doesn't it seem like we're slowing down?" Bongo asked Lt. Jones.

"Yes, it does, a little," the skipper replied. "The big schooner does seem to be leaving us behind, which one might expect because of her length, but the others are also catching up with us. I don't see why, as we have everything hanging out but the laundry."

Soon the boat acted as though a sea anchor was dragging astern, but the men couldn't see any obstruction at all. It was Abby who put two and two together.

"Good heavens, I think we're sinking!" she exclaimed.

There was no doubt about it any longer, as the other two boats eased past them with a fair show of speed and cheery waves from their crews. "Everything OK?" someone shouted.

"Where's the chief," Lt. Jones asked. "Commander, please see what's going on down below. And Abby, could you take the wheel, please? I want to look over the boat."

Both Peter and Bongo slid down the short ladder into the galley, off which the small engine compartment lay with its hatch door wide open.

"Chief, are you in there?" Bongo shouted.

"Aye sir, please come and help," was his muffled reply.

Bongo crowded into the engine space, leaving Peter in the galley for lack of room. Glancing through the hatchway Peter could see a pair of legs protruding from the bilge, and Bongo reaching for a hand that was waving jerkily. Bongo pulled on the hand and an oil-stained and sodden chief petty officer emerged from the bilge, apoplectic and choking.

"Gawd a'mighty, we're in deep trouble! Do we have a radio to send a May Day message?" The chief stood up which forced Bongo back into the galley. "There's a plank washed off the hull. I tried to patch the hole with boards from the galley, but the hole is too big and they just washed away. The sea is coming in fast, and we'll be flooded real soon. Best get on deck and see to the lifeboat, Commander!"

There was of course no sign of a radio on board, and the so-called lifeboat was a tiny wooden thing that might hold three of them at best. Apparently, no one had thought they'd ever need it. "Drop the sails!" the skipper ordered, as he realized what was happening. "Drop the main and jib please, Mr. Perry and Commander Perkins. Bring her 'round into the wind, then stay on the wheel, Abby, you're doing fine. Chief get the mizzen down would you and look to the small boat. Over the side with it, please."

Lt. Jones was calm and collected, which was a relief to everyone. "Look," he said, "I saw a flare gun near the chart table, and some flares I think. Fire one off, Chief, once you have the lifeboat in the water and made fast. In fact, fire them all off!"

Taurus V was now dead in the water, and there was no sign that anyone on shore had seen their perilous situation. Two flares shot into the air, one white and one red. The dinghy was alongside, looking not at all like a lifeboat.

292

"Look everyone," Lt. Jones ordered, "we'll swamp that little boat with more than three people, and they need to be lightweight people at that. Here's who goes into the boat and why: the first is Abby, 'cause she's too pretty to get her hair messed up in the water; next is the Chief, 'cause he's too old to go swimming; third is Commander Perkins 'cause he's our senior officer. OK, that means Mr. Perry and I will take a bath as soon as you three are aboard."

Bongo spoke up at once: "Skipper, I'm over-riding you. You're our leader and too valuable to be splashing about in an unfocussed sort of way. Perry and I will be the swimmers. No more talk."

"All right then, we don't have time to discuss it. You can see we're sinking but being wooden there's a likelihood she may not actually go down all the way. We may even be able to climb back onto the hull some kind of how, but we need to get away from the boat now in case she turns turtle or just falls over to one side, where someone might get hurt. So OK, Chief, please board the dinghy and then you can help Miss Abby aboard. I'll join you then and rely on the other two gents to cast us off and jump in the sea.

This they all did; Abby was certain the chief was fondling her buttocks as he eased her down the rope ladder, but she was too nervous about everything to make a fuss over it just then. Peter dove into the water and swam over to the little boat. Then it was Bongo's turn; before he jumped he told the others that the committee boat seemed to be turning around and heading their way, but it was a slow old barge and they were at least ten miles from them. The three other sailboats were still going flat out downwind for Tulagi.

As Bongo swam to the dinghy Peter said "Why are you pushing me? There's plenty of room on the other side.

"I'm not pushing you, silly Brit."

"Then who is?" Peter insisted. "There it is again."

Bongo looked beneath the surface and came up spluttering: "It's a damned huge shark, that's what it is."

He submerged and hit the beast on the nose with his fist, and all the force he could muster.

CHAPTER EIGHT

★ ★ ★

The End Game

Iwo Jima Flag Raising
(photo by Joe Rosenthal - NARA unrestricted)

"There Is No Substitute for Victory"
General Douglas MacArthur

"The mystery of war enshrouds the deeper mystery of death"
William Manchester USMC, *Goodbye, Darkness;*
MacArthur's official biographer (*American Caesar*)

*** ON THE CASUALTY LIST ***

By Tuesday of the following week, everyone but Bongo Perkins had been released from hospital after the disastrous capsizing of A/V *Taurus V.* The unfortunate Commander Perkins was still drifting in and out of consciousness from loss of blood, after the aggressive shark took away his left forearm. Peter Perry was at Bongo's bedside when his friend first regained a semblance of his old self for a short spell.

"Oh Bongo, how sad we are that you had to suffer for helping the rest of us escape a mauling from that brutish animal, and the other sharks," Peter spoke sincerely.

"Crap, old pal, I'm not too devastated by the missing arm, but losing that Rolex really gets to me. It was just eight years old, for heaven's sake. They are supposed to last a lifetime!"

Peter smiled. "A perfect Bongo-ism. I must write Bill and Frank right away and tell them what you just said."

"Well, tell them about the damned plank coming off the boat then. What kind of seaworthiness is that? Are we insured?"

Abby came into the room just then, dressed in her whites for duty. She felt Bongo's forehead and offered to give him another sedative. The stump of his left arm was wrapped thoroughly in bandages, and had been trimmed, cauterized and sewn up by the chief surgeon. Nevertheless, there was blood oozing through the bandages.

"Try to sleep, Commander. We've given you three transfusions already, but you may need another one soon. I'm ashamed that it took so long to tie a tourniquet around your arm, but everyone was in a state of confusion at that time, trying to climb back up the slippery capsized hull and fend off the other sharks with oars. Your bleeding was really attracting them."

"I can imagine," Bongo replied drowsily. "But I remember we could see the hole from the missing plank with the hull turned like that. Did the chief look at it to see if he could figure what happened?"

"Of course, and Lt. Jones too. They think the plank was unscrewed and then put back in place with nails. Perhaps sabotage on Tulagi or perhaps sloppy repair work over in Louisiana. When the boat rounded the buoy the stresses on the hull changed, and out popped the plank. It was just a short plank at that, sistered onto a full-length piece for some reason. But it had been freshly caulked like the rest of the hull—they saw evidence of that."

Bongo dropped off to sleep then, so Peter and Abby quietly left him. "Peter, I'm really shocked about poor Bongo, and I think Colonel McKee is also. He asked to speak with you at his office whenever you have a moment."

"Yes, I had better give the colonel an update on all this. I'd like to get Lt. Jones over from Tulagi to speak to the colonel as well. Can I send a message from here? Seems to me this might have happened while the boat was in dry-dock for those few days, without a guard."

"But who could have done the sabotage?" Abby asked. "Surely not the chief or his crew."

"Perhaps some local fellows at night then," Peter suggested. "They're pretty capable with boat construction. It's interesting than none of the other workboats turned back to help us. Surely someone saw what happened."

"Who won the wretched race then?" Abby asked.

"Why, the big schooner, just as we expected. But back to Bongo," Peter said, "I understand they're planning to send him home on leave for two months, as soon as he can travel. He may have trouble staying in the Navy with that arm missing."

"Yes, darling, but please don't forget about Colonel McKee. He sounded quite anxious to speak with you, and I think alone."

***

Colonel McKee was more upset than Peter had realized. "Perry, this nonsense with the sailboat is quite disturbing. The hull has now been patched and righted, and towed to Aola for proper repair by our chaps. You should be able to hand the boat over officially to Colonel Noel in another two weeks, so I've been told. He is most grateful for your generosity and that of the other three people who financed it—not to mention the enormous sum of gambling receipts—and he is as relieved as I am that there was no loss of life involved."

"Yes, sir, you've been most kind to assist with the aftermath, as it were. We all appreciate it," Peter said solemnly.

The colonel was not finished: "The fact that there was serious and permanent injury incurred by a US naval commander in my jurisdiction is a point that gives me serious concern as base commandant of Allied forces in the Solomons. In my mind this unfortunate condition has come about because of, number one—sabotage by one or more as yet unidentified persons; and number two—incompetence on the part of US naval personnel, who should have had more sense than to take this boat to sea without the prescribed safety equipment on board. I refer of course to Lieutenant Jones the Tulagi harbormaster, and his assistant Chief Petty Officer Lubinski."

"Oh, I see," said Peter, although he didn't quite understand.

"Perry, I had considered requesting a court martial for those two men, but in view of their goodwill in undertaking the adventure with you—no malice aforethought and so forth—I am now inclined to just ask the US Naval District commander on Espiritu Santo to issue a written reprimand for their records. I wanted you to hear the news before I made it public. I strongly feel that Commander Perkins' deplorable condition warrants at least some such action."

"Colonel McKee, I had not thought about the misadventure in that light before, but I think you are correct that we should have had life jackets, life rings, a larger or additional lifeboat, a wireless of some sort and additional flares, but in honesty we were all so excited about the regatta it was as if there were no war for a few days, just the pleasure of the competition."

"Absolutely right, Perry, I think Colonel Noel and I were caught up in the spirit of the event too, but that's no excuse for shoddy safety measures. Noel has since had all the other local craft inspected, and each of them was found wanting. Even on the Thames River in London for a Sunday regatta, there are safety standards, by Jove. Now let me express another point: the name none of us has mentioned in all this is that of your lovely wife. My God, man, what would we all be feeling now had it been Miss Abby in the jaws of that damned shark, eh?"

"Unthinkable, Colonel, I try very hard not to focus on it. But to change the focus a little bit, let me tell you what Commander Perkins said when he recovered consciousness this morning: that he didn't mind losing the left arm so much, it was his missing Rolex that troubled him most; university gift from the parents, you see!"

The colonel guffawed loudly. "Perry, you're lucky to have a Yank friend like that; one in a million he is. I shall pop by to see him tomorrow. The Rolex, by Jove! Hah. P'raps we'll issue a reward and get the natives started on a shark hunt; you never know what we might find in the bellies of those beasts. Might even make this workboat race an annual event and call it the Rolex Cup!"

*** CHRISTMAS ON GUAM ***

After the utter devastation from Guam's bombardment and invasion the past July, it was still quite usual to see the bleakness of former cities and towns as the Christmas season arrived. Not very much had been constructed, apart from rows of Quonset warehouses by the harbor, but the Agaña River had been rerouted so that a huge mass of rubble from the capital city could be trucked, bulldozed and shoveled into the sea. Those acres of pulverized remains included the former government house and the cathedral, and all other buildings around the old square. There was so much rubble involved that it created a sort of reclaimed land promontory in the sea, where the quaint old town of Agaña had once been the focus of Guamanian life since Spanish days.

[Americans of course pronounced it Agana; who could blame them? If only the Spanish had mollified their pride centuries ago and used 'ny' to spell the sound of their precious 'ñ', a letter that did not appear on any American or British typewriters, then the Anglo-Saxon world could have easily coped with words like Aganya—Ed.]

So Agana or Agaña is where Peter found himself once again, after the infamous Guadalcanal workboat race, as Christmas 1944 approached, just days away. He was unable to join Abby back on Guadalcanal, as things were just too busy now that new construction had finally begun in earnest. Abby did manage to write Peter that Bongo had been airlifted to the US for leave and rehabilitation with his parents in Boston. She was as busy as Peter, with a seemingly endless stream of wounded US soldiers and sailors from the Philippines, as General MacArthur drove onward through Leyte toward Luzon and the capital, Manila. It was a challenge just finding time to write.

Peter became swamped with project evaluations. Seabees had almost cleared the population centers of rubble and had laid out several temporary housing encampments for the Army Air Corps, Navy, and Marines—and even some rudimentary camps for the few thousand wretched Chamorro refugees, who had somehow survived Japanese atrocities and intensive US naval bombardment, only to face an extremely bleak Christmas in the temporary shelters. But Guam was slowly recovering its natural beauty as the chaos of war was dealt with, and its decrepit fresh water supply was brought under control by Marine Corps engineers.

One Saturday morning, stuck in a Quonset hut with a pile of proposals and technical drawings to review, Peter heard a knock on the screen door and rose to see who was there. "Yes, can I help?" he said seeing a short, slim, dark-complexioned young man outside the screen.

"Sorry to bother sir, but are you Mr. Perry? I am Domingo Salas from the Catholic Diocese. Could we please have a word?"

"Why of course Mr. Salas; please do come in." Peter shook hands and waved the young man to a chair at his desk. "May I offer something to drink? I'm sorry my staff are not here on Saturdays."

"No thanks, Mr. Perry, I do not wish to take much of your time, as I know you are just recently arrived on Guam."

"Yes, that's true," Peter shrugged and smiled, "about two months ago, and what's worse I was just away once again until this week. But how may I help?"

"Mr. Perry, I am but recently arrived myself, although I was born here in Agaña. My late parents and grandparents were Guamanian, as I am—in fact my father ran the hotel management school for Pan Am on the Orote Peninsula. Did you know Pan Am's hotel was the very first one on Guam? Fortunately for me I was sent away to university in California before the war started. But I can hear from your accent that you are English, Mr.

Perry. How can it be that an Englishman is running the US contracts office here?"

Peter thought the young man, scarcely thirty, was being deliberately precocious, and wondered why. He shrugged and remained silent.

"I apologize, Mr. Perry. I am being rude. I've had to deal with a lot of military bureaucrats and functionaries these past few days. One of them sent me over to see you, when I requested reconstruction help for the local people who survived the inhuman bombardment last July. Most military types seem to feel they did the civilians a favor by blasting the island around the clock for thirteen days, before they came ashore to deal with our Japanese captors. I can see their point, but they seldom try to see mine."

"Mr. Salas, I don't know about this bombardment, but I see you are quite upset about it. Please allow me to invite us to a quick lunch, if you will kindly suggest somewhere nearby. I am so new here that I still bring my lunch to work from the mess hall."

***

Marine Corps Season's Greetings for 1944

"Christmas Day, December 25th, 1944, is Admiral Nimitz's third anniversary as Commander-in-Chief Pacific," his advance staff told the young Guamanian press reporters, two eager but nervous Chamorro students whose teachers were determined to launch a two-page newspaper for Agaña residents.

"The admiral will arrive here on Guam during January, but for security reasons we cannot tell you exactly which date. You can say in your article that the war in the Pacific will soon be over, and Japan will be completely defeated."

Christmas Day being a Monday, many on the new base were given a two-day holiday, which brought forth a plethora of baseball competitions and a reasonably good turnout for church services. At Domingo Salas' invitation, Peter joined the Catholic congregation with the Chamorros. He very much enjoyed the relatively cooler climate of Guam compared to Guadalcanal, and wrote often to Abby, urging her to request a transfer, because the new general hospital at Agat was almost ready for staffing.

It was during his second week of attending the local Catholic congregation's Saturday afternoon celebration, under battered palm trees near the beach—their church building having been partly demolished—that Peter, who was nominally an Anglican churchgoer, met the rest of the Salas family. Domingo proudly introduced his uncle Benjamín, his aunt Claudia, and his younger brother Raúl.

"The four of us are all that's left now. My parents and two older brothers died this year in the fighting and bombardment, and we lost my little sis back in '41 when the Japs invaded Guam. She was only fourteen, but they raped her and killed her."

"I'm terribly sorry for your awful tragedies," Peter said, quite moved. "How were you able to return to Guam from California so soon after the Americans did?"

"It was thanks to the USO, oddly enough. They are planning to bring some entertainers here next month, and I was lucky enough to meet one of the big-name people in Los Angeles who does the planning and scheduling. He is a Chamorro like me, and had been in the States for more than twenty years. When I told him of my parents' deaths, and my uncle and aunt's dire situation, he pulled some strings and got me here on a NATS flight around the end of August. You would be sick to see what this place looked like back then."

"Gosh, I can imagine. How were you able to make ends meet?" Peter asked.

"The Catholic church helped me a little at first, then as I got to know the bishop, he offered me a job to assist with the rehabilitation of his Chamorro flock. I am the archdeacon now, which simply means an assistant to the bishop. The Catholics were our only real hope for the past half century, you see, as American governors came and went like a revolving door, and then the Japanese invaded with their Saipan Chamorro lackeys. Between the Japs and the Saips, they stole our homes and forced my people into compounds in the jungle for over two years. After the bombardment, they were planning to kill all the locals to hide evidence of their bad behavior. Some Marine patrols found the Chamorro camps just in time."

"Domingo, I'll see what I can do through this US contracts office to help with the temporary shelters you need, while the villages are being rebuilt. We often have leftover materials of various sorts, that are simply warehoused until some other project needs them. I'll let you know in a day or so. Meanwhile can you perhaps organize some construction workers for us? I can tell you that anyone willing and able to work from January onwards will be assured of a job, once the projects get going."

"Thank you so much, Mr. Perry. Here, this is for you; it's a photo of the plaza as it used to look in 1936. Guam was a happy place then, in spite of the well-meaning Navy governors who didn't really understand us local people. It was the Church that was our guardian angel."

*** *IWO JIMA* ***

Very much to Peter's surprise, Bongo appeared at his office in the middle of February 1945, with a customary greeting.

"Open up, busy Brit. You can't hide indoors while the war is on. Come with me and take a look at what the Seabees have done for Admiral Nimitz. You know he arrived here two weeks ago, right?"

"Good grief," Peter responded, nodding. "Why on earth have you come back to work so soon? How is your arm, or what's left of it?" Peter eyed the neatly folded khaki sleeve that Bongo had pinned up near his left shoulder.

"I guess I'm doing OK," his friend replied, "and everyone thinks this Purple Heart I got from the Fiji wound is for the missing arm, so I have a lot of fun making up sea stories to keep the masses entertained. I've got half a dozen variations, depending on the audience. My parents were pretty bent out of shape, though."

"I can imagine they were," Peter replied, chuckling, "How do you keep track of the time now, without the famous Rolex?"

"My dad gave me his," Bongo grinned, showing his right wrist, "But I still find myself looking at the wrong arm. Look, what do you say we cut out now and have a late lunch at the new club? There are a couple of fellas waiting for me there that you might remember, and we can stop and say hello to the Navy's newest rear admiral on the way."

"All right, then. I really am busy these days, but since it's Friday I suppose one could sneak away early. Just let me tell my assistant to close up. Gosh, it's good to see you again, Bongo."

"Well, hurry up, slothful Brit; we've a driver waiting outside."

On the way to the new CINCPAC compound, which locals were already calling 'Nimitz Hill', Bongo recounted the tale of his trip back to Boston, and his battle with the Navy to let him return to active duty.

"Admiral Silvers finally had to pull some strings to keep me from getting the boot. He got me some sort of medical dispensation as part of a cooked-up study to see whether one-arm commanders can still button their flies. The solution is a zipper; no telling where this could lead."

Peter, whose construction projects did not include the new CINCPAC headquarters, was quite impressed at the usual Seabee efficiency, but not overwhelmed by the esthetics of the new buildings, a mixture of Quonset and Dallas huts. Nevertheless, the views of the coastline and Agana Bay from the little hill were superb, and this he noted aloud.

Bongo agreed: "The old man picked out the site himself when he came through here last year. He has a keen eye for that sort of thing. The architecture is pretty dismal though, but it's just a temporary deal until the war is over. Nimitz and MacArthur—the general is now in Manila—are both waltzing towards Tokyo, you might say. It's that old cartwheel dance again, now set to louder and faster music."

Bongo led Peter through Security and over to Admiral Silvers' office, but the admiral's orderly handed them a note that apologized "for having to miss saying hello to Mr. Perry, due to pressing business."

"The newest batch of photos must have arrived from Interpron-2," Bongo explained. "I'll tell you more about this at the club."

When they arrived at the Naval Officers Club, Peter was delighted to see Lt. Cdr. Mike Osborn and Lt. (jg) Andrew Culver, Abby's brother, waiting in the lobby.

"I thought you might be pleased," Bongo grinned at Peter. "Even better, young Culver here has just been promoted to lieutenant, though he obviously hasn't had time to do his shopping." pointing to the single silver bar still on Andrew's collar.

"Does Abby know yet?" Peter inquired, shaking Andrew's hand.

"Uh-uh, I only just heard about it myself," Andrew grinned. "I have Commander Osborn here to thank for this nice surprise."

"Nonsense, Culver, you earned that second silver bar by hard work. That's why you're more than a NATS assistant this time. Here on Guam, Lt. Culver runs the Apra seaplane operation completely by himself. It's the old Pan Am base, as you folks may know," he said to Bongo and Peter. "We operate flights from two land-plane fields on Guam as well."

Amid the handshaking and back-slapping, Bongo announced that he would host the meal, which was self-service that day on a cafeteria line. "Always pick up the cheap tabs, clever Brit; remember that." Everyone laughed at the sage advice.

After they had eaten and retired to a quieter corner for coffee, Bongo looked around before restarting the conversation.

"OK," he said quietly so they wouldn't be overheard, "you know that we're launching those super-bomber B-29s from Saipan already, and blasting the Jap cities, right?" The others nodded and paused while Peter, smiling, signed for the coffee.

"Well we're definitely pounding the crap out of the cities, but their AA and fighters are shooting down some of our bombers, and others are flying back badly damaged. We've lost a dozen already, crashed into the sea, so we need an intermediate airfield in the middle of their flight path for the damaged ones to land on. Aircraft carriers are too small for those monster Superforts, so our Marines are busy taking another island away

from the Japs at this very moment, having gone ashore just two days ago."
He paused to take a coffee from Peter.

"The name of the island is Iwo Jima—better remember it. The Nips are dug in with masses of troops and artillery. It's a god-awful dust-covered volcanic horror, but there are three airfields plenty big enough for B-29s. And, of course, it is really well defended with caves and tunnels, even more complex than Peleliu. You probably won't hear about it through channels until after it's over, but I wanted you to be aware, especially you NATS people, as they will be flying the more seriously wounded to Guam by plane, now that your hospital is about finished.

"And Peter, here's something that might interest you. The skipper of one of our subs, USS *Archerfish*, sank a large Jap carrier late in November '44, that was sort of cruising unescorted along the Japanese coast all by itself, but no one at ONI believes him, simply because we didn't pick up any radio traffic about this ship, and because we have no record of a large, unknown, IJN fleet carrier. I personally think it must have been *Shinano*, the third *Yamato*-class battleship that was converted to a carrier by Admiral Yamamoto before he died. Time will tell, but that's probably 'two down and one to go' for Lt. Naburo's score card. Still remember that unlucky fellow?"

Peter nodded, pensively. "Of course, and I think often of him and his parents in Hawaii. Col. McKee told me about the *Musashi* being sunk in the Philippines. Apparently *Yamato* got away again."

"So, Commander, what about your arm?" Mike Osborn interrupted. "What the heck happened?" Bongo glanced at Peter and winked before replying.

"It's a terrible story, really," Bongo began. "I hope young Culver has the stomach for it." Peter rolled his eyes and excused himself to visit the toilet.

*** *BACK TO CORREGIDOR* ***

The following evening, a Saturday, the four friends reconvened for supper at the club. This time Andrew Culver sported his new Navy lieutenant bars, which were the subject of the first toast. Bongo told them the news from the Philippines:

"After pushing through Leyte, General MacArthur was intent on moving his headquarters from Hollandia to Manila just as soon as the Philippine capital was subdued," Bongo said, "but unfortunately the Japs did not declare Manila an open city as the general had done in 1942. Many historical buildings have been badly damaged by street fighting.

"The general had intended to set up shop in the old Manila Hotel like before, so he was quite put out at the destruction caused by evicting the Nips from inside the city. In fact, he was highly pissed off, you might say. This I got from an Army spook with whom I exchange jokes and gossip."

"I can imagine that," Mike Osborn said. "They say MacArthur loves the Philippines and has hardly ever been back to the States. So is everything secure there now, and under reconstruction?"

"Not quite. Do you guys know about Corregidor?" Bongo asked. Mike and Andrew shook their heads.

"Well, it's a five square-mile island fortress right at the entrance to Manila Bay. Our General Wainwright held out there until April '42 with some Army troops and the old Fourth Marines from Shanghai. That was several weeks after MacArthur left for Australia. There were Army and Navy nurses on the island too, because they had a hospital down in the tunnels. Our people were pretty much starved out before they surrendered, and probably half of them died afterwards. God knows what happened to the nurses." Peter blinked at the thought, and Andrew swallowed hard.

"Sorry," Bongo paused, then concluded: "On February 7th, MacArthur's GIs finally recaptured Manila, but Corregidor still needed to be retaken, if for no other reason than revenge for the Japs having captured it from us. Over six thousand Japs were defending it, and it took two weeks for GI paratroops and landing forces to eliminate them. That finally happened yesterday, more or less, a few days after the Marines landed on Iwo Jima, lest we forget."

*** NURSES MOVE TO GUAM ***

Almost all of Guam's previous medical facilities had been destroyed in the lengthy US bombardment, not that they were in very good condition after three years of Japanese misuse, but one building survived in fair enough condition for refurbishment—a former tuberculosis hospital in the village of Agat. Marine engineers went to work on it, while the Seabees were busy rebuilding the port facilities.

It was a miracle that public health on the island did not deteriorate drastically during the Japanese occupation, or while temporary US hospitals were being built or rebuilt at Agat and Anigua. This phenomenon was attributed to a resurgence in native herbal medicine use; there seemed to be no other explanation, the Navy doctors reluctantly admitted.

Eventually, enough medical staff had been conscripted from New Zealand for Guadalcanal, so that more senior nurses like Abby could be transferred to Guam, which was closer to the pending battlegrounds of 1945—Iwo Jima and Okinawa. Peter was beside himself with happiness as the first group of Canal nurses stepped down the ladder from their R4D cargo plane, flown by Navy Lt. Joey Foster, who kissed one of them after the engines shut down.

Then Peter was embarrassed when he found himself the center of attention, as Abby led her colleagues over to meet him at the arrival Quonset. Finally, Lt. Cdr. Osborn interceded, and chased off the other nurses to collect their duffel bags, where Joey Foster was waiting with ground transportation and a big smile.

"Oh Abby, at last you're here," Peter effused. "I hope you like Guam as much as I think you will. This is my friend Mike Osborn, who is in charge of NATS operations. I just realized that you two hadn't met before even though you were both on Nouméa at the same time."

"How are you, Abby? Welcome to Guam," the NATS commander said, returning her salute. "Peter has told us so much about you. I hope you enjoyed the flight from Guadalcanal."

"Thank you, Commander Osborn, it was just fine," Abby smiled. "And I understand from Joey Foster, our pilot, that NATS is flying into the combat zones now, to help evacuate some wounded by air from Iwo Jima. We had a flight nurse in training with us on the Canal recently, after graduating with her class at NAS Alameda."

"Yes, that would be young Ensign Jane Kendeigh, I imagine. Everyone calls her Candy, heh-heh. Just 22 years old, they say she was quite a sensation on Iwo Jima a few days ago, as the first-ever Navy flight nurse, aboard the first-ever NATS flight into a combat area. It was not all that long after the flag was hoisted on Mount Suribachi—I suppose you've seen that great photo by Joe Rosenthal in the papers?—but even today heavy fighting continues at the other end of the island, you know."

Abby was slightly miffed that Peter, too, seemed caught up in the story about the cute Navy nurse. Commander Osborn continued, clearly relishing the telling:

"Well, her plane even had to circle Iwo for 90 minutes before it could land, while a big naval bombardment was going on. Ensign Candy—er, Kendeigh—is based here on Guam with our elite air evacuation squadron VRE-1. She's become an expert on triage, which is figuring out in which order the wounded men should go to the operating room. You'll have to meet her one of these days, Peter."

Abby didn't look particularly happy at that suggestion, and quickly changed the subject:

"Commander Osborn, I believe my brother is working here for NATS. Would you happen to know how I could get in touch with him? He is Lt (jg) Culver."

"Yes of course; he is on my staff in fact. I'll get a message to him at once. Andrew has just been promoted, you'll be glad to know."

"Darn, he still outranks me then," Abby pouted.

*** REBUILDING THE MARIANAS ***

Abby was much envied by her fellow nurses for having worked out a way to get married in 1944 while on overseas duty, but then—surprisingly—in January '45, the official US ban on marriage for overseas servicewomen was lifted.

Several nurses took advantage of this relaxation of rules, to get themselves engaged on Guam, usually to military or naval colleagues such as pilots, doctors, engineers or corpsmen. Soon the first weddings took place under restored US civil law, but the problem for all the married couples, including Abby and Peter, was finding married quarters for setting up house.

There just wasn't anything available through the Navy and constructing homes for the few married couples in their custody was a very low naval priority. Peter, once again, solved the problem for Abby and himself, but was slow to realize that he had done so.

Recently he had been issued with a jeep, painted white to show that it wasn't military. One Sunday, he and Abby drove to the Catholic service at the beach site only to find a notice tacked to a palm tree, stating that the people had moved back into their old church building, which the Seabees had insisted on repairing.

"Good morning, Peter and Abby," Domingo welcomed them after the service ended. "Are you both keeping well? Isn't it a nice surprise to be back inside our old parish building? Well, we also have a special surprise for you two after lunch."

"Oh, what could that be?" Abby blurted out. Domingo just smiled and signaled her to be patient. Peter chuckled and did the same, so they sat and fidgeted, asking Domingo about his family while a simple lunch was served by some cheerful ladies from the parish. Abby helped them clear away after the meal and waved to Peter from the kitchen door. Peter grinned back at her, shrugging slightly.

Soon Father Isaias, the parish priest, joined their table for a coffee, then beckoned Domingo and the visitors to follow him along a path leading behind the church building. Abby by this time was quite giddy with anticipation and clutched at Peter's sleeve. They passed a little stand of spindly trees with bulbous orange fruit hanging low, and a patch of interesting-looking vegetables.

"Oh look, Abby, paw-paws," Peter exclaimed. "I haven't seen those since Canton Island."

"You mean papayas," Abby answered. "I ate some in Hawaii on our layover for Nouméa."

"No those are paw-paws, I'm certain. Look, let's ask Domingo; that'll settle it." He gestured to his Chamorro friend, pointing at the little orchard.

"*Fruta bomba* is what they are called here, because the fruit looks like small bombs," Domingo said. "They almost grow wild. They are very good for your digestion, by the way. Maybe the Spanish brought them here from Cuba, I'm not quite sure."

The path turned off into what might once again become an attractive grove of native hardwood trees one day, and ended at a row of dwellings that had, like the church building, been recently repaired by the Seabees. Fr. Isaias led them to a door at the far end, and opened it to display a well-designed two-story apartment, complete with basic kitchen and bathroom amenities.

"Well, here it is," Domingo beamed, "your new home on Guam!"

"What on earth…," Peter began, while Abby clapped her hands for joy. "I don't understand."

"Peter, your overwhelming assistance when we were desperately seeking help has saved many of our local people from deprivation, without a doubt. The materials you arranged for your company to donate have provided housing for many a Chamorro family, and have helped the Seabees repair our church and this row of clergy quarters. We are all grateful and hope you will allow us this one pleasure in return. We know how hard you have been searching for a place to live together with your dear wife."

Peter and Abby were amazed, and couldn't help hugging each other and Domingo, who continued: "You know that our priests are all celibate, like the good padre here"—Father Isaias nodded—"therefore their housing units are simple and small, but comfortable, one above the other. This larger unit at the end is not a two-clergy duplex, but rather a two-story hostel where Bishop Benito and his assistants can stay together and hold meetings, when they make visitations to our parish. But they will happily stay with various congregation families instead, for as long as you and Abby remain on Guam—even if it's for a hundred years!" Domingo laughed.

"I'm sorry for the simple furnishings, but we'll work on that later. For now, welcome to your new home. You can park your jeep at the churchyard whenever you like."

"Bless each of you and this house," Father Isaias added, beaming, as Peter carried Abby across the threshold.

*** *OKINAWA* ***

During the month that followed, as the Perrys grew used to the church neighborhood and gradually acquired odds and ends of furnishings for the bishop's hostel, delightful springtime weather began to envelope the island. Guam took on a subtle green glow which was accentuated by the surrounding clear blue ocean.

It had been considerably cooler up at Saipan, where Peter had just flown by Navy PBY to a meeting of the various Mariana Islands military and civilian reconstruction teams, planning how to best share available equipment and materials efficiently. Having to deal with a group of far-flung islands created a special logistics problem not foreseen by US planners, when they totaled up the land surface as if it had all been contiguous.

As he listened through the various discussions and presentations, Peter was awed by the extent to which the Marianas were being rebuilt in under a year's time. During a break for lunch, he sat with some Army engineers who explained the type of work they did, compared to that of the Navy Seabees. Peter remembered the conversation afterwards and related the gist of it to Abby.

"We tend to handle things differently from the Seabees," a major had explained. "I have the greatest respect for those Seabee fellows, especially for their speed and their courage under fire. They'll come charging onto a new island, often right behind the Marines, take a look at the terrain, then start the bulldozers going to carve out an airfield, a motor pool parking lot, or a dock site, whatever is needed. Suddenly, bingo, you blink your eyes and it's all finished, and they've moved on to the next job.

"Well, what we do instead is study the contours, the flood plains and rivers, the rainfall data and any geological oddities, then we take all that into account before starting any actual excavation work. Often we get aviation outfits like VD-2 to help us with contour photos, because it's a snap for those boys to fly over our site on the way to a job and take a few shots for us with their stereo cameras. Then we ask their analysts to study the photos and produce a nice contour table for us, with all the numbers laid out. We could never afford a service like that if this were a civilian job," he laughed. "Did you say your name was Berry?" the major asked Peter. "I enjoyed your presentation."

"Thanks very much, Major; the name is Perry, with a 'P'. I represent the US contracts office, strangely enough for an Englishman. As I told the group, what we do is select civilian contractor-bidders to put up the permanent buildings and bridges, that sort of thing, using local labor where possible. I can see we'd better be certain our foundations are laid on Army rather than Navy plots from now on! I suppose typhoons must give you fits when planning for water movement."

On the way back to Guam, the Dumbo flew them over Tinian and fairly close to Rota, and Peter was glad for a look at those other two islands.

Tinian seemed to be a mass of long landing strips where the enormous B-29s came and went, whereas Rota was still occupied by Japanese troops, someone said. *Poor blighters must be starving*, Peter thought to himself. *I wonder if they are cannibals by now.*

When Abby met him at the Guam airfield, she told Peter that Okinawa had just been invaded.

"April Fools' Day too, I hope that's not an omen," Peter said. "And Easter Sunday as well. It does explain why all the shipping disappeared from here a week ago."

A few days later, Bongo asked Peter to lunch with Commander Osborn. "Mike, it's a long time now since Peter and I first met you in Fiji. I have a feeling that the war is ending at last. We all know that Hitler's on his knees in Germany, and we're already jockeying for position with Stalin for carving up Europe. Okinawa is by far our biggest one over here, and the momentum just might carry us onward to the emperor's palace. But as usual the Japs are dug in far better than we figured, and the Army has stalled out near Naha, the capital, so our momentum is temporarily lost. Probably the Marines will go help them out after they get their end of the island secured.

"But what I mainly wanted to tell you guys is that our carrier planes sank the super-battleship *Yamato* yesterday. I'll show you a couple of photos in a sec. I spoke to a wounded carrier pilot last night from TF58.1, who saw the beginning of the attack, and the *Yamato* dodging bombs and torps like a deer in the car headlights."

"This completes Lt. Naburo's great achievement, then," Peter said. "I wonder if he's alive to know it."

Seeing Mike Osborn's puzzled look, Bongo explained: "It's OK to talk about this now. Our pal Peter here brought a secret photo to Admiral Nimitz, way back before we met you. It was of the monster battleship *Yamato* being fitted out at dock in Japan, not long before her sea trials. A young Hawaiian Nisei took the photo and smuggled it out to Tarawa, from where your friends the Overwoods took it onward to Canton Island and then sent Peter off with it to Hawaii. We have no further word about the Hawaiian lad, whose name is Naburo. He was stranded in Japan when the war started and was conscripted into the Jap Navy after they found out he was a photography expert. Well, that was their first mistake; Naburo, the Overwoods, and Peter gave the US Navy two years to get ready for *Yamato* and her two sisters."

"What a story," Mike Osborn exclaimed. "This should go in the *Navy Times* after the war. Is there more?"

"It should indeed, and yes there is more," Peter agreed. "Look Bongo, since all this probably isn't classified any longer, how about giving me your permission to track down Naburo's parents if Abby and I go back through Honolulu. I would feel better if they knew what their son did for our side in this war, especially after the way the Japanese-Hawaiians were treated at home. Could you perhaps get approval from the admiral?"

"I'll definitely work on that, anxious Brit, right after I get back from Okinawa. I'm catching a ride there in the morning with Mike's very first medical evacuation flight, and I'll probably stay three or four days to look around. Did you notice that I'm on the manifest, Mike?"

"No I didn't, Commander, but that's fine. You'll have some good company then—a cute Navy nurse who was also the first one on Iwo Jima before it was secure. She and a corpsman will bring back around fifty wounded on the R5D."

"Ha, yes we all know about the amazing Miss Candy," Peter chuckled. "Abby doesn't want me to fall under her spell, but you're fair game if she's the type who likes one-armed bandits, Bongo."

"Thanks pal, but I think I've had enough of Navy nurses for one lifetime," Bongo groused. "Sorry, Peter, no offense meant to Abby; she's a great one, old friend."

***

Three days later, Bongo was back on Guam with another NATS flight. He had enjoyed chatting with Candy going over to Okinawa, but the return flight nurse was less communicative. True to form, he invited himself to the Perry's hostel for supper, but brought along a bottle of old Spanish wine that he got from Joey Foster at the airfield.

"Good evening, Bishop Pedro and Sister Abigail, I trust you are staying at arm's length in view of the church's very clear prohibitions."

"Just never you mind, chief inspector," Abby said, taking the bottle with a smile. "The bishop is upstairs in his study, if you'd care to join him."

"Abby, please join us too; I wanted to tell you both about my Okinawa trip." Seeing Abby glance at the little kitchen, Bongo added: "Well, after dinner then?" When the time came, after a plate of tough goat ribs and two glasses each of heavy Spanish Rioja, Bongo was waxing more and more theatrical.

"Friends, Okinawa is the biggest spectacular ever launched by Nimitz in the Pacific. All the others since Pearl Harbor, if added together, don't even come close to the armada of 1,200 ships, the squadrons of carrier planes and the legions of men put ashore in 72 hours. The ground campaign is mostly an Army show this time, but Nimitz is still the supreme honcho. The Marines have two divisions in the fight as well, and another in reserve. The center of the island where our boys landed is secure, as is the northern half which the Marines cleaned up in short order. But the south is at a stalemate with well-armed Japs dug into caves and tunnels like a giant ant hill.

"Army Lt. General Buckner is in charge there and charge he does—repeatedly—head on into a wall of fire. The enemy doesn't budge, and other generals and admirals are giving Buckner more advice than he can handle, so he just keeps head-butting with the Japs. Meanwhile there's a huge population of civilians getting in everyone's way, and the covering ships offshore are being plastered by Jap suicide planes. Thank goodness *Yamato* is out of the way. She never quite made it to Okinawa but would have raised hell if she had.

"I was taken around on a jiffy little vehicle called a Weasel. It's more or less like a Jeep on tank tracks instead of wheels, which some genius designed for bringing commandos across the snows of Norway, of all things. Peter, we must get one of these intriguing machines for our Texas pals after the war. They are amphibious and I don't know what else. Great for duck hunting, I bet."

Peter was looking at his watch and making secret signs to Abby, so Bongo took a hint and his leave in quick succession, thanking Abby for the meal before strolling back to his Jeep by the church.

"See you tomorrow, Pope Peter!" he called over his shoulder.

*** DEATH OF A PRESIDENT ***

On April 12, 1945, a sick and weary FDR passed away early in his fourth term as President of the United States, gratifying some of his Republican political enemies but bringing forth in most Americans a feeling of deep sadness, and even grief. A victim of crippling polio, the man whose personal strength and courage, genius and guile, had kept both America's enemies and allies at bay throughout the warring years in Europe and Asia, was gone. Perhaps it was the stupendous invasion of Okinawa on April first that finally caused him to falter.

If President Franklin Delano Roosevelt failed in any major way during his lengthy and stressful incumbency, it was perhaps in his over-generous support of the Soviet Union, which he saw as a vital ally throughout the war. This generosity was not reciprocated by Marshal Josef Stalin, who would cause former Vice President Truman much misery as FDR's successor.

*** VICTORY IN EUROPE ***

While the fierce battle raged on in Okinawa, victory was announced in Europe on May tenth, to a wave of euphoria at home and abroad. The beast called Hitler was dead from suicide in Berlin; it was the beginning of the end for World War Two.

Peter and Abby were excited by the news from Europe, which opened up the possibility for Peter to secure a good job in Germany with the reconstruction teams. His selection looked almost certain. Abby would then resign her Navy commission and search for a nursing role wherever in Europe Peter was assigned. Peter cabled his Sydney contacts, but was told to stand by for another month or two, until funding for Europe had been voted by the US Congress.

On June 29, 1945, the United Nations charter was signed in San Francisco by fifty nations, planning ahead for the imminent surrender of Japan, and a new world order. But Japan clearly wasn't going to go out with a whimper.

*** RUSSIA SNEAKS IN ***

Having fought with fanatical intensity to save Okinawa from the Allies, in spite of a depleted arsenal and a homeland under siege, Japan heard the other shoe fall on August fifth, as Russia and the Soviet Union declared war on the Mikado's tattered Empire.

The USSR entry was both to fulfill a pledge made by Stalin to FDR at the Yalta Conference in February—that Russian troops would invade Japan no later than three months after Germany's defeat—and also a land-grab from a weakened former adversary that had defeated the mighty Russian fleet in 1905.

Masses of Soviet veterans attacked the once-powerful but now-depleted Kuantung Army in Japan's stolen territory of Manchukuo, formerly Manchuria. Russia would hand over these Japanese prisoners to China after the war. They then occupied the northern half of another Japanese colony—the Korean Peninsula—while the US took over the southern half, per FDR's prior agreement with Stalin for a 'Joint-Allied border at the 38th parallel'.

Less well-reported at the time, Russian troops also grabbed—without prior US agreement—the southern part of Sakhalin Island that Russia had shared 50/50 with Japan since the last century. The Japanese portion, known as Karafuto, was promptly emptied of Japanese and Ainu populations, and a small White Russian community was packed off to Siberian labor camps. The entire large island of Sakhalin, lying just to the north of Japan, became a Russian bastion, which alarmed the Americans as much as the Japanese. It seemed to happen in the blink of an eye.

Then B-29s from Tinian dropped onto Japan the world's first atomic bombs used in warfare. *Enola Gay* flew over Hiroshima on August 6th; when that failed to produce a surrender, *Bockscar* dropped the second bomb on Nagasaki three days later. Both cities were flattened, with huge numbers of dead and disfigured. Then the Mikado finally listened to his ministers.

*** JAPAN SURRENDERS ***

There was incomplete consensus among the Allies as to whether Japan chose to surrender because of pressure from the Soviet army, virtually at her door on Sakhalin Island and northern Korea, or from the threat of more atomic bombs from the US, after those that destroyed Hiroshima and Nagasaki around the time of the Soviet declaration of war. Russian opinion generally assumed the former, whereas Americans were certain it was the latter. No doubt it was a combination of the two threatening situations, plus Japan's awareness of the US buildup on Okinawa for an invasion of Kyushu, that finally convinced the Emperor to accept Allied demands for an unconditional surrender.

Japan announced its capitulation on August 15, 1945. The Emperor's speech was broadcast to his surviving subjects at home and abroad, many of whom found it difficult to understand, and to believe.

Ahead of final surrender ceremonies to be formally held in Japan, Victory in Japan (VJ) Day celebrations took place wherever in the world the good news was received.

Exceeding even the joyous VE Day euphoria in May that year, hundreds of thousands of newly-drafted US troops and veterans from the European Theater, who were otherwise destined to be shipped out for the invasion of Japan—and thereby possibly killed—ran riot in the streets of major US cities on VJ Day, 1945. Combat troops already in the Pacific, who would probably have been the first ashore on Kyushu, fell to their knees in thanks for the miracle.

Excited celebrations also took place at the overseas Pacific bases, especially those that happened to have a USO troupe at hand to kick off the event, but perhaps one of the smallest gatherings of all was at Interpron-1's campsite near Yonabaru Airfield on Okinawa, where a few of its officers gathered for a celebratory shot of bourbon. Interpron-1 had arrived on Okinawa in June, having been reactivated in Hawaii. Its former and more senior flight partner squadron, VD-1, had been left in the US, and replaced by VD-3.

Once the cease-fire was confirmed, immediate instructions were issued by Pacific Command for Japanese military aircraft to paint over their red 'meatball' insignia with green crosses, before proceeding into Allied territories. Japanese aircraft failing to enter Allied airspace thus identified would be considered as non-conforming rebels, and promptly shot down.

The order was carefully observed. Two such green-cross planes brought Japanese functionaries to Ie Shima for transfer to US aircraft and onward to Manila, where General MacArthur's staff would instruct them on requirements for the official upcoming surrender events in Japan.

The official surrender ceremony itself took place in Tokyo Bay on September 2nd aboard 'Mighty Mo', the battleship USS *Missouri* (BB-63), until then the flagship of the US Third Fleet (at times known as the Fifth Fleet). Prior to the ceremony, Admiral Halsey retired his flag from America's newest and last-ever battleship, that had been launched in 1944, signifying the end of an era in several ways.

Five-star General of the Army Douglas MacArthur, newly appointed by President Truman as Supreme Commander of Allied Powers in the Pacific (SCAP), addressed the large gathering of assembled international dignitaries on board the battleship. SCAP would co-sign the surrender documents with 5-star Admiral of the Fleet Chester Nimitz, Commander of the Pacific Fleet. MacArthur spoke in sonorous tones to a worldwide audience: "It is my earnest hope—indeed the hope of all mankind—that from this solemn occasion a better world shall emerge out of the blood and carnage of the past, a world founded upon faith and understanding, a world dedicated to the dignity of man and the fulfillment of his most cherished wish for freedom, tolerance, and justice."

Many senior US and Allied commanders stood in the surrounding ranks. The only Marine officer assigned to a front row was Lt. General Geiger, who had briefly commanded the Tenth Army on Okinawa after Lt. General Buckner's death.

*** POST-SURRENDER TASKS ***

Scarcely had totalitarianism faded away in Germany, Italy, and Japan than world communism rushed in to fill the vacuum. Because Sakhalin's proximity threatened Japan with clandestine communist infiltration, Bongo and a Russian-speaking Marine Raider bodyguard were requested by Admiral Silvers to drop into the former Karafuto zone of Sakhalin by parachute, to scout out Russian activities and report back as soon as possible after pickup by a submarine.

Bongo flew to Okinawa to meet his bodyguard, who had arranged for a Marine C-47 to deliver them to RAAF Iwakuni air base in Japan, whence an Australian plane would take them up to Sapporo in northern Hokkaido.

A waiting submarine, the same that would return to collect them two weeks later, would drop them off at a beach on southern Sakhalin, the parachute drop having been cancelled due to concerns about Bongo's missing limb.

They would be issued with cold-weather gear at Iwakuni, as the climate in Hokkaido and Sakhalin was already quite frigid under the approach of winter. Bongo was interested to learn that the minority indigenous Ainu people of Hokkaido were also native to Sakhalin, which they considered to be part of their ancestral homeland.

A third member of the team, that would join them on Sapporo, was an Ainu sergeant who had formerly been in the Japanese Army. The tall and stocky veteran was eager to help the Americans remove Russian invaders from the island of his birth. Aussies at Iwakuni couldn't pronounce his name, so they just called him "Sergeant O'Blokee," in the notes that Bongo had been given with a summary of his dossier. Bongo had also read the Marine Raider's service record and noted he had been with Carlson on the famous Guadalcanal long patrol.

Bongo felt he would be in very capable hands with his two teammates. The evening before his departure from Okinawa, he enjoyed a few drinks with Frank Evans and Bill Clark of Interpron-1, whom he hadn't seen since Guadalcanal. He was surprised to run into them at Yonabaru Airfield when registering for his little team's flight the next morning.

"So how are you Texans doing? I thought your outfit was disbanded after you left the Canal," Bongo said.

"So we had hoped," Frank answered, "but they recalled us back to Hawaii after we were home on leave. Interpron-1 got expanded about four times its Guadalcanal size, can you believe? We even absorbed Interpron-3 into our ranks. I guess Nimitz wanted a monster photo team for the push into Japan. We're almost 300 people now, and that's not counting the VD-3 fliers, right Bill?"

"Yup, 228 ornery enlisted and 60 bored officers. We teamed up with VD-3 after we got here around June; those guys had a soft life on Canton Island and California before, but now they must work for a living. They already photographed Formosa, the coast of China and most of Japan, and even took photos of Hiroshima right after the bomb. And now that we finally have Interpron-1 all collected together in tents at Yonabaru Field, instead of spread out at Yontan and all creation, everyone just wants to pack up and go home—including me. But Frank here and a few salty old enlisted guys are the only ones with enough points accrued for that. He's leaving this weekend, and I just made Lt. Commander, so I'm the new CO of an unwanted outfit that's bordering on mutiny. Well, not really mutiny, but they're restless as all get-out. There's only so many baseball games and USO shows, right?"

"Poor old Bill," Frank smiled, patting Bill's shoulder, "I'm so sad for him. Well how about you, Bongo? I'm sure sorry about your arm, and all. We finally got Peter's V-Mail a month after the race on Guadal."

"No worries, folks. My boss just a gave me one last job to do, then I'm going to Mare Island Naval Hospital, San Francisco, where they teach old cripples like me how to use artificial limbs. After that I guess I'll be a civilian like you two characters. I was thinking of writing a book, as a matter of fact. Peter thought that would be a good plan for me; luckily I'm right-handed."

"Well Bongo, here's to your final assignment, and a successful rehab afterwards," Bill offered. "We've both enjoyed knowing you, and Frank was just saying the other day that his pal Boudreau in New Orleans was looking for a shrimp boat partner now that the war's over, in case you're interested. Come by and see us in Houston some time."

***

In early December 1945, Peter and Abby were preparing to leave Guam for Hawaii, where Abby would be processed out of the US Navy according to her recent resignation. From there, they would travel to San Francisco by ship and Boston by train, to meet her parents. Each of them had over a month's accrued leave, part of which they would enjoy in New England prior to the flight to Germany and their new jobs.

"Peter, I'm actually glad to be leaving the Navy for another reason than the new life in Europe."

"Oh, what's that then?" Peter asked.

"It's the silly regulation against women marrying while in the service. You remember, it was done away with in January but now it has been reinstated. I know several of the nurses who made plans to marry soon, but now they can't get permission all of a sudden. If they go ahead with their plans, they'll have to resign from the Navy. One of them is Jane Kendeigh, as a matter of fact. Well, I feel like I'm resigning in protest, for their sakes."

"Good for you, Abby. Let's just pretend that's the reason you're leaving the Navy then."

"Yes, but I would also feel bad if that were really the case, you see, to be leaving the Navy in protest against something. The Navy helped turn my life around, and I am forever grateful for that. I'm grateful to Andrew too, for persuading me to join the Nurse Corps, and of course to you most of all, my dearest husband."

"Well, steady on there, old girl. You'll have me all emotional too in a moment."

Abby laughed aloud, mimicking Peter's accent. "Oh quite so, none of that emotional nonsense."

Peter hastened to change the subject. "Speaking of Andrew, have you heard from him since he was transferred to Okinawa last month?"

"Yes, I just got a letter—I meant to tell you. Andrew ran into some men from Interpron-1, who told him Frank and Bill had both gone back to the US for good. They also told Andrew they had seen Bongo a month ago, but now he is supposedly missing in action somewhere!"

"What! MIA! What could that mean? The war is over, isn't it? I've been wondering why we haven't heard from the old rascal. I don't think Admiral Silvers is still here in Guam, but I'll go to his office tomorrow and check. Otherwise, I wouldn't know who else to ask, since Robert McGowan is away on sea duty now, and I'm probably not supposed to know Bongo officially. Abby, this is a calamity—our old shipmate!"

"It certainly is a calamity," Abby agreed. "Peter, I guess we'll just have to write Bongo's book for him now."

***

On Sunday June 25, 1950, massed troops, artillery, tanks, and planes from Russia's client state, North Korea, crossed the 38th Parallel to invade South Korea, the US client state. Capturing Seoul with ease and pushing the South Korean Army all the way down the peninsula to Pusan (Busan), the army of North Korea nearly pulled off a spectacular victory, but

MacArthur soon dealt them a hidden Joker called Inchon—one of his most brilliant tactical accomplishments of all time.

A conflict with global Communism had begun; would it lead to World War III, the newly minted United Nations wondered? A once-again demobilized United States struggled to respond. *Déjà vu.*

"Be Prepared; that's the Boy Scout's marching song"
Tom Lehrer, 1953

EPILOGUE

To celebrate still being alive despite human foibles, a group of actors from our story, some with family members, held a reunion at beautiful Champagne Bay on Espiritu Santo. The chosen date was April 12, 1975, 30 years after President Roosevelt's death. The cast included:

- Peter (67) and Abby (63) Perry of Maynard MA, who worked in Europe during the reconstruction years, and then dabbled in California private enterprise with modest success. At Abby's urging, Peter joined the high-flying mini-computer company Digital Equipment Corp (DEC), working for his brother-in-law Andrew until retirement.
- Andrew Culver (58), DEC Senior VP of Facilities, and his wife Barbara (58), who also were residents of Maynard MA, the site of DEC's headquarters.
- Hans (78) and Yvonne (70) Lazet, the reunion hosts on Santo with their children and grandchildren. Peter learned from them that Philippe Orly and Ralph MacAdam were deceased. Stéphanie (42) and her Australian husband Brian (47) owned several tourist resorts on Santo, whose capable manager Liat (48) was still a single Tonkinese woman. Brother Raymond (41) ran the contractor business; André (40) was a rancher.
- RADM USN (Ret.) Robert McGowan (62) and his wife Umiko (55) from Nagoya Japan, who were consultants to several Pacific islands including Efaté, with the Asian Development Bank.
- VADM USN (Ret.) Herman 'Hi Yo' Silvers (75), widower from San Diego CA, who was **Guest of Honor**. While in the navy

he helped army Col. Donovan start the OSS, which eventually became the CIA.

- The Rev. Thaddeus Jones (60) and his wife Beulah (62), civil rights activists from Birmingham, Alabama.
- Colonel USA (Ret.) Elias Crighton (64), bachelor, skier, millionaire stockbroker and long-time fundraiser for Rev. Jones, who provided food and lodging for the entire group as a tax write-off. He also organized a tour of the abandoned airfields on Santo, that then-lieutenant Jones had helped build.
- Former LCDR USNR Mike Osborn (65) and ex-stewardess Leilani (67), who had both retired from Pan Am and were residing in Florida near Dinner Key. They were acquaintances of Pan Am chairman Najeeb Halaby, whom Mike met in the 1940s when Halaby was a navy test pilot. The Osborns adopted two Fijian children in 1955 and traveled often to the Pacific region, staying in touch with Graham and Lois Overwood until the latters' deaths in the early 1960s. *[Halaby's daughter Lisa became Queen Noor of Jordan in 1978–Ed.]*
- John Perry (39), MIS manager at DEC Sydney, who lived with his Chinese girlfriend Ai Li at Rose Bay and saw Wendy and Doris (his mums) often. Doris lost her child, John's half-sister, at birth.
- A day late in arriving after being tracked down by Admiral Silvers, and initially confronted by hotel security as a presumed beachcomber, MIA Elmer "Bongo" Perkins (66) was enthusiastically welcomed. Having planned to leave the navy in 1946 to work in Thailand and China for Donovan and Jim Thompson, he instead spent 25 years in Russian prisons after being arrested on Sakhalin Island, then escaping and being recaptured in the USSR itself. Bearded, one-eyed, one-armed and single (the fickle Ellie Norbush having soured him on marriage), Bongo planned to dictate his memoirs after the forthcoming 40th reunion of his class at Dartmouth College.

Following the happy get-together on Santo, most visitors planned to renew their acquaintances with other places in the region such as Nouméa, Guadalcanal, and Guam.

326

John Perry invited Peter and Abby to visit Sydney, but they felt it best to decline.

Before leaving the Santo reunion, Bongo distributed—as a souvenir for the other guests—copies of a declassified picture of the infamous WWII Japanese battleship *Yamato*, taken when it was nearing completion at the Kure Naval Base, saying that young IJN Lt. Naburo's microfilm was from roughly the same period of time.

Kure Naval Base 19 September 1941

This photo (*Yamato battleship under fitting-out works.jpg*) is part of the records in the Yamato Museum (PG071320). Search with the kanji characters of *Yamato* (大和) for the name (second field), and 昭和 for the period (last field). The photo can also be viewed at the US Naval Historical Center (Photo # NH 63433), courtesy of Shizuo Fukui, and is in the Public Domain.

END NOTES

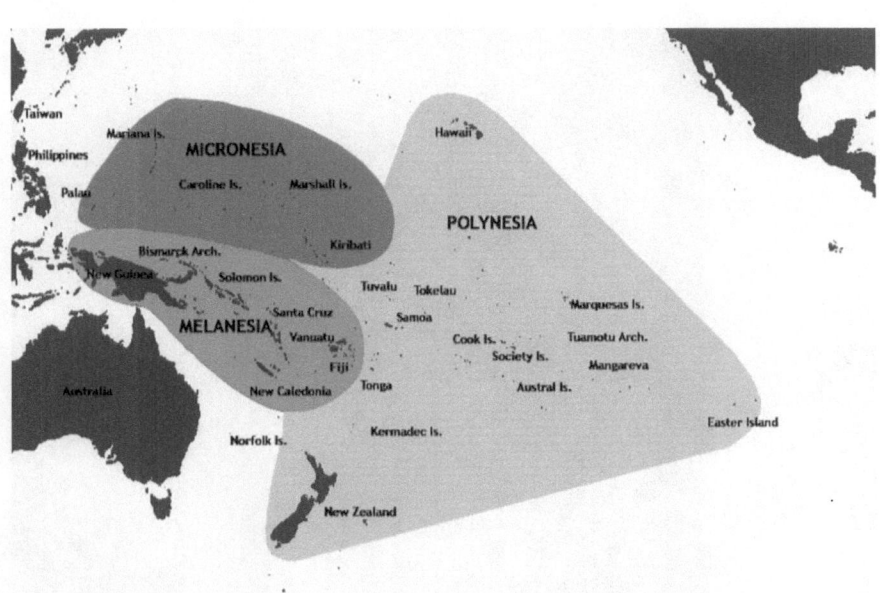

Pacific Cultures Map by Kahuroa

POSTSCRIPT

Before thirty years had passed, the Second World War (*The War to REALLY End All Wars*), which followed closely after the First World War (*The War to End All Wars*), was supplanted by bloody campaigns in Korea and Vietnam. In concert with those new disasters, a few other changes gradually affected the former Pacific Theater of WWII, as a 'cold war' evolved between the USSR and the USA:

- Russia was first into space, but the US was first on the moon.
- French forces in Vietnam were defeated by Viet Cong rebels under Ho Chi Minh and General Giap in 1954, prompting a French withdrawal from their Indochina colony. Following an appeal for military assistance made by South Vietnam to President Truman, US involvement with Vietnam gradually escalated under successive presidents Eisenhower ('53–'61), Kennedy ('61–'63), Johnson ('63–'69), and Nixon ('69–'74). US and worldwide public opposition to such involvement became bitter and extreme, and an anti-establishment drug culture took root in the United States that has been its ongoing curse.
- Following Guam's refusal to reunite with the Northern Mariana Islands (as under Spanish rule), Guam became a US Commonwealth and the rest became a US Trust Territory, from which the surviving Japan-settled Taiwanese and Okinawans were forcibly repatriated after the war. The rebuilt capital of Guam was given its original Chamorro name Hagåtña, which of course the Americans pronounce Hagatna (and the Spanish used to pronounce Agaña).

- US President John F. Kennedy was assassinated in November 1963, soon after the Cuban missile crisis. His brother, attorney general Robert Kennedy, was assassinated a few years later.
- The great Pacific War leaders, General of the Army Douglas MacArthur and Admiral of the Fleet Chester Nimitz, died in 1964 and 1966 respectively.
- First World War ace and Medal of Honor recipient Eddie Rickenbacker passed away in 1973, having been rescued in November 1942 with crew members, after twenty-four days at sea following a B-17 crash near Canton Island. He was president of Eastern Airlines from 1938 to 1963.

More Related Notes

Canton Island is today spelled Kanton (a.k.a. Aba Riringa, meaning 'the land of sunshine'), part of the Pacific island nation of Kiribati comprising the former Phoenix, Line, and Gilbert (but not Ellice) British island colonies. The capital of Kiribati is Tarawa, site of a particularly fierce battle in November 1943 when the Second Marine Division expelled Japanese occupiers.

Kanton is also part of PIPA (Phoenix Island Protected Area), the world's largest oceanic nature reserve. In 1999, the United States was invited by Kiribati to enjoin the US Outlying Islands of Howland, Jarvis and Baker into PIPA, which in 2014 they agreed to do but without giving up US sovereignty. The current population of Kanton, the only inhabited Phoenix island, is around forty or so I-Kiribati (Gilbertese people), living in a village they named Tebaronga on Northside, quite a change from the 1943 high of around four thousand military personnel during *Operation Galvanic*, the Allied invasion of Tarawa.

In 1946, Canton Island saw its Pan Am refueling business resumed, though primarily for land-based flights, and the island continued a parallel role as a LORAN and weather station that had evolved during the war. The British Residency was reinstated also, the main function of which became the supply and housing of Gilbertese (I-Kiribati) labor for the entire island. A shared US/British school was formed, the hospital was modernized, and finally by 1954 the wreck of the *President Taylor*, which for twelve years had been a rusting eyesore just outside the natural lagoon entrance where it ran aground during *TF Holly*, was finally demolished down to the waterline for scrap by some Americans who lived aboard their yacht inside the lagoon, and educated their children at the local school.

The author visited Canton Island briefly in April 1947 aboard a DC-4 (VH-ANA) of Australian National Airlines and crossed the lagoon to breakfast at the old Pan Am Hotel (spam and eggs). That visit made a lasting impression, not least because of the hulking *President Taylor* wreck lying virtually outside the hotel.

Canton Island ceased to be a Pan Am refueling station in 1959. Its facilities were sold to Qantas, which just a year later closed the base completely as jet aircraft became available and stopover refueling was no longer needed. However, Canton gained a new lease on life as NASA tracking station #11 for the Mercury and Gemini programs, and still later as a missile tracking station of the US Air Force until 1976. At that point the nation of Kiribati was formed, with the US relinquishing all claims to Canton and Enderbury. Most Kiribati islands are now threatened by rising sea levels.

The former airport's main runway, although without scheduled flights today, still rates the IATA code CIS, and is considered suitable for emergency use. A secondary 1943 Fighter strip was abandoned. A wartime runway on Baker Island was also abandoned.

The so-called Benjo Sewage System on Canton Island is fictional but raises a seldom-discussed issue that challenged all shore-based military and naval organizations throughout the Pacific Theater, and throughout history of warfare for that matter. The most common solution was the digging of pits and trenches, a thankless task for the most junior people in the chain of command. It was quite difficult to dig into Canton Island coral.

Pan Am: Pan American Airways restarted its Pacific air services on August 28, 1946, with the addition of Sydney to its Southern Pacific route. None of its luxurious Boeing B-314 Clippers survive today. The astonishing foresight of Pan Am's Yale-educated founder, Juan Trippe, launched a seaplane service across the vast Pacific in the 1930s to blaze two trails that the Allies would use to help defeat the Japanese war machine in the 1940s.

Trippe's vision and contribution are largely forgotten today, although it was Pan Am that eventually brought air travel to the masses, first introducing the Boeing 707 in 1957 to herald the jet age where intermediate fueling stops were no longer required; and later 'the Jumbo' Boeing 747 that could carry many more passengers per trip. But the 747 was also Pan Am's undoing: its commitments to Boeing—when the 1982 oil shocks curtailed holiday travel—caused the airline to eventually run out of cash and credit. Pan American Airways thus became a victim of free enterprise self-cleansing, going out of business a decade after Trippe's 1981 death. Some nostalgic donors including the author help maintain an online museum under the auspices of the Pan Am Historical Foundation, whose helpful director and webmaster, Doug Miller, looks after https://www.panam.org/.

Singapore, in its eternal quest for a water supply independent of neighboring Malaysia, has since 2003 experimented with sewage being recycled into drinking water—which is marketed as NEWater—a concept proposed long ago by the pre-war public health officer for Singapore, Dr. Nathaniel Canton (no relation to the Chinese city or the Phoenix island), in collaboration with the then-senior engineer for Singapore's municipal water department, Mr. Hubert Price, the author's father. Faced with shortages of the life-sustaining liquid, several other communities around the world are nowadays reclaiming sewage in spite of the 'gross-out' obstacle in people's minds.

USCGS / USS (*Roger B.*) *Taney:* Launched in 1936, Coast Guard cutter *Taney* was on active service for an amazing 50 years, serving in World War Two, the Korean conflict, and the war in Vietnam. Since 1986, the proud ship has been the focal point of a maritime museum in Baltimore, Maryland.

I-23: Japanese submarine *I-23* was thought by the IJN to have been lost with all hands somewhere off Oahu on February 24, 1942. In our story the sub was perhaps captured and scuttled in March '42 off the west coast of Suva, Fiji.

The US Contracts Office that employed Peter Perry is fictional, but such an organization could certainly have existed to complement the talented Navy Seabees, the Army Corps of Engineers, and Marine Corps Engineers to produce buildings and infrastructure of a more lasting nature than the ubiquitous Quonset and Dallas huts, the desperately needed wharves and docks, and the jiffy bridges and Marsden-clad airfields.

MV *Mirrabooka:* Launched in 1928, motor vessel *Mirrabooka,* a twin-diesel engine passenger-freighter, was sold in 1955 by its Swedish owners Rederi A/B Transatlantic. She had sailed the world in concert with her sister ship *Parrakoola,* with a focus on Australian trade. Rederi A/B Transatlantic launched another, slightly smaller, *Mirrabooka* in 1961, which plied the same waters as her namesake. In Australian aborigine dialect, *Mirrabooka* means 'Southern Cross'; *Parrakoola* is thought to means 'one more of the same', which would be a good response in an Aussie pub.

Hawaii: From December 7, 1941, until October 24, 1944, the Territory of Hawaii was placed under martial law as preconceived by the FBI. Almost every facet of local life was controlled by a military administration that behaved more like an occupying than a defending force. Behind the scenes lurked five big conglomerates that controlled Hawaiian economics, ever grateful to the Army for wage freezes and labor mobility restrictions. In 1946, the Supreme Court declared 6-2 that martial law on Hawaii during WWII was unconstitutional and illegal. Hawaii became a US state in 1959 (as did Alaska). Its state flag still bears the British Union Jack in the top left quadrant, in memory of its discovery by British Captain Cook.

Fiji: Pan Am, the British Colonial Office, and the Royal New Zealand Air Force collectively opened a seaplane base in Lauthala Bay (Laucala in today's spelling) near Suva on November 5, 1941, barely a month before WWII caused Pan Am to abandon its complete network of Pacific Clipper routes. After the war, Pan Am began flying DC4s to Australia through Nadi Airport in Fiji, and the seaplane base at Lauthala was operated solely by the New Zealand military until the mid-1960s when its shore facilities became part of a new campus for the University of the Pacific (UPC). Fiji was a British colony from the late 1800s until independence on 10/10/1970.

New Hebrides: The New Hebrides Islands were not granted their independence by the condominium of Great Britain and France until July 30, 1980, as the Republic of Vanuatu, hence those lovely islands, which included the familiar wartime names of Efaté and Espiritu Santo, were still the New Hebrides during the aforementioned nostalgic cast reunion. Being favorite destinations by then of Australian cruise ships, yachtsmen, and scuba divers, the growing tourist income stream helped the islands garner support for their eventual independence. As predicted, some Kanaks were not happy with the outcome and attempted to circumvent it.

New Caledonia and Sir Harry Luke: The US army arrived in New Caledonia ahead of the navy, to assist and relieve Australian commandos in early 1942. On March 12, the first of three mobilized but disparate national guard infantry regiments reached Nouméa via Australia, where they had been reloaded into smaller ships that could negotiate the Nouméa nickel docks. Winning a write-in contest to suggest a suitable name for the new army division, one of the men came up with 'Americal', a contraction of America and Caledonia. The name stuck and these civilian soldiers, after getting badly needed training there in the French colony, would eventually be sent to relieve battered Marines on Guadalcanal. Still later, after a rehabilitation tour in Fiji, the Americal Division would distinguish itself in the brutal fight on Bougainville that helped neutralize Rabaul. The division commander, MGEN Alexander Patch, established his residence and initial headquarters in Nouméa's *Grand Hôtel du Pacifique*, requisitioning most but not all of its guest rooms for his staff.

The initiative of Fiji-based Sir Harry Luke, British High Commissioner for the Western Pacific, may be credited with helping New Caledonia tilt away from Vichy control in 1940, when he arrived from the New Hebrides islands for an official visit at Nouméa. Sir Harry's visit helped foment a political uprising of Free French populist sentiment that hastened the departure of the former governor and others to Indochina.

In referring to people of mixed ancestry in the Pacific islands, Sir Harry often tried to promote the term 'Euronesian' as a replacement for 'Eurasian', which had negative racist connotations. We use Euronesian in this story where appropriate.

Sydney: Trams no longer run across the Sydney Harbor Bridge, having yielded their right-of-way to masses of cars and buses, but the grand old bridge is as stately as ever with its younger icon, the Sydney Opera House, standing resolutely nearby. Today one can climb the bridge span for a magnificent view of Sydney Harbor. Not long after the war, the airport was moved from Rose Bay to Botany Bay, affording the old neighborhood more tranquility.

The author had the privilege of dwelling in Sydney for five excellent years as a student during and after World War Two. Bondi and Manly beaches were favorite destinations, as was boy scout camp in Queensland.

Guadalcanal: The huge Allied base near Point Cruz during WWII became the Solomons' capital, Honiara. Former Henderson Field is today's Honiara International Airport, the other wartime airfields having been abandoned. Many warships reposing in Iron Bottom Sound have been located and identified by noted underwater explorer Robert Ballard. *[There is also a Henderson Field on Midway Island, from where Major Lofton Henderson USMC met his death attacking the Japanese fleet in 1942—Ed.]*

The US Marine Corps: In spite of the Marine Corps' heroic actions and sacrifices in the Pacific Theater of WWII, the US Army attempted to have the smaller organization dismantled after the war, apparently due to inter-service jealousy. Famous army generals Eisenhower and Marshall in collaboration with President Truman made a serious attempt to consign the Marines to oblivion and to take away from Congress the responsibility of overseeing future military and naval affairs. Upon learning of this plot, Marine generals Vandergrift, Twining, and Krulak alerted members of congress to the pending subterfuge, upon which Congress acted to both reassert its civil authority over the military and to save the Marines to fight another day. ***Semper Fidelis!***

Orthography Notes:

- US spelling is used throughout this series of books, even for British dialogue. This may cause confusion and even alarm among British readers, for which the author apologizes.

337

- In the style of the war years, names of the various military services (Navy, Marines, etc) are capitalized, whereas nowadays it is no longer as customary (except for Marines!).
- Even though official spelling for Hawaiian place names is generally of the form Hawai'i and O'ahu, the simpler modern forms of Hawaii and Oahu are used herein to avoid reader distraction. Absolutely no disrespect to Hawaiian readers is intended.
- The spelling system used in Kiribati was apparently introduced by 19th century missionaries who were short of certain type fonts for their printing presses. Hence the combination 'ti' was used to represent the sound 'sh', being derived from the 'ti' in 'nation'. With this knowledge one can recognize Kiribati as the local pronunciation of 'Gilberts', and Kiritimati as 'Christmas' (e.g. Christmas Island).
- Similar missionary font shortages in Fiji and Samoa—among them the letter 'n'—resulted in a Fiji place name that is pronounced 'Nandi', being written as Nadi. In Samoa the city of Pago Pago is pronounced 'Pango Pango.'

FICTIONAL CHARACTERS

Fictional characters (civilian, military, and naval in appropriate groupings and approximate order of appearance, with their initial responsibilities and ranks, if any):

Peter Perry, English civil engineer and reserve army captain.
Wendy Joules Perry, Peter's Jersey-born wife.
John Perry, Peter and Wendy's son.
Graham Overwood, British representative for the Phoenix Islands.
Lois Overwood, Graham's English wife.
Gordon and John, the Overwoods' Gilbertese assistants.
Chamorro Joe, Pan Am bartender and guitarist on Canton Island.
Messrs. Fong and Naburo Sr., Hawaiian business partners.
Cyril the Nukulau postmaster in Fiji.
Manuel, a Filipino waiter at NATS Canton Island.
Doris and Fred Smyth, the Perrys' neighbors in Sydney.
Edgar (Ned) Perry, Peter Perry's younger brother.
Marjorie Barrett Perry, Ned's Canadian wife.
Hans Lazet, Java-born Dutch civil engineer.
Ralph MacAdam, New Zealand-born Australian civil engineer.
Ronald Beamish, an Australian, as US contracts manager in Nouméa.
Hamish MacDougall, Beamish's managing director in Sydney.
Philippe Orly, businessman and politician on Espiritu Santo.
Yvonne Orly Bardot, Philippe's widowed sister.
Stéphanie, André and Raymond Bardot, Yvonne's children.
Mrs. Belfast, boarding house owner in Melbourne.
Roland Axelsson, acting captain of MV *Mirrabooka*.
Thomas Malmgren, a previous captain of MV *Mirrabooka*.

Jurgen Schroeder, Danish-born bosun of MV *Mirrabooka*.
Watanabe-san and the Spanish consul's daughter in Melbourne.
Bruno Carstens, Anglo-Efaté businessman.
Charles Rivens and Jean-Marc Forrester, colleagues of Carstens.
Domingo Salas, Roman Catholic archdeacon for Guam.
Father Isaias and Bishop Benito, Domingo's clergy colleagues.

NZ Army Col. Percy McKee, commander of the Fiji defense garrison.
US Army Col. Horace O'Reilly, commander of the Canton Island. garrison.
US Army Major Elias 'El' Crighton, Corps of Engineers at Santo.
US Army 2d Lt. Thaddeus Jones, Co. B, 810th Bn., Corps of Engineers.

IJN Lt. Naburo, Jr., Hawaiian-born photography expert.
USNR Lt. Cdr. Elmer 'Bongo' Perkins, naval intelligence officer.
USN Capt. 'Hi-Yo' Silvers, intelligence aide to Admiral Nimitz.
USN Capt. Brian Weaver, naval operations on American Samoa.
USN Lt. Cdr. Starkey, NATS operations officer on Canton Island.
USNR Lt. Mike Osborn, NATS operations officer in Fiji.
USN Lt. Robert McGowan, naval intelligence officer.
USNR Ens. Ellie Norbush, Nurse Corps, Efaté and Nouméa.
USNR Ens. Andrew Culver, NATS ops Canton, Nouméa, Okinawa.
USNR Ens. Abigail 'Abby' Culver, Nurse Corps, Pacific Theater.
USNR Lt. Joey Foster, shuttle pilot and presumed smuggler.
USNR Lt. Franklin Jones, harbormaster at Tulagi.
USN CPO Martin Lubinski, asst. harbormaster at Tulagi.

ABBREVIATIONS

AA–Anti-aircraft
ANZAC–Australia New Zealand Army Corps
APD–modified destroyer-transport
APL–American President Lines
ATC–Air Transport Command
AWOL–Absent Without Leave
A/V–Auxiliary Vessel
BAR–Browning Automatic Rifle
BOQ–Bachelor Officers' Quarters
BSIP–British Solomon Islands Protectorate
CINCPAC–Commander-in-Chief Pacific
CNO–Chief of Naval Operations
CO–Commanding Officer; Colonial Office(r)
FBI–Federal Bureau of Investigation
GI–Government Issue, i.e., the army troops
HMAS–His Majesty's Australian Ship
HMS–His Majesty's Ship
IJA–Imperial Japanese Army
IJN–Imperial Japanese Navy
LCM–Landing Craft Mechanical (a.k.a. 'Mike' boats)
LSD–Landing Ship Dock
LSI–Landing Ship Infantry
LST–Landing Ship Tank
LVT–Landing Vehicle Tracked
MP–Military Police
MV or M/V–motor vessel (as in MV *Mirrabooka*)
NATS–Naval Air Transport Service

OD–Officer of the Deck (navy); Officer of the Day (army)
OSS–Office of Strategic Services
RAAF–Royal Australian Air Force
RAF–Royal Air Force
RAN–Royal Australian Navy
RNZAF–Royal New Zealand Air Force
R&R–Rest & Recuperation
SCAP–Supreme Commander of Allied Forces in the Pacific
SOPAC–South Pacific Command
SP–Shore Patrol
SS–Steamship (as in SS *Monterey*)
SWPA–Southwest Pacific Area
TWX–Teletypewriter Exchange
UDT–Underwater Demolition Team
US–United States of America
USA–US Army
USO–United Services Organization
USAAF–US Army Air Force
USCG–US Coast Guard
USMC–US Marine Corps
USN–US Navy
USS–US (naval) ship (as in USS *Indianapolis*)
VIP–Very Important Person
XO–Executive Officer

BIBLIOGRAPHY–
FURTHER READING

A

Alone on Guadalcanal, Martin Clemens, 1998: Memoir of a Coastwatcher.

American Caesar, William Manchester, 1978: Official Biography of General Douglas MacArthur.

An American Saga, Robert Daley, 1980: Juan Trippe and his Pan Am Empire.

B

Battleships, William H. Garzke and Robert O. Dulin, 1985: Axis and Neutral Battleships in World War II.

Brute, Robert Coram, 2010: Life of Victor Krulak, US Marine.

C

Cameras over the Pacific, John G. Bishop, 1999: Marine Photographic Squadron VMD-254.

Can Do! William Bradford Huie, 1944: The story of the Seabees.

Canton Island, Carl Oates, 2003: History of Canton Island until it was renamed Kanton, as part of Kiribati.

Carrier Admiral, J.J. Clark with Clark G. Reynolds, 1967: Naval career of Admiral J.J. "Jocko" Clark.

Clash of the Carriers, Barrett Tillman, 2005: An account of the 'Marianas Turkey Shoot'.

Combined Fleet Decoded, John Prados, 1995; US Naval Intelligence and the Japanese Fleet.

D

Dornier Wal; "a Light Coming Over the Sea", M. Michiel van der Mey; LoGisma revised edition, 2012: A history of European seaplanes

F

First to Fight, LGEN Victor H. Krulak USMC (Ret.), 1964: The US Army's failed attempt to eliminate the Marine Corps.
From a South Seas Diary 1938-1942, Sir Harry Luke, 1945: Diary of his stint as High Commissioner.
Future Indefinite, Noël Coward, 1954: Memoir of his early years, including a stopover on Canton Island.

G

Gilbert Islands in WWII, Peter McQuarrie, 2012: History of the Gilbert Islands 1920s to 1970s.
Goodbye Darkness, William Manchester, 1978: Memoir of the Pacific War.
Guadalcanal, Richard B. Frank, 1992: Definitive account of the landmark battle.

H

Hell's Islands, Stanley Coleman Jersey, 2008: The Battles of Guadalcanal.
Hell's Kitchen Tulagi 1942-1943, Thomas J. Larson, 2003: Memoir of a naval communicator at Tulagi.
Helmet for My Pillow, Robert Leckie, 1972: First Marine Division memoir.
Hostages to Fortune, Arthur Nicholson, 2005: Sinking of the *Prince of Wales* and *Repulse.*

I

Intrepid Aviators, Gregory G. Fletcher, 2012: Story of the navy fliers that sank *Musashi* in 1944.
Into the Valley, John Hersey, 1943: Descriptive report of a Guadalcanal skirmish.
Islands of the Damned, R. V. Burgin, 2010: Memoir of a First Marine Division non-com in WWII.

L

Last Stand of the Tin Can Sailors (The), James D. Hornfischer, 2004: The extraordinary story of the Naval Battle off Samar.

Lonely Vigil, Walter Lord, 1977, Coastwatchers of the Solomons.

Long Way Home (The), a Journey into History with Pan Am Captain Robert Ford; Ed Dover, Revised Edition 2008

Lost Island, James Norman Hall, 1944: Tale of an unspoiled Pacific island sequestered for Allied defenses.

M

Marine Tank Battles in the Pacific, Oscar E. Gilbert, 2001: Comprehensive history of Marine armor and actions.

N

Neptune's Inferno, James D. Hornfischer, 2011: The US Navy at Guadalcanal.

No Bended Knee, Merrill B. Twining, 1996: Memoir of the Battle for Guadalcanal.

O

Okinawa 1945, Simon Foster, 1994: Final assault on the empire–the British account.

Okinawa 1945, Gordon L. Rottman, 2002: Illustrated synopsis of the last battle.

On the Warpath in the Pacific, Clark G. Reynolds, 2005: Admiral "Jocko" Clark and the fast carriers of TF58.1.

P

Pan Am at War, Mark Cotta Vaz and John H. Hill, 2019: How the Airline Secretly Helped America Fight World War II.

PT-105, Dick Keresey, 1996: History of PT Boats in the Solomon Islands.

R

Return to Paradise, James A. Michener, 1951: Revisiting the Pacific Islands.

S

Scapegoat, Martin Stephen, 2014: The Death of *Prince of Wales* and *Repulse*.
Skygods, Robert Gandt, 1995: The Fall of Pan Am
Songs from the Girl Back Home, Ruth Dixon, 2004: The USO Camp Shows.
South Pacific Cauldron, Alan Rems, 2014: World War II's Great Forgotten Battlegrounds-
Star Quality, Noël Coward, 1951: Short stories including *Mr. and Mrs. Edgehill (a fictional* Canton Island*)*.
Storm Landings, Col. Joseph H. Alexander USMC, 1997: Marine Corps landings in the Pacific Theater of WWII.

T

Tales of the South Pacific, James A. Michener, 1946: Famous WWII short stories of the region.
Tanks on the Beaches, Robert M. Neiman and Kenneth W. Estes, 2003: First Tank Battalion memoir.
The Magnificent Bastards, Lucy Herndon Crockett, 1954: A novel of Nouméa and Guadalcanal.
The Pacific, Hugh Ambrose, 2010: Companion book to the HBO miniseries.
They Were Ready, Terry L. Shoptaugh, 2013: History of the US Army's 164th Infantry Regiment, a component of the Americal Division.
They Were Expendable, W. L. White, 1942: History of PT Boats in the Philippines.
Touched with Fire, Eric Bergerud, 1996: The land war in the South Pacific.

U

US Marine Corps Tanks of WWII, Stephen J. Zaloga, 2012: Illustrated synopsis of WWII tank actions.

W

We Band of Angels, Elizabeth Norman, 1999: American nurses trapped on Bataan.
With the Old Breed, E. B. Sledge, 1981: Memoir of a mortar man at Peleliu and Okinawa.

PERMISSIONS

It is the author's hope that this historical novel will succeed in portraying 'the way it was' for people who lived in the Pacific region during the Second World War, 1941-45. To this end, a series of maps, photos and such items are included to add a visual aspect to the opus in the hope that such embellishment might enhance the reader's understanding and curiosity about this fast-fading but momentous historical event, perhaps thereby encouraging him or her to pursue works by other authors, such as those listed in our bibliography.

With the kind assistance of the publisher, the author has done extensive investigation to gain assurance that each of the WWII-vintage photos, maps and so forth used in this work is in the public domain and thereby free of copyright, or otherwise that permission has been expressly provided. On this basis the work will be published in a limited volume of digital and print quantities. Should it later transpire that copyright does exist for any item of the above-mentioned visual aids that were assumed to be in the public domain, the author hereby agrees—at a minimum—to acknowledge the proven copyright holder in print or else to delete said item from subsequent editions. This statement is made in good faith to ensure that the publisher is not to be held responsible for any oversights by the author in this regard.

no written permission is required to use them. In general, all government records are in the public domain and may be freely used." Additionally, according to the United States copyright law (United States Code, Title 17, Chapter 1, Section 105), in part, "[c]opyright protection under this title is not available for any work of the United States Government". Material provided by any branch of the military service (e. g. government employees) is in the public domain. See also https:// en.wikipedia.org/wiki/ Wikipedia:Public_domain_image_resources.

Disclaimer in Lieu of Permission: *Neither the United States Marine Corps nor any other component of the Department of Defense has approved, endorsed, or authorized this book.*

ABOUT THE AUTHOR

★ ★ ★

Courtesy JohnDoherty.com

Antwyn Price was born in Singapore of British parents. He attended Fort Street School in Sydney, St Mark's School in Dallas, then Harvard College and the University of Oklahoma. A US Marine of the late 1950s and a multilingual worldwide resident thereafter, he has authored several other works about WWII in the Pacific region and has been a frequent speaker on the topic.

Antwyn and his wife Elizabeth now reside in San Antonio, Texas, having spent several years in great cities of the USA (Los Angeles and Boston), Latin America (Mexico City and San Juan PR), SE Asia (Taipei and Singapore), and Europe (Brussels and London.

A TRIBUTE FROM PAN AM

Antwyn Price, who has an unusually insightful perspective on the geo-politics of the Pacific, has worked to give us a unique view of the events in the Southwest Pacific during the conflict. He's taken a cast of fictional characters, given them (mostly) believable human qualities, backgrounds, and jobs, and thrown them into the real maelstrom of the war in the Pacific.

Price's background includes a childhood partially spent "down under" in Australia, as well as time spent in the US Marine Corps, so he has a firm grasp as far as both the real "where" and the "who" are concerned.

Pan American Airways, which before the war had dedicated both substantial treasure and human effort to opening some of the locales in the book to commercial aviation, has a silent but steady presence in *Paradise*. Mr. Price provides an homage of sorts to Pan Am through numerous references to the airline's recently curtailed activities and surviving infrastructure that was everywhere in evidence in the book's settings.

Overall, *Paradise in Ruins* is an eminently entertaining entrée to some fascinating history that has been overlooked for decades, and is well worth reading.

By Doug Miller, board member of PAHF, the *Pan Am Historical Foundation*

EAST ASIA WIT

CHINA

MYANMAR

LAOS

HAINAN

THAILAND

VIETNAM

KAMPUCHEA

ANDAMAN SEA

GULF OF THAILAND

Aceh

MALAYSIA

Melaka

Sarawak

Singapore

SUMATRA

Plaju

INDONESIA

Sunda *Subang*

Jakarta

Ciater Pass

Bandung **JAVA**

Cilacap

NORTH KOREA
SOUTH KOREA *JAPAN*

MAP AREA

Maputo

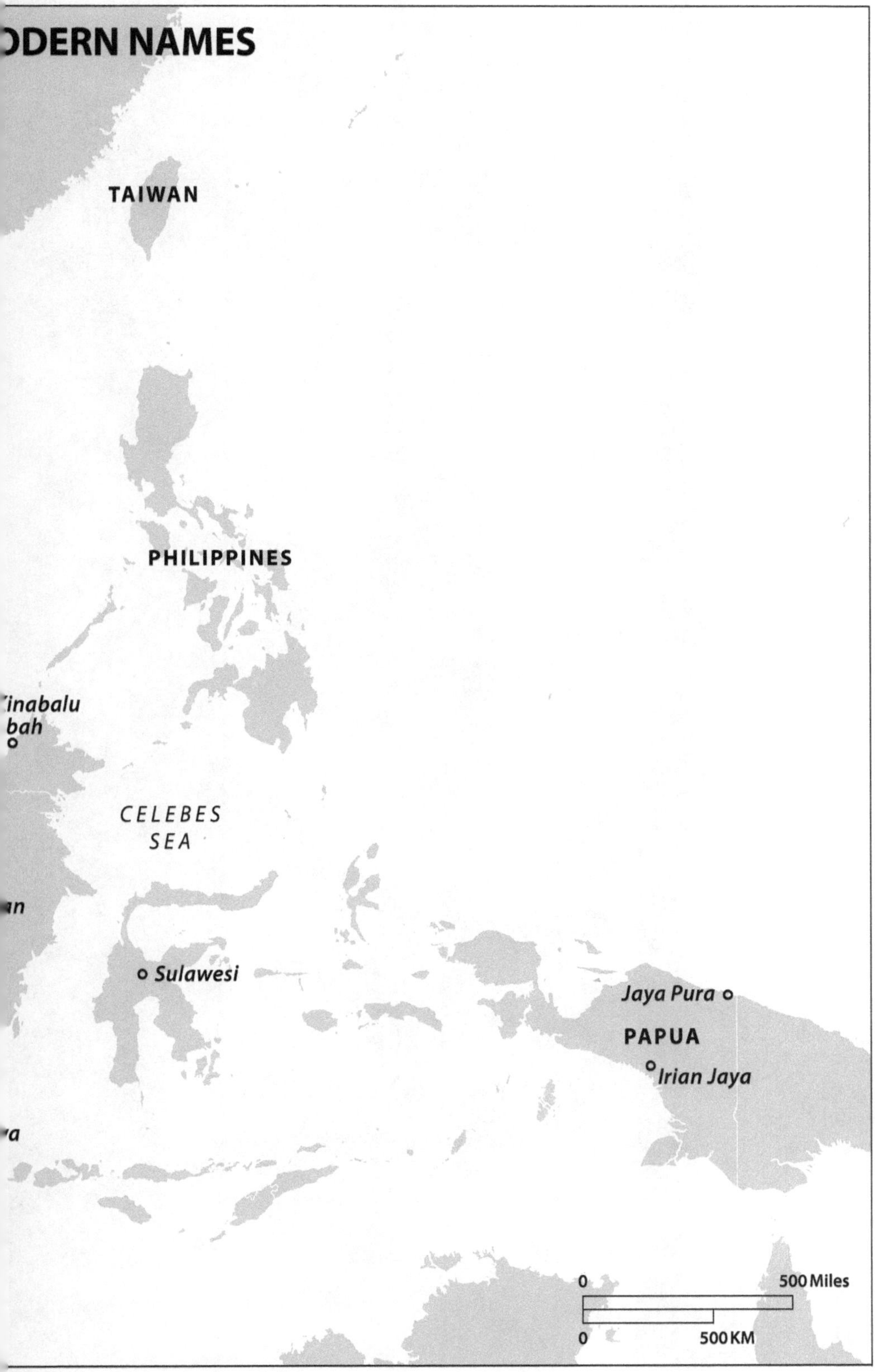

TAIWAN

PHILIPPINES

inabalu
bah
o

*CELEBES
SEA*

an

o *Sulawesi*

Jaya Pura o

PAPUA

o *Irian Jaya*

a

0   500 Miles

0   500 KM